THE NEW
money®
BOOK OF
PERSONAL
FINANCE

WITHDRAWN

THE NEW money®
BOOK OF
PERSONAL
FINANCE

Saving, Planning, Investing, and Borrowing—
All the Information You Need in One
Easy-to-Follow Guide

Edited by Sheryl Hilliard Tucker
and the editors of MONEY magazine

WARNER BOOKS

An AOL Time Warner Company

Warner Books, Inc., 1271 Avenue of the Americas, New York, NY 10020
Visit our Web site at www.twbookmark.com.

An AOL Time Warner Company

Printed in the United States of America
First Printing: October 2002
10 9 8 7 6 5 4 3 2 1

Library of Congress Cataloging-in-Publication Data

The new money book of personal finance: saving, planning, investing, and borrowing—all the information you need in one easy-to-follow guide / from the editors of Money magazine.
    p. cm. — (America's financial advisor series)
  Rev. ed. of: The money book of personal finance / by Richard Eisenberg and the editors of Money magazine. c1996.
  Includes index.
  ISBN 0-446-67933-X
    1. Finance, Personal. I. Eisenberg, Richard, 1956- Money book of personal finance. II. Money (Chicago, Ill.) III. Money, America's financial advisor series.

  HG179.E395 2002
  332.024—dc21

                                                 2002016828

Special Edition ISBN: 0-446-53167-7

Book design and text composition by L&G McRee

ACKNOWLEDGMENTS

Updating a personal finance and investing book as comprehensive as this one is a much more complicated and time-consuming project than I had ever imagined. Although new laws and the Internet have transformed the world of personal finance and investing, the foundation of wealth-building advice and strategies found throughout the original version of this book, *The MONEY Book of Personal Finance*, are still sound today. My hats off to the team of MONEY editors and writers who produced the original version of this book in 1996 (and the revised edition in 1998) under the adroit leadership of the former MONEY executive editor Richard Eisenberg.

I extend my sincere gratitude and special thanks to a team of dedicated MONEY editors, writers, reporters, art directors, and freelance journalists whose tireless efforts have helped me incorporate the 2001 tax laws and rules, a slew of new investing and money-management strategies, a wide range of resources, and most importantly, the powerful research tools and financial calculators found on the Internet into *The New MONEY Book of Personal Finance:* They are: Syndi Becker, Andrew Feinberg, Judy Feldman, Karen Hube, Tara Kalwarski, Roberta Kirwan, Derek Manson, Cara M. Moultrup, Maryann Salvato, Michael Sivy, Walter Updegrave, and Jason Zweig.

In addition, I would like to acknowledge the following MONEY staffers whose reporting, writing, and editing help form some of the new advice, worksheets, tables, and resource boxes found throughout this revised edition: Aravind Adiga, Marion Asnes, Andrea

Bennett, Jon Birger, Joan Caplin, Peter Carbonara, Adrienne Carter, Jean Sherman Chatzky, Brian L. Clark, Glen Coleman, Amy Feldman, Jim Frederick, David Futrelle, Pablo Galarza, Erica Garcia, Leslie Haggin Geary, Eric Gelman, Jon Gertner, Lisa Gibbs, Maya Jackson, Walecia Konrad, Ken Kurson, Laura Lallos, Jeanne Lee, Denise B. Martin, Scott Medintz, Jeff Nash, Nick Pachetti, Ilana Polyak, Michael J. Powe, Stephanie D. Smith, Ellen Stark, Penelope Wang, Cybele Weisser, Amy Wilson, and Suzanne Woolley.

This book would not be a reality without the Warner Books team of Rick Wolff, Dan Ambrosio and Penina Sacks and MONEY's vice president of business development Andrew Schultz. Thank you for your patience.

And finally, many thanks to MONEY's managing editor Robert Safian for giving me the time, the team, and the support to complete this project.

Sheryl Hilliard Tucker
Executive Editor, MONEY

CONTENTS

SECTION ONE

GETTING STARTED

CHAPTER 1

How Are You Doing?

Taking control of your finances. The very sound of it delivers a jolt of self-confidence. Once you're in control of your finances, after all, you can do what it takes to reach your most important money goals. But don't be in a hurry. Many people mistakenly think that the way to become financially independent is to plunge into stocks or mutual funds and hope for some winners. Actually, the secret to financial success is educating yourself about all the key areas of personal finance—from taxes to investing to debt management to estate planning—and then taking the right steps in each.

Before you make any moves to improve your financial lot in life, you need to know how you're doing currently. By putting down on paper the true numbers representing your finances—your assets, your liabilities, and your net worth—you'll see where you need to get started improving your situation.

Determining Your Assets, Liabilities, and Net Worth

So, do you know how you're doing, really? Chances are, you have a vague notion. For instance, you may be pretty certain that your debts are higher than they ought to be. Or that you could be investing a bit more. Perhaps you've been squirreling away money for years and have amassed a substantial amount. By filling in the following worksheets, you'll know for sure.

Sizing yourself up means looking at three important financial indicators: your **assets**, your **liabilities**, and your **net worth**. Your assets are all the things you own: the money you have in the bank, your furniture, your home, your investments. Your liabilities are the debts you owe. Your net worth is what you get when you subtract your liabilities from your assets. In some cases, particularly if you are young and haven't accumulated much yet, your net worth is a negative figure.

Complete the following "**Calculate Your Net Worth Worksheet**" and you'll learn exactly how much you have in assets and liabilities and, ultimately, your current net worth. To fill in the blanks, you will need to pull together your financial records. This could take a few hours, and admittedly, it's not a lot of fun to do. Once you've completed the exercise, however, you'll have all the data you need to help you make some important calculations, such as the amount you'll need to save and invest to retire comfortably or to send your children to college. What's more, you'll be able to tell which types of assets you should build up and which types of liabilities you should whittle down. You'll learn more about investing and debt management later in the book.

CALCULATE YOUR NET WORTH

Pull out your financial statements to fill in the current market value of your assets and the amount of your liabilities in the spaces provided. Complete this exercise at least once a year to track how much your wealth is growing.

- **Your Assets:** To tote up your assets, first collect all your year-end bank, brokerage, mutual fund, mortgage, and employee benefits statements.
- **Your Debts and Net Worth:** Now you're ready to figure out what you owe. What you're paying on all your debts and what you're truly worth. Get out your December 31 statements for all mortgages, loans, and revolving credit cards. Add up their outstanding balances, subtract that amount from your Total Assets, and you will get your net worth. You can make your net worth grow by controlling your spending, reducing your debts, and increasing savings and investments.

ASSETS	AMOUNT
CASH AND SAVINGS (savings accounts, money-market funds, Treasury bills)	1. _____
TAXABLE INVESTMENTS (excluding retirement accounts) Stocks and stock mutual funds	_____

Bonds and bond mutual funds _____

Stock options (if exercised today) _____

Value of privately owned business _____

Investment real estate _____

Cash value of life insurance policies _____

Other investments _____

Total taxable investments 2. _____

RETIREMENT ACCOUNTS

IRAs _____

Employer savings plans: 401(k), 403(b) _____

Self-employed plans: Keogh, for example _____

Annuities _____

Estimated value of company pension _____

Total retirement accounts 3. _____

HOME AND PERSONAL PROPERTY

Home _____

Vacation home _____

Cars, recreational vehicles _____

Art, collectibles, jewelry, and furnishings _____

Other personal assets _____

Total home and personal property 4. _____

TOTAL ASSETS (Add lines 1, 2, 3, and 4) 5. _____

LIABILITIES

Mortgage debt (balance of mortgages
and home-equity borrowings) _____

Car loans/leases _____

Student loans _____

Credit-card balances _____

Other loans (401(k), installment,
personal lines of credit, and the like) _____

Other debt _____

TOTAL LIABILITIES 6. _____

NET WORTH
(Subtract line 6 from line 5) 7. _____

Budgeting and Cash Flow

Now that you know how you're doing you can begin looking for ways to do better. Start by getting a handle on where your money goes every month. This way you can begin plugging your money leaks and find ways to spend less, save more, and boost your net worth.

Nobody likes to keep a running budget of expenses. The process is a pain and generally winds up as an annoyance. That said, jotting down how and where you spend your money can be an eye-opening experience. How often have you said to yourself: "I just don't know where the money goes. I make a decent living, but there's nothing left at the end of the month." By keeping tabs on your expenses, you'll be able to solve America's greatest unsolved mystery: the case of the vanishing paycheck.

So, try this mini-budgeting program and think of it as cash-flow management. For two months, starting the first day of next month, keep a written record of every time you spend money. (Yes, one month would be easier, but some expenses such as clothes don't show up monthly; by giving yourself two months, you're more likely to end up including the full range of your spending.) Jot down exactly how much you spent and what you spent it on. In addition, make note of every time you take cash from the bank or your automated teller machine and write down the amount.

If the old paper and pen approach seems way too Stone Age for you, go digital with computer software such as Quicken or Microsoft Money or tap into the great tools and calculators at their Web sites www.quicken.com and moneycentral.msn.com, respectively. Both programs (which sell for $30 to $90) or other, free Web sites have a computerized ledger for entering purchases and worksheets to help you create a budget. (For a paper budget, see worksheet beginning on page 9.)

Chances are, you'll be astounded to see where your money actually went. You might find that you spent an exorbitant amount on food, particularly for restaurants or workday lunches. You could also be surprised to see how much it cost to clothe your family or drive them around. The cost of upkeep for your home and your utility bills may also be sky-high.

Similarly, you may be shocked to see how little you saved or invested. Continue on such a path and you'll have a devil of a time meeting your long-term financial goals, such as paying for your child's college education or retiring with a lifestyle that matches your dreams.

Reining in your spending isn't easy, but it's not impossible, either. Some fixed expenses are hard to reduce, such as your health, disability, and life insurance premiums, but not impossible. Chapter 2 offers great premium-reducing strategies that might work for you. Most of your other expenses, however, are what economists call **discretionary**. That means you could spend more or less on them if you choose. Ask yourself the following 20 questions and odds are you'll find at least one expense that you can snip without feeling much pain:

20 QUESTIONS TO TURN SPENDERS INTO SAVERS

1. How can I eat out less often?
2. How can I spend less money when I eat out?
3. How can I cut back on my vacation spending this year?
4. How can I reduce my entertainment expenses and still have some fun in my life?
5. How can I get my boss to pick up more of my business expenses?
6. Can I lower the cost of child care and education without harming my kid in any way?
7. What can I do to cut my household's medical expenses without endangering my family's health?
8. How can I spend less shopping? (Hint: Try less expensive stores, more sales, fewer trips to the mall, and hand-me-downs for your kids.)
9. How can I lower the cost of commuting to work?
10. What can I do to reduce my car expenses? (One idea: Do more work on your car instead of taking it in. Another: Wash it yourself and save the car wash fee.)
11. What can I do to reduce the cost of upkeep for my home?
12. How can I pay less in debt? (Consider charging less on your credit cards or trading in a loan or a card for one with a lower interest rate.)
13. How can I lower my home heating and cooling, telephone, and cable TV bills?
14. What can I do to pay less to the IRS and the state tax man and keep more for myself?
15. Could I fight my property tax bill and get it lowered?
16. How can I reduce my dry-cleaning bill? (How about laundering and ironing more clothes yourself?)
17. Can I cut the fees I pay to my bank, mutual fund, or stockbroker? (Try consolidating accounts so you're not hit with so many different fees.)

18. Could I lower my mortgage payments by refinancing?

19. Are there discounts I could receive to cut my homeowners and car insurance premiums?

20. Can I buy less expensive gifts without looking stingy?

Throughout this book you'll find budget-cutting ideas that will answer many of those questions. Chapter 18, for instance, is devoted to making you a wiser consumer. But only you know for sure what you can give up or scale back. Only you know the alternatives in your area to your favorite restaurants and stores.

If you're truly serious about spending less and having more cash to save and invest, set monthly or annual limits for certain expenses. For instance, you might force yourself not to spend more than, say, $100 a month on telephone bills (including your cell phone) or $200 a month on clothes. Or you could limit your annual vacation spending to, say, $2,000. That might require you to give up a vacation altogether. Alternatively, you could just find a less expensive way to relax. Make sure you let yourself have some pleasures, though. Otherwise you'll eventually get so fed up with your budget constraints that you'll bust loose and spend wildly to compensate.

You may find it easier to put yourself on a budget by deciding in advance what you will do with the savings. This means converting your budgeting into a specific financial goal. It might be using the savings to pay down your debt or to invest for your child's looming college bills. Whatever the goal, give yourself something to shoot for. That way you won't feel as though you're simply punishing yourself.

After you have a spending plan you can live with, stick with it for three months. Then, repeat your initial exercise and see how you're doing. Find out exactly how much you are spending in every category again. You may even be able to kick in for a luxury or two that you've done without. After 12 months you ought to be so used to this spending regimen that you'll no longer mind the cutbacks you have made.

A final budgeting tip: Don't carry around too much cash, since you may be tempted to spend the money. If you normally take out $150 from the bank each week for spending money, try withdrawing $125 for a few weeks and see how you manage. If you're in the habit of constantly yanking cash out of your bank's automated teller machines, cut your visits in half. If you must, change your routine so you're not anywhere near your bank's ATMs. If you can't see the machine, you can't take money out of it.

CASH-FLOW STATEMENT

The following form is a cash-flow worksheet that you can use to evaluate where your money has been going. Take a hard look at your finances over the past two months—and fill out the worksheet as completely as you can. If you can't verify some of the information, make as accurate an estimate as you can. Keep in mind, though, that what you don't know can hurt you, so try to research what you've been spending as completely as possible. Your final result should ideally be a positive number, but be prepared for the possibility that you are currently spending a little bit more than you are bringing in.

INCOME	Month 1	Month 2
Income 1 _____	$ _____	$ _____
Income 2 _____	$ _____	$ _____
Income 3 _____	$ _____	$ _____
Total Income	$ _____	

EXPENSES

Withholding

	Month 1	Month 2
Federal Income Tax	$ _____	$ _____
State Income Tax	$ _____	$ _____
Social Security Tax	$ _____	$ _____
Medicare Tax	$ _____	$ _____

Investments/Savings

	Month 1	Month 2
Employer-Sponsored Retirement Plan	$ _____	$ _____
IRA	$ _____	$ _____
Other _____	$ _____	$ _____
Other _____	$ _____	$ _____
Other _____	$ _____	$ _____

Housing	Month 1	Month 2
Rent or Mortgage	$ _____	$ _____
2nd Mortgage	$ _____	$ _____
Property Taxes	$ _____	$ _____
Homeowners or Renters Insurance	$ _____	$ _____
Gas	$ _____	$ _____
Electric	$ _____	$ _____
Water/Sewer/Trash	$ _____	$ _____
Telephone	$ _____	$ _____
Home Maintenance	$ _____	$ _____

Transportation		
Auto Payment 1	$ _____	$ _____
Auto Payment 2	$ _____	$ _____
Fuel	$ _____	$ _____
Auto Maintenance & Repair	$ _____	$ _____
Auto Insurance	$ _____	$ _____

Food		
Groceries	$ _____	$ _____
Dining Out	$ _____	$ _____
Lunches/Snacks	$ _____	$ _____

Medical		
Health Insurance	$ _____	$ _____
Doctor Visits	$ _____	$ _____
Dental Visits	$ _____	$ _____
Medications	$ _____	$ _____

Family Expenses	Month 1	Month 2
Vacations	$ _____	$ _____
Entertainment	$ _____	$ _____
Recreation	$ _____	$ _____
Clothing	$ _____	$ _____
Dry Cleaning	$ _____	$ _____
Tuition/Day Care/Child Support	$ _____	$ _____
Professional Services	$ _____	$ _____
Personal Expenses/ Grooming/Hygiene	$ _____	$ _____
Contributions	$ _____	$ _____
Gifts	$ _____	$ _____

Other Insurance

	Month 1	Month 2
Life Insurance	$ _____	$ _____
Disability Insurance	$ _____	$ _____
Umbrella Policy	$ _____	$ _____

Other Debt

	Month 1	Month 2
Debt 1 _____	$ _____	$ _____
Debt 2 _____	$ _____	$ _____
Debt 3 _____	$ _____	$ _____

Miscellaneous Expenses

	Month 1	Month 2
Expense 1 _____	$ _____	$ _____
Expense 2 _____	$ _____	$ _____
Expense 3 _____	$ _____	$ _____
Total Expenses	$ _____	$ _____
Difference	$ _____	$ _____

YOUR HOUSEHOLD BUDGET

Your work to this point should have given you a clear perspective on your current financial health. You've looked at your assets, your debt load, and your cash flow (including your spending habits). Now it's time to create a budget. Keep in mind that a budget is not a record of what you spent—it's a plan for what you will spend.

Use the following form (or a software program of your choice) and your completed Cash-Flow Statement to create a budget for the coming month(s). Try to set reasonable limits for yourself in each category, and give some thought to how you will control impulse spending in those areas. Identify some current expenditures that you could reduce, with minor changes in your habits. Discuss the budget with your family. Define weekly or monthly limits that all can agree to for these targeted categories.

One of your primary goals, of course, is to have some money left for savings and investment. If your first draft doesn't provide you with this result, reevaluate your proposed expenditures.

INCOME	Budget	Month 1
Income 1 _____	$ _____	$ _____
Income 2 _____	$ _____	$ _____
Income 3 _____	$ _____	$ _____
Total Income	$ _____	

EXPENSES (from total income)

Withholding

Federal Income Tax	$ _____	$ _____
State Income Tax	$ _____	$ _____
Social Security Tax	$ _____	$ _____
Medicare Tax	$ _____	$ _____

EXPENSES   **Budget**   **Month 1**
Investments/Savings

Employer-Sponsored
    Retirement Plan $ _____ $ _____

IRA $ _____ $ _____

Other _____ $ _____ $ _____

Other _____ $ _____ $ _____

Other _____ $ _____ $ _____

Housing

Rent or Mortgage $ _____ $ _____

2nd Mortgage or $ _____ $ _____
    Home Equity Loan

Property Taxes $ _____ $ _____

Homeowners or
    Renters Insurance $ _____ $ _____

Gas $ _____ $ _____

Electric $ _____ $ _____

Water/Sewer/Trash $ _____ $ _____

Telephone (include cell phones) $ _____ $ _____

Home Maintenance $ _____ $ _____

Transportation

Auto Payment 1 $ _____ $ _____

Auto Payment 2 $ _____ $ _____

Fuel $ _____ $ _____

Auto Maintenance & Repair $ _____ $ _____

Auto Insurance $ _____ $ _____

Food

Groceries $ _____ $ _____

Dining Out $ _____ $ _____

Lunches/Snacks $ _____ $ _____

Medical

Health Insurance $ _____ $ _____

Doctor Visits $ _____ $ _____

Dental Visits $ _____ $ _____

Medications $ _____ $ _____

EXPENSES	Budget	Month 1
Family Expenses		
Vacations	$ _____	$ _____
Entertainment	$ _____	$ _____
Recreation	$ _____	$ _____
Clothing	$ _____	$ _____
Dry Cleaning	$ _____	$ _____
Tuition/Day Care/Child Support	$ _____	$ _____
Professional Services	$ _____	$ _____
Personal Expenses/ Grooming/Hygiene	$ _____	$ _____
Contributions	$ _____	$ _____
Gifts	$ _____	$ _____
Other Insurance		
Life Insurance	$ _____	$ _____
Disability Insurance	$ _____	$ _____
Umbrella Policy	$ _____	$ _____
Other Debt		
Debt 1 _____	$ _____	$ _____
Debt 2 _____	$ _____	$ _____
Debt 3 _____	$ _____	$ _____
Miscellaneous Expenses		
Expense 1 _____	$ _____	$ _____
Expense 2 _____	$ _____	$ _____
Expense 3 _____	$ _____	$ _____
Total Expenses	$ _____	$ _____
Difference	$ _____	$ _____

Your Finances by Your Age

A useful way both to see how you're doing financially and to figure out what you ought to be doing with your money is to understand what you should be focusing on financially today, depending on your age.

PEOPLE UNDER AGE 30: THE STARTING OUTS

1. **Stop living paycheck to paycheck and start saving regularly.** Ideally, you'll want to salt away 10% of your income. Then you can start investing in the stock market, through mutual funds.
2. **Start investing as early as you can.** For instance, if you put aside only $2,000 a year in an Individual Retirement Account earning 8% for just the 10 years from ages 25 to 34, you'll have nearly $315,000 by the time you're 65. If you wait to age 35, however, and then start investing $2,000 a year in the IRA for a full 30 years, you'll have only about $245,000. Similarly, try to contribute the maximum allowable amount to your employer-sponsored retirement savings plan, such as a 401(k) plan. (For more on great tax-deferred retirement savings vehicles, see Chapter 11.)

PEOPLE 30 TO 44: THE CLIMBERS

1. **Get serious about cutting your spending and debt.** This is the time of your life to break bad spending and debt habits. Otherwise you'll likely be stuck with them for life and you'll find yourself struggling to reach your financial goals.
2. **Don't forget about insurance.** It's easy to put off buying life and disability insurance. Don't. You want to be certain that if something happens to you, the people you care most about won't be hurt financially.
3. **Pump up your savings for your retirement and your children's college education.** Check out tax-sheltered plans for both in Chapters 10 and 11.

PEOPLE 45 TO 54: THE PEAK EARNERS

1. **Don't let looming college bills prevent you from saving for retirement.** When tuition payments approach, it's easy to decide to forgo contributions to employer-sponsored retirement savings plans—such as your 401(k) or 403(b)—

IRAs, and Keoghs. That would be a mistake, however. Borrow more for college, if you must. But you need to look out for yourself as well as your kids.

2. **Meet with your aging parents to discuss their finances.** Your parents may need some help with the likes of investing wisely, dealing with Medicare or Social Security, holding down medical bills, or simply making ends meet. You may even want to try to save a bit for their potential nursing home bills.

PEOPLE 55 TO 64: THE PRE-RETIREES

1. **Meet with a financial adviser to discuss how to handle a pension and 401(k) or 403(b) payout.** You might want to take all the money at once. Or, you might prefer to get the pension in monthly installments for the rest of your life. Whichever way you go, there will be tax and investment implications.

2. **Make sure you're clear about IRA withdrawal rules.** Although recent laws have made this process a lot less complicated, you'll still want a pro to help you work out the details.

3. **Wise up about Social Security, particularly as you approach 60.** You'll need to decide when to start getting your first checks. Plus, you should determine how much of your benefits will be taxable and whether income you earn in retirement might reduce the size of your Social Security checks. For more on these topics, see Chapter 11.

PEOPLE 65 AND UP: THE RETIREDS

1. **Focus on preserving your assets and preventing them from losing value to inflation.** That means keeping about half of your investments in stocks or mutual funds that buy stocks. You can put the rest in safe bonds, mutual funds that buy bonds, or the bank.

2. **Don't buy a home for retirement in another part of the country until you've fully checked out the area.** It's smart to rent for a year or so before you buy. That way you'll have time to see whether you like the climate, the setting, the people, and the attractions.

Setting Your Financial Goals

No matter how old you are or how much you make, you'll want to zero in on the key financial goals you hope to achieve. Too often, people have just vague notions about what they want financially. Their goals are things like "I want to have a lot of money." Or "I don't want to die poor." Or "I want to be comfortable." Or "I want mutual funds that will go up." Trouble is, these goals are too squishy to help you much.

Instead, you ought to get more precise and decide exactly what it is you want to have and when you want to have it. For instance, your goal might be "I want to be able to retire at 65 and live as well as I did before retirement." Or "I want to buy a house in my city within three years." Or "I want to have enough saved to pay for 75% of my son's college education when he is a freshman."

The best way to make the right goals is to figure out what's important, what isn't, and when you want to achieve your goals. Once you've placed priorities on your financial goals, you can start adopting appropriate strategies to hit your marks. For example, if reducing debt is much more important to you now than goals requiring you to save and invest—such as buying a house or financing education—you'll want to focus on your credit cards and loan payments. If you've been negligent in properly insuring yourself and your family, you'll want to make that a top priority and concentrate on building up protection.

Similarly, it's crucial to divide your goals into short-term, medium-term, and long-term commitments. That will help you see how quickly you need to work. For instance, if you have teenagers, paying for college is a short-term goal. So you'll need to find ways to increase your savings, borrow wisely, find scholarship or grant money, or some combination of all of these.

Complete the following two worksheets by checking off the appropriate money goals and you'll get a clear idea of both your true financial goals and your timetable for reaching them.

After you've created these master goal lists, remember to return to them from time to time. After all, your goals may change, or—with any luck—you'll be able to cross some off your list over time. At the very least, draw up new goals worksheets once a year. Be certain to make revisions when you have dramatic life changes, such as the birth of a child, a marriage, a divorce, a new job, a layoff, a move, or the purchase of a home.

SETTING PRIORITIES FOR MY MONEY GOALS

OBJECTIVE	NOT IMPORTANT	SOMEWHAT IMPORTANT	VERY IMPORTANT
Reduce debt	_____	_____	_____
Build an emergency reserve fund	_____	_____	_____
Increase insurance coverage	_____	_____	_____
Buy a house	_____	_____	_____
Make home improvements	_____	_____	_____
Buy a vacation house	_____	_____	_____
Buy a car	_____	_____	_____
Make another big purchase	_____	_____	_____
Have children	_____	_____	_____
Finance children's education	_____	_____	_____
Live more luxuriously	_____	_____	_____
Take an expensive vacation	_____	_____	_____
Take an unpaid leave from work	_____	_____	_____
Start a business	_____	_____	_____
Take early retirement	_____	_____	_____
Live well after retirement	_____	_____	_____
Other	_____	_____	_____

TIMING MY MONEY GOALS

OBJECTIVE	SHORT TERM	MEDIUM TERM	LONG TERM
Reduce debt	_____	_____	_____
Build an emergency reserve fund	_____	_____	_____
Increase insurance coverage	_____	_____	_____
Buy a house	_____	_____	_____
Buy a vacation house	_____	_____	_____
Buy a car	_____	_____	_____
Make another big purchase	_____	_____	_____
Have children	_____	_____	_____
Finance children's education	_____	_____	_____
Live more luxuriously	_____	_____	_____
Take an expensive vacation	_____	_____	_____
Take an unpaid leave from work	_____	_____	_____
Start a business	_____	_____	_____
Take early retirement	_____	_____	_____
Live well after retirement	_____	_____	_____
Other	_____	_____	_____

YOUR FINANCIAL-PLANNING CHECKLIST

One last way to get a read on how you're doing financially: a financial-planning check-list. This one was prepared by the Consumer Financial Education Foundation. Circle the YES or NO answer for each and see how you score when you finish:

1. Are you saving money?   YES   NO
2. Do you know how much you spend each month?   YES   NO
3. Do you pay all of your bills each month on time?   YES   NO
4. Is your net worth improving over time?   YES   NO
5. Do you have a satisfactory credit rating?   YES   NO

6. Do you have enough life insurance?	YES	NO
7. Do you have adequate medical coverage?	YES	NO
8. Do you carry disability income insurance?	YES	NO
9. Are your investments diversified?	YES	NO
10. Do you invest according to your own tolerance for risk?	YES	NO
11. Do you have a growth component (such as stocks or stock mutual funds) in your investment portfolio?	YES	NO
12. Do you rely on financial information from an objective source?	YES	NO
13. Do you learn as much as you can before you invest?	YES	NO
14. Do you review your investments regularly?	YES	NO
15. Do you take taxes into account when you spend and invest?	YES	NO
16. Do you file tax returns on time?	YES	NO
17. Do you know how much money you'll need to live on when you retire?	YES	NO
18. Do you know how much you'll receive in Social Security benefits when you retire?	YES	NO
19. Do you contribute the maximum amount you are allowed to your employer's 401(k) or other pension plan?	YES	NO
20. Do you know how much you'll need in personal savings to fund a comfortable retirement?	YES	NO
21. Do you have a will?	YES	NO
22. Have you considered ways to minimize estate taxes that may be due on your death?	YES	NO
23. Do you have a secure (hopefully fireproof) file for your important documents?	YES	NO
24. Have you recorded the location of all your assets?	YES	NO
25. Have you prepared advance directives such as a durable power of attorney, living will, and health care proxy?	YES	NO

Score (one point for each YES):

20–25 points: You have taken solid steps toward establishing financial security.
15–19 points: You have begun the journey to financial stability—continue and focus.
Less than 15 points: You need to take control of your financial life.

No matter what you scored the following chapters will help you improve in all of the areas covered in this checklist.

CHAPTER 2

Your Financial Foundation

Now that you know how well you're doing financially, you're ready to learn the basics about personal finances. One mistake people often make is skipping over the basics and plunging headlong into investing. Bad idea. It's essential, first, to learn how to keep good financial records, use a bank wisely, and purchase the insurance protection you need for yourself and your family. Once you have these bases covered, you can move to the next stage: managing your money and making it grow.

Keeping Good Financial Records

It's a drag to see all those papers taking over the desk by your bed. But it's even more of a drag to be audited by the Internal Revenue Service and suddenly realize that the crucial receipts you need to prove that mammoth tax deduction are now mingling with the landfill on the other side of town.

Think of it this way: The moderate amount of discipline that smart record keeping requires is good practice for moving on in your financial life. If you don't have the discipline to file away crucial bills and chuck useless ones, for instance, how will you have the discipline for the far more demanding task of saving large chunks of your money for retirement?

Let's start with documents you probably already have lying around in boxes. If you're like most people, you can safely toss many of them. Here are the ones to keep and store in a fireproof file cabinet or in a safe-deposit box:

- **Real estate documents.** These include the title to your home, the deed of purchase, your mortgage contract, and your sales contract. (It's best to keep these in a bank safe-deposit box.) Also save any receipts for capital improvements or property repairs you have made, such as reroofing or adding a deck. You'll need these records to minimize the taxes you might owe someday after selling your home for a profit.

- **Receipts for valuable items such as furniture, silverware, furs, and jewelry.** If you lack a receipt for, say, those diamond brooches your grandmother left you, have the jewelry appraised and save the appraisal forms. You'll need them to fill out an insurance claim if your house burns down or is burglarized.

- **Records of all personal property you own.** It's best to keep photographs or a videotape of these items, along with written estimates of their value. Your home-owners or renters insurer will be far more willing to accept your insistence that you owned four mint-condition Hepplewhite chairs if you can show him or her recent photos of them in your dining room. (It's a good idea to keep copies of all this at your office or in a bank safe-deposit box as well as at home, just in case.)

- **Warranty statements covering your major appliances or electronics, along with a receipt proving the date of purchase.** Write down the make, model, and serial number for all items, if applicable.

- **Old tax returns.** It's crucial to keep copies of your income tax returns for the past three years. That's because the IRS can typically probe that far back if it chooses to audit you. But it's a good idea to keep all your tax returns: They can be helpful reminders of previous financial moves you made. For more information about the IRS and record keeping, get IRS Publication No. 552, *Record Keeping for Individuals* (800-829-3676; www.irs.gov).

- **Old tax-related documents.** The three-year holding period also applies to documents that substantiate claims you made on your tax returns. In a tax audit, if you cannot document an expense you deducted, you may lose the write-off. So save receipts or canceled checks that prove your deductible expenses. Save your year-end W-2 forms from your employer and 1099 forms from your freelance clients for three years.

- **Insurance policies.** Keep all policies you still hold, from life to liability, at home. But it's a good idea to create a list of all your policies and your agents and keep it in your safe-deposit box.

- **Legal documents.** You also need to keep copies indefinitely of your will and, if you have them, your living will and power of attorney. Have your lawyer keep the originals; you should retain your copies at home. And be sure to get rid of old wills. Otherwise, after you die there could be confusion about which will is the one you wanted.

- **Credit-card statements.** Save these for a year or so. That way, if a charge erroneously appears on your bill more than once, you'll be able to prove you already paid it. Also, if a product you bought breaks and needs to be returned, you'll remember where you bought it. The statements can also come in handy at tax time.
- **Bank checking and savings account statements, including canceled checks.** Holding on to your checks helps you keep track of where your money goes. The checks can also work as proof of payment if necessary. For instance, it helps to have a check if your landlord says you didn't pay last September's rent and you know you did. Keep these statements and checks for three years, indefinitely for home improvements.
- **Investment records.** Save monthly statements from your mutual fund companies and your brokerage firm—print out your online statements at least quarterly. These statements will establish what you paid for an investment, so you'll have the information to compute the taxes when you sell it. After you get your annual summary statement, you can toss the monthly statements—as long as the annual statement shows all your transactions for the past 12 months. Exception: Save all trade confirmations and dividend-reinvestment statements for three years after you file a tax return declaring a gain or loss from selling securities. Save your annual statements indefinitely. If you have certificates of ownership for stocks, bonds, or other investments, keep them in a safe-deposit box at the bank.
- **Retirement accounts.** Hold on to all annual statements from tax-advantaged retirement accounts such as 401(k)s, 403(b)s, 457s, Individual Retirement Accounts (IRAs), Keogh retirement accounts, Simplified Employee Pensions (SEPs), and Simple IRAs. The statements will document your contributions and your earnings.

    It's especially important to keep annual statements from any nondeductible IRAs you may have. Reason: You'll need them to show the IRS which part of any future withdrawal was funded with after-tax money. Otherwise you'll wind up being taxed twice. And if you make a nondeductible IRA contribution, be sure to keep a copy of your IRS form for it, No. 8606.
- **Debts.** Aside from your mortgage contract, you'll also want to save records for your student loans, home-equity loans, car loans, bank loans, and other large debts. Then, when they're paid off, just keep the statement that says so.
- **Miscellaneous documents.** Also keep in your safe-deposit box the following: the title to your car, your birth and marriage certificates, your children's birth certificates, and deeds to cemetery plots you own.

Records You Can Toss

Here are the types of records you don't need to keep:

- Old, expired insurance policies
- Receipts for cars you don't own anymore
- Pay stubs from earlier years
- Expired product warranties
- Old annual reports and proxy statements

Records You Should Start Keeping for Tax Time

Now it's time to get organized with the financial documents that will come rolling in this year. Doing so will make end-of-the-year tax moves much easier. For instance, if you maintain careful records of your family's medical expenses every month, toward the end of the year you'll be able to see if they'll exceed 7.5% of your adjusted gross income—the level at which they become deductible on your tax return. If they do, you can, say, shift upcoming January medical appointments to December in order to deduct them.

Don't worry. You needn't create a whole room or some fancy system for these records. Just pick up a large accordion file or a handful of individual manila folders and spend a few minutes labeling them by their deductible category. (Refer to Schedule A of last year's tax return to see what all these categories should be.) Don't forget to create a folder to stow your old tax returns, too.

For those who like to file things electronically, consider using money-management software or Web sites like Intuit's Quicken (www.quicken.com) and Microsoft Money (moneycentral.msn.com). Both make it easy to consolidate far-flung stock and mutual fund investments into one ledger, track bill payments and tax write-offs, store emergency records, and do your banking online.

Here are a few tips to be sure you don't miss anything important whether you're keeping records in a paper or electronic folder:

- **Medical expenses.** Keep all receipts for health insurance premiums, prescription drugs, eyeglasses, and contact lenses, and for fees to your doctors, dentists, psychotherapists, and hospitals.

- **Charitable donations.** Remember to hang on to canceled checks for your cash contributions plus receipts for used clothing and other property donations. If you throw a $10 bill in the collection plate at church every Sunday, keep a log of that, too. Don't forget that one-time donations of $250 or more to a charity require a written acknowledgment. Also keep a record of trips you make to perform volunteer work. You can deduct those travel expenses; see www.irs.gov for the specific rate.
- **Miscellaneous expenses.** These expenses become deductible only once they exceed 2% of your adjusted gross income. So be sure to keep receipts and canceled checks documenting fees to financial planners and tax advisers; subscriptions to trade and professional journals; costs related to looking for another job in your current profession; and safe-deposit box rental fees.
- **Your income.** In this folder toss in your pay stubs, of course. But be sure also to throw in records of all other earnings from any other sources of employment, such as freelance work or consulting. Otherwise you might wind up forgetting about the work at tax time. Guarantee: The IRS won't forget.

After you've completed your tax return for the previous year, you can junk any records of expenses that you couldn't deduct, such as medical receipts if the expenses didn't exceed 7.5% of adjusted gross income. Put the papers you did use in preparing your return into a file labeled by the tax year. As an added bonus, if you use a tax preparer, organizing your records this way before sending them to him or her should save so much time that you may be able to save as much as 50% off last year's bill. That should have you smiling all the way to the bank.

Banking Smart with Your Checking and Savings

A bank was probably your first connection to the world of personal finance. Remember that childhood savings passbook, stamped by a teller every time you deposited $5 from your paper route? Things have changed since then, but banks still provide a host of basic—and crucial—services, from checking to savings to borrowing. Surprisingly, however, many people fail to get the most out of their banks.

If you are already a customer of a small, friendly bank where the staff knows your name and responds quickly to your needs, consider yourself lucky. But while good service is important, so is getting the most for your money. So don't feel you have to do all your bank business—from your checking to your credit cards to your mortgage— with the same institution. A dedicated relationship with one bank can sometimes work in your favor; for example, if you have your checking and savings accounts at one bank, that institution may lower or even waive its annual credit-card fee for you in gratitude. That said, you usually come out ahead if you shop around for the best deal on the individual services you need—including online services.

These days almost all U.S. banks offer some online services. If all you want is round-the-clock access to your accounts and to pay bills online, open up an account with an established bank that offers a variety of online services. But remember, while plenty of banks let you pay bills online, not every company you have accounts with is set up to present their invoices or bills or accept payments via the Web.

If you are looking for higher interest rates on your CDs or money-market accounts, you may want to check out a Net-only bank. But most don't offer all the convenient features of their bricks-and-mortar peers.

The most basic service that banks offer is the **checking account**. The purpose of a checking account is to give you a place to park your cash safely and let you spend it (via writing checks or making withdrawals) whenever you like. The bank with the best checking account for you is one that's conveniently located, has automated teller machines (ATMs) near where you live and work, and has the lowest possible fees.

More than ever, it's essential to check out a bank's fees before opening a checking account—and review fees on the account you already have. In the past few years banks have been hiking their fees on checking accounts like mad. They've also become increasingly creative in finding new ways to charge. Nowadays, unless you keep a balance of at least $2,400 in your checking account, your bank will probably charge you a monthly fee (the average for this fee is about $11) and maybe an additional fee of 34¢ for each check you write. Balances are figured in different ways, so be sure to ask a bank officer about the institution's method before opening an account.

A word to the wise: Some banks charge service fees according to your lowest balance during the month. That way, fees kick in if your bank requires a minimum monthly balance of $1,000 for free checking and your account, which averages $2,000, dips to $900 for a single day. Look instead for a bank that bases its fees on your average daily balance.

Also, ask any bank you're considering for a list of all fees associated with checking accounts. You may find that the bank is making up for a low monthly account fee by socking customers with big charges for bouncing checks ($24 or more), confirming account balances, stopping payment on checks, transferring funds by telephone, and—most insidious of all—using ATMs.

According to a 2001 study by Bankrate.com, ATM fees have climbed 6.5% since 1998. Most charge an average of $1.50 or so for making withdrawals from ATMs that are owned by another institution, but in addition, 90% of institutions that own ATMs charge non-account holders for each transaction. Note: Many Internet banks reimburse for any ATM surcharge fees, either for a certain number of transactions (about four) per month, or up to $6 or so each month.

Another strategy to cut your ATM fees (beyond looking for banks and machines that do not charge fees at all) is to take advantage of accessing cash through point-of-sale transactions. Most institutions that offer point-of-sale debit transactions (such as supermarkets that accept debit cards to pay for your groceries) do not charge extra fees to do so. For example, if the cashier asks you if you'd like to use your debit card, and if you would like cash back, you can ask for an extra $20 or so, at no extra charge. This strategy is likely to come in handy when you are out of town, or in a different part of town than you usually shop, which are the times you are most likely to be forced to use a foreign ATM. (For more specific information about ATM fees, see the U.S. Public Interest Research Group's Web site, www.stopatmfees.com.)

You can get a complete list of most bank fees charged by the large banks at the Bankrate.com Web site (www.bankrate.com).

On the positive side, most banks will pay interest on your checking account (well, not much interest, actually), provided you maintain a minimum balance of about $700 or more. Such accounts may be called NOW (negotiable order of withdrawal) accounts. Interest rates are normally pegged to your balance: the higher your balance, the higher the rate. In recent years the average interest-paying checking account has yielded around 1%.

If it's interest you're after, another alternative is to open a linked savings account at the same bank that supplies you with checking. As long as you maintain a minimum savings balance of around $1,000 to $3,000, some banks will waive all their checking account fees.

Checking accounts at credit unions are referred to as **credit union share draft accounts**. This kind of account is a lot like a bank checking account, except it generally pays more interest while charging no, or low, fees. In fact, the average credit union's checking fees are about half those of the typical bank. Best of all, most credit unions will give you free checking with interest no matter what your balance is. You don't belong to a credit union? No big problem. It's becoming easier and easier to get into one. Ask your friends or business associates if they're a member of a credit union you could join. Another place to look is your alumni association. Or you can ask the Credit Union National Association (www.cuna.org) how to locate your state credit union association, which can refer you to local credit unions you may be able to join. Just make sure that the credit union you choose is covered by the U.S. government's Federal Deposit Insurance Corporation (FDIC) insurance.

A **savings account**, of course, keeps your money safe but readily available for withdrawal, either at the teller's window or through an ATM. Deposits of up to $100,000 are insured by the FDIC. In other words, in the unlikely event that the bank or savings and loan fails, the feds will pony up your missing cash. (If you'd like to deposit more than $100,000, divide your money among different banks so you'll get full FDIC coverage on all of it.)

Oh, yeah—a savings account also pays interest, recently averaging about 1.5% to 2%. If you keep enough money on deposit, that is. Once your balance dips below $200 to $500 or so, some banks stop paying interest and even start charging account-maintenance fees. (Banks often waive these penalties for kids; alas, grown-ups have no such luck.)

When shopping for a savings account, be sure to analyze the way it calculates its yields, because methods of compounding interest vary. Try to use a bank that pays interest on the balance accumulated in your savings account every day, rather than on your average monthly balance or (even worse) on your lowest balance each month. And it's best to use a bank that compounds interest daily: All things being equal, the more often your interest is compounded, the more money you make. A quick way to cut through interest rate double-talk: Ask an officer at three different banks you're considering what $1,000 deposited today would be worth in a year if you leave all your interest on deposit. Go with the bank whose answer is highest.

There are also four safe alternatives to checking or savings accounts that will pay you more in interest:

ALTERNATIVE 1: A MONEY-MARKET ACCOUNT

If you've got at least several thousand dollars to sock away, consider stepping up to a **money-market deposit account** at your bank, S&L, or credit union. Such accounts often require minimum deposits of $1,000 or more but normally pay slightly higher rates than those on traditional checking and savings accounts. Yields rise and fall with short-term interest rates; the accounts often pay about two percentage points less than those of money-market mutual funds (see Alternative 2 below).

The money-market account is often free and you may get free checking, but you may be limited to writing only three to six checks a month.

You're not limited to the banks in your hometown or even in your home state, however. So to get the highest possible yield, consider opening an out-of-state money-market account (for a monthly list of the highest-yielding money-market accounts from safe institutions, see **MONEY** magazine's "By the Numbers" column). The difference can be substantial: When the national average money-market rate is, say, 1.5%, you might be able to find a bank or S&L paying 4%. Institutions that court out-of-state depositors often have toll-free numbers; call to request application forms. Smaller regional banks trying to drum up business often offer some great deals, and Internet banks can be tough to beat.

ALTERNATIVE 2: A MONEY-MARKET MUTUAL FUND

A **money-market mutual fund** is a pool of money managed by an investment firm; you actually become a shareholder when you get into a money-market mutual fund. The money is typically invested in short-term IOUs from government agencies and corporations. Money funds, as they're often called, generally yield a few percentage points more than bank checking accounts and at least one percentage point more than bank money-market deposit accounts. They aren't federally insured, but the managers of the funds work to ensure that no shareholder ever loses money.

Most money funds make you keep a $5,000 minimum balance or let you write checks only for amounts of $250 or more. But there are a few exceptions. For instance, a few let you write an unlimited number of checks if your balance is at least $1,000. Some even have no minimum balance and let you write checks for amounts as small as $100. You typically make deposits into the money funds by writing a check and sending it through the mail to the fund trustee, or through automatic transfers from your bank. If you live in a high-tax state such as California or New York, you might want a municipal bond fund exempt from federal and state taxes. (Go to www.investinginbonds.com to calculate your best route.) Taxable money funds tend to yield a little more than one percentage point over tax-exempt funds.

Fund vs. account: For cash you might need on short notice, go with a money-market mutual fund, not a bank money-market account. The difference? Interest rates tend to be higher on money-market funds. There's another difference: The bank account is FDIC insured, while the money fund comes with no guarantee that you won't lose your principal. That might lead squeamish investors to stick with a money fund that invests only in U.S. government securities. But, it's highly unlikely that any money fund will "break the buck" (dip below the $1 share price at which investors buy in) because SEC regulations ensure that these funds invest in the safest instruments around. Yes, an issuer may default on its debt but any major fund company left holding worthless notes will make it up to shareholders. Mutual fund companies such as Fidelity or Vanguard have insurance policies to cover defaults, as well as reputations to protect.

The big fund companies also tend to keep fund expenses below the 0.5% norm, and low expenses are the only guarantee that a fund's yield will remain competitive. You can find the highest-yielding money funds listed in newspapers, on the Internet, or in each month's issue of MONEY (see "By the Numbers"). But look carefully at these deals, because some companies temporarily waive fees to draw customers. Check the fund prospectus, and call to ask if a fee increase is imminent. Of course, some money funds do waive fees indefinitely.

Discount brokerages like Schwab and E-Trade offer decent money-market rates, but if you're working with a traditional firm, make sure your spare cash does not go into a money-market fund with high expenses that subsidize a commission to the broker.

ALTERNATIVE 3: A BROKERAGE OR BANK CASH-MANAGEMENT ACCOUNT

Also known as an **asset-management account**, this may be the perfect arrangement for you if you own stocks or bonds and make at least a few trades every year. A cash-management account is a combination money fund, brokerage account, and checking account. As a rule, you need to keep at least $10,000 in cash or securities in the account. Also, you may be asked to pay an annual fee of $50 to $125.

ALTERNATIVE 4: CERTIFICATES OF DEPOSIT

If you're willing to lock up your cash for a period of time in exchange for a higher rate of interest than you would get from a savings account, ponder a bank or savings and loan **certificate of deposit (CD)**. A CD has a fixed maturity—the most common terms are for three months, six months, one year, 2½ years, and five years. At the end of the term, you can either withdraw your principal and interest, or roll over the proceeds into a new CD for another term earning whatever yields are at the time. Generally, the longer you commit your money, the higher the interest rate. For instance, if a six-month CD is yielding 4%, a five-year CD might well yield about 6%. If you withdraw the money before the CD matures, you'll pay a penalty equal to roughly three to six months' interest. So CDs are appropriate only if you're confident you won't need to raid the account soon. (CDs do not offer a check-writing feature.)

For a list of the highest-yielding CDs (which are often sold by online banks), check out www.bankrate.com. Every week, the site surveys more than 4,000 banks, credit unions, and other financial institutions and then lists the best deals in the U.S. on its site. Typically, you must call the institution to get an application for a CD, but some let you download an application to your computer directly from the site.

As long as you stick with institutions backed by the Federal Deposit Insurance Corporation and limit your deposits to less than $100,000 at any one institution, you will be completely protected against loss of principal. The CDs you purchase from a brokerage firm like Merrill Lynch or Charles Schwab are actually ones that have been issued by banks. So they're insured up to $100,000. And, as at a bank, you pay no commission to get them. Brokers tend to require minimum investments of $1,000 to $5,000.

Since issuers play lots of games with these certificates, watch out for these two CD traps:

1. **Interest rates that don't reflect your true return.** There are almost as many ways to compound interest as there are banks. Some compound your interest (or pay interest on your interest) each day. Some do it each month, each quarter, or each year. And others pay **simple interest**, which means they don't compound at all. A simple-interest CD isn't necessarily a bad one; it all depends on the rate the institution is paying. You could wind up earning more on a simple-interest CD than on one compounding quarterly, for example. To compare apples with apples, when you're shopping around for a CD, ask the financial institution for the certificate's **annual percentage yield**, which shows what really matters. The annual percentage yield will tell you the precise percentage increase you'd earn on your investment if you kept the CD for 12 months. Another way to compare CDs is to ask one simple question: How much money will I have at the end of the term of the certificate? That way, if you're planning to deposit, say, $10,000 in a CD, you'll see who will have paid you the most interest by the time the CD comes due.

2. **Excessive penalties.** If you withdraw your money before the CD matures, however, you'll pay a penalty, equal to roughly three to six months' interest. Some penalties are based on the cost to the institution to replace the funds you withdraw and can be calculated in a number of ways. One example: If you want to cash in a three-year, 4.5% CD after one year and the bank's current interest rate for two-year CDs is 5.5%, then its replacement cost would be 2% of the face value (or 1% times two years). That kind of penalty can be extremely costly if interest rates have risen since you bought the CD.

   Aside from asking about withdrawal penalties before you make a CD deposit, you can minimize the bite of a withdrawal penalty by spreading your stash among several CDs. Then, if you have to cash out a portion of your money early, you won't pay a penalty on the entire principal; you can just take out a little from each of your CDs.

Another note of caution: Avoid **callable CDs**, which the issuer can redeem before maturity. After one or two years, the issuer can in effect return your money. Since that's most likely to happen if rates have fallen, you'll have to reinvest the money at a lower rate.

Getting the Right Insurance

Spending money on insurance policies is an act of faith: You are buying promises that you hope will never have to be kept. But because none of us can predict the future, it's crucial that you protect your assets (and therefore your family's well-being) from risks. Insurance is the way to do it. What follows is a guide to getting the insurance you need for the price you can afford.

Buying Health Insurance

It's amazing how many people think they can do without health insurance. They're making a big mistake. If you're uninsured, a serious accident or debilitating illness can wipe out you and your family financially. And yes, young people get sick, too. In short, insurance that protects you against major health catastrophes is absolutely crucial.

If you're like most working Americans, your employer supplies you with **group health insurance coverage**. Most employers will give you a choice of several plans, typically the traditional fee-for-service indemnity plan and a few managed-care plans such as HMOs, PPOs, and POS plans (explained below). The old-fashioned **traditional fee-for-service plan** covers visits to any doctor you choose. For an annual premium (sometimes paid by the employer, sometimes paid by the employee, and sometimes shared between them), group plans typically pay about 80% of your medical expenses after you pay an annual deductible of, say, $200 for a single person or $400 for a family of four. (A **deductible** is the amount you must pay toward your bills each year before your insurance kicks in. Once it does kick in, the small percentage of your medical expenses that insurance doesn't cover—and that you must pay for—is called your **copayment**.) Luckily, many group plans establish an out-of-pocket limit for your annual share of the bills (for example, $1,500), meaning that if you belong to that plan, $1,500 will be the most you should have to pay toward medical care in any year. Of course, if your plan excludes certain treatments, such as dentistry or drug abuse counseling, you'll have to pay the entire cost yourself.

To control costs, employers are either dropping the traditional higher-priced fee-for-service plans or passing along more costs to their employees. In fact, studies indicate that employees should expect a rise in premiums over the next few years. Therefore, it's important to get the right coverage at the right price. The alternatives to a traditional fee-for-service plan are called **managed-care plans**. There are a few main types of managed-care plans: **health maintenance organizations (HMOs)** and **preferred-provider organizations (PPOs)** or **point of service (POS)** plans.

Which should you choose? If you care less about cost cutting and more about the ability to see whichever hot specialist you've heard about—or if you're devoted to a current doctor who does not belong to your company's managed-care network—stick with your old fee-for-service plan. However, if you are looking for the least expensive plan (and one that provides fuller coverage for preventive care) consider a managed-care plan.

HMOs are the strictest managed-care plan: In general, HMOs don't require you to pay a deductible—and with HMOs you can avoid having to fill in lots of paperwork. However, typically only visits to doctors who are members of their network are covered automatically; you must get approval to see outside specialists. (For information on Medicare HMOs see Chapter 21.)

PPOs and POSs have higher monthly charges (typically $6 to $20 more) than HMOs and you will also have to shell out slightly higher out-of-pocket costs. PPOs and POSs usually charge copayments of just $5 to $15 for doctor visits, prescription drugs, and laboratory tests. However, unlike HMOs, PPOs and POS plans allow you to see specialists who are in their network (and you'll typically pay 10% to 20% of the bill) or they will allow you to choose to go out of network, but then you are often required to get a referral first and you may be paying up to 30% of the bill. It's a simple trade-off: Extra flexibility equals extra cost. So if you don't have any tricky medical conditions or you have young kids and will thus likely take them in for lots of potentially costly checkups, an HMO is probably your best choice.

SIZING UP A MANAGED-CARE PLAN

If your employer offers a new managed-care plan, and you need to decide whether to join, ask the following four questions:

1. **How good are the doctors?** First, get the plan's doctor directory and see if there's a doctor in it you know. If so, call the physician and ask his or her opinion of the other doctors in the plan. That will give you a clue about the quality of the group.
2. **What kind of preventive services are offered?** Some plans figure you'll get preventive care if you want. Others are more proactive, keeping records on patients and letting you know if, for instance, you're due for a mammogram. The more the HMO, PPO, or POS watches out for you in advance, the more you can feel sure the group cares about your health.
3. **What kind of accreditation does the group have?** Two voluntary accrediting agencies have started to certify managed-care plans based on strict measures of

quality. They are the National Committee for Quality Assurance (888-275-7585; www.ncqa.org) and the American Accreditation HealthCare Commission (202-216-9010; www.urac.org). This isn't to say that a plan without accreditation isn't a good one. But one that has ponied up the fee to get accredited and then met the standards demonstrates a quality plan.

4. **What's it really like to be a member?** Ask to see a copy of a patient satisfaction survey or a similar questionnaire that will let you know how it feels to be a member. Ask about doctor turnover. The average turnover for fee-based doctors, like the kind in many PPOs and POS plans, is 5% a year. It's about 10% for salaried physicians, who tend to work at HMOs. If you learn that the plan's turnover rate is higher than that, that could be a signal that the doctors in the group aren't very happy.

BUYING HEALTH COVERAGE ON YOUR OWN

What if you work for a company that does not provide group health insurance? Or you're self-employed? Or unemployed? There's no way around it: Buying health insurance on your own means you'll face some hefty bills. Sadly, there is simply no such thing as a bargain individual health policy. At least not yet. When it comes to forking over cash for your own individual health insurance policy, the first thing you must do is figure out how much coverage you truly need. When buying health insurance, as with any kind of insurance, you should insure only against losses that you couldn't absorb without derailing your family's finances. Remember: There's a seesaw effect between deductibles and premiums. The higher the deductible you choose—meaning the more you're willing to pay out of pocket—the lower your premium will be. The lower the deductible, the higher the premium. It's a waste of money to pay high insurance premiums for costs you could handle yourself without too much pain.

Your primary concern, then, should be **catastrophic coverage**. That is, if you're hit by a car or develop cancer and rack up total medical costs of $500,000, you want to make sure that your insurance will pick up as much of that staggering amount as possible. So buy a health insurance policy that has a maximum annual payout of at least $500,000 or (preferably) $1 million. It should cover the full cost of basic hospital services and surgery as well as most doctor bills and prescription drug costs. Also make sure never to buy a policy without a ceiling on your out-of-pocket expenses ($1,500 per year is typical). After you reach the ceiling amount, your insurer should pick up 100% of remaining bills. Finally, make sure the policy you buy is guaranteed to be renewable. That way the insurer can't cancel your policy just because your health deteriorates.

If you're turned down by a number of insurers because you have a preexisting condition such as diabetes or heart disease, check out your state insurance department and find out which companies offer policies for individuals in your area. Certain nonprofit insurers often have open enrollment periods when they take all applicants, regardless of their health. And they charge pretty much the same rates for everyone of the same age and sex in the same area. Another possibility is a health insurance pool for the "uninsured," available in most states. The downside: You'll probably pay higher premiums and have higher deductibles. But at least you'll be covered.

One of the scariest experiences for people changing jobs or leaving the corporate world is the prospect of losing health coverage. If you are unsure whether you'll have health insurance in your new position, tell the benefits department of the company you're about to leave that you'd like to extend your old coverage under the terms of the **Consolidated Omnibus Reconciliation Act (COBRA).** As long as the company you are leaving has 20 or more employees, COBRA guarantees you the right to continue your health insurance coverage for up to 18 months. The 18 months will give you plenty of time to shop for an affordable longer-term policy. Unfortunately, although your employer probably paid much of the premium while you worked there, under COBRA you must pay the total cost of the premium yourself. Still, it's almost certainly cheaper than any plan you could buy on your own.

Individual coverage is determined by where you live and every state has a legal system unto its own. What's available depends on the insurance laws and characteristics in your state. An invaluable source of state-by-state information is available at www.healthinsuranceinfo.net, a Web site run by the Georgetown University Institute for Health Care Research and Policy.

Even if your new job offers health insurance, extend your coverage under COBRA for a few months anyway. Reason: Many employers' health coverage doesn't go into effect until you've been working there for three months or so. If you're about to retire, you have different concerns. Once you reach age 65, the federal government's Medicare health insurance program kicks in. Medicare comes in two parts: Part A, which you get automatically and most people get for free, covers bills for hospital stays and care in hospices and skilled nursing facilities (after a related three-day hospital stay). Part B, for which you must sign up and pay a premium (in 2002 the premium is $54 a month), covers 80% of doctor bills, outpatient surgery, lab tests, X-rays, certain drugs, and other costs that don't exceed the "approved" amounts—those that Medicare has decreed are standard in your area.

But it is wise to learn the limits of Medicare. The federal health program for the elderly and disabled covers only short nursing home stays and home care when skilled care is needed (for instance, yes for therapy after hip replacement surgery; no for the custodial care Alzheimer's patients often need). Helpful Web sites on Medicare: www.medicarerights.org and www.aarp.org.

If you're retired, check with your former employer to see whether its health plan will continue to give you and your family the care you need. If not, sign up for Medicare Part B. If you have an individual health insurance plan, definitely sign up for Part B when you turn 65. Your existing individual plan will metamorphose into a so-called **Medigap policy**, which pays only certain medical bills that Medicare doesn't.

You may also want to check out long-term-care insurance if you are concerned about the high cost of staying in a nursing home or having home health care for a long period of time. Turn to Chapter 21 to find out more about Medigap and long-term-care insurance.

SIX WAYS YOU CAN LOWER YOUR MEDICAL COSTS

1. **Ask professional, fraternal, alumni, or religious groups you belong to whether they sell group health insurance to members.** Group coverage is often—but not always—less expensive than individual coverage. If you don't belong to any such group, look into joining up.
2. **Consult an independent insurance agent who sells comprehensive major medical policies for individuals from a variety of companies.** He or she may be able to turn up a policy that you couldn't. Tell the agent you want policies only from financially sound companies.
3. **Consider joining an HMO rather than buying an individual policy from an insurance company.** You may have to give up a little freedom in your choice of doctors, but you'll help keep your medical costs down.
4. **Choose the highest deductible that you can afford.** If you figure you can probably afford $1,000 in medical bills this year, take a $1,000 deductible; it might be 25% cheaper than a similar policy with a $100 deductible.
5. **Become a smarter medical consumer.** Actually, this is sound advice for everyone these days. The more you understand about your own health, the more you can save. According to studies by the actuarial benefits consulting firm Milliman USA, at least 15% of doctor visits are wholly unnecessary. Speaking of doctors, you may be surprised to know how much doctor fees can vary in the same area. Studies show that charges for the same service can differ by more than 700% among local doctors. Lately it's been getting a little easier—though not too easy—to compare prices, since some local consumer and business groups have been putting together price guides.
6. **Get healthier, too.** You might be able to slash your health premiums by as much as 50% by stopping smoking or losing weight or taking action to lower your blood pres-

sure or cholesterol level. Don't expect your insurance agent to tell you about such discounts. It's up to you to ask.

Buying Disability Insurance

What, you may think, me become disabled? Unfortunately, chances aren't as slim as you may think. At age 35, you have a fifty-fifty chance of being unable to work for more than three months before you turn 65, according to data from the Society of Actuaries. And, according to the Insurance Information Institute, at age 40, the average worker faces only a 14% chance of dying before age 65 but a 21% chance of being disabled for 90 days or more. Think of it this way: A disability policy is the way to insure what's likely your largest asset—your earning power. Here's how to get the coverage you need:

Generally speaking, you should have enough disability coverage to replace at least 60% of your gross income while a long illness or injury prevents you from working. In fact, that's usually the most coverage that insurers will sell you (though some will sell as much as 70%). If they provide much more coverage, they figure, you'll have little incentive to return to work. The best policies start paying benefits no more than 90 days after your disability occurs and continue to pay until you can work full-time again or reach age 65.

Large corporations often offer their employees a group long-term disability plan (typical percentage of pretax salary replaced: 40% to 60%, up to a specified ceiling). If you don't own such a policy, ask your benefits department if one is available. Your employer may also offer short-term disability coverage to bridge the gap between when your sick leave runs out and a long-term disability policy kicks in. Some states, including New York and California, require that most employers provide short-term disability benefits (usually for 26 weeks).

But if you work at a company that does not offer disability coverage at all, you're self-employed, or you work for an employer whose benefits fall below the 60% threshold, look for an individual disability policy sold by a life insurance company. Buy the highest-quality coverage you can get and be prepared to pay a bundle for the policy; the cost for women especially is rising because fewer and fewer insurers offer unisex policies.

The fee for your annual disability premium will depend on your age, occupation, how much income you want replaced, and how many months you're willing to wait before benefits kick in. Take a 40-year-old, nonsmoking, $80,000-a-year professional man. At the specialty disability insurer UnumProvident (www.unumprovident.com), premiums for his policy, which begins paying 90 days after he becomes disabled with a maximum benefit period to age 65, will cost roughly $1,500 a year. Some policies sell for a lot more. For instance, in 2001, a 45-year-old male executive might pay another insurer $230 a month for a policy that provides up to $5,000 a month; a female surgeon might pay $425 a month for a similar benefit. When you shop for a policy—available through insurance agents and financial planners—keep these points in mind:

- **Own-occupation coverage.** This means that the policy will pay in the event that you develop any disability that prevents you from performing your own occupation, even if you are still able to do other kinds of work. For example, with such coverage, an airline pilot who went blind would collect benefits even though blindness wouldn't prevent him from being, say, a deskbound administrator. You can keep receiving benefits even if you earn money doing something else, as long as you are under a doctor's care. This coverage may cost up to 20% more than a policy that will pay benefits only if you are unable to work at any occupation suitable to your training and experience. And this feature is becoming harder and harder to find.
- **Residual benefits.** This mouthful simply means that you can return to work part-time while you are recuperating and still collect partial benefits. If your policy doesn't have residual benefits built in, pay the extra fees to have it added as a rider.
- **A noncancelable contract.** This feature means that the company must insure you without raising premiums or lowering benefits as long as you continue to pay the premiums. Like own-occupation coverage, noncancelable contracts have been becoming scarcer.
- **Guaranteed increase.** This is simply the option of buying more coverage later without having to undergo a medical exam.
- **Guaranteed level premiums.** By getting guaranteed level premiums, you'll prevent the insurer from raising premiums later. Again, this coverage is getting scarcer.
- **Annual cost-of-living adjustments.** With this feature, your benefit payments will rise with inflation every year.

There are several ways to trim your premiums. For starters, you can accept the longest waiting period (also known as **elimination period**) available. The waiting period is the length of time you must be disabled before the insurance company starts paying benefits. Accepting a 180-day rather than the standard 90-day waiting period, for example, can save you several hundred dollars a year. Other cost cutters: You can select a shorter benefit period or reduce the number of options (riders) included with the policy.

If you automatically get employer-provided long-term disability coverage, your employer may let you buy more. But the insurer it uses may not offer the lowest available rates, so it pays to compare premiums among several insurers. At the very least, check with any professional organizations to which you belong, such as the American Institute of Certified Public Accountants. Such groups often can negotiate cheaper rates than a large company.

If you plan to leave the corporate world to strike out on your own, you may not qualify for disability insurance anymore—at least at first. Because people starting their own businesses don't have any income yet, they can't insure it against disability. Homemakers, with no earned income, have the same problem. One solution: Buy an individual policy before you quit your job.

Many people don't realize that the Social Security system provides disability benefits, too. But you must be in pretty bad shape to qualify: You've got to prove that your disability will keep you from working at any kind of job for more than a year or is fatal. Furthermore, these payments don't kick in until five months after your disability sets in. Your salary and the number of years you've worked determine your benefit amount.

Buying Homeowners or Renters Insurance

No matter where you live or whether you own your home or rent, you need to have insurance to protect your belongings against loss from theft and against damage by fire and other hazards. Homeowners insurance also covers the value of the home itself. In addition, property insurance on your home provides personal-liability protection for members of your household, covering you for claims against you involving injuries to people on or off your property.

Many renters and condo or co-op residents think they can get away without buying insurance for their apartment. They think differently after a burglary or other disaster, though. Don't be chintzy about paying to cover what you own. Renters insurance covers only your possessions so it's relatively inexpensive—a typical policy costs $169 a year for $15,000 worth of property. In a condominium or co-op, master policies cover the structure, including your bare walls, floors, and ceilings. But often you must insure anything on those surfaces, from rugs to chandeliers—even drywall and wallpaper.

For homeowners, the amount of coverage you should buy is whatever would be enough to pay for rebuilding your house if it were leveled by disaster. Standard homeowners policies cover your home's contents for half the dollar limit you place on the house. Most companies provide coverage for 50% to 70% of the amount of insurance you have on the structure of your home. So if you have $100,000 worth of insurance on the structure of your home, you would have between $50,000 and $70,000 worth of coverage for your belongings. The best way to determine if this is enough coverage is to conduct a home inventory. Your insurance agent can help you figure rebuilding costs, or you can hire a real estate appraiser for about $150.

Your annual premium depends on many different factors, among them the value of your house; its age; whether your area is prone to natural hazards such as hurricanes or earthquakes; the crime rate in your neighborhood; and what materials your house is made of (fire-vulnerable wooden houses cost more to insure than stone ones, for example). Annual premiums might run $500 to $1,000 for a $150,000 house, depending on coverage and where you live.

The best kind of coverage to get is known as **HO-3 (homeowner 3)**, or "full coverage," insurance. It protects your house against all perils not specifically excluded by the policy. (HO-1 and HO-2 policies are cheaper, but they cover fewer risks.) Depending on where you live, common exclusions are damage from floods, earthquakes, sewer and drain backups, war, and nuclear accidents. Your insurer may cover you for some of the excluded perils—at extra cost, of course. For instance, earthquake insurance—advisable for all Californians—runs about $400 to $900 a year for a $200,000 house, depending on where you live. (For more information on earthquake insurance, call the California Department of Insurance at 800-927-4357 or visit www.insurance.ca.gov.)

If you want to buy flood insurance, ask someone at your town hall whether your community is among the 18,000 or so that participate in the federal government's National Flood Insurance Program (www.fema.gov). That list includes almost every place with a serious risk of floods. To better gauge your vulnerability, ask your homeowners insurance agent to show you a flood insurance rate map; that will show you if you live in a minimal, moderate, or "special" hazard area. (If your risk is high, buy.) Cost: about $375 a year for a $100,000 house, depending on how much coverage and where you live. The coverage is available through your regular homeowners insurance agent; for insurers, call 800-427-4661 or check www.floodalert.fema.gov.

Even though **cash-value coverage** is the cheapest way to go, avoid it. These policies pay only the current value of any part of the house you lose. Instead, opt for **guaranteed replacement cost coverage** for your home. This simply means that you're insured for the full cost of replacing your house. (Most insurers cap coverage at 120% to 150% of the value of your house. Purchase extra if you believe your insurer's appraisal is low or your home has handcrafted cabinetry or other expensive features.) Your coverage will rise yearly with inflation. Not every home is eligible for guaranteed replacement cost coverage, though. Some insurers won't provide it for properties built more than 40 or so years ago. One reason: The intricate moldings and other detail work common in old houses can be very expensive to replace.

If guaranteed replacement cost is not an option, go for the second-best type of coverage: **replacement cost**. It covers the full cost of replacing your house, but with a price cap. If you buy one of these policies, it's important that you're covered for 100% of your rebuilding costs. Never let that amount fall below 80%. If your coverage is at or above the 80% mark, your policy may not pay the entire cost to rebuild your house if it's completely destroyed—but it will pay the entire repair cost if a portion of your home is damaged, such as after a fire. If your house is insured for less than 80% of its replacement cost, insurers will reimburse you for only that percentage of what is lost. For instance, if you've insured your house for only 60% of its value and your roof blows off, your insurance will pay only 60% of the cost of replacing the roof.

What if you have lots of expensive jewelry, silverware, furs, or a valuable stamp collection? You're right to ask, because most policies have a low $1,500 to $2,500 limit for these items. Hardly enough for such valuables. The solution: Buy a **floater**, or **personal property rider**, to make up the difference. Another advantage of a jewelry rider: It covers you for losses that occur on or off your property. So if a mugger takes off with your $10,000 engagement ring, you're covered. However, don't rely on your memory—photograph or videotape your possessions, and keep this dated record in a safe-deposit box or other secure place outside your home.

You may need more **liability protection** than the $300,0000 a typical standard policy provides. If you have a dog, a swimming pool, a home-based business, teenage children, a high-profile job, or a job that has the appearance of deep pockets, you're open to a lawsuit, warns the Independent Insurance Agents of America. (For more information, see the section on umbrella liability insurance later in this chapter.)

If you work from home, you need a home-business endorsement to cover your equipment and liability.

In the past few years a number of homeowners insurers have jacked up their premiums or stopped offering coverage altogether in certain areas around the country. If you find that your insurer has announced a giant rate hike, call your state insurance commissioner to see if the proposal is likely to go through.

If you can't find private homeowners or renters insurance at any price, you may be able to get coverage by joining your state's **risk pool**. Call your state insurance department for more information. Premiums may be steep, though. Often they go for 10% to 100% more than those on the open market.

EIGHT WAYS TO CUT YOUR HOMEOWNERS INSURANCE COSTS

1. **Equip your home with smoke detectors, deadbolts, and burglar alarms, and tell your insurance company about them.** These steps can reduce your homeowners premiums by 5% to 20%.
2. **If you own a new home, ask about special breaks.** Some insurers lower premiums by 5% to 25% for customers whose homes are less than five years old.
3. **Raise your annual deductible.** Hiking it from the standard $500 to $1,000, for instance, can save you as much as 15% per year; a $5,000 deductible, 25%.
4. **Check to make sure the facts on your policy statement are correct.** If the stated square footage is bigger than your house's actual square footage, say, or if the policy says your home has wood-frame construction when it's really concrete, you're being overcharged. Call your insurer to correct the problem.
5. **Phone agents or check Web sites to review six insurers to find the cheapest policy with the coverage you want.** This advice is especially crucial now that major disasters such as hurricanes can hike rates as much as 30%. To shop on the Web, visit Netquote (www.netquote.com) and Homesite (www.homesite.com). The agents you call can be independents who represent a number of companies, or salesmen who work for a single insurer. Companies represented by independent insurance agents are almost always more expensive, mainly because your premium must cover their commissions.

   Don't sacrifice safety for savings, though. A cheap policy won't be worth much if your insurer has gone under by the time you need to make a claim. Stick only with an insurer rated A+ or better by the insurance ratings service A. M. Best or AA- from Standard & Poor's (www.ambest.com; www.standardandpoors.com/ratings). You can also find these reports in most libraries.
6. **Don't pay for floaters you don't need.** If you bought a floater for a $5,000 fur coat you got five years ago, for instance, but have since given the coat to charity, be sure the insurer isn't still charging you for the coverage.
7. **Ask agents about insuring your home and your car with the same company.** Some insurers snip premiums on homeowners policies by 5% to 15% if you double up this way. But don't go this route until you check to be sure the insurer's car insurance premium is fairly priced.
8. **Finally, if you have guaranteed replacement cost coverage, keep a close watch over your annual premium adjustments.** The company will raise your rates each year to keep pace with inflation. If the price hikes are getting too hefty, look for a better deal elsewhere.

Buying Auto Insurance

Are auto insurance premiums costlier than ever? Is a car alarm noisy? Unfortunately, auto insurance premiums will continue to soar along with the costs of lawsuits, medical care, and car repairs. That's why it's crucial to become a smart auto insurance shopper. Even six-month premiums in big cities such as New York and Los Angeles often climb into the thousands of dollars, especially if you are under 25, own more than one car, or have a teenager in the house.

To find a suitable, affordable auto policy, first decide what level of coverage you want. Car insurance comes in a package that consists of the following provisions:

- **Liability protection.** Like homeowners insurance, auto insurance protects you against liability. Here, the coverage protects you against claims for injury and property damage brought by other drivers, pedestrians, or property owners who allege that you caused an accident. Your auto insurer will defend you in or out of court against any claims. The insurance company pays the legal expenses and, if necessary, the damages, up to the dollar limit specified in your policy.

   Most policies have three separate dollar limits for each of the following: (1) each person injured in an accident; (2) all people injured in the same accident; and (3) property damage, typically damage to the other driver's car. Most states require drivers to take a minimum of between $15,000 and $30,000 of coverage per person in an accident, with a cap of between $40,000 and $60,000 per accident. (This gets complicated; hang in there.)

   A typical bare-bones policy covers $25,000 of liability per person, $50,000 per accident, and $10,000 for property damage; the shorthand name for the insurance would be 25/50/10 coverage. But that's not enough coverage for most people. Unless you have virtually no assets, be sure to purchase at least $100,000 of liability per person, $300,000 per accident, and $100,000 for property damage, or 100/300/100. This enhanced level of coverage will cost you about 20% to 30% more per year, but the protection is worth it.

- **Collision and comprehensive coverage.** If you carry collision coverage, your insurer will pay for the repairs to your car in the wake of a smash-up. Comprehensive coverage takes care of damage from fire, storm, vandalism, or theft. Few banks and finance companies will approve you for a car loan unless you buy both kinds. Together, collision and comprehensive coverage can get expensive: They typically represent at least 30% to 40% of your total premium.

   Both of these coverages are subject to a deductible, the amount you must pay out of your own pocket before the insurance kicks in. Beefing up your deductible can really cut your car insurance premiums. By raising your deductible from $100 to $500, for example, you can cut your collision premium by about a third; raise it to $1,000, and you'll cut this part of your premium in half. A tip: Deposit in the bank the money you're saving by upping your deductible, earmarking it to pay for fender-benders that don't reach the new deductible level.

If your car is more than five years old and on the decline, consider skipping collision and comprehensive coverage altogether. The reason: Your insurer will pay you no more than the car's market value if it's totaled or stolen. When the annual cost of your collision and comprehensive insurance exceeds 10% of your car's **blue-book value**— the amount you'd get if you sold the auto—drop the coverage. Your insurance agent can tell you the current blue-book value of your car.

- **Uninsured/underinsured motorist coverage.** It has become a fact of modern American life: In many places, the streets are thick with drivers cruising blissfully without car insurance—or without enough insurance. The provision known as uninsured/underinsured motorist coverage means that if you have a close encounter with an uninsured, underinsured, or hit-and-run driver, your insurer will pay for injuries to your passengers, your own "pain and suffering," and other expenses that health plans don't pick up. If you don't buy this coverage and get hit by one of these scofflaws, you'll have to pay for everything your medical insurance doesn't cover plus other expenses resulting from the accident. Clearly this is protection you want to have. You can buy as much coverage as you carry under the liability section of your policy, but it's a good idea to fork over the $40 or so a year that $100,000 of uninsured/underinsured coverage will cost.

- **Personal injury protection (PIP).** You must purchase this type of coverage if you live in a state with no-fault insurance laws, which generally require your insurer to pick up medical costs for your injuries regardless of whether you or someone else caused the accident. Your agent can tell you whether you need PIP.

HOW TO CHOOSE A CAR INSURER

If you haven't shopped in three years for insurance, check what's out there. Get quotes from at least four carriers. First try a free database such as InsWeb (www.insweb.com), which offers quotes from up to eight insurers, or Quicken InsWeb (www.insuremarket. com), which provides up to 16 quotes. The larger the database, the better. If you're willing to pay for a more comprehensive database, go to the *Consumer Reports* Web site (www.consumerinsure.org). The site's database compares up to 25 policies in 27 states. It costs $12 for the first vehicle, $8 for the second.

- **Use a direct writer.** Companies like State Farm (www.statefarm.com) and USAA (www.usaa.com) that deal directly with consumers without using independent agents are called **direct writers**. In theory, they can pass on their savings by eliminating the middleman.
- **Read your junk mail.** Direct marketers like GEICO (www.geico.com) and Progressive (www.progressive.com) save on overhead—and pass on the savings—by marketing by phone, mail, or the Internet.
- **Let your state be your guide.** Two-thirds of state insurance departments and the District of Columbia offer shopping guides for auto insurance on the Web; half offer homeowners' guides. Your state's guide may identify little-known companies with competitive rates. Insure.com (www.insure.com) offers links to most state guides.
- **Check affinity groups.** Your business association, club, or employer may offer group auto insurance at a discount.

Be sure to ask for any and all discounts you might be entitled to receive. The discounts might save you 5% to 25% of your premiums. Get the conversation started by telling your agent if any of the following factors apply to you:

- You'll insure more than one family car with the same company.
- Your car has safety features such as air bags, automatic seat belts, or an antitheft device.
- Your car isn't a racy high-performance vehicle.
- You've taken a state-approved defensive-driving course.
- You're a senior citizen.
- You're a middle-aged woman and are the only driver in your household.
- You participate in a carpool.
- You park in a garage rather than on the street.

CAR INSURANCE IF YOU HAVE TEENS IN THE FAMILY

If you have a teenager—which can double your insurance costs—look for discounts that he or she can help you get. Ask your insurance agent about discounts such as if your teen gets good grades or passes a driver's education course. Also, adding your child to your own policy will generally cost less than getting a new one just for your son or daughter. Be sure to tell the insurer if your teen is not the principal driver of the car but only pilots it occasionally, since occasional-driver status is often cheaper. Consider restricting your teen to driving your oldest or least expensive car and don't forget to tell your agent that he or she will be driving an old but safe clunker rather than a speedy sports car. If the kid has his or her own used car, you can always lower premiums by purchasing only liability coverage (though if it's a newer or late-model used car, you may want the extra protection). Finally, if your child is going away to college without a car—and the campus is at least 100 miles from home—request a discount for the months he or she will be away.

Buying Umbrella Liability Insurance

If you own a car or a home, of course, your homeowners and auto policies provide some liability coverage—typically $100,000 to $300,000 for your homeowners policy and about $50,000 for your auto policy. (Renters insurance policies provide some liability coverage, too.) But if you can afford it, you ought to buy additional liability coverage—known as **umbrella liability insurance**—from a homeowners or auto insurance agent. After all, if, say, you or a member of your household cripples a bigwig executive by plowing into him on a ski slope, you could be the target of a massive lawsuit that far exceeds those limits. Or if your teenager throws a party in your basement while you're away and a friend breaks a leg on the stairs, you could be held responsible and your liability could be enormous.

An umbrella liability policy covers any claims that come because you or members of your household have damaged others out of negligence—or libeled, slandered, or defamed them—in excess of the limits on your other policies. Buying such insurance is especially important if you fit one or more of the following profiles:

• You have substantial assets and are thus a prime target for a big lawsuit.
• You employ hired help who are not licensed or bonded, such as a cleaning woman, baby-sitter, or gardener.
• You often have people house-sit for you.
• You rent out a room in your home.
• You have a home-based business.

To be safe, if you have as little as $200,000 in assets, it's wise to purchase a total of $1 million in liability coverage (the minimum for umbrella policies). If you have, say, $500,000 in assets, you're better off with $2 million or more. The cost of the coverage depends on where you live and how many cars, boats, and homes you own. Generally, a $1 million policy might cost $200 to $300 a year. The next million dollars would cost an added $75 annually; you'll pay about $50 for every million thereafter. (Umbrella liability coverage on a home-based business will cost about $30 extra a year.)

To shave the cost of an umbrella liability policy, see about raising your liability coverage to the highest allowable levels on your homeowners and auto insurance policies. Then buy an umbrella policy for just the remainder you'd like covered. Also, look into buying your umbrella policy from the same insurer that provides your auto and/or homeowners coverage. In return for all this business, many companies will knock about 15% off your umbrella policy premium.

Buying Life Insurance

Amazing but true: Buying life insurance is one of the most important moves you can make to solidify your personal finances, yet it is also one of the most complicated. It's extremely difficult to compare life insurance policies. On top of that, life insurance has its own jargon that is enough to make anyone head for the aspirin bottle. It doesn't help, of course, that buying life insurance means coming to terms with your own mortality. Great.

Nevertheless, if you have dependents but your assets wouldn't provide for them adequately after you die, you need life insurance. By contrast, if you're single and have no dependents, you probably don't need to buy life insurance since no one is relying on your financial support. A life insurance agent may argue that you should buy a life insurance policy to cover the cost of burial when you die. But you should have enough in savings for this expense.

How much life insurance do you need? The simple answer: enough to sustain your family's present standard of living and let them meet their financial goals in the event that you're no longer around. If you're married and the only breadwinner, your life policy's death benefit—the face amount of the policy, collected by your beneficiaries after you die—together with your other assets should be large enough to deliver lifetime income for your spouse. If you have kids, you'll need to provide income for them, too, until they leave home, as well as a tuition fund if you intend to pay their way through college. If both you and your spouse work and earn income that the family relies on, both of you need coverage.

But putting a dollar figure on the exact amount you need is trickier than you may think. The rule of thumb that says you should insure yourself for five to seven times your annual gross income is far too simplistic. Instead, meet with a life insurance agent or a financial planner who can do the calculations to match your situation. Many personal finance and insurance Web sites can also handle the calculations right on your personal computer—with no salesman in the room! Visit www.money.com/life on CNN-money's Web site or complete the worksheet below.

HOW MUCH LIFE INSURANCE DO I NEED?

To figure out how much life insurance you need, you must first answer some tough questions. How little could your survivors live on? Would your family move from your home? Could your spouse ever replace your income? This worksheet, developed with the help of insurance adviser Peter Katt, is flexible. For one, it gives you the option of providing for your heirs for only a few years—or indefinitely.

A. SURVIVORS' ANNUAL LIVING EXPENSES
Based on your current budget, estimate the minimum your family needs to live on. You can exclude mortgage payments and college savings if you opt to fund those obligations with your insurance proceeds (see line D below). Account for additional child care expenses if necessary.   _____

B. EXPECTED ANNUAL INCOME
Include survivors' earnings, pension benefits, and Social Security for dependent children (call 800-772-1213 for an estimate).   _____

C. LIVING EXPENSE SHORTFALL
Subtract line B from line A.   _____

D. ONE-TIME EXPENSES

Include funeral expenses, legal fees, and any financial obligations you would like to fund, such as your children's education and current debts. If you plan to pay off your mortgage here, subtract monthly mortgage payments from your living expenses (line A).

_____

E. INCOME REPLACEMENT

There are two ways to replace your income, one permanent and one temporary. Your survivors can invest your insurance proceeds to produce income (option 1) or draw down the money over several years (option 2).

_____

Option 1: To calculate the amount you would need to invest to make up the shortfall, divide line C by an expected rate of return (expressed as a decimal). For instance, a conservative portfolio of government bonds would earn 4% (or 0.04).

_____

Option 2: If your survivors would need short-term help only, multiply the annual shortfall on line C by the number of years you need to cover.

_____

F. PRINCIPAL GOAL

Add line D to line E.

_____

G. AVAILABLE ASSETS

Add any group life insurance benefits and your investments. Exclude qualified retirement plans like IRAs and 401(k)s, 529 college plans, and your home. One exception: Include a portion of your home equity if your survivors would sell and move to a less expensive home.

_____

H. INSURANCE NEED

Subtract line G from line F.

_____

You already may have some of the life insurance coverage you'll need through a policy provided by your employer at work. If the amount you calculated by the worksheet is more than you can afford, consider trimming the amount by cutting back on certain goals (for example, maybe you don't want to leave each of your kids a $100,000 inheritance after all). Still, the basic amount of coverage a family of four needs can easily reach into the millions.

To decide which kind of life insurance policy is best for you, the first thing to understand is the difference between the two major types: term insurance and cash-value insurance.

Term insurance is pure insurance: Your premium payments go toward the guaranteed death benefit for your survivors. Well, almost exclusively. A portion also pays the agent's commission and the insurance company's overhead and profit. The term policy is good—in insurance terms "stays in force"—as long as you keep paying the premiums. When you stop paying, you're no longer insured.

Cash-value insurance, on the other hand, is a hybrid. It's life insurance combined with a savings fund. Part of the premium you pay goes toward the death benefit, the commission, and so forth, just as with term insurance. But a large piece of your premium goes into a tax-deferred investment fund. The balance you build up in this investment fund is known as the policy's **cash value**. The cash-value has a guaranteed interest rate, typically 4% to 5%, but the policy is likely to earn more than that for you. Depending on the policy, you can eventually borrow against your cash value or even withdraw it. Insurance agents sometimes like to call cash-value coverage "permanent insurance."

So which kind of insurance is better: term or cash-value? For most people, term is the clear winner. If you're young or money is tight, opting for a cash-value policy is downright foolish. That's because for the same death benefit, term insurance is far less expensive, especially in the early years. And the commissions are far less steep (commissions on cash-value policies generally run five to 10 times higher than those on term policies). If you're 35 and want to buy $500,000 worth of life insurance, your annual term premiums will run about $850 to $1,500.

The most basic type of term insurance is called **annual renewable term**, which in most cases guarantees that you can renew your contract each year without a medical exam. Its premium rises each year as you age. Women pay less; smokers pay much more. You generally cannot renew the policy after age 70, at which point you probably won't need life insurance anymore anyway. If you go with an annual renewable term policy, make sure the contract guarantees that you'll be able to keep it regardless of changes in your health. Another kind of term: **guaranteed level-premium term**, which has premiums that remain constant for a period of years, then spike up.

Price hikes for annual renewable term are not as scary as they may sound. While the premium rate keeps rising, the amount of coverage the typical family needs will likely level off and then decline. That's because as your children grow up and your savings and investments accumulate, you typically need to own less insurance, not more. And cutting back on the death benefit amount means lowering the premiums.

If you're shopping for a term policy, don't be taken in by one just because it has the cheapest first-year premium. Instead, make sure the agent shows you its projected annual cost five, 10, and 20 years into the contract (through what's known as a policy illustration) and the maximum premium charge in each case. You can also find this information on insurance Web sites. A policy with the lowest initial premium may cost more as the policy ages than a similar policy with a higher initial charge. Your agent may recommend a level-term policy with set premiums for an extended period, such as 10 years. Since the premium is basically an average of the cost for the entire period, you'll pay more in the early years of a level policy than with a traditional annual renewable term. That's fine, but go for level-term only if you expect to keep the coverage for the entire period. (And note: Some level-term policies don't guarantee the premium for the entire term; check before you buy.)

The typical cash-value policy carries a much higher premium than a term policy because that premium must cover two things: insurance plus savings. That high premium ordinarily stays the same each year. But unlike term, cash-value insurance can be kept until you're at least 95. If you decide to purchase a cash-value policy, be sure you'll hang on to it for at least 10 years. Otherwise the policy's fees and agent commissions will eat up far too much of your cash-value fund.

There are many different types of cash-value policies. Among the most common are **whole life, universal life**, and **variable life** policies. Here's how they differ:

- **A whole life policy**, the traditional form of cash-value insurance, invests mostly in bonds and earns a fixed, modest rate of return. This is the kind of policy your father or grandfather might have had. Premiums are fixed and in the early years tend to be higher than the cost of providing the protection; in later years they're usually less. The policyholder has no say in how the company manages these funds; long-range returns are comparable to those of bond funds.
- **Universal life policies** let you adjust your premium and death benefit every year to suit your changing circumstances, so long as you keep enough cash value to cover administrative expenses and mortality charges. Part of your premiums are invested in short-term securities similar to those in money-market mutual funds, paying money-market rates of interest.
- **Variable life** invests your cash value in your choice of stock, bond, or money-market funds. Returns fluctuate according to the markets and the fund manager's investing skill. Variable life policies generally deduct sales charges and other annual expenses that can cut their cash-value returns in half over the first 10 years you own them.

If you're shopping for a cash-value policy, be especially careful: Such policies are so complex that it's extremely difficult to compare the costs and benefits of different insurers' offerings. At a minimum, ask each agent what assumptions he or she is using to calculate policy illustrations. Some illustrations assume that cash-value accounts will earn an average of 8% a year for 20 years, for example, even though the kinds of things they invest in may now yield only 6%. Also ask the agent to verify that the interest rate figures are net of expenses, since that's what you'll really earn. Tell the agent to show you what would happen to your cash value if the insurer earned two percentage points less than anticipated, just to be sure. Also get a worst-case scenario—what the cash-value buildup would be if the insurer ended up paying the mere guaranteed rate, typically 4% to 5%. For $50, the Consumer Federation of America (www.consumerfed.org) will evaluate any cash-value policy's illustration, including expenses and commissions.

No matter which type of life insurance policy you want, don't sacrifice safety for price. If your life insurer goes belly-up, your coverage will be worthless. So stick with an insurer that gets a safety grade of no lower than A+ from rating agency A. M. Best (www.ambest.com) or AA- from Standard & Poor's (www.standardandpoors.com). Books detailing both agencies' ratings are also available at most public libraries.

THREE WAYS TO LOWER YOUR LIFE INSURANCE COSTS

Follow these suggestions to help save money on your life insurance premiums:

1. **Get healthier.** Quitting smoking can cut your life premium in half; losing excess weight can save almost as much.
2. **Call a price-comparison shopping service or use one online.** Several companies exist that will report the lowest rates available to you from a variety of different insurers. Price quotes are free; you can usually buy the policy you want directly from the company offering the price quote. Online services can also help you buy life insurance wisely, by advising you with calculators that help you figure out how much coverage you need, providing databases that can suggest appropriate types of policy, and identifying the least expensive one. A few such firms: Quotesmith (it scans more than 150 insurers: 800-556-9393; www.quotesmith.com); SelectQuote (16 insurers: 800-343-1985; www.selectquote.com); InsWeb (www.insweb.com), the insurance content provider for MSN Money (moneycentral.msn.com) and Quicken.com; and QuickQuote (www.quickquote.com). A few companies focus

exclusively on providing information about term life insurance: TermQuote (75 insurers: 800-444-8376; www.termquote.com) and InstantQuote (www.instantquote. com).

3. **Get some quotes from low-fee insurance companies.** Certain low-load insurers such as Ameritas Acacia and USAA, both of which sell by telephone, charge sales fees that amount to just 10% to 20% of your first-year premium and perhaps 2% of subsequent premiums. Check USAA (800-531-8000; www.usaa.com) or Ameritas (800-552-3553; www.ameritas.com). If you work with a fee-only financial planner, that pro can locate low-load policies for you, too. You'll pay a flat fee of perhaps $200 to $500 or a rate of something like $100 to $150 an hour.

Insurance You Don't Need

You may well be thinking, Gee—I sure need a lot more insurance than I have now! Well, maybe you do. And maybe you don't. According to the nonprofit Consumer Federation of America (CFA), fully 10% of the half a trillion or so dollars that Americans spend on insurance is unnecessary.

Remember, the purpose of insurance is to protect your family against financial catastrophe. So you should insure only against losses you can't absorb without serious pain— not against small losses that you can meet by tapping your savings. Nor should you buy policies that insure you against just one risk, such as dying in an airplane crash or contracting one specific illness. Such narrow policies are usually very expensive for what you get back in benefits.

Among the policies you should spurn—or dump if you already have them:

• **Life insurance for your kids.** It's amazing how many people take out policies on their young children's lives considering how little reason there is to do it. You should insure a person's life only in order to protect his or her dependents against the loss of that person's income stream. So unless your kid is supporting you, save your money.
• **Dread-disease insurance.** Policies that pay only if you get cancer, for example, cost a whopping $250 or so a year. Better to pay the premium for a policy that will cover you no matter what disease you get.
• **Hospital indemnity insurance.** Such heavily advertised policies promise to pay you, say, $50 to $200 a day for every day you spend hospitalized. But a typical hospital stay costs $1,150 a day. And any decent comprehensive health insurance policy should

cover hospitalizations adequately. Besides, you may have other medical expenses outside the hospital. What's more, these policies don't protect you against medical-cost inflation, because their dollar limit is locked in place.

- **Credit life and credit disability insurance.** It's a rare person who hasn't heard the credit insurance pitch from car dealerships, finance companies, or banks offering loans. "This policy will make your loan payments if you die or become disabled. And won't you feel better with that peace of mind?" Probably not—once you realize that credit insurance is usually a crashingly bad buy, costing perhaps $300 on a $10,000, four-year car loan.

  About half of all credit-card issuers offer such insurance, too, usually pushed in flyers included with your monthly bill (cost: about 60¢ on every $100 of your credit-card balance each month). The insurance generally pays off revolving credit-card debt if you die, become disabled, or lose your job. But there's one big problem: The policies generally pay off your entire debt only if you kick the bucket. If you're disabled or laid off, they'll pay just the monthly minimum on your card—typically a puny 2.5% of your balance—usually for no more than a year. Meanwhile interest keeps accruing on the balance.

  Instead of buying such insurance, simply beef up your personal emergency savings fund to cover small debts. As for large debts, make sure your life and disability coverage is adequate to cover them.

- **Mortgage protection insurance.** Similar to credit life insurance, this type of policy would make your house payments for six to 12 months if you were laid off. But it's too overpriced to be appealing: Premiums usually amount to 3% to 4% of your annual mortgage payment.

- **Home warranties.** Builders or real estate agents offer these contracts, which protect you against major defects in your home. Such warranties are expensive, though. They can cost up to $500 or more a year. And they are usually filled with exclusions. Another risk: The builder selling you the warranty will go out of business. If you're worried about defects in a house you're looking at, have a home inspector check it out instead.

- **Extended-service contracts on cars.** These complex and overpriced policies pay if certain big-ticket components in your car break down, which is unlikely during the first few years of ownership.

  The same goes for extended-service contracts on appliances and consumer electronics. But you're duplicating coverage for at least part of the time: The manufacturer's warranty usually lasts from three months to two years. Fact is, more than 80% of service contracts go unused.

- **Towing insurance.** Typically piggybacked onto your auto insurance policy, this coverage pays, say, $75 for getting your sick car to a repair shop. But if you belong to an auto club such as AAA, you almost certainly have towing coverage already. Many luxury carmakers also throw in free towing for the first few years of ownership.

- **Collision-damage waivers for rental cars.** These waivers, costing from $10 to $15 or so a day, can add 50% to the cost of your car rental. But for most people, accepting the coverage is completely unnecessary: Your own auto policy probably covers any car you rent (check to make sure). And some gold credit cards, as well as most American Express cards, automatically provide such protection when you charge your rental car.

- **Flight insurance.** Credit-card issuers often throw in free life insurance when you charge an air ticket (at least $100,000 in coverage when you charge your ticket to American Express, for example).

- **Trip-cancellation insurance.** If your sciatica flared up just in time to force you to cancel your prepaid vacation last year, you might be intrigued by such a policy. Not so fast. The policies usually won't pay if your cancellation is due to recurrence of an old ailment.

CHAPTER 3

Getting Help
You Can Trust

Fortunately, managing your finances isn't something you need to do alone. Although the Internet offers great investment, tax, insurance, and financial tools (you'll find dozens of helpful Web sites listed throughout this chapter and the book), you will probably be more likely to reach your financial goals if you hire some crackerjack advisers. Who should you consider for your financial team? A tax preparer, insurance agents, one or more lawyers, perhaps a broker, financial planner, or even a money manager. If you are planning a move, a sharp real estate agent can help you get the best price when selling your home and direct you to suitable shelter if you're buying.

You don't have to be rich to hire advisers, either. The key is finding the right pro for your needs and your wallet. For instance, although you could pay a certified public accountant (CPA) as much as $850 to fill out your federal and state tax returns, you might do just as well with a storefront preparer such as H&R Block or Jackson Hewitt charging fees that start at $50 or so. A helpful rule: To find an appropriate, honest adviser, start by asking your friends or business associates whom they use and begin interviewing them. What follows is kind of an annotated search engine to help you turn up the financial advisers you need.

Choosing a Tax Preparer

Which type of preparer to hire and how much you'll pay depend on the complexity of your tax return and your financial life. You have three basic options: **storefront preparers, CPAs**, and **enrolled agents**. You needn't hire a tax lawyer just to fill out your return or to get sensible tax-planning advice. A tax lawyer is worth a call, however, once you arrive at the intersection of taxes and the legal system—for instance, if you are about to get a divorce or buy or sell a business.

Try not to look for a tax pro in the heart of tax season, during March or April. By that time most of the better preparers are already booked. You'll also have a tough time getting one to sit with you for a free consultation. The best time to seek out a tax adviser who will provide tax-planning advice is in June or July (many take well-deserved vacations in May). If you want someone only to fill out your returns, start your search in January, once you have the necessary data for the previous year's finances. The skinny on your tax adviser choices:

- **Storefront preparers.** These are the people at places such as H&R Block, Jackson Hewitt Tax Service, and Liberty Tax Service. Some are part-timers, some work full-time year-round preparing tax returns. Nearly all are conservative about the write-offs they'll let you claim. Storefront preparers are the least expensive way to go. Figure on spending between $50 and $150 for a basic tax form, probably $200 or so for one that's a bit more complicated. A knowledgeable storefront preparer can certainly fill out a 1040 with ease (you ought to be able to fill out the simple 1040EZ or 1040A by yourself), along with Schedule A and Schedule B for itemized deductions, interest, and dividends. However, once you get into more complicated areas, such as home offices, small businesses, rental real estate, and the sale of stocks, bonds, or mutual funds, you might consider stepping up to either a CPA or an enrolled agent.
- **Certified public accountants (CPAs) and enrolled agents (EAs).** These are the pros to consider when you're looking for help with a complicated tax return, year-round tax-planning advice, and someone who might be able to help you if you need to do battle with the IRS. In fact, a CPA or EA can become one of your trusted allies throughout your life. This pro may turn into the sounding board you need when deciding things such as: Should I get a home-equity loan? Does it make sense to borrow from my 401(k) savings plan? Would I be better off in a tax-free municipal bond mutual fund or a fund that invests in U.S. Treasury securities?

Certified public accountants who specialize in taxes (not all CPAs do) and enrolled agents are similar in many respects. Both have received rigorous training. A CPA must pass a state accountancy exam and then take continuing education classes to keep up. To find a qualified CPA in your area, call 800-999-9256; or go to www.cpapfs.org.

An EA has either worked at the IRS and earned a special license or passed a stiff two-day IRS test. Both can represent you in front of the IRS. You'll pay either one more than a storefront preparer, because of their training. Enrolled agents often charge a little less than tax partners at big-city accounting firms. Many charge by the hour— $60 and up. If that's how yours gets paid, do whatever you can to bring your accountant or enrolled agent organized records. Otherwise you'll be throwing money away paying the adviser to sort through your receipts and determine which ones are important. As noted earlier, it's a good idea to ask friends or business associates for the names of advisers they use. Since there are only about 30,500 enrolled agents in the country, however, you may not know of anyone using one. To get names of enrolled agents in your area, call the National Association of Enrolled Agents at 800-424-4339; www.naea.org, or write to the group at 200 Orchard Ridge Dr., Suite 302, Gaithersburg, MD 20878-1978.

Ideally, you want a CPA or EA whose clients have incomes and jobs similar to yours. For instance, some know small-business taxes backward and forward; others don't. You also want to find a tax pro who will be just as aggressive about claiming write-offs as you would yourself—no more, no less. The tax code has many gray areas, particularly when it comes to things such as home offices and business expenses. Some preparers are willing to take chances and claim iffy deductions, figuring the IRS won't notice or that they will have a decent chance of defending them in an audit. Others favor a safer letter-of-the-law approach that could cost you more in taxes. When interviewing prospective tax advisers, find out how aggressive they are and see how you feel about their stance.

Ask, too, who will actually be preparing your return. At many accounting firms, low-level preparers and even temps make the first run filling out returns. They then pass their work up to the experienced CPAs, who sign the returns. There's nothing necessarily wrong with this approach; you just don't want to be surprised to find out that the person you thought was your preparer has farmed out your 1040.

Don't become wholly ignorant about taxes once you hire a tax adviser, however. The more you know about the tax code, the better the questions you can ask your preparer. It's worth picking up an annual tax guide sold in bookstores or checking out tax-helpful Web sites such as www.irs.gov.

Choosing Insurance Agents

Although you can buy insurance through the Internet, you still may want an insurance agent to help you click through the clutter, especially if you're not interested in spending hours plugging numbers into financial calculators or comparing various offers.

It's hard to think of anything more important than protecting yourself and the people you love. That's why buying insurance is so important and why you need to have trustworthy insurance agents. The preceding chapter told you how to shop for life, health, disability, auto, and homeowners insurance policies. Now a few words about getting the right agents who will sell you the policies. There are two types of agents: **independent agents**, who sell policies for a variety of companies; and **exclusive agents** or **captive agents**, who work for just one insurer. Theoretically, an independent agent should be better for you, since he or she can search among different companies for the least expensive policies with the broadest coverage from the safest insurers. Real life doesn't always work that way, however. An independent might be tempted to sell you the policy paying him or her the highest commission. Also, a captive agent's policy might be better than any policy sold by an independent. So don't rule out any agent because he or she works for too many or too few insurers. Instead, when interviewing agents, talk with both independents and exclusives. Again, your best bet is to get a referral. Some specifics for particular types of policies:

- **Life insurance.** While most life insurance agents are honest, you should always do your homework before choosing an agent. Five tips in finding a scrupulous agent:
  1. **Be sure the agent represents one or more insurers with top safety grades from independent analysts.** It won't matter how kindly your agent was if your insurer goes out of business. You'll want to get a policy from an insurer rated no lower than A+ from A. M. Best or AA- from Standard & Poor's.
  2. **Ask the agent to explain clearly how much insurance you need, why you need that much, and why he or she recommends a particular insurer and its policy.** If you don't get straight answers that you can understand, move on to another agent.
  3. **Look for someone who is a chartered life underwriter (CLU) or a chartered financial consultant (ChFC).** These designations are no definitive defense against moral turpitude, but they do suggest that the agent was serious enough about the profession to take the courses necessary for the moniker. The American College, an insurance school in Bryn Mawr, Pa., awards both the CLU and the ChFC.

4. **Don't buy from someone pitching insurance as an investment.** Remember: The reason to buy life insurance is to replace a lost income, not to get rich.

5. **Consider hiring an independent insurance adviser, not an agent, to help you choose a policy.** For instance, the Consumer Federation of America will evaluate any cash-value policy for $50 (www.consumerfed.org). The Life Insurance Advisers Association (800-521-4578) will put you in touch with a fee-only agent. For general life insurance questions, you can call the National Insurance Consumer Helpline (800-942-4242; www.acli.org) of the American Council of Life Insurance.

- **Health and disability insurance.** Many of the same agents who sell life insurance offer health and disability policies. So the first two life insurance tips apply here, too. In addition, however, when buying a health or disability policy, stick with agents who represent larger insurers. The bigger the policyholder base, the easier it is for the insurer to spread its risks and thus keep your premiums down. If you're looking for a health policy and have a medical problem, be sure to meet with an independent agent. This type of agent is more likely to find you an insurer who will sell you coverage.

- **Homeowners insurance.** Your homeowners insurance agent is the person who will go to bat for you if you need to file a claim after a casualty loss. Interview a half dozen agents. You're likely to find that in many cases you'll get the best price from a captive agent working for a single insurer with its own in-house sales force. As with life, health, and disability policies, buy homeowners coverage from a financially solid company. So make sure the agents you call sell policies from insurers rated no lower than A+ from A. M. Best or AA- from Standard & Poor's. While many states have so-called guaranty funds to protect customers if their insurers fold, many limit reimbursement to $100,000 to $300,000.

- **Car insurance.** The advice here echoes that of finding a decent homeowners agent, since both types of policies are sold by casualty insurers. You can get free online quotes from direct sellers such as Amica (www.amica.com) or GEICO (www.geico.com). However, you may prefer to hire the services of an agent you know who will help you collect if your car is in an accident or gets stolen.

One indicator of a helpful agent: When calling around for premium prices, see if the agent volunteers information about policy discounts. If you don't hear any, ask what discounts are available and watch what happens. A decent agent will either tell you without prompting about insurers' discounts for, say, policyholders with antitheft devices, or at least explain the discounts when asked. Nearly all insurers offer some kind of discounts today, so a cagey agent is one to be avoided.

Choosing a Broker or Investment Adviser

In the height of the bull market of the late 1990s, many investors started bypassing their stockbrokers to make their own trades (with cheaper commissions) through online brokers—from pure Internet players such as E-Trade and Ameritrade or traditional or discount firms like Merrill Lynch or Charles Schwab that provide online services. However, after the market crash of 2000-2001, the do-it-yourself trading fever died down a bit as serious investors realized that broker advice for some trades may be worth the higher fees.

Today, brokerage firms prefer calling their employees "account executives" or "account specialists" or "financial consultants," implying that they provide customers with more than just stock-picking tips. That's because smart brokers should be able to help you build a portfolio that meets your financial goals—now and in the future. Most people invest to accumulate money for a purpose, not just for the thrill of the trade.

Finding the right broker takes time. You're looking for someone with a proven track record and experience investing for people like you—whether you're a beginner or a high-net-worth executive. After getting the names of brokers recommended by people you know, do a little research on them—even before you meet any face-to-face. You'll want to be sure that the broker hasn't done his customers wrong. The best way to do this is by calling your state securities administrator (the phone number is in your phone book) and the National Association of Securities Dealers (800-289-9999; www.nasd.com). Ask both if the broker is licensed in your state and if there have been any complaints or disciplinary actions against him. The state agency should give you a copy of the broker's Central Registration Depository (CRD) file, listing any complaints or disciplinary actions taken against the broker.

Once you've found several brokers with clean records, make appointments to meet with them. At these free sessions, you'll want to see both how knowledgeable the brokers are about investing and how much the brokers want to know about you. As with an accountant or enrolled agent, you're looking for someone whose temperament and tolerance for risk match yours. Tell the broker up front about your investing goals, financial status, and risk tolerance, since this is the only way your broker can get a true sense of what you should be investing in. Then ask this key question: What kinds of investments would you recommend for me and why? If the investments seem too risky for you or too safe, you need to find a better match.

Unlike, say, tax preparers or lawyers, brokers have quantifiable performance records you can review. By checking out how well the broker's recommended stocks, bonds, and mutual funds have done, you'll be able to see whether you're likely to make money with him or her. And that, after all, is the bottom line. Ask the broker for 12 months' worth of performance for three clients whose objectives are like yours. Then have your broker compare those returns with the appropriate yardsticks. For instance, if you want to invest in stocks or stock mutual funds, stack up his returns against the Standard & Poor's 500 stock index.

Another way to eliminate inappropriate brokers is by discussing compensation. Now and after you've hired a broker, ask what kind of commission he or she would make from the recommended investments. You're not looking to cheat the broker out of a decent livelihood; you just want an explanation that will tell you whether the fees are reasonable. Brokers tend to keep a significant percentage of the commissions they receive; their firms get the rest. Ordinarily, brokers collect the highest commissions on complicated and risky investments that require some effort to sell. But if your broker recommends any investment paying a commission that seems too high, ask whether a less costly alternative could help you achieve the same financial goal.

Find out, too, about additional charges you might get socked with by the brokerage firm. Some firms charge 2% to 3% a year to maintain an account. Some brokerages charge a customer extra fees to keep the account open if the brokerage considers it inactive, to set up an IRA, or to get and keep your stock certificates. Brokerages have been piling up these junk fees in recent years, so you'll want to check out the charges before you select a broker.

Once you have found a broker you like, fill out the "My Investment Profile" form on pages 64–65 and give a copy to him or her. This way, you'll both know exactly what you want out of the relationship.

The key to having a successful and prosperous relationship with your broker is to keep in touch regularly—and don't be afraid to ask questions. When the broker recommends an investment, find out why. You want to be sure that the investment fits your needs and isn't just one the broker is touting to earn a fatter commission. From time to time, some brokerages offer sales incentives such as contests with prizes if their brokers sell a certain amount of a particular investment, such as a specific stock, mutual fund, limited partnership, or annuity. Most firms also increase brokers' commissions if they sell stocks that their firm is eager to clear out of inventory or if they sell their own in-house mutual funds rather than other funds. (A few brokerages, prodded by the Securities and Exchange Commission, are moving away from such practices.)

When your broker recommends an investment or you have one you want to buy, be sure to ask whether you're eligible for a discount. For example, if you invest at least $25,000 in a single mutual fund, you may qualify for a break point that lowers the commission you pay by one to one and one-half percentage points. When buying stocks, ask if your brokerage firm can shop around various dealers who make a market in given securities to get you the best price. Most full-service brokerages also authorize salespeople to slice trading commissions for their best customers by 20% to 50%.

Make sure you get your money's worth from your broker, too. If you're paying for the services of a full-service broker, you ought to be receiving research reports on investments that interest you—from the brokerage's own analysts or from outside firms such as Standard & Poor's, Value Line, and Morningstar. Feel free to ask your broker questions about the outlook for the economy and the securities markets, if you trust his or her judgment. Always discuss your investment strategies and concerns. At least once a quarter, review your portfolio with your broker, identifying investment winners and losers and plotting future moves.

When your broker suggests a particular investment, ask if it could be especially difficult or costly to unload later. If it could, that may well be an investment you can do without. For example, you might be stuck with a narrowly focused fund that is invested in securities that you hold elsewhere in your portfolio. With annuities and some mutual funds, your problem could be the cost of selling your holding. For example, if you sell shares of some mutual funds within five years, you'll get hit with a fee of 1% to 5%.

Resist efforts by a broker to trade too often. Because brokers earn a commission on every sale, they have an incentive to encourage trading. But you're almost always better with a **buy-and-hold strategy**. If you sell an investment within a year or so, brokerage commissions may eat up any profits. To discourage your broker from **churning** your account—that is, trading actively simply to rack up commissions—ask him how long he expects you to hold any investment and why. Your being so conscientious will convince a broker that if he has any churning impulses, you're not interested.

If you want to give your adviser the power to buy and sell investments for you, you need to consider what that means. One key issue: Do you want to be notified before every transaction? Your account can be discretionary, which means the adviser can buy and sell without contacting you first (although you'll still be mailed a confirmation after every trade), or nondiscretionary, which means the adviser needs approval for every trade. If you have a discretionary account, you'll be asked to sign a **limited power of attorney**. That gives, say, an independent financial planner who manages your account the ability to download your statements daily, place trades, send out money to your address of record, and debit fees from your account. (You can opt to restrict the power of attorney to certain activities.) What it never allows the planner to do is to send money from your account to another person's account or to change your address. Our advice: Never let your broker trade without your approval.

MY INVESTMENT PROFILE

This disclosure form, created with assistance from Thomas Benson of Diogenes Group in Naples, Fla., and J. Boyd Page of Atlanta's Page, Gard, Smiley & Bishop will help ensure that you and your broker are on the same wavelength. By filling in the worksheet, you will help your broker understand your risk tolerance, objectives, investment knowledge and experience, and financial goals. Make a copy of this and give it to your broker.

My name _____

Brokerage firm _____

My account number _____

Risk tolerance (circle appropriate level)

LOW (CDs and bonds)   HIGH (options, margin trading)

1   2   3   4   5   6   7   8   9   10

My objectives (don't rate any two classifications the same):

CAPITAL PRESERVATION

1	2	3	4	5
Less Important			Important	

GROWTH

1	2	3	4	5
Less Important			Important	

INCOME

1	2	3	4	5
Less Important			Important	

TAX SAVINGS

1	2	3	4	5
Less Important			Important	

LIQUIDITY

1	2	3	4	5
Less Important			Important	

Value of my investments:

Stocks $_____   Bonds $_____

Pensions $_____   Cash $_____

Real estate $_____   (money funds, CDs)

(other than residence)   Other $_____

My investment knowledge and experience:

Extensive   Moderate   Minimal   None

Investments I've made (circle if applicable):

Stocks   Taxable bonds   Tax-free bonds   Junk bonds

CDs   Mutual funds   Partnerships   Penny stocks

Short sales   Preferred/warrants   Options   Futures

I am relying on my broker for investment ideas . . .

Not at all   Partially   Totally

In any year, I'm willing to lose no more than $_____

I consider myself to be generally a . . .

Long-term investor   Short-term investor

I do not wish to pay more than _____% of my account in commissions in any year.

Broker's name and how we met _____
_____

Expected role and function of broker _____
_____

My big upcoming expenses (include estimated amount and date) _____
_____

Other instructions (when to sell securities; maximum sales charges I'll pay) _____
_____
_____

_____   _____

Broker's signature, date   **My signature, date**

Don't forget to discuss your **risk tolerance** and **time horizon** with your broker. Do you want to invest in stocks that you can hold for five years or more, or do you want to be an active trader? When will you need this money? Do you consider yourself a conservative or an aggressive investor? How often do you check the value of your investments? How have you reacted during this bear market? Did you sell? If you can't stomach a 20% or 15% or even 5% drop in your portfolio, your adviser should know. Remember, the quality of advice you get from a pro depends in part on the quality of information you share about yourself.

What should you do if you have a dispute with your broker? First, take a deep breath, since getting brokerage wrongs righted is not easy. Don't sit and stew. Federal law says claims against brokers must be filed within three years of buying a security or one year of discovering a problem, whichever is less. Some states give you more time, however. Start your battle by complaining to your broker directly. If that strategy doesn't work, meet with the brokerage's branch manager and write a letter to the firm's regulatory compliance department, spelling out your problem. The more precise your complaint, the better. Merely saying that you lost money or you don't like your broker won't get you anywhere. But if you can demonstrate that your broker took your money and put it into investments that weren't suitable for you or churned your account, you may have a solid case. If your complaint remains unresolved two months later, escalate by consulting a securities lawyer. For details about going to arbitration or through mediation, usually your only recourse under a standard brokerage agreement, call the National Association of Securities Dealers at 212-858-4400; www.nasd.com. One arbitration tip: Be sure to insist on a face-to-face hearing. You're more likely to win when arbitrators conduct a formal hearing rather than merely review documents submitted by both sides.

WHAT TO ASK ANY TYPE OF INVESTMENT ADVISER

Your first line of questioning should be about qualifications. You should ask not only what credentials a broker or investment adviser has but also how long he or she has been doing this kind of work, and where. This may give you a hint of how varied the person's experience is.

• **What's your investment philosophy?** This is a key area in determining whether you and your adviser are compatible. So be prepared to discuss your philosophy (if you have one), as well. That's because if you're a long-term investor, for instance, you don't want to partner with someone who will pull you in and out of the market. To get an idea of how actively an adviser trades, ask how many trades are made per year for the typical account. Remember, by now you should have thought about your risk tolerance and time horizon. If you're hiring someone to manage your investment portfolio, another consideration is whether the adviser will tailor the portfolio for you—or fit you into a standard asset mix. Also ask questions like: What research do you use? If an adviser is recommending stocks and funds, ask: What are your picks based on? Do you do the research yourself, use analysts at the firm, or tap some outside source?

- **Do you own the stock you recommend?** The answers to this and the previous questions should give you a sense of how independent a thinker the adviser is—and how confident of the investment.
- **How much personalized attention will I get?** Even though many major financial firms are extending money management to more investors, the attention you'll get—and the experience of your adviser—will vary considerably, based on how much money you invest. At large firms, services for accounts of less than $100,000 increasingly tend to be automated. At Merrill Lynch, if your account is under $100,000, your calls may be handled by a call center staffed by registered representatives. That system frees up advisers to put more focus on clients with more complex needs—and more money for Merrill to manage.

When you're interviewing a prospective broker or adviser, ask how many clients he or she has and who your primary contact will be—the adviser or an assistant. How many accounts did the firm have three years ago, compared with today? If the practice has grown quickly, how has the firm managed that growth? Has the staff grown to meet the demand?

Choosing a Financial Planner or Adviser

Do you need a financial planner? Maybe. A planner can be an invaluable playmaker for you, keeping a wide focus on your finances and instructing you on how to reach your goals. A talented planner may, in fact, act as the quarterback for your team of financial advisers, working closely with your specialists in taxes, insurance, investing, and the law. It's worth hiring a financial planner once your household income approaches $75,000 or so. Some people hire financial planners only when they need advice about a particular issue such as evaluating an early retirement offer, paying for college, or budgeting better. That's a smart strategy, too.

The trouble with financial planners, however, is that anyone can call himself one. Unlike a CPA or a lawyer, a financial planner is not required to undergo any specific training. Brokers and insurance agents are trying to be full-service advisers, and banks are jumping on the same bandwagon. Meanwhile, firms like Fidelity, Charles Schwab, and Vanguard are devoting more resources to the advice business. Even property and casualty insurer State Farm is moving into the advisory business, offering wealthy clients help with estate planning and charitable giving. The federal Securities and Exchange Commission ostensibly regulates registered investment advisers, but many planners don't even bother to register with the agency. What's more, SEC staffers are so busy, they rarely monitor financial planners until one gets into trouble. States regulate financial planners a bit more, but even their regulators don't do regular inspections of planning firms. So it falls to you to do some due diligence before hiring a planner.

The lack of clear boundaries between financial firms may give you the impression that it doesn't matter which adviser you pick. We disagree. The choice does matter—not because one firm or one set of credentials guarantees success, but because you need someone whose expertise and style are compatible with your needs.

WHAT TO ASK YOURSELF
BEFORE HIRING A FINANCIAL PRO

To home in on what you want out of an adviser, ask yourself these questions:

- **How much help do I want?** Depending upon that answer, an adviser can recommend how to allocate your assets, suggest stocks and funds to buy, or do the trades for you. The first question to ask yourself is whether you're looking for day-to-day money management, broad financial advice on a wide range of topics, or the answer to a single question. The relationship can be one-time, or ongoing, someone you can call whenever you have a question.
- **How much control am I willing to give up?** Some investors prefer to manage their own money but still value the insights and discipline their adviser provides. Others want their pro to formulate an investment plan—and then implement it. The degree of hand-holding is a matter of personal style. (If your adviser is also handling your investment transactions, see suggestions in the broker sections on discretionary and nondiscretionary accounts, risk tolerance, and time horizon.)

WHAT TO ASK YOUR FINANCIAL ADVISER OR PLANNER

Here are some specific items you want to discuss with a prospective planner:

- **Do you specialize, and if so, how?** Many planners try to be a jack-of-all-trades and take any client who can pay the freight. Some, however, work primarily with a particular type of client such as small-business owners or widows. Others tend to focus on one area of financial planning such as retirement planning or college funding. Be sure the planner has experience working with people whose financial lives are similar to yours.
- **Who's your typical client?** Finding out the adviser's average account size will help determine whether he or she has experience working with clients with needs similar to yours. Ask the adviser to describe a typical client—and a nightmare client (if that person is you, move on). Ask for the names of other clients you can contact, preferably ones in situations like yours. No client to whom an adviser refers you is likely to be a dissatisfied one, of course. But you can get a sense of how the adviser works.
- **How are you compensated?** Any reputable planner won't flinch when you ask this important question. It's imperative to find out ahead of time both how you'll be charged and how much.
- **What's for sale?** Not every adviser sells every type of investment. Some stick to funds, others branch into individual stocks and bonds, and still others specialize in variable annuities and life insurance (especially advisers who work for insurance companies). Even within asset classes an adviser may offer little beyond his parent company's products. Wide choice doesn't ensure better results, but being directed to a limited line of products should raise questions. If your adviser always offers up the same fund family or insurance company, ask whether he or she has an incentive to sell those products.
- **Who are three of your clients similar to me?** You'll want to talk to them about their opinion of the planner. Tell the planner you'd also like to see at least one recent written financial plan (of course without the names and other private information). You want to make sure your planner customizes the plans and that he or she isn't offering cookie-cutter advice. That's the best way to ensure that an adviser will focus on your specific concerns and finances. If you mentioned that you want to plan for your children's education, for example, were you asked to be more specific? There's a big difference between planning for four years at a state college and planning for private prep school and the Ivy League.

- **Can I have a copy of your ADV?** Before you visit an adviser—and certainly before you turn over your money—run some simple background checks. Any adviser who manages assets of $25 million or more must register with the Securities and Exchange Commission. A registered investment adviser should be willing to give you his or her registration form, or Form ADV, which lists education and employment history and any regulatory problems or client complaints (in Part I) and services, fees, and investment strategy (Part II). Advisers who manage less than $25 million must register with their state securities agency. For details on how to find background information from state and federal regulators and other online resources, see the box below.
- **What are your qualifications?** Advisers and planners can be found under many different guises, not all of which are created equal (as the box below illustrates). Anyone can claim the title "financial planner," and new titles pop up all the time. At Merrill Lynch, for example, brokers became known as "financial consultants" in the mid-'80s and now are called "financial advisers," "private-wealth-management advisers," or "private-wealth managers," depending on their training and experience.

WHO'S WHO IN THE FINANCIAL ADVICE BUSINESS?

- **Certified Financial Planner (CFP)**
  EXPERTISE: financial planning, including estates and retirement.
  WHO AWARDS: CFP Board of Standards.
  REQUIREMENTS: a 10-hour, two-day exam and three years of client experience (with bachelor's degree; five years without) (www.cfp-board.org).

- **Certified Investment Management Analyst (CIMA)**
  EXPERTISE: evaluation and selection of money managers.
  WHO AWARDS: Investment Management Consultants Association.
  REQUIREMENTS: a week-long course at the Wharton School of Business and a four-hour exam covering asset allocation, risk management, and the like; three years of related experience (www.imca.org).

- **Chartered Financial Analyst (CFA)**
  EXPERTISE: stock and bond analysis; portfolio management.
  WHO AWARDS: Association for Investment Management and Research.
  REQUIREMENTS: three six-hour exams in three years—on such topics as financial accounting and quantitative analysis—and three years' experience as an investment pro (www.aimr.org).

- **Chartered Financial Consultant (ChFC)**
EXPERTISE: financial planning, insurance.
WHO AWARDS: the American College.
REQUIREMENTS: eight planning courses and three years' business experience.
FACT: The same school awards CLUs (see below), so many ChFCs come from the insurance industry (www.amercoll.edu).

- **Chartered Life Underwriter (CLU)**
EXPERTISE: life insurance.
WHO AWARDS: the American College.
REQUIREMENTS: eight courses and three years of insurance experience.
FACT: Most CLUs are life insurance agents; a third are also ChFCs (www.amercoll.edu).

- **Personal Financial Specialist (PFS)**
EXPERTISE: financial planning, taxes.
WHO AWARDS: American Institute of Certified Public Accountants.
REQUIREMENTS: Must be a CPA and pass a six-hour exam (www.cpapfs.org).

- **Registered Financial Consultant (RFC)**
EXPERTISE: financial planning.
WHO AWARDS: International Association of Registered Financial Consultants.
REQUIREMENTS: a graduate degree in finance or business and four years of full-time experience in the financial industry (www.iarfc.org).

- **Registered Investment Adviser (RIA)**
EXPERTISE: investment advice.
WHO AWARDS: Securities and Exchange Commission (more than $25 million under management) or state securities agency.
REQUIREMENTS: must file disclosure documents with appropriate regulators (www.sec.gov).

- **Registered Representative (commonly referred to as broker)**
EXPERTISE: sale of securities.
WHO AWARDS: National Association of Securities Dealers.
REQUIREMENTS: the Series 7 exam in trading procedures for general securities or Series 6 exam for variable annuities and mutual funds (www.nasd.com).

THE PRICE OF FINANCIAL-PLANNING ADVICE

The financial-planning field is divided three ways, based on compensation practices. There are **fee-only planners**, who earn their living by charging customers either a flat fee or a percentage of their assets under management. There are **fee-and-commission** or **fee-based planners**, who charge fees and also earn commissions based on the investments and insurance policies they sell. Both types of planners will charge you for creating a written, comprehensive plan that looks at your whole financial picture from taxes to investments to estate planning. Finally, there are **commission-only planners**, who get paid only from the commissions they earn on what they sell you.

If you can afford one, a fee-only planner often is the best kind to hire. By not accepting commissions, the planner can be unbiased in his or her advice. To find a fee-only planner near you, call the trade group known as the National Association of Personal Financial Advisors or NAPFA (888-333-6659; www.napfa.org). NAPFA's membership directory includes names, addresses, and phone numbers of fee-only planners around the country, as well as the number of years they have been in the financial-services industry and any professional designations.

If you can't find a fee-only planner you like or can afford, try a fee-and-commission planner. It's best to avoid commission-only planners; they have too much temptation to stick you in high-fee investments. Should you wind up hiring a fee-and-commission planner, don't be shy about asking for advice whenever you need it. You always pay for the advice. With many financial products the commission is embedded; you don't see an itemized fee on your statement.

Finally, even if you've been working with an adviser for years, you should calculate your expenses every year. Only then can you judge whether the advice you're getting is worth the price you're paying.

- **Financial plan.** Several factors affect the cost of a one-time checkup, including what you're worth and the scope of the advice you're after. For instance, a family with an income of $75,000 to $250,000 and assets worth $600,000 that's looking for education and retirement planning would pay about $300 to $750. Someone who makes $250,000 a year, has assets over $1 million, and wants a comprehensive plan, including estate and tax advice, should expect a tab from $1,000 to $5,000, depending upon the amount of assets held.
- **Advice by the hour.** According to the latest survey by the CFP Board of Standards, from 1999, the average hourly rate charged by a CFP is $120.
- **Ongoing management.** The key is how much money you give the adviser to manage. According to Tiburon Strategic Advisors, the average fee levied by inde-

pendent advisers is 0.9% of assets for accounts of $1 million to $2.9 million, 1.2% for $500,000 to $999,999, and 1.4% for $250,000 to $499,999. However, at top brokerages, you may pay as much as 3% on a $50,000 portfolio; the larger your account, the lower the fee. Plus, you get a break if you have other business with the firm, such as a mortgage.

- **Full-service brokerage.** You'll typically pay a commission of 1% to 2%, depending in part on the number of shares and the value of the trade.

Warning Signs for When to Dump Your Financial Pro

Sometimes walking away from an adviser is a smart financial move. Here are seven red flags:

- **Makes unrealistic promises.** You've heard it before: If it sounds too good to be true, it is. An assurance of consistent double-digit returns means that your adviser has an overly rosy view of the market—or of his or her abilities. In the same vein, a promise that you'll never lose money is suspect. You want solid reasoning and objective analysis, not happy talk.
- **Gives a hard sell on annuities.** Your adviser may push annuities or other insurance products for their tax advantages. But the high annual fees—and hefty surrender charges if you sell in the first few years—mean that annuities are rarely the best tax-sheltered option. Instead, fund a 401(k), an IRA, or, if you're saving for college, a state 529 savings plan.
- **Ignores tax considerations.** If a new adviser takes a look at your portfolio and suggests that you sell all your old funds to buy new ones, he or she may be putting commissions ahead of the tax consequences of selling.
- **Claims somebody else is paying bills.** Even if your adviser says that the fund company or the insurance company is paying the commission, you can be confident that you're paying one way or the other, probably through higher annual expenses or premiums.
- **Discourages background checks.** Advisers shouldn't balk at providing any relevant documents, such as both parts of the Form ADV, if you want to look into their background. (Of course, you may want to get information on your own. See the box on pages 70–71 to find out how.) A pro should also freely give you references to clients with similar finances and, if appropriate, a sample plan with the client's identifying information blacked out.

- **Doesn't ask you the right questions.** If you want a broad financial plan and an adviser talks of nothing but what's for sale, that person may not be the best fit for you. An adviser should be willing to talk about the process of financial planning, not just the products involved.
- **Wants to move quickly.** If an adviser stresses the need to act at your first meeting—or expresses impatience when questioned—be on guard. What's the hurry? An adviser needs to know your risk tolerance and goals in order to provide sound advice. And a good one won't take your questioning as an affront. You're paying for the advice, and you're entitled to ask all the questions you want.

Getting action against a financial planner who defrauded or looted you is even tougher than fighting a bad broker. No formal body censures wrongdoers. The best advice: Try to work out a settlement with the planner or with his or her firm. If that doesn't work, you'll have to go to arbitration or sue. That's when good record keeping becomes critical. You'll bolster the chances of winning your case if you have kept notes about the planner's promise that a certain dicey investment is low-risk, for example. If you win, you might even consider putting that chunk of money into an investment you select all by yourself.

Choosing a Money Manager

If all you need is an adviser to help you invest and you've got plenty of bucks, you might want to hire a **money manager**. Usually, money managers require at least $250,000 (sometimes far more) to invest, though some will take $50,000. The advantage of using a money manager rather than just buying professionally managed mutual funds on your own is that you have more control over how your cash is invested. For instance, you could tell the money manager not to buy certain types of stocks for you, such as tobacco companies. This brain won't come cheaply, though. Many money managers charge 2% of the amount you invest, which is generally more than the fee of an average stock mutual fund.

Brokerage and financial-planning firms will find a money manager for you, if you like. Instead, get an independent specialist known as an **investment management consultant** or talent scout to find one for you. Chances are you'll wind up paying less in fees and have more personal contact this way. For the names of talent scouts near you, call the Institute for Certified Investment Management Consultants (800-449-4462;

www.icimc.org). Once you have the names of a few money managers, read through their ADV forms and ask them to supply you with performance figures going back at least five years for portfolios similar to the one you would like. After you have hired a money manager, monitor his or her performance quarterly. If, after a year, the manager hasn't beaten the appropriate market averages, you may want to make a switch.

A **managed account** or **separately managed account** (formerly known as a wrap account) is an increasingly popular way for people who can't afford a money manager to buy the services of one. Most brokerage firms now offer managed accounts. They work like this: You hand over a chunk of money—typically $100,000 and up—and the money manager selected by the brokerage firm decides which stocks, bonds, or sometimes mutual funds to buy for you and moves your money around at will. Cost: up to 3% of the assets you invest. You needn't pay 3%, however, and shouldn't. Instead, negotiate the fee with your broker. You may well be able to get it down to 1.5% or so. The average brokerage annual managed account fee is 2.3%; mutual fund managed accounts tend to charge 1% to 1.5% plus annual expenses of 0.5% to 2%. Your broker must give you a brochure explaining the compensation arrangement for the account and how the manager's track record is calculated. (These brochures aren't required for accounts that invest exclusively in mutual funds.)

Should you open a managed account? That depends on how much money you have to invest. These accounts make the most sense for people investing $250,000 or more. Once you have that amount of money, you have the best chance of cutting down the fee. What's more, you can then diversify among two or three money managers.

If you decide to get a managed account, be sure you can select among managers with different investing styles. Be sure each manager's performance record has been calculated and verified according to the standards of the Association for Investment Management and Research, a trade group for money managers (800-247-8132; www.aimr.org). You'll also want to find out how much personal attention you can expect to receive from the manager.

Choosing Lawyers

Sooner or later, you'll need a lawyer. In fact, you'll most likely wind up needing more than one lawyer—one for your real estate closings and routine matters such as reviewing contracts and another for estate matters like wills and trusts. If your marriage sours, you may need a divorce lawyer. You might even hire a tax lawyer if you find yourself in a serious fight with the IRS or you're about to sign a business deal with significant tax implications.

The cost of hiring a lawyer can vary enormously, depending on the expertise of the pro and the amount of time you'll demand. Lately, growing numbers of people have turned to **prepaid legal plans** as a way to save on legal fees. These plans, often offered through employers and credit-card companies, are kind of like legal HMOs. You pay a set annual fee of $200 or thereabouts, which entitles you to a specified amount of service from lawyers in the prepaid plan's network. These plans can be handy if you need a lawyer for fairly mundane matters such as a real estate closing or a simple will. They're not terrific, however, if your legal needs are more complex. Being limited to using just the lawyers in the group is also restricting, particularly if you would prefer to hire specialists who don't belong to the plan.

When hunting to hire a lawyer on your own, start the way you would look for any adviser: Ask your friends and business associates for names of pros they've used. Find out whether they thought the lawyer's fee was reasonable and if the attorney did everything he or she promised. A helpful organization is Nolo Press, a publisher of self-help law books and software (800-728-3555; www.nolopress.com).

This electronic aid offers advice about shopping for a lawyer from its *Cradle to Grave Legal Survival Guide* book. Court TV's *Lawyer Check* (www.courttv.com/legalhelp/check.html) is a free online site that gives state-by-state listings as to where to check attorneys' disciplinary records. Another resource: the *Martindale-Hubbell Law Directory*. This book, actually a shelfful of books, lists attorneys throughout the United States and notes their specialties. You can find *Martindale-Hubbell* in the public library or a law library or on the Internet at www.martindale.com. The American Bar Association's guide, *The American Lawyer: When and How to Use One*, is also useful ($2.50; 312-988-5522; www.abanet.org). Don't waste your time getting referrals from the local bar association, however. Lawyers pay to get listed with such groups, so you're really getting nothing more than a bunch of names of lawyers who've paid to advertise their services.

When interviewing lawyers you might want to hire—the first consultation is usually free—check out their experience, aggressiveness, and fees. Don't use a lawyer fresh out of law school; let someone else be the guinea pig. Instead, work with lawyers who have been practicing at least five years. Choosing a suitable lawyer is much like finding the right tax preparer: You're looking for someone who is as much of a tiger as you prefer. For instance, some lawyers are extremely tough in real estate negotiations, demanding extraordinary concessions from buyers or sellers, even if that means walking away from a deal. Others are more willing to bargain a bit to cut a quick contract. Before taking on a lawyer, have a discussion about how tough he or she plans to be. Ask, too, for names of several clients and call them to find out how satisfied they were.

Most lawyers charge by the hour. You might pay as little as $50 an hour or as much as $400, depending on the firm. For simple matters such as a house closing or reviewing a lease, you may be cited a flat fee of $500 or so. A will could run about $1,500. Some lawyers ask clients for a **retainer**; this is an up-front deposit that might range from $500 to $5,000. If yours does, make sure to get in writing exactly what the retainer covers. For a personal injury case, expect the lawyer to charge a **contingency fee**. This means he or she will collect a portion of any amount you receive, generally 30% to 40%.

Divorce lawyers are a special breed. Most are tough and expensive. The National Coalition for Family Justice in Irvington, N.Y. (914-591-5753; www.ncfj.org) is a self-help group for divorced persons and can help you locate a lawyer in your area. Before hiring any divorce lawyer, however, get a rough estimate of what the total bill will be. Also, make sure the lawyer agrees in writing not to file any motions or papers before you have had time to review them.

You may be able to avoid hiring a divorce lawyer altogether or at least save on some legal fees by ending your marriage through either a **mediation** or **arbitration specialist**. When you hire a mediator (cost: about $500 to $3,000), this expert meets with you and your soon-to-be ex and works out terms of the divorce. Often, the mediator is a lawyer or a family therapist. Once your lawyer and your spouse's lawyer agree to the mediator's agreement, the divorce is final and binding. For the names of mediators near you, contact the Association for Conflict Resolution (202-667-9700; http://acresolution. org). Arbitration, which runs a little more (figure $750 to $4,000), entails hiring a pro to listen to both sides of the marital dissolution and then determine the terms for the divorce. For names of arbitrators, contact the American Arbitration Association (800-778-7879; www.adr.org).

CHAPTER 4

How to Lower Your Taxes

According to estimates from the Citizens for Tax Justice, an independent tax-tracking organization in Washington, D.C., the average two-income American household now pays 25% of its income in federal, state, and local taxes. So, for instance, that means should you be granted a $1,000 raise, you'll take home $750.

Clearly, taxes make it tougher to reach your financial goals, although the $1.35 trillion tax cut signed into law in 2001 was the deepest in two decades, slashing tax rates and adding a host of other perks, like expanded retirement accounts and incentives to save for your kids' education. However, every single reform will vanish in a decade unless Congress unwinds the law's sunset provision, which essentially puts the old pre-2001 tax code back in place in 2011.

No matter what happens to these tax cuts in the future, it is clear that, coupled with inflation, taxes steadily eat away at your wages and investment gains. So to build up your net worth, you have to bring your taxes down. That means getting a basic understanding of the tax rules and then putting together a well-thought-out, carefully implemented tax plan. It's easier than you might think.

Determining Your Tax Bracket

The key to shrewd tax planning is knowing your **tax bracket**. This number is essential because it tells you how much of any extra earnings—from investments or moon-lighting—you actually get to keep. Furthermore, only by knowing your tax bracket can you pinpoint what your home mortgage interest or business driving costs you after taking tax savings into account. Depending on your filing status (single, married, etc.), different levels of income will be taxed at different rates. The United States uses a **marginal tax rate system**. That means that all income up to a certain limit is taxed at one rate and any income over that limit and under the next limit is taxed at a higher rate. Under the present graduated U.S. tax system, as income rises, so does the percentage of income that goes to the government. In theory, the federal tax law has only six tax rates for employment earn-ings and interest earned. (See table below for the tax rates from 2002 through 2011.)

INCOME TAX RATES (2002–2011)

The Economic Growth and Tax Relief Reconciliation Act of 2001 lowered tax rates, as listed below. Note that some of the rates are scheduled to continue to drop throughout the decade. When figuring out how much tax you will owe, your income and your filing status (whether you are filing single, married and jointly, or separately but married) tell you what rate you need to use. To determine your own tax bracket, go to www.irs.gov to see the most recent IRS tax rate schedule.

Year	Tax Brackets					
2002	10%[1]	15%	27%	30%	35%	38.6%
2003	10%	15%	27%	30%	35%	38.6%
2004	10%	15%	26%	29%	34%	37.6%
2005	10%	15%	26%	29%	34%	37.6%
2006	10%	15%	25%	28%	33%	35%
2007	10%	15%	25%	28%	33%	35%
2008	10%	15%	25%	28%	33%	35%
2009	10%	15%	25%	28%	33%	35%
2010	10%	15%	25%	28%	33%	35%
2011	—	15%	28%	31%	36%	39.6%

[1]From 2001 to 2007, 10% bracket applies to first $6,000 of income for singles, $12,000 for marrieds filing jointly, and $10,000 for heads of households. From 2008 to 2010, 10% bracket applies to first $7,000 for singles, $14,000 for marrieds filing jointly, and $10,000 for heads of households. **Sources:** Economic Growth and Tax Relief Reconciliation Act of 2001, CCH, Joint Committee on Taxation.

Of course, federal income tax is merely the most notorious levy. For a complete picture of your tax bite, you'll need to add in state and local income taxes. For instance, if your federal tax rate is 27% and your state tax rate is 9%, your combined marginal tax rate is 36%.

Three Types of Income to Calculate Your Tax Bill

You also need to understand the three broad categories of income to determine how much tax you must pay.

- **Gross income.** This is the income you receive before taking out any deductions, credits, or exemptions. Gross income includes wages and salary, dividends and interest from investments, tips, alimony, pension payments, gross business income, unemployment benefits, scholarships for room and board. Interest from tax-free municipal bonds, tax-free Social Security benefits, and tax-free scholarships are not included.
- **Adjusted gross income (AGI).** Your AGI is your total gross income minus certain deductions. These include deductible contributions to qualified retirement plans such as IRAs and Keoghs, student loan interest, moving expenses, self-employment tax or self-employment health insurance premiums, and alimony.
- **Taxable income.** To calculate your taxable income, subtract all your adjustments, deductions, and exemptions from your AGI. These deductions might include itemized deductions, personal exemptions, unreimbursed employee business expenses or medical bills, mortgage interest, or moving expenses.

Capital Gains

Each time you sell an investment and make a profit you owe capital gains taxes on your earnings. The tax rates and rules for sales of your investments can be complicated because how much you'll pay in tax is determined by two factors: your federal income tax bracket and how long you've owned the investment.

CAPITAL-GAINS TAX RATES

This capital gains table covers stocks, bonds, mutual funds, and real estate investments.

Type of Capital Gains	Tax Bracket	Number of Years Investments Were Held	Tax Rate
Short-Term Capital Gains	All filers	Investments held one year or less	Gains taxed at ordinary income tax rates
Long-Term Capital Gains	10% and 15%	Investments held one to five years	10%
	27%, 30%, 35%, 38.6%		20%
Qualified Five-Year Gains	10% and 15%	Investments held longer than five years[1]	8%
	27%, 30%, 35%, 38.6%		20% or 18%

[1] The gains will be taxed at 20%, unless the five-year holding period began after December 31, 2000, either through acquisition date or a deemed sale election in 2001. Source: CCH.

Smart Federal-Income-Tax Saving Strategies

Funny thing about taxes: Most people approach them backward. They sit down between January 1 and April 15 and start sifting through the records of things they've already done, looking for ways to save. The problem is, by then it's too late to take advantage of many of the tax-saving opportunities that do exist. A smarter way to approach the task would be to look ahead, not behind. You should chart a year-round tax strategy that will yield the lowest possible tax bill come next April 15. Sitting down and filling out your return is only the last step in such a strategy.

The 2001 tax laws created some new tax-saving techniques, so smart tax planning can pay handsome rewards. Run through this list of 30 tax-saving ideas (grouped into categories) to make sure you're taking advantage of all the opportunities that work for you.

YOUR TAX GAME PLAN

1. **Don't wait until it's too late.** Begin tax planning early. This gives you time to take advantage of strategies that may not be available later in the year. Also, it sometimes takes several months to realize maximum benefits or implement the strategy. For example, wait until July to look for a new home and you probably won't reap any tax benefits until at least October—count on a month or so for house hunting and around two months to close. That will give you only two or three months of mortgage interest to deduct, costing you thousands of dollars in write-offs.

2. **Don't overwithhold.** One of the biggest tax mistakes people make is having the wrong amount of taxes withheld from their paychecks during the year. Having too much money withheld can be a kind of forced savings plan that transforms into a hefty refund at tax time. But think about it: Why should the IRS have its hands on your money all year long instead of you? If you got a big refund after you filed your last tax return or recently had a baby or bought a house (two occasions that produce tax savings—and joy), fill out a new W-4 form at work and revise your withholding allowances on the Deductions and Adjustments Worksheet.

3. **Maintain tax-smart records.** Keeping track of your deductible expenses can save you a shoeboxful of tax dollars. If you use your car for business, for example, the IRS lets you deduct either a flat amount per mile (for example, in 2001 it was 34.5¢) or—if you keep careful records—write off your actual operating expenses. The business portion of your gasoline, auto insurance, repairs, and other costs may net you hundreds of dollars more in tax savings than the government's standard mileage rate.

   Nowhere is poor record keeping more costly than in an audit. Without records, the IRS may disallow your write-offs. Audit-proofing your records means paying by check or credit card (and keeping a receipt) or requesting cash receipts. If you entertain for business, back up restaurant stubs with notations or diary entries showing the date, place, amount, name of person entertained, and business purpose.

   Keep records on anything related to your home. That includes paperwork on the sale of your home. Although you won't owe taxes on gains on your principal residence up to $500,000 if you're married ($250,000 if you're single), if you're audited you may need documentation to prove that your gains didn't exceed these thresholds. What's more, you might be lucky enough to have a profit over those amounts when you sell. So when you do sell, you'll still want to reduce any taxable gain by adding to your original purchase price the amount you've spent on improvements over the years (and have the records to verify). You may also need the records to deduct the interest on a refinanced loan. Bona fide improvements include remodeling your kitchen, adding central air-conditioning, refurbishing a basement, landscaping, and installing a spa. Repairs, painting, and routine maintenance work do not qualify as improvements, though. Sorry.

4. **Make sure you take all of your deductions, credits, and exemptions.** But first you need to understand the difference between a tax deduction and a tax credit. A **deduction** isn't as valuable as a credit. That's because a deduction reduces the amount of your income subject to tax, so that only a percentage of the expense gets recouped as tax savings. These include home mortgage interest, employee business expenses, charitable gifts, and medical and dental expenses.

A **credit**, however, reduces your tax liability dollar for dollar. Put another way, if you owe $5,000 in taxes but have a tax credit of $500, you would owe only $4,500 in taxes. See the "Your Family" section below for four popular tax credits.

Exemptions are types of income you don't have to report for taxes. These include gifts, inheritances, life insurance proceeds, child support payments, personal injury damages, disability benefits, rental security deposits (unless you don't refund the money), new-car rebates, and utility company rebates for buying energy-conservation devices.

5. **Bunch your deductions if you will have trouble itemizing.** You may find that you don't have quite enough write-offs to exceed the standard deduction (in 2001 this was $7,350 for married couples filing jointly; $4,400 for singles). In that case, see whether there are some deductible expenses you expect to incur next year that you could make this year to let you itemize and get some extra write-offs. (Some often overlooked deductions: legal fees relating to the production, collection, or advice about taxable income and investment expenses such as financial planner fees, IRA custodian fees, subscriptions to investment publications, or the cost of safe-deposit boxes in which you store securities or tax documents.) Conversely, if it's pretty clear you won't be able to itemize, try to postpone to next year expenses that you could write off if you itemized. That's because next year you might just have enough deductions to itemize.

6. **Defer taxes.** Certain kinds of investments let you postpone paying taxes on earnings to a later year, when you may be in a lower bracket. One sure advantage of tax deferral is **tax-free compounding**. Series EE and Series I U.S. savings bonds offer

this feature, as do annuities. You can defer paying taxes on the interest on savings bonds until the bonds are cashed. With an annuity, taxes aren't due until the income is actually paid out. Another tax-delaying tactic: Buy Treasury bills that mature next year. Although you get your T-bill interest when you buy the security, you don't need to report the income on your federal tax return until the T-bill matures.

Quite a few tax laws provide breaks only if your income is below certain levels. To qualify for certain breaks, you may need to lower your adjusted gross income or push income into the following year. Here's an example of how this can work. In 2002 the AGI threshold to qualify for a child tax credit ($600 per child) is $121,000 for married joint filers. So if a married couple with two children under 17 have an adjusted gross income of $124,000 in 2002, they will not qualify for a child tax credit of $1,200. However, if they lower their AGI by $3,000 they will be eligible for the $1,200 credit. One way to do this: They could increase their pretax contributions to their employer-sponsored retirement plans and flexible savings accounts this year, which will lower their adjusted gross income. They could also defer payment of bonuses until the following year.

YOUR INVESTMENTS

7. **Pad your nest egg with tax-sheltered retirement savings plans.** If you are an employee, your best single tax-slashing move is to contribute the maximum to an employer-sponsored 401(k) savings plan. Your contributions, as well as their earnings, escape federal and most state and local taxes until withdrawn. A bonus: You won't owe Social Security—known as FICA—tax on the money your employer donates. (For more on Social Security and retirement plans, see Chapter 11.) Your second best bet: Take advantage of tax-shelter features of IRAs.

8. **Contribute to an IRA or Keogh plan early in the year.** If, like so many taxpayers, you wait until April 15 to make an IRA contribution and then claim the deduction for the previous year, you're passing up 15½ months of compounding. That's a big loss. Just watch: If you invest $3,000 on January 1 of every year into an IRA earning 8%, you will have $142,879.70 at the end of 20 years. But if another saver decided to wait until April 15 of the following year to start investing his $3,000, by December of the year in which the "late" saver has made his last contribution, the difference between the two accounts would be $16,290.87. Merely contributing the same amount in the same investment 15½ months apart makes a difference of almost $1,000 a year. Think how great the difference would be in a Keogh plan for self-employed people where you can invest up to $40,000 a year. Even if you can't make

the full contribution on January 1, invest as much as you can as early as possible. You must open a Keogh plan by December 31 to deduct your contribution for the year; you can wait until tax time to open the IRA for the write-off, though you shouldn't.

9. **Consider tax-exempt securities.** Income from municipal bonds is free from federal taxes. Better still, invest in municipal bonds issued in your own state and you can save state and perhaps local taxes as well. Focus on after-tax yield when comparing the returns on different income investments. For example, if you are in the 30% bracket, a municipal bond paying 5% is equivalent to a taxable investment earning about 7.1% (see Chapter 5). Seniors may pocket even more tax savings from municipals. Although tax-free interest counts when figuring how much of your Social Security benefits are taxable, the lower yields on tax-exempts will hold down the extra tax.

10. **Round up all mutual fund transactions.** To avoid getting socked by the IRS with a negligence penalty, carefully review all the Forms 1099-B you receive from your mutual funds during the year. You may have more gains or losses than you think. You also incur gains or losses each time you pick up the phone and switch from, say, a stock fund to a bond fund in the same fund family.

11. **Don't overstate mutual fund capital gains.** If you calculate the **tax basis** (the cost on which your capital gain or loss is based) of your mutual fund shares and come up with a round number like $10,000, you've probably erred in Uncle Sam's favor. You likely forgot that your dividends and capital-gains distributions were automatically reinvested in new shares. Because you reported those amounts as income in prior years, you will wind up paying taxes on them twice if you don't add the reinvestments to your basis. Here's how to figure your taxable gain: First, start with your original purchase price. Then, add together any amounts the fund reported to you during the year as undistributed capital gains and ordinary income dividends. Next, subtract any nontaxable dividends that represented a return of your investment. The result is your basis. Subtract that figure from the sale price. Voilà! Your taxable gain.

12. **Unload your most expensive shares first.** When selling stocks, bonds, or mutual funds you've bought over time, cut your taxable gains by identifying the shares you want to sell—that is, the ones that cost you the most. This strategy works best when fund prices have fluctuated dramatically. Review your brokerage or mutual fund statements to find the dates when you paid the most for each share or bond. Then write a letter of redemption to your broker or mutual fund, specifying which shares you're selling according to the date you paid. Keep a copy for your records and ask your broker or fund for confirmation in writing. If you don't specify which block you are selling, the IRS may use what's known as the **first in, first out** method **(FIFO)**. That simply means the first shares you bought will be pre-

sumed to be the first shares you sold, which could force you to pay more in taxes than necessary. If that sounds too complicated, you do have another option, at least when it comes to selling your mutual fund shares. When selling funds, the easiest method to calculate your gains, by far, is **average cost**—your total investment divided by the number of shares. Most fund companies provide a year-end gain or loss calculation based on your average cost. But one final note: If you use average cost, you can't use any form of specific identification (such as FIFO or highest cost) for subsequent sales of the same fund. You may, however, switch from specific shares to average cost.

13. **Look for mutual funds that are tax-efficient.** These are the ones that produce the highest returns for investors, net of taxes on income and capital-gains distributions. The average diversified stock fund had a tax-efficiency ranging from 84% to 88% over three, five, and 10 years, according to the Morningstar mutual fund research firm. Translation: Shareholders returned to Uncle Sam 12% to 16% of the annual gains they received from their funds. (You can find a fund's tax-efficiency rating by going to www.morningstar.com or checking out the Morningstar mutual fund publications at your library.)

14. **Shift your profitable investments to your kids.** If you are ready to sell shares that have appreciated in value, make a gift of them to your child instead. Your child can then sell the stock, paying tax at his or her rate on the capital gain (the profit from an investment), which is likely to be 8% or 10%—rather than your rate of 18% or higher. Under the new capital-gains rules, you are taxed on long-term capital gains at either the 18% or 20% tax rate, even if you're in one of the higher brackets. Short-term gains (those under 12 months) are still taxed at your income tax bracket. One exception to these rules: Collectibles such as art, antiques, and coins aren't eligible for the new, lower capital-gains rates; they're still taxed up to 28% for long-term gains. Red alert: If your children are under age 14, their investment income above $750 (in 2002) will be subject to the so-called **kiddie tax**. In other words, that amount of income will be taxed at your top rate.

   If your investment drops in value, you can sell it for a capital loss and offset up to $3,000 in losses against your capital gains. This move effectively reduces your capital-gains taxes. If it turns out you don't have any capital gains, you can offset up to $3,000 in losses against your regular income, known as **ordinary income**. You can carry over to future years any losses that exceed $3,000.

15. **Swap, don't sell.** If you are thinking of selling rental real estate you own, consider a nontaxable **like-kind exchange** instead. If you sell, you may well have a huge capital gain because of the depreciation you have claimed over the years. For example, if you sell for $1 million a building with an **adjusted basis** (its cost minus depreciation) of $100,000, you would pay an 18% or 20% capital-gains tax, or

amount of any unpaid principal and interest will be subtracted from your death benefit. If you choose to pay the interest, you can do so whenever you wish.

29. **Prepare for the worst.** You never know when disaster may strike, but you can be prepared if it happens. Inventory your valuable possessions, take photographs, or make videotapes and keep them together with purchase records and appraisals in a secure place outside your home, such as in a safe-deposit box or your office. This way you'll have proof if a deductible casualty or theft loss occurs.

30. **Deduct long-term-care costs if you can.** A little-known 1996 law now lets some of the premiums or fees you pay for long-term-care insurance or services qualify as a tax-deductible itemized expense. Only the expenses combined with other medical outlays that exceed 7.5% of your adjusted gross income can be written off, though. The amount you can deduct rises with your age and the medical-cost inflation rate.

Smart State-Income-Tax-Saving Strategies

You can't do serious tax planning unless you take state and local taxes into account, too. States and municipalities, forced by Congress to shoulder more and more of the burden of social programs, have been hiking levies dramatically in recent years. The result? State and local taxes can no longer be ignored. Fortunately, you can fight back. In some cases you can do so just by making the federal-income-tax-saving moves previously mentioned. That's because federal and state tax returns often piggyback on each another. Most states exact a percentage of what you pay to the feds or use your federal return as a starting point in computing your state tax. Lower your federal tax and you then automatically chip away at your state tax, too.

That's just the first step, though. Now comes the hard part: sifting through your state's tax code for any odd twists and turns you can exploit. For instance, some expenses that aren't federally deductible are allowed as write-offs by many states. A few examples are political contributions, a portion of your rent, and medical expenses that fall below the federal deductibility threshold of 7.5% of adjusted gross income. Some states also offer their own tax credits not available from the federal government, such as a renter's credit or, in several states, credits for installing energy-saving equipment. Ask your tax pro or consult a state tax handbook, available in most libraries, for a listing of your state's deductions, exemptions, and credits.

Here are 10 ways to fight back against steep state taxes:

1. **Invest in municipal bonds.** Most municipal bonds issued by your state pay interest that is exempt from federal, state, and local taxes. This can be especially valuable in states that tax interest at a high rate, such as California, Connecticut, and New York.

2. **Buy Treasury securities.** Not only are they the safest investments, their interest is exempt from state and local taxes. That lets you pocket up to seven-tenths of a percentage point in extra yield if you live in a high-tax state. For the same reason, look at money-market funds that hold only Treasuries; such funds offer yields very close to those on the best-performing nongovernment money funds. After taxes, however, the government money funds pay nearly a point more in high-tax states. Caution: The words "U.S. Government" in a mutual fund name don't necessarily mean all of its earnings are tax-free in your state. For example, many states tax interest earned on U.S. government–backed mortgage securities known as Ginnie Maes. The fund will usually enclose a list with its year-end statement, showing the percentage of its income that is exempt from tax in your state.

3. **Don't pay tax on tax-exempt income.** Social Security benefits are fully exempt from state taxes in California, Illinois, New York, Pennsylvania, and about 20 other states. Pension income is also exempted, or at least partially exempted, in 16 states. The pensions of specific employees (usually military personnel) are not taxed in 14 states. Lottery winnings—you should be so lucky—are also tax-free in a few states.

4. **Benefit from favored capital-gains treatment.** Two states currently protect a percentage of capital gains: Massachusetts has lower rates for gains on assets held for longer than one year, and no tax on gains from assets held over six years. Wisconsin protects 60% of the gain from assets held for more than one year.

5. **Take full advantage of your federal deductions for state and local taxes.** If you itemize deductions on your federal return, remember to write off the state and local income tax withholding shown on your Form W-2, as well as your real estate tax and any personal property tax. Don't overlook such items as the state estimated tax payment for the previous year that you made last January and taxes for a prior year that you paid as a result of an audit or because you filed an amended or late return. State disability insurance withheld in California, New Jersey, New York, and Rhode Island is also deductible. Finally, ask your tax adviser or local tax agency what local charges, such as water or sewage fees, may be federally deductible.

6. **Know where your state is stricter than the feds.** Don't assume that the federal rules automatically apply to your state. Among the snares: 10 states and the District of Columbia will not grant an extension for filing your state income tax return simply because you requested a federal extension. Also, the estimated tax penalty

may be different in your state from the one the feds use. Under federal law, if you make **estimated tax payments** (quarterly taxes due if you don't have enough withheld) and underpay your federal liability by $1,000, you're hit with a tax penalty. The cutoff can be much lower at the state level, however. The feds say that you must make quarterly estimated tax payments to the IRS if you expect to come up with a tax due of $1,000 or more at the end of the year and your withholding won't cover 90% of your tax or 100% of last year's tax, whichever is less.

7. **See whether it pays to file separate state returns for you and your spouse.** To ease the tax bite on two-earner couples, 11 states let married persons file separately, even if they file a joint federal return.

8. **Research the taxes of a locale before you move.** Don't jump from the frying pan into the tax fire. A full 18 states refuse you the right to special 10-year averaging on lump-sum pension distributions (for more on the advantage of averaging pension distributions, see Chapter 11).

9. **Plan your estate.** Some states impose estate or inheritance taxes independent of federal estate taxes. The result: Even a modest estate may be exposed to death taxes. Consult an estate-planning lawyer for ways to reduce or eliminate death duties through charitable gifts, trusts, and other strategies.

10. **Move to a no- or low-tax state.** If you are blessed with economic freedom of choice, you can always take tax flight. Some states have no income tax at all. They are Alaska, Wyoming, South Dakota, Nevada, Texas, and Washington. Florida has no personal income tax but does levy an annual 0.1% wealth tax on portfolios above $20,000. New Hampshire and Tennessee impose a flat tax on interest and dividends only.

Smart Property-Tax-Saving Strategies

Americans are up in arms against property taxes. In recent years, California, Colorado, Michigan, New Jersey, and Oregon, to name a few states, have been swept up in anti–property tax sentiment. You do not have to mount a wide-scale taxpayer revolt to cut your own property taxes, though. By following the five tips below, you may be able to stage your own personal tax protest and save money, too.

1. **Find out whether you qualify for any special property-tax breaks.** Many states reduce property taxes for being 65 or older, a veteran, or disabled. Make sure you take advantage of any general homeowner's exemption as well.

2. **Check the accuracy of your home's assessed value.** Review your property

record card on file at your local assessor's office. This card lists such characteristics as lot size and number of rooms. If you find an error on the card—the assessor overstated your home's square footage, for example—a visit to the assessor can usually win you a tax reduction.

3. **If you do not spot an obvious error, determine whether your home's value has been overstated.** Maybe your house has suffered damage or housing prices have plunged in your area. To find out if your property-tax bill is inflated, ask your local tax assessor for your home's official assessed value. Compare that number with the result you get when you multiply your property's fair market value by your town's residential assessment ratio. That figure, which is also available from your assessor, is the percentage of fair market value subject to tax. To estimate your home's fair market value, ask a real estate agent or your assessor for recent sales prices of comparable homes in your neighborhood. If the assessed value you computed is less than the official assessed value, it's time to appeal. (For fair market values in most areas, see www.domania.com.)

4. **Document your case.** No tax official is going to take your word for it when you plead for a reduction. If you're fighting your assessment, you will need written verification of the sales prices of three to five comparable homes. Drive by those houses to make sure they are similar to yours. Then photograph the exteriors to strengthen your claim. If your home has deteriorated or been damaged since the last assessment, take pictures of it, too.

5. **Appeal an unfair assessment.** Make sure you follow your local appeals procedure to the letter. The first step is usually an oral plea before the local assessor. If that does not succeed, you must fill out an appeals form and request a hearing before the local, county, or regional board. Ask for the board's schedule and try to attend one meeting to get a feel for the process before your appeal is heard. When it's your turn, bring the documents and photographs you have assembled to back up your oral testimony. If the appeals board rejects your challenge, you can go to court or the state review board, but you will probably need to hire a lawyer.

Eight Tax-Return Filing Tips

Knowing the tax law is only half the battle. Your tax planning will pay off only if you know how to present the results to the IRS. Observing the correct mechanics for filing your tax return will speed up your refund, save you interest and penalties, and keep you out of the clutches of an IRS audit. Before you drop your return irretrievably in the mailbox, make sure to do the following:

1. Use the long form 1040 instead of the 1040A or 1040EZ to be certain you don't overlook any tax-saving deductions or credits.
2. Double-check your math.
3. If you're married, include your spouse's Social Security number.
4. Check the "65 and over/blind" boxes if you are claiming the extra standard deduction for being elderly or blind.
5. Claim the earned income credit if you are eligible.
6. Attach explanations of any item you think might be questioned.
7. Report the Social Security number of any dependent you will claim.
8. Consider having your refund directly deposited into your bank account.

Using Tax Software and Web Sites

Preparing your return electronically does away with the tedious calculations and math errors that can make April so taxing. Using a computer also lets you experiment with different combinations of depreciation, expensing, and Keogh or IRA contributions to save the most tax. Plus, software and Web sites let you correct your return in seconds if you discover overlooked deductions or income just as you are ready to mail the completed return. If you do your return by hand, the thought of redoing the entire return from scratch could be enough to keep you from claiming additional tax savings. Finally, tax software and Web sites can help you gauge the answers to key tax questions such as: What are the tax effects of buying or leasing a car? How much can I save in taxes by investing in rental property? What taxes will I owe when I get my pension plan distribution?

Before you rush out to buy software or jump on a site, consider the pros and cons of each. If you file early and don't need a lot of help, use the sites. They're convenient and the fee is lower than the cost of most software. Filers who want a bit of handholding or are concerned about putting financial information on the Net will do best with software they can install on their PC. Two favorite software programs (2001 prices) and sites: Intuit's TurboTax ($39.95 before $10 rebate) at www.quicken.com and H&R Block's TaxCut ($29.95) at www.taxcut.com.

Remember, no matter what method you use to prepare your return, you still have to gather all the information about your income, deductions, and credits. Sadly, you cannot escape this scut work whether you do your return with a pencil, use a computer, or turn the whole mess over to a tax preparer. Another piece of friendly advice: If you've never used tax software before, it will take a while to get the hang of the program.

Tax software and sites perform two functions. They store and organize your income and expense records and use this information to prepare your return or analyze tax strategies. Although the major tax programs and sites are far from being clones, they all offer certain basic features:

- **Selecting the right forms.** If you don't know a Schedule E from a Form 2106, one of the brightest benefits of tax software and the Web is their ability to tell you which forms you will need. Each will ask you a series of questions and from your answers will list the forms to be completed. When you are done, the program checks to see if you have been thorough and tells you when a form seems incomplete.
- **Matching the right number to the right line.** Software and Web sites also let you select a tax item from a list, such as church contributions, and carries the dollar amount you enter to the correct line of the correct form.
- **Mathematical accuracy.** With tax software and sites, you can usually avoid worrying about any math errors. The exception: when there's a bug in the program. In that rare case, you're at the mercy of the company that owns the software or the site to help you resolve your problem.
- **Internal consistency.** That $2,532 capital gain on Schedule D will show up where it's supposed to—on line 13 of the Form 1040—and as $2,532, not $2,352 or some other transposed figure.
- **Spotting omissions.** You don't have to worry about forgetting to include a critical piece of information to make your return complete. Case in point: To claim a child care credit, it's not enough to enter the amount you spent, you also need to include the name and identification number of the child care provider. If you forget, your software or site will remind you so that no line is left undone.
- **Technical advice.** At a minimum, you get the IRS instruction booklet online, with specific form and line instructions keyed to those places on the screen. The amount of additional advice you get depends on the software.
- **Tax forms.** No more last-minute trips to the library for forms the IRS never sent. They're all in your computer; at least they are if your software or site includes your state's forms, too. If you have a laser printer, you can print forms that look just like the IRS versions, with your tax information already typed in. You can download forms at

www.irs.gov. If you don't have access to the Internet you also can get forms by fax, twenty-four hours a day, by calling 703–368–9694.

- **Importing financial data.** You will save hours at tax time if your tax information is already stored in a banking software program. The tax program then can read your income and deductions from your checkbook files and transfer the data directly to your tax return. Make sure the tax program you choose supports your banking program.
- **Auditing.** When you have finished your taxes, the program checks for inconsistent or incomplete items, which could draw unwanted attention from the IRS.

Electronic Filing

If the IRS has its way, we will all be filing our returns electronically. Electronic filing—the system that zaps your tax information almost instantly to IRS computers over telephone wires—is now available nationwide. The software and sites offer electronic filing features.

Electronic filing has led to a booming business in loans against your tax refund. The tax preparer will give you a check for your refund amount minus fees within a couple of days if you file electronically. Unless you desperately need the money, though, do not bite. These quick refunds are really very expensive short-term, loans. The fees, which range from about $30 to $65, get you the use of your money only for an extra two to five weeks. If you pay $40 to get a $400 refund loan, for example, you're paying more than 10% interest on what amounts to a three-week loan. Even if you need the money immediately, you should be able to find a cheaper source of credit.

Dealing with the IRS

What combination of tidal forces or plain bad luck subjects you to an audit in the first place? No one outside of the IRS knows exactly, but this much is for sure:

- **The higher your income, the more likely you are to be audited.** Other factors also play a significant role in the chances of being audited, such as small-business (Schedule C) returns and the presence of items that are the subject of special scrutiny (such as Earned Income Tax credit claims).

- **Deductions larger than the national norm often are scrutinized, too.** If, for instance, you report charitable contributions or employee business expenses that are far higher than what most people with your income claim, the IRS is likely to want to know why.

   Lately, the IRS has begun focusing more on returns through what it calls an "economic reality" approach to auditing. If the IRS thinks that your write-offs seem unusual based on your lifestyle or occupation, your return may be flagged for an audit.
- **Where you live may make you more or less susceptible to an audit.**
- **You may be the target of an IRS special project.** In recent years, these projects have focused on tax shelters, home-office deductions, direct-sales businesses (such as being an Amway or Shaklee distributor), and the "underground economy"—unreported income by persons who moonlight for cash or barter.

Many people believe that if the IRS does not call them in for an audit within six months after their return is filed, they are home free. Receiving your refund check does not mean you are immune from audit, however. The IRS has three years from the date your return was filed or due, whichever is later, to audit your return. (There is no statute of limitations for fraud, however, or for failure to file a return. If your reported income is understated by 25% or more, the IRS has six years to audit.)

When your return information doesn't match what's reported by third parties—employer, bank, etc.—you are most likely to get a letter to that effect, asking you to agree to an additional assessment.

There are two types of audits:

- **Field audits** usually target businesses, and for these an IRS agent comes to your home or business to review your records or to ask you to provide an explanation for the discrepancy.
- **Office audits** are the most common type, and for these an individual gets a personal invitation to come down to the local IRS office. The audit notice will tell you to call for an appointment or to come in at a specified date and time. Read this notice closely. It contains valuable information about who may represent you at the audit and outlines your appeal rights. It also tells you the items on your return that are being questioned—usually broad categories, such as medical or employee business expenses. Included with the notice will be information guides noting the types of records you'll need to verify the items being audited. Office audits are usually limited to two or three issues, so you won't be expected to haul in all your records and prove every entry on your return.

If you are unable or unwilling to appear in person, you may mail in your records. A word of warning, though: An audit conducted by mail can be much more costly than one done in person. Unless your records are perfect and self-explanatory, you stand a good chance of losing the deduction, because you won't be present to answer the auditor's questions.

Usually, once an audit is started, it cannot be stopped. There is one exception, though: the repetitive audit. If you went through a nonbusiness audit for the same issues in either of the two preceding tax years, emerged without owing tax, and still get audited again on them, you can alert the IRS and tell the agency that it can't audit you about these write-offs this time.

Assuming there's no way out, though, you need to prepare. First, get a copy of the tax return under audit and pull together all the documents that support the items being questioned. Try to reconstruct any missing records. Get copies of canceled checks from your bank, duplicate receipts from your credit-card company, church, synagogue, or doctor, for example, or letters from people who can back up your claims. For instance, if you deducted business expenses, get your boss to write a letter verifying their legitimacy.

Your records do not have to be perfect. If you cannot dig up proof, try to prepare a convincing argument. The auditor usually must give weight to your oral testimony, except for disputes over business entertainment expenses.

If record keeping fails, the following guidelines may save the day:

- **Don't volunteer information.** What you do not know about the tax law can hurt you. Answer the auditor's questions, but do not feel compelled to elaborate.
- **Leave your emotions and hostility at home.** Be courteous and cooperative. That does not mean you have to automatically give in when the auditor disallows your donation to Goodwill or your trip to Miami. In fact, being too eager to agree can raise suspicions.
- **Look for areas of compromise.** The auditor will probably be willing to bargain in order to close your case. If you are flexible and know when to give a little, both you and the auditor may come away from the audit satisfied with the final bill.

Should you brave the IRS by yourself or, if you hired a tax pro to prepare your return, should you have him or her do the talking? It all depends on what the IRS wants to know. If you had a preparer or adviser fill out your return, when you get an audit letter from the IRS, show it to that person. Then ask for his or her guidance. If the issue is a simple one, you may be able to handle it on your own and save another fee to your tax preparer, either by sending back a letter to the IRS or by meeting with the auditor.

However, if the IRS wants to ask a lot of questions, you're being audited on a gray area of the tax law, or you took a write-off you shouldn't have, it's best to let your tax adviser handle the audit for you. In fact, you'll probably be better off not even going to the audit, since you could inadvertently say something to the auditor that could be held against you.

After all the evidence has been presented, the auditor will make a decision. This judgment may come at the end of the audit or after you have provided more information at the auditor's request. If you are in the IRS office, the auditor will give you his or her ruling and explain any proposed changes to your tax liability. Otherwise you will get an audit report by mail. Call the auditor if there is something you do not understand.

Three outcomes are possible: (1) no extra tax due; (2) additional tax due; or (3) a refund. In four out of five cases, the wheel of fortune lands on more tax due.

If you agree, fine. What if you don't have the cash to pay the extra taxes? An **installment plan** may be appropriate for any person who cannot make full payment of the tax owed, whether or not this results from an audit. The streamlined installment agreement process is available to anyone who owes less than $25,000 and will be able to pay it off within five years. These agreements do not require a collection manager's approval and do not involve the filing of liens. Use Form 9465, "Installment Agreement Request." Taxpayers may get installment plans for more than $25,000 or more than five years, but these are subject to managerial approval and will usually involve the filing of a tax lien.

There is a $43 setup fee for an installment plan, plus a late payment penalty of 0.5% per month (0.25% if the taxpayer filed on time and did not receive a levy notice), plus interest, which is currently 7% a year, compounded daily. The interest rate is subject to adjustment each calendar quarter.

If, however, you think you'll never be able to pay the full amount, try to work out a settlement with the IRS. Fill out Form 656, known as the **Offer in Compromise** form, and type in: "Doubt as to collectibility of the full amount of tax, penalty, and interest." In addition to Form 656, those seeking an Offer in Compromise based on doubt as to collectibility must submit a financial statement (Form 433-A for individuals).

But bear in mind that the auditor's findings are not necessarily final; you don't have to accept them. You have 30 days after you receive the audit report to decide whether to accept or appeal the proposed changes. The initial appeal is to the IRS Appeals Office. If you do not reply within the 30 days, or if you do not reach an agreement with an appeals officer, you will receive a "Notice of Deficiency." You will then have 90 days to appeal to the Tax Court (150 days if your address is outside the U.S.). The Tax Court's small-case procedure applies to those with disputed amounts of $50,000 or less for any one tax year or period. Under that procedure, the Tax Court's decision is final—you cannot appeal it.

During the 30-day period, you may submit additional information you believe might change the auditor's mind.

If you have no other information to help your cause, you may either agree or disagree with the audit report. If you decide to agree, sign a copy of the report and mail it back. Keep the other copy for your records. You may send the IRS a check for the tax due with the signed report or wait for a bill for the extra tax, plus interest and penalties, from the IRS Service Center.

If you decide the audit report is unfair or incorrect, tell the auditor within the 30-day period that you want to appeal. The IRS gives you several choices if you want to keep fighting. You can ask for an informal appeal to the auditor's supervisor. If you go that route and are still unhappy or you prefer to skip this stage, you can go to the IRS Appellate Division. This is called a **formal appeal**. Then, if you lose at the appellate level, you can take your case to court. This decision should be made with the help of an experienced tax professional, however, since going to court can be extremely expensive and time-consuming.

Getting the Most Out of Your Tax Pro

In Chapter 3 you learned how to choose a tax adviser. Now a few words about using him or her to greatest effect. Plan on seeing your preparer at least twice a year—once to have your return prepared and once to explore ways to reduce next year's taxes. A good time for your planning session is May or June, to give you enough time to implement your preparer's suggestions during the rest of the year. A second planning meeting in early November may be warranted if you are active in the stock market, own a business or rental properties, have income over $100,000, or had unexpectedly large earnings or capital gains during the year. If you fit any of those descriptions, last-minute tax tips can shave your bill to the IRS and your state.

Just meeting with your tax pro is not enough, however. You need to arrive prepared. If you are dealing with a new preparer, give him or her copies of your last two or three returns. Besides painting a fairly complete picture of your tax situation, your returns may contain valuable information about property you are depreciating and about losses or credits you can carry over into future years. Be sure your records are complete and up-to-date. Your preparer cannot invent numbers to put on your return. Unless you supply accurate information, money you spent on deductible items will be lost. Remember that your income is even more important to the IRS than your deductions. So make sure your professional has copies of all of your W-2 forms and your 1099 forms when preparing your return.

If you are coming in for tax-planning advice, bring an estimate of your year-to-date income, federal and state tax withholding, and deductible expenses. Also carry along the latest monthly or quarterly statement from each of your investments; a summary of year-to-date capital gains and losses; a record of estimated taxes paid; and a record of deductible retirement account or savings plan contributions you made.

Write down any questions you have before coming in, such as whether there are any changes in the tax law that affect you or whether you will be subject to the **alternative minimum tax** (a special tax system with a flat tax rate levied on some upper-income people to ensure that they pay their fair share of taxes). Always ask if there is anything you should be doing to save taxes.

Use a tax manual to bone up on any areas of the tax law that affect you. This is especially true when you come in during the filing season, because your busy preparer will have only a limited time to question you. If you do not know that the cost of removing trees killed by southern pine beetles may be deductible, it is unlikely your preparer will uncover it unless you get around to chatting about your landscaping.

Mention changes in your family situation, too. Unless you send your preparer a baby announcement, he or she will not know you have a new exemption to declare. Keep your preparer informed of any marriage, divorce, births, or deaths in your family, children who leave home, and changes of address.

Unless you quake at the thought of an audit, make it clear that you want all the deductions you are entitled to receive. Once your return is prepared, feel free to question any decisions you do not understand or challenge. Ask for a reference to the tax law supporting his or her opinion if you are still unconvinced. Remember that your preparer is only a phone call away. Seek his or her advice before making any major financial move, such as buying a house or funding your child's education. Just give your pro enough time to research the tax angles.

Finally, act on your professional's advice. Don't ignore it. After all, in the long run, how much you save in taxes is up to you.

SECTION TWO

REACHING YOUR FINANCIAL GOALS

CHAPTER 5

How to Boost
Your Savings

Wouldn't it feel great to kiss your biggest money worries good-bye? Imagine being able to pay off all of your credit-card debt, buy a second home, afford your kids' college tuition bills, and know that you will be able to retire in comfort. It's not impossible if you get into the savings habit early. By setting aside money regularly, you will be able to solve most of your financial problems—and afford the good stuff in life. What's more, a monthly savings program will help you feel more confident about handling an unexpected financial emergency and meeting financial goals.

Of course, it could take you a decade or longer to finance life's biggest expenses, such as four years at a private college or your retirement. But you can amass thousands of dollars—even hundreds of thousands of dollars—over time by setting aside just a few dollars a day and letting that money earn money (see the table below). For example, you can build up $10,000 in cash in five years by saving and investing only $133 each month if the money earns 7% on average. That's less than $34 a week or the cost of a dinner for two.

HOW SMALL SAVINGS CAN ADD UP

This table will show you how much your savings can build, depending on the amount you salt away weekly and how long you do it. Choose the amount you think you can save from the row across the top. Then, determine how many years you think you could continue saving. The intersection of those two boxes will show you how much you'll have at the end of your chosen time period—before taxes.

	Amount You Save Each Week				
Earning 7% for...	$1	$5	$10	$15	$20
5 years	$ 319	$ 1,597	$ 3,194	$ 4,791	$ 6,388
10 years	$ 796	$ 3,979	$ 7,957	$ 11,936	$ 15,914
15 years	$ 1,506	$ 7,530	$ 15,061	$ 22,591	$ 30,122
20 years	$ 2,566	$ 12,828	$ 25,655	$ 38,483	$ 51,310
25 years	$ 4,146	$ 20,728	$ 41,455	$ 62,183	$ 82,910
30 years	$ 6,502	$ 32,509	$ 65,091	$ 97,528	$130,037
40 years	$15,257	$ 76,285	$152,570	$228,855	$305,140
50 years	$34,730	$173,649	$347,299	$520,948	$694,598

HOW LONG WILL IT TAKE TO SAVE $10,000?

Monthly investment	————— Growth Rate —————		
	3%	5%	10%
$ 100	7.8 years	7.4 years	6.7 years
$ 200	4.1	3.9	3.7
$ 300	2.8	2.7	2.6
$ 500	1.7	1.7	1.6
$1,000	10 months	10 months	10 months

HOW LONG WILL IT TAKE TO SAVE $100,000?

Monthly investment	————— Growth Rate —————		
	3%	5%	10%
$ 100	50.6 years	41.4 years	29.4 years
$ 200	30.8	26.8	20.6
$ 300	22.4	19.9	16.3
$ 500	14.6	13.5	11.4
$1,000	7.8	7.4	6.7

Note: Calculations assume annualized growth rate and 30% tax bracket.
Source: MSN Money.

Thanks to the beauty of **compound interest**—when your interest earns its own interest—the earlier you start saving, the less you'll have to set aside each month or year to reach your goals. To save $100,000 for, say, a child's college fund 15 years from today, you'd have to save $316 a month, assuming your money earns 7% a year on average. But if you waited 10 years before starting to stash funds away, you would have to save $1,397 a month ($16,764 a year!) to meet that goal. Trouble is, you probably have a number of humongous financial headaches coming at you in the future. You may need a seven-figure nest egg to get you through retirement and a six-figure stash to afford a young child's future tuition, to cite just two. That's why financial advisers often say you should start saving for retirement as soon as you start working and you ought to begin putting money away for college right after your child is born. Easier said than done.

The first way to begin boosting your savings is finding more cash to save. The best way to do that is to get rid of all or most of your high-interest-rate debt. The reason is simple: You will never get rich earning 3% on your savings while you are paying creditors 17%. Turn to the net worth statement you filled out in Chapter 1. (You might want to mark the page with a Post-it or paper clip, since there will be more references to it throughout this chapter.) Do you have any double-digit debts other than a mortgage on your home? If so, list the loans (excluding your mortgage) or credit-card balances in the "Your Debt Worksheet" in Chapter 6 and estimate the extra amount you could put toward paying off each of these debts each month. Then, try to fully pay off your loans and credit cards with the highest interest rates as quickly as you can.

In general, try to avoid using your plastic unless it's absolutely necessary. If you carry a balance on a number of credit cards, you might contact the National Foundation for Credit Counseling (www.nfcc.org) for low-cost and free counseling services—one-on-one sessions, face-to-face, online, or over the telephone.

Creating a Cash Cushion

Before you start figuring out how much to save for the future, you'll want to calculate how much you'll need to squirrel away to create your emergency fund. It's extremely important to have an emergency reserve fund just in case you suffer an illness, unemployment, or any other financial setback. As a rule, it's best to keep an amount equal to three to six months' living expenses in this fund, either in a bank account or a money-market mutual fund. Use the worksheet below to figure out roughly what size emergency fund you should keep. To fill in the blanks, you may want to refer back to your "Cash-Flow Statement" and "Budget" worksheets in Chapter 1.

EMERGENCY FUND WORKSHEET

1. **Add up your total annual expenditures.** (You should have totted up those figures in Chapter 1.) $_____

2. **Add up the amount you spent last year on vacations, gifts, savings, and investments.** (This figure represents outlays you could forgo in the event of a financial crisis.) $_____

3. **Subtract line 2 from line 1.** $_____

4. **Divide line 3 by 4.** (This will give you an estimate of your necessary expenditures for three months.) $_____

5. **Divide line 3 by 2.** (This will give you an estimate of your necessary expenditures for six months.) $_____

Fine-tune your emergency savings to fit your own circumstances. For example, you'll need to consider your job safety and any misfortunes that could occur that would not be covered by your health and disability insurance. Your emergency fund should be large enough to cover living expenses until your long-term disability insurance kicks in, which might take from two to six months. The reserve also should carry you through any periods of unemployment, so you'll have to make some assumptions about your employability. If you are a highly paid executive in a slow-growth industry, you may want to keep cash reserves equal to a year's worth of living expenses. But if your skills are in demand and you have ample insurance, just a few months' worth of expenses may be sufficient.

After you have decided how large your cash cushion should be, use your net worth statement on pages 4–5 to add up the balances you now have in cash and cash equivalents, such as checking accounts, savings accounts, credit union accounts, money-market mutual funds, Treasury bills, and CDs with maturities of a year or less. The total ought to be at least enough to cover the minimum emergency fund needs you listed on the worksheet above. If not, start growing your cash reserves to cover the shortfall. Although some financial pros advocate that you do this before you begin putting away discretionary savings—money for buying a house, paying for a child's education, or funding your retirement—others say that you should continue funding your retirement and put the rest of your savings toward building your emergency fund.

Figuring How Much You Need to Save

One of the most common financial questions people have is: Am I saving enough? That's a tough question to answer, since the amount you need to save depends on so many factors: your age, your goals, whether you expect to borrow to reach your goals, your income, and the rate of return on your savings, for starters. A general guideline is that you should try to save at least 10% of your gross income each year. That may sound impossible. If so, don't just throw up your hands. Instead, try a strategy of saving 4% to 8% of your gross income in your twenties and doubling that percentage in your thirties and forties. In your fifties, when your children's college bills have been paid off and thus your expenses have dropped but retirement looms, you should attempt to squirrel away 20% of your pay. But rather than rely on general rules, you'll help safeguard your future by plugging in some real numbers for your financial situation. The key is to determine what your financial goals are and when you want to pay for them. For specific college savings and retirement worksheets see Chapters 10 and 11. (You can also find savings calculators on the Web at www.money.com.)

A Guide to Your Savings Alternatives

Once you know how much you need to save, the next step is deciding where exactly to put your savings. And don't think you have to keep all your savings in the same place. In fact, you probably will want to spread it around a bit by keeping your emergency reserve fund in a super-safe, if low-yielding, account and your long-term savings in something a little racier with a higher return.

The rate of return on your savings will play a big role in how much you need to save. The best evidence of this is something called the **Rule of 72**. You divide 72 by the interest rate you expect to earn and that will tell you how long it will take to double your money. If you earn 5% a year, you'll have twice as much in less than 15 years. If you earn just 3% a year, however, it will take 24 years before your savings double.

The following is a quickie run-through of the best savings alternatives for every one of your goals. Most of the choices described here are the safe, traditional savings vehicles most appropriate for short-term savings needs; some already have been discussed a bit in Chapter 2. Stocks, bonds, and mutual funds, which are important components in any long-term savings plan, are discussed in greater detail in Chapters 13, 14, and 15. The goals and the appropriate ways to save for them:

WHAT'S YOUR TIME HORIZON TO SAVE?			
If Your Savings Goals Are . . .	Type of Account	Typical Minimum Deposit	Comments
Less than two years away	Savings account	Varies by financial institution	Some banks stop paying interest and charge fees if balance dips below $200 to $500.
	Money-market deposit account[1,2]	$1,000 or more	Generally percentage point or so more than savings accounts.
	Money-market mutual fund[2]	$5,000 or more	Generally percentage point or so more than bank money markets
	U.S. govern-ment–only money fund[2,3]	$3,000	Invests in Treasury bills and other government obligations that mature within a year.
	Tax-free money-market fund[2,3]	$3,000	Invests in short-term municipal securities. Interest is free from federal income taxes. Best for high-income tax bracket.
	Certificate of deposit[1]	$500	Common terms: 3, 6, 12 months. The longer the maturity, the higher the yield. Penalty for early redemption.
	U.S. Treasury bills[3,5]	Face value of $1,000	Maturities of 4, 13, or 26 weeks.

If Your Savings Goals Are . . .	Type of Account	Typical Minimum Deposit	Comments
Two to three years away	Certificate of deposit[1]	$500	Maturities of 2½ and 3 years.
	U.S. Treasury notes[3,5]	$1,000	Maturity of 2 years. Pays more than bank CDs of same maturity.
	Ultra-short-term bond funds[4]	$3,000	Invests in high-quality corporate and government debt with maturities of 3 to 12 months. Yield 1 or 2 percentage points higher than money fund.
	Short-term taxable and tax-free[3] bond funds	Varies by financial institution	Average maturities of 1 to 3 years. 2 percentage points higher than money funds.
Three to seven years	Certificate of deposit[4]	$500	Maturity of 5 years.
	Intermediate term bonds	$1,000	Maturities generally of 5–7 years.
	Treasury notes[3,5]	$1,000	Come only in 2-, 5-, and 10-year maturities.
	Intermediate-term bond funds	$3,000	Automatic diversification of all types of bonds; value of bond-fund shares changes daily.

If Your Savings Goals Are . . .	Type of Account	Typical Minimum Deposit	Comments
Three to seven years (cont.)	U.S savings bonds[3,5]	Denominations range from $50 to $10,000	Best for 5-year or longer time horizon. Federal taxes are due when you redeem bonds. Do not provide current income; you get payout when you cash bond. Proceeds can be tax-free if used for college tuition.
	I Bonds[5]	$50	Denominations range from $50 to $10,000. Total return is guaranteed to beat inflation.
	Intermediate-term mortgage-backed securities	$25,000	These are packaged mortgage loans usually issued or guaranteed by agencies such as the Government National Mortgage Association (Ginnie Mae), Federal Home Loan Mortgage, and Federal National Mortgage Association (Freddie Mac and Fannie Mae). Interest is not exempt from state income tax. Only Ginnie Maes are backed by the U.S. government.

If Your Savings Goals Are . . .	Type of Account	Typical Minimum Deposit	Comments
More than 8 years	10-year Treasury notes[3,5]	$1,000	Highest maturity available is 10-year note. Typically offers a higher yield than a shorter-term savings vehicle.
	Tax-deferred college savings plans	$25 a month	See Chapter 10.
	Tax-deferred retirement savings plans	Varies by plan	See Chapter 11.

[1]Insured by the Federal Deposit Insurance Corporation. [2]Check writing available. [3]U.S. Treasuries and U.S. Treasury funds are exempt from state and local income tax. [4]May charge sales fee or load. [5]Available online at www.treasurydirect.gov.

Fifteen Painless Ways to Save

1. **Put your savings on autopilot.** The most effective way to build savings is to have the money removed from your paycheck or bank account before you can get your hands on it. And since you don't see these funds or have the option to spend them easily, you won't miss them much. You can sign up for an automatic investing plan just by filling out a simple form at work or by mail from home.

   - **U.S. savings bond payroll deduction plans.** At some companies you can ask your employer to withhold an allotment of money from every paycheck and invest the cash in a Series EE savings bond (maximum: $15,000 a year, per individual, per savings bond). Because you don't get the interest until you redeem the bonds, you're forced to save the earnings, too. Your payroll department can give you the enroll-ment form specifying how much to withhold. Some employers will also let you withhold and invest part of your paycheck in I Bonds. (See description of I Bonds in table on page 114.)

     One clever strategy: After your baby is born, fill out a new W-4 federal income tax withholding form at work, to adjust your withholding for an additional exemp-tion for a dependent. The reduction in withholding will leave you with about $65 more a month in your paycheck. Instruct your payroll department to use that $65 to buy savings bonds. By doing so, you'll ensure that your bundle of joy will have more than $20,000 to put toward tuition when he or she is ready for college.

   - **Mutual fund automatic savings plans.** Based on your instructions, a fund com-pany will automatically transfer a set amount each month—usually at least $100—from your checking account to one of its mutual funds. These programs are a great way to make you save for a future goal, such as your child's college education. You can withdraw the money whenever you want for whatever reason. But you don't have to remember to write the checks to invest.

     By signing up for an automatic investing plan, you can sometimes avoid having to meet a mutual fund's minimum initial investment of $1,000 to $3,000. To get started, simply fill out a form authorizing the fund to deduct a set amount from your bank account or paycheck at regular intervals, typically either monthly or quarterly. You can ensure that the fund gets your correct bank account number by returning the form with a blank personal check and writing "void" across it. Many mutual fund companies, such as Vanguard, will let you have money shunted directly from your Social Security check into their funds. At any time, you can switch off the flow without penalty by calling the fund. If you set up an automatic investing program with a fund group that levies up-front sales charges known as **loads**, how-ever, you will still have to pay the normal sales charge on your periodic investments.

- **Mutual fund reinvestment plans.** If you automatically reinvest the dividends and capital gains paid to you by a mutual fund, your profits can mount. To get your earnings reinvested automatically, call your mutual fund company and request an application.
- **Stock dividend-reinvestment plans.** Many publicly traded companies offer dividend-reinvestment plans (DRIPs). As their name suggests, these plans take your stock dividends and use them to buy even more stock for you. Setting up a DRIP will add to your record keeping, however; you must usually hold the shares in your name, rather than at a brokerage in so-called street name. To get started, ask the DRIP company or your stockbroker for a DRIP form.

  Sites such as BuyandHold.com and ShareBuilder.com function as DRIP clearinghouses, allowing you to choose from a large number of stocks at commissions of $5 or less.

2. **Earn a higher return on your savings.** The higher the interest rate on your savings, the less you have to salt away each month to meet your goals. Remember that Rule of 72? One way to earn more interest on your savings is to put your money in a CD or bond with a longer term than you had originally planned. Another idea: Make your annual IRA contribution every January instead of at the start of the following year. That way your savings will earn an extra 12 months' interest tax-deferred.

3. **Use a home-equity loan to pay off high-rate debts.** Replace consumer debts at, say, 18% with a home-equity loan at 10%, and you'll cut your interest costs by more than a third. In addition, the interest on a home-equity loan can be fully deductible on your income tax return. Let's say you consolidate $10,000 credit-card cash advances with a home-equity loan at 10%. Counting the tax break, a taxpayer in the 30% bracket in 2002 would save $1,160 (assuming that they itemized).

4. **Pay in cash.** This high-discipline technique will teach you a lot about the difference between what you want and what you really need. Moreover, by paying in cash, you avoid paying finance charges. For example, trimming your credit-card balances by $500 this year can save you almost $100 in interest if your card issuer charges 18.6% interest.

5. **Make higher down payments.** When financing your next major purchase—a new car, new kitchen, whatever—put up as much money as you can and keep your borrowing down. By not financing $5,000 at 12% over three years, you can save a cool $979.

6. **Use your flexible spending account (FSA),** if you have one. Don't pass up the opportunity to pay for medical and dependent-care expenses with pretax dollars through these accounts (see Chapter 9). The money in an FSA can be used to pay for any medical expense that is not covered by your health insurance, such as deductibles, copayments, eyeglasses and contact lenses, or any treatment that may not be a part of your health plan. A family of four is almost certain to spend $1,000 or

more a year on doctors, dentists, and prescription medicines, in deductibles or co-payments alone. Tax savings if you pay these bills from an FSA can be at least $280.

7. **Skip one big expense a year.** You might be able to realize some meaty savings simply by skipping your winter vacation, trading in your turbocharged sports car for an econobox, or ditching your exclusive health club membership and switching to the YMCA.

8. **Squirrel away your next raise.** This tip is an example of the rule financial planners love to tout: Pay yourself first. To squeeze out money for your savings, earmark your next raise as savings toward a specific goal. If you earn $40,000, for instance, a 5% raise will give you $2,000 to set aside toward your baby's college fund.

9. **When you come to the end of your payments on a loan or credit-card balance, send the same amount each month to a mutual fund that you have chosen for a particular savings goal.** Because the payment was already factored into your budget, you won't miss it. Smart, huh?

10. **Don't pay for financial services you could get for free.** Using only no-fee checking accounts, no-fee credit cards, and no-load mutual funds can save you $100 a year or more. For instance, checking accounts often run $60 to $100 a year; annual fees for credit cards can be as much as $300.

11. **Give yourself an incentive.** When you meet your targeted savings goal for the month, reward yourself and your family by spending any leftover savings on a treat.

12. **Pay yourself back—with interest.** If you have to tap your savings, aim to pay yourself back with interest. For instance, say you need to withdraw $250 of your savings and you figure it will take you two months to pay it back. At the end of two months, throw into your savings another $40 or so.

13. **Deposit your stash where you can't easily get at it.** The biggest enemy of savers may very well be the automated teller machine, or ATM. Your ATM lets you have instant access to your money any time of the day or night, but the more you withdraw, the less you have left in your savings. So try to limit your ATM visits to one a week.

    Also, consider locking in your savings with vehicles like CDs or IRAs, which carry penalties on early withdrawals. Those lockup penalties actually serve as a useful deterrent against unnecessary savings withdrawals; in some cases you won't be able to withdraw cash at all unless you can prove financial hardship.

14. **Moonlight for moola.** Figure out what you could do in your spare time to bring in some extra cash. Then take some or all of that found money and save it toward an important financial goal.

15. **Hold a garage sale to raise cash.** By getting rid of an old computer, TV, stereo, dining set, or exercise machine, you could earn $300 to $3,000 more in just a day or two.

CHAPTER 6

How to Manage
Your Debt

The classic Jimmy Stewart movie *It's a Wonderful Life* has a touching scene where George Bailey, an ambitious dreamer, describes how loans improved the lives of folks in Bedford Falls. Henry Potter, the resident Scrooge, grouses that loans fill the heads of the "discontented, lazy rabble . . . with a lot of impossible ideas." Residents of Bedford Falls should be a "thrifty working class" and wait and save money before buying a house, he cracks. "Wait for what?" Bailey asks. "Until their children grow up and leave them? Until they're old and broken down? Do you know how long it takes a working man to save $5,000?"

Sadly, you would need more than 43 times that amount, or $216,000, to purchase the average home in America today. But Bailey's argument is still true: Debt is a powerful tool that can improve your lifestyle. When you take out a loan or buy something on credit, you are able gradually to pay for things you want to use or enjoy now. You can have what you want when you want it—a new car, a college education, or a home for your family.

Fortunately, borrowers have many more choices today than they did during the '20s, when Potter and Bailey debated the pros and cons of debt. Credit-card issuers, retail stores, mortgage companies, banks, savings and loans, credit unions, auto dealers, brokerage houses, and consumer finance companies are scrambling to lend you money. Anyone with a credit card can now finance even the most routine expenditures—groceries, prescription drugs, and newspaper subscriptions. Not surprisingly, Americans have come to live by the mantra: Buy Now, Pay Later. According to CardWeb.com, of the households that have at least one credit card, the average American household owes $8,123.

From a balance sheet standpoint, the less debt you have, the better. That's because the money you spend on interest charges is cash that could otherwise be saved or invested for your future. What's more, if you one day can't manage your debt payments, you may have to declare bankruptcy, which could cripple your ability to borrow, rent an apartment, or get a job for as long as seven years. So go ahead and borrow—but do it wisely.

How Much Debt You Can Afford

Fill out the following worksheet to calculate your **debt-to-income ratio**, which will tell you how much debt you can realistically afford to carry. Generally, your total debts excluding your mortgage should eat up no more than 10% to 15% of your take-home pay. You may be able to handle a 20% debt level if you make a healthy living and are not likely to incur new debts anytime soon. Including a mortgage, your debt payments shouldn't exceed 36% of your gross monthly income. When you're at or beyond your debt limit, you'll need to get your debt-to-income ratio down. That means: Refuse future invitations to borrow, put your credit cards in a drawer, and look for ways to reduce your current debt load.

Are You Too Deep in Debt?

To see if you've got more debt than you should, take the following quiz. If you answer yes to three or more of these questions, you're in trouble:

1. Do your monthly credit-card and loan payments (excluding mortgages and car loans) exceed 20% of your pay after taxes?
2. Have you ever borrowed from one lender to pay another?
3. Have you ever been forced to ask a friend or relative to co-sign a loan?
4. Do you hold more than 10 credit cards, including cards issued by gasoline companies and department stores?
5. Are you making only minimum monthly payments on credit cards?
6. Are you unable to say how much money you owe?

YOUR DEBT WORKSHEET

To fill out this worksheet, you'll need to assemble your latest month's bills and statements from lenders, credit-card companies, and stores where you have charge accounts. (Ignore first mortgages on your home and credit-card accounts that you habitually pay in full.) Also, turn back to your cash-flow statement in Chapter 1 to find your annual disposable income for line 2. It's the amount you had last year after taxes.

LOANS AND CHARGE ACCOUNTS (EXCLUDING MORTGAGES AND CREDIT CARDS PAID IN FULL)	LAST MONTH'S PAYMENT
_____	$_____
_____	$_____
_____	$_____
_____	$_____
_____	$_____
_____	$_____
_____	$_____
_____	$_____
_____	$_____
_____	$_____
_____	$_____

1. Your total monthly payments $_____

2. Your total annual disposable income divided by 12. Do not include bonuses, since you can't depend on them. Unless you are living on investment income, exclude dividends, interest, and capital gains, too. $_____

3. Total monthly payments you can safely handle. If you are over 65 or the sole wage earner in your family, enter 10% of line 2. If you are married and you and your spouse work or you are under 35, enter 15% or 20% of line 2. $_____

4. Amount of room in your budget for additional debt (line 3 minus line 1). If the figure is negative, it's the amount of your current debt over the danger limit. $_____

CANDIDATES TO REDUCE YOUR HIGH-COST DEBTS WORKSHEET

Call your lenders or look at your latest statements to find the interest rates and monthly payment information you'll need to fill in this simple worksheet.

CREDIT CARD OR LOAN	AMOUNT YOU OWE	ANNUAL INTEREST RATE	MINIMUM REQUIRED MONTHLY PAYMENT	TARGET MONTHLY PAYMENT

Choosing and Using Credit Cards

Credit cards can be a big convenience. You can charge a purchase when you don't have the cash and don't want to pay by check. Many credit cards also let you pay off purchases over time. Indeed, fully 60% of the nation's 100 million cardholders carry balances from month to month. Like snowflakes, however, no two cards are exactly alike. And the cards you're holding right now may not be the best ones for you. Odds are you probably own more cards than you need. So here's a short course in how to choose and use credit cards.

The first thing to know is the difference between **credit cards** and **travel and entertainment cards**. Credit cards, such as Visa, MasterCard, Discover, certain American Express cards, department store cards, and gasoline cards, let you make monthly payments of less than the amount you've charged. But you'll pay interest on your unpaid balance, perhaps as much as 18% to 21%.

You may be surprised to learn that Visa (www.visa.com) and MasterCard (www.mastercard.com) are umbrella organizations comprising independent financial institutions that issue so-called bank cards and set their own terms for borrowers. So the Visa card from the bank on the corner could be much different from the one issued by the bank across town. Generally, there are bank credit cards with high interest rates but no or low annual fees and cards with high annual fees but low interest rates. If you tend to carry a balance, you'll want to look for a card with a low interest rate. If you never or rarely carry a balance, look for a card with no annual fee, possibly one that offers a bonus or perk for every dollar you charge. (Each month, **MONEY**'s "By the Numbers" section lists the best credit cards with and without annual fees. Also, see www.cardtrak.com and www.bankrate.com.)

Many credit-card issuers offer premium or special cards often called **gold** or **platinum cards**, which typically come with higher credit limits, higher annual fees, and extras like free traveler's checks, purchase-protection insurance, and frequent flier miles. The additional cost of a gold card is probably not justified unless you expect to use the card's extra services, such as discounts on selected hotels and rental cars. If an issuer offers you these perks on a card with a low interest rate and a low or no annual fee, however, don't hesitate to opt for a gold or platinum.

In addition to financing purchases, you can also use a Visa or MasterCard to get a loan in a flash. You can go inside a bank to get a, say, $200 to $500 credit-card **cash advance**, or get the same advance through many automated teller machines, for a fee of 3% of the amount you're taking out (minimum fee: $10). It's best to take out a cash advance only when you're truly desperate for quick dough, though, since the cost of this type of borrowing is so high. Furthermore, you'll probably owe the credit card's standard interest rate from the day you take out the cash advance. According to Cardtrak. com, an industry research company, someone who takes a $300 cash advance and pays $10 in fees, and one month's interest at 18.5%, will pay an effective interest rate of 59%! Many times, however, card issuers will charge a higher rate of interest for a cash advance.

Travel and entertainment cards, like American Express (www.americanexpress.com) or Citigroup's Diners Club and Carte Blanche cards (www.dinersclubus.com), require you to pay your entire balance every month. (Diners Club has an $80 annual fee, and Carte Blanche has a $300 annual fee.) As a result, you don't owe interest on these cards unless you're late with your payments. They typically have no preset credit limit and charge an annual fee of $55 to $300. American Express offers four types of charge cards: green ($55 a year), gold ($75), platinum ($300), and the black Centurion card (by invitation only at $1,000). Green, or classic, card members can withdraw up to $1,000 every seven days (assuming they are a customer in good standing); gold card members can withdraw a limit of $2,500 every seven days; and platinum card members can withdraw up to $10,000 every 30 days. These withdrawals can be accessed as express cash (as long as you have signed up for the service) or emergency check cashing.

The cards all offer an increasing array of benefits and services such as optional enrollment in a membership rewards program. The green card offers car rental damage and loss protection, travel insurance, and purchase protection. The gold card will send you a summary of charges at the end of the year. In addition to these benefits, the platinum and the Centurion offer additional travel planning and reservation assistance as well as enhanced travel emergency assistance. Centurion offers personal shopping assistance, a concierge-like service.

But are travel and entertainment cards worth their relatively steep annual fees? Probably not, unless you think you'll use a lot of their perks or can't live with your credit cards' predetermined spending limits. These days most merchants that accept plastic honor all the major brands. However, Visa and MasterCard are accepted at more places outside the United States than American Express.

Debit cards, also known as check cards, look like regular MasterCard and Visa cards but are linked to your bank checking account instead of a line of credit. They work like an electronic check. When you use one, the amount you spend is withdrawn directly from your account, usually after one to three business days. Banks that are part of the Visa or MasterCard associations issue debit cards with their logos that can be used at any store that accepts those credit cards. So if you're at a restaurant, short on cash, and don't want to rack up charges on your credit card, you don't have to excuse yourself for a run to the nearest ATM. Simply whip out your debit card, and voilà! the meal is paid for. Bear in mind that you can't build a credit history with a debit card, since you aren't actually borrowing money. Before getting a debit card, however, find out if your bank charges an annual fee or any transaction fees when you use the card. Many do. At $1 a pop, the convenience of a debit card may be less of a deal.

Another wrinkle in the world of plastic is the **bonus** or **rebate card**. Issuers linking up with manufacturers, airlines, oil companies, and the like have been handing out rewards in the form of rebates to customers charging all manner of goods and services. There now are about 2,500 rebate cards, and consumers are snapping them up: About 250 million are in use by consumers, or roughly 45% of all bank credit cards. The rebate marketing war has touched off a guerrilla counterattack by clever people who've learned to manipulate the system to maximize their bonuses. Among card issuers, such people are known as "gamers," because they treat rebates like a game. To win the rebate game, you need to charge a lot. Even more important, you need the means and self-discipline to pay off your credit-card bills in full each month. Otherwise the interest rate on rebate cards, which can run as high as 19.8% compared with 9% for a typical low-rate card, will undermine any profits.

If you hanker to play the rebate game like a pro or just improve your weekend game, follow these five rules:

1. **Get the right cheap rebate card for you.** Check at www.cardtrak.com or www.bankrate.com for low-rate and no-fee cards. Then switch to one or call your card issuer's 800 number and threaten to transfer your balance to a card charging less. It will probably match the deal.

2. **Charge nearly everything—even purchases you wouldn't normally put on a card.** You can rack up bonuses by using rebate cards to pay for things like groceries, day care, college tuition, and medical bills. Just make sure you pay off your balances each month to avoid incurring finance charges.

3. **Keep track of your charges and retire each card as you reach its maximum annual rebate.** For example, most airline cards limit you to 50,000 or 60,000 miles per year unless you are a frequent flier with that particular airline, so be sure to note when you have reached the maximum.

4. **Use one card to pay off another and thus double your rebates, as long as the rules permit it.** Some award you rebates for using the convenience checks that you often get when you first open a credit-card account. These checks are linked to your credit-card account, so you can use them to pay off charges accumulated on some other rebate card. In effect, you simply transfer your balance from one card to the other and get two rebates for one set of purchases. (But always read the fine print carefully. Some credit-card issuers have changed their policies and do not always

allow customers with rollovers to get the low interest rate that is advertised up front in the big type.)

5. **Don't take the game too seriously.** Remember that credit-card companies have the upper hand; they can change the rules whenever they please. So play the game strictly for fun.

Secured cards are generally a sensible choice for people who can't get regular credit cards because of a bad credit history. A secured card looks and works just like a regular credit card, but to get one you must make a collateral deposit of a few hundred dollars in an interest-bearing savings account. You can then get a Visa or MasterCard from the bank as long as you leave your deposit there. If you fail to pay your bills, the bank will snatch your deposit. However, if you close the secured-card account in good standing, you will get back your full deposit. Beware issuers who ply their secured card on TV or through 900 numbers, however. Their cards tend to come with high fees and rates. Shop for a better deal at www.cardtrak.com and at www.bankrate.com. Note: Debit cards for teens have become increasingly popular. With the teen cash cards offered by Master-Card and Visa, parents transfer money into an online account. Kids 13 and older can spend the money by using the debit card at any establishment that accepts MasterCard and Visa. Teens can also use the card at ATMs to get cash. Annual fees for these cards range from zero to $24, depending on the issuing bank.

Whether you're looking for or have a standard card, a premium gold or platinum card, a rebate card, or a secured card, scrutinize the following:

• **The annual percentage rate.** The annual percentage rate (APR) is the total cost of credit expressed on an annual basis. You can find a credit card's APR on an application or its monthly billing statement. About 55% of credit cards today have variable interest rates, usually pegged to 10 percentage points or so above the **prime rate** (the rate banks charge their best customers). Be careful: Many cards that advertise rock-bottom, single-digit APRs have rates designed to last for only a few months before they soar by as much as 10 points. If you wind up taking one of these "deals," cancel your card before the initial rate expires.

Variable-rate cards sometimes masquerade as cost savers, since they purport to charge APRs that rise and fall with interest rates. But some of these cards sport a minimum interest rate that's actually a maximum rip-off. And some cards have "floors" below which rates cannot go. For instance, say a bank offers a secured MasterCard rate of prime plus 10.5%. That might sound as though it amounts to roughly 18%. But if the fine print says that the bank has a minimum rate of 18.9%, that is what cardholders would actually pay unless the prime rate is 8.4% or higher. Furthermore, some cards may offer what they call a "fixed" rate card, but the rate can actually change if something should change, say, in your credit rating.

- **The annual fee.** Many bank card issuers charge an annual fee of $20 to $35 for standard cards and from $50 to $300 for premium gold or platinum cards. Here's a secret: If you have a decent credit rating, you might be able to get this fee waived. When it shows up on your bill, call your card's issuer and, as politely yet fervently as you can, demand that the issuer stop assessing the fee. The issuer may waive it to keep your business. You may even be able to get American Express or another travel and entertainment card to do the same, especially if you threaten to cancel.
- **The grace period.** A card's grace period lets you avoid its finance charge if you pay the balance in full before the due date. Usually the due date is about two weeks after you have received your monthly statement. Most cards offer a grace period that annoyingly vanishes whenever you carry a balance. So, if you charged your kids' fall wardrobes last month, for instance, but didn't pay the entire balance at the end of the month, you'll start accruing finance charges on whatever you buy today almost as soon as you leave the store.
- **The junk fees.** Most card issuers charge you a fee when you make a late payment (average fee: $27.50), exceed your credit limit (average: $26.75), or take out a cash advance (typically 3% with a $10 minimum). Watch out for cards that spare you an annual fee, then sock it to you with other steep charges.
- **The minimum payment is not your friend.** If, like the average cardholder, you carry a balance of $1,100, paying off just 2% a month instead of 2.8% will add $120 to $400 to your annual interest bill. If possible, send in a payment that's at least double what your issuer requires.
- **The balance-computation method.** Here's a riddle: When is 18% not 18%? The answer: When two credit-card issuers calculate their interest rates differently. There are basically four ways card issuers can compute a balance: (1) the **average daily balance (excluding new purchases) method**, in which the issuer totals the balances for each day in the billing period without counting your new purchases; (2) **the average daily balance (including new purchases) method**, in which an issuer figures your average balance after counting your most recent purchases; (3) the **two-cycle average daily balance (excluding new purchases) method**, which totals your average balances for two billing cycles not including new purchases; and (4) the **two-cycle average daily balance (including new purchases) method**, figured the same way after taking your recent purchases into account.

If you occasionally carry a balance, you'll usually pay the least amount of interest when an issuer uses the average daily balance (excluding new purchases) method. Consider this: Suppose that four times a year you charged $1,000 on a credit card with a 19.8% interest rate and made the minimum payment of $28 when the charges appeared on your bill. The following month you charged another $1,000 and paid off the entire balance when your next bill arrived. The interest you owe over a year could vary by as much as $130:

TYPES OF CREDIT-CARD BALANCES

Type of Credit-Card Balance	Interest
Average daily balance (excluding new purchases)	$ 66
Average daily balance (including new purchases)	$132
Two-cycle average daily balance (excluding new purchases)	$131
Two-cycle average daily balance (including new purchases)	$196

Shopping for a Car Loan

The car-buying experience can be so aggravating that when it comes time to finance the purchase, you may be tempted to go with the dealer's loan just to get it over with. (For advice about car leasing, see Chapter 18.) Nearly 80% of all car buyers arrange financing through the dealer. Jumping at the dealer's financing isn't wise, though. You may be able to borrow elsewhere at far better terms—and the Web can be a gold mine of resources. That's because dealers often stack two percentage points on top of the APR (annual percentage rate) that a bank would charge. So before you walk into the showroom, check with at least six lenders, including the institution where you have a checking or savings account and lenders on the Web, to see what kind of deal you can swing. Then you'll know whether the car dealer's loan is best for you.

Sometimes car dealers dangle enticing loans with ridiculously low interest rates. These loans, however, often come with three strings: They are available only on certain models; you cannot qualify for any cash rebate if you accept the financing; and you can usually get the lowest rate only by signing up for a loan of no more than two years or so. That could make your monthly payments higher than you can afford, since shortening the term of a loan raises the size of the monthly payments. Here are a few alternatives:

- **If negotiating is too unappealing or time-consuming, you can pay a car-buying service to do it, for fees ranging from $155 to $395.** Check out AutoAdvisor (800-326-1976; www.autoadvisor.com), CarBargains (800-475-7283; www.carbargains.com), or CarQ (800-517-2277; www.carq.com). And several car-buying Web sites are marketing themselves successfully on the basis of convenience and freedom from hassles. A few popular sites are: www.autobytel.com, www.carpoint.com, and www.carsdirect.com.
- **Credit unions.** Car loan rates at credit unions are usually at least a percentage point less, on average, than rates at banks and S&Ls. Major credit unions also provide a car-buying advisory service developed by the Credit Union National Association (see www.carfax4cu.com). A report costs $12.95 and provides car-quality ratings, rebate information, and dealer costs for various options, as well as history on used cars.
- **Your bank or S&L.** Sometimes banks and S&Ls give their depositors a slight break on car loan rates if they agree to have their payments deducted directly from their accounts.
- **Home-equity loans.** More than 20% of all home-equity loans today are used to buy cars. Surprised? Actually, it's quite understandable once you look at the tax side of the car-financing equation. Interest payments on a home-equity loan are tax-deductible no matter what the money is used for; interest on a car loan is not deductible. If the interest rate on a home-equity loan is 8.6%, say, your after-tax rate might wind up being 6.2%, far lower than the rate on a typical car loan.

Before applying for a car loan, decide on the length of the term that you want. The shortest term is two years, but you may be able to stretch out your payments for as long as 10 years. Stay away from auto loans with terms longer than five years, despite their low monthly payments. By the fifth year, the amount you still owe could be more than the depreciation value of the car, putting you in what's known as an upside-down position. If you sell the car, you might have to come up with additional cash to pay off the loan.

Other car-financing tips:

- **Ask if there will be any penalties for paying off the loan early.** If you can choose between two loans with similar rates, go with the one that most easily lets you get rid of the loan ahead of schedule.
- **Mention your credit history if it's spotless, especially if you borrow from a car dealer.** According to the Consumer Bankers Association, about a third of lenders offer slightly lower rates for borrowers who never or rarely make late payments on their other loans. Typically, they'll knock 1% or so off their standard interest rate.
- **Try to make a down payment of at least 20%.** Lenders often add a quarter of a point to their rates for borrowers who put down less.
- **If you're a young, first-time car buyer, tell your car dealer.** Some dealers try to help people like you by using less stringent guidelines in deciding if you qualify for a loan. You may also be allowed to make a smaller down payment than normal.

Shopping for a Mortgage

For many people, the search for a mortgage can be overwhelming. You often must compare a variety of loans with different interest rates and terms to find the best mortgage for you. Miss out on the best deal and you could be stuck paying thousands of dollars in extra interest over the next 15 or 30 years. Bear in mind that in the early years of a mortgage, the bulk of your mortgage payment is going toward interest. In successive years, more and more of your payment goes to pay the principal. How much do one or two percentage points of interest or a difference of $50,000 matter for a mortgage? Check out the table on page 131.

The Internet can help you figure out how large a mortgage you can afford and where to get a loan. These days, roughly 80% of lenders with Web sites will let you know how large a mortgage you are likely to qualify for; however, these pre-qualification programs don't guarantee that you'll actually get the loans. Sites like www.hsh.com and e-loan.com are great for learning what your monthly payments would be for different types of mortgages. You also can get timely data on mortgage rates in your area at www.hsh.com and at www.bankrate.com. Such services may notify you if mortgage rates have risen or fallen since you last checked in. (See box on next page for Web sites.)

ONLINE MORTGAGE RESOURCES

You can find good mortagage calculators and information at:

- **Bankrate.com (www.bankrate.com)** offers information on mortgage rates in most areas of the U.S.
- **Mortgage.com (www.mortgage.com)** factors all interest rate changes into tables or graphs.
- **HSH Associates (www.hsh.com)** gives all kinds of mortgage information, including timely data on mortgage rates in your area.
- **Quicken Loans (www.quickenloans.com)** will ask you to complete a loan interview, then give you a list of mortgage options for which you are pre-approved from a pool of wholesalers. Even if you decide not to apply online, going through this process will get you thinking about your financing options.

MONTHLY PAYMENTS FOR A 30-YEAR FIXED MORTGAGE

Mortgage Amount	6%	7%	8%	9%	10%
$ 50,000	$ 300	$ 333	$ 367	$ 402	$ 439
$100,000	$ 600	$ 665	$ 734	$ 805	$ 878
$150,000	$ 900	$ 998	$1,101	$1,207	$1,316
$200,000	$1,199	$1,331	$1,468	$1,609	$1,755
$250,000	$1,499	$1,665	$1,835	$2,013	$2,195
$300,000	$1,799	$1,997	$2,203	$2,415	$2,633
$350,000	$2,098	$2,329	$2,568	$2,817	$3,073
$400,000	$2,398	$2,663	$2,937	$3,219	$3,511
$450,000	$2,698	$2,994	$3,302	$3,621	$3,949
$500,000	$2,998	$3,326	$3,669	$4,023	$4,388

Source: HSH Associates.

The table below provides a brief description of a sampling of mortgages. Find the one that suits you best.

WHAT'S THE BEST MORTGAGE FOR YOU?

FIXED LOANS
> 15-year fixed
> 20-year fixed
> 30-year fixed

Fixed-rate loans have interest rates that remain unchanged during the life of the loan. The shorter the term, the less costly the loan, since you pay lower total interest. Longer-term loans require smaller monthly payments, so it's easier to qualify for, say, a 30-year loan than a 15-year loan.

BALLOON LOANS
> Five-year balloon
> Seven-year balloon
> Five-year balloon-reset
> Seven-year balloon-reset

Balloon and **balloon-reset** loans are worth considering if you intend to sell your home or refinance within seven years. You make fixed monthly payments for a set period, usually five or seven years, at which point the loan balance comes due. Consider a balloon mortgage if you plan to sell your home before the onerous lump sum is due. Balloon-reset loans offer low initial rates. At the end of five or seven years, you have the option of paying off the balance or renewing the loan for 25 or 23 years, normally at a rate that's slightly higher than that of the prevailing fixed-rate loan.

ADJUSTABLE LOANS
One-year adjustable
Three-year adjustable
3/1 adjustable
5/1 adjustable
10/1 adjustable

Adjustable-rate mortgages, or **ARMs**, typically have rates that change every one, three, or five years. Your monthly payments start low since ARMs' initial rates are usually two percentage points or so below those on fixed-rate loans. But your rate and payments then rise or fall depending on changes in other interest rates. 3/1, 5/1, or 10/1 ARMs adjust once after the first three, five, or ten years, then change annually.

To begin the mortgage process, ask your real estate agent to recommend some lenders and see if your friends have used local lenders. Your agent might also be able to direct you to a mortgage broker, a kind of clearinghouse for home loans, or a Web site like the ones listed earlier in this section. Also, find out from your agent if any firms publish lists with data on mortgages offered by lenders in the same area. For example, every week HSH Associates puts together surveys of loans offered by 25 to 80 lenders in most states (www.hsh.com). Cost: $11 for each survey. If you can't find such a list, check your local paper's real estate section for advertisements to give you a sense of the mortgage market in your area. Then call a half dozen or so lenders to find out their current rates and terms.

Most lenders are reputable and honest. Still, before you go with any, it's a good idea to make sure the firm is on the up-and-up. Beware of lenders or mortgage brokers who ask you to pay stiff fees up front. Call your state banking department as well as the local Better Business Bureau to find out if any of the lender's customers have filed complaints. When an honest lender goes out of business, it will hand off its mortgages to another firm. However, if you are dealing with a fraudulent lender, your chances of getting money back depend on what's left when the scamsters are caught.

The type of mortgage you should choose generally depends on how long you plan to remain in the home and how you feel about your payment changing from month to month. There are two basic varieties: (1) **fixed-rate loans**, which have interest rates that do not change over the life of the loan and generally run for 15 to 30 years; and (2) **variable-** or **adjustable-rate mortgages** (ARMs), whose rates can rise or fall along with other interest rates. Most ARMs have 15-year or 30-year terms. An ARM's rate generally cannot rise by more than two percentage points a year or six points over the life of the loan, however. A 15-year mortgage has two attractions: Your interest rate on a 15-year mortgage will probably be about a quarter of a percentage point lower than that of a comparable 30-year loan; and your total interest payments will be cut in half. The drawback is that 15-year loans have higher monthly payments. At recent rates, you would face a $1,010 monthly nut on the average $100,000 15-year mortgage, compared with $823 on a 30-year fixed-rate loan—a 23% difference. All in all, if you can afford a 15-year mortgage, go for it.

Adjustable-rate loans typically have initial interest rates that are about two percentage points lower than fixed loans plus lower initial monthly payments. At recent rates, for example, the initial monthly payment on a $100,000 ARM was about 20% lower than the payments on comparable 30-year fixed-rate mortgages, or $659 versus $823. Payments on adjustable-rate mortgages can increase substantially, though, if interest rates rise. Typically, you lock in the initial interest rate on an ARM for six months or a year. But a **hybrid ARM mortgage** can allow you to lock in for three years or longer. Then every year or so the lender will raise or lower the rate in tandem with an index, such as the one-year Treasury constant maturity rate.

The first-year ARM rate is usually set at a discount from the index, so even if interest rates remain flat, a borrower's ARM would go up in a year. That's right: After the first year of your ARM, your interest rate and monthly payments will rise even if other interest rates haven't increased.

You may have to sign up for an ARM if your income is too low to qualify for a fixed rate. (As a rule, you can qualify for a mortgage on a home that costs up to about 2½ times your gross income. Also, your monthly debt payments, including your mortgage, cannot exceed 36% of your gross monthly income.) If you do not expect to own the house for more than five years, an ARM can be especially appealing, since there is little risk that your rate will rise substantially over that short period of time. Before you commit to any adjustable mortgage, see whether you can live with it under the worst-case scenario. With a 6% ARM that maxes out each year—jumping to 8% in year two, 10% in year three, and 12% in year four—you still end up with a four-year average rate of 9%, which would beat a 30-year fixed-rate average of 9.2%.

A few other mortgage variations are worth considering. If you think mortgage rates might be heading down in a few years, check out a **convertible loan,** which starts out as an ARM but gives you the option of switching to a fixed rate between the second and fifth years of the loan. The interest rate is initially about one percentage point higher than that of a comparable ARM, though still lower than what you would pay for a fixed-rate mortgage. At conversion, you will owe a fee of about $250.

If you plan to be in your house for five to seven years or so, a **two-step** or **balloon-reset mortgage** might be the call. The monthly payments stay at the same level for the first five or seven years. At that point, there's a one-time adjustment based on market conditions, then the payment is again fixed for the duration of the loan. Typically, the new rate is the yield of the 10-year U.S. Treasury constant maturity plus 2.5 percentage points. The rate on a balloon-reset mortgage is often one-half to three-quarters of a percentage point less than that of a 30-year fixed. For example, if a 30-year fixed rate is 8.61%, a balloon reset might charge 8.07%.

If you would rather lock in a discounted interest rate for a longer period than two-step loans offer, check out a loan called a **10/1 hybrid**. A 10/1 hybrid loan can be a smart choice if you plan to move within 10 years. It locks in a rate for 10 years, but generally at a lower rate than the traditional fixed-rate loan. After 10 years, the rate adjusts annually as if it were a one-year ARM.

A **biweekly loan** is another way to slash your interest costs. It requires that you make half your monthly payment every two weeks. Because most months are longer than four full weeks, or 28 days, you'll end up making two extra half payments a year. These extra payments will shave up to 12 years off the life of a 30-year loan. Problem is, many banks don't offer biweekly mortgages as such. Those that do may charge a higher interest rate that could offset your savings, making it essential to compare your lender's rate on biweekly loans and standard loans. However, many lenders will arrange to make your loan a biweekly loan on a regular basis, for a one-time fee. You can also achieve similar savings by making one or two extra payments a year. Avoid third-party firms that will convert your standard mortgage to a biweekly, but may charge you a one-time fee plus an extra amount for each payment.

If you want to pay less in interest and unload your mortgage ahead of time, you can shorten the life of your loan on your own simply by tacking on more to your monthly payments. For example, if you added $25 to your regular monthly payments of $805 on a $100,000 30-year 9% fixed rate loan, you could save $29,440 in total interest and shorten your loan by almost four years. Most lenders will let you make these extra payments, although some will impose a **prepayment penalty** if you do so during the first few years of your mortgage. That's why you'll need to check with your lender before making extra payments. If there is a penalty, ask to have it waived. Then explain how much more you'd like to pay and how often, finding out the way the lender will want you to submit your extra payments.

Minimum down payments are typically 5% to 10% for fixed-rate loans and 10% to 20% for adjustable loans and balloons. If you put down less than 20%, however, you'll need to buy **mortgage insurance**. That usually means paying the first year's insurance premium at closing—up to $950 on a $100,000 loan with 5% down—plus coughing up a few extra bucks each month as part of your mortgage payment.

Some financial professionals recommend putting down as much as possible and getting the shortest-term loan you can afford to save on interest. The alternate argument is that you should borrow as much as possible and invest the money you save. To make this strategy successful, however, you need the self-discipline to actually invest the extra cash in a way that will generate an after-tax return higher than the after-tax cost of your mortgage. (To figure your after-tax cost, subtract your marginal tax rate from 1 and multiply the result by your interest rate.)

Getting a mortgage is never easy, but first-time buyers have it roughest of all. They don't have cash from selling a previous residence to help them come up with the down payment or other mortgage closing costs. In fact, first-time buyers often find that it's the down payment and closing costs, not the monthly payment, that are the biggest obstacle to getting a mortgage. For solutions to problems faced by first-time home buyers, see the following table:

HELP FOR FIRST-TIME MORTGAGE BORROWERS

PROBLEM: You can't come up with enough cash for the down payment.

SOLUTIONS:
1. **Find a lender that will approve you for a loan with a lower down payment.** Many banks accept down payments as low as 5%. Lowering the down payment, however, means increasing the size of the mortgage, which could make it harder for you to qualify. If so, check out the 5% down, Fannie-Neighbors/Community Homebuyer's, which allows a debt-to-income ratio of up to 40%. Fannie Mae, the largest source of financing for home mortgages in the U.S., has low-down-payment programs for first-time buyers whose household income is less than the local median. One features monthly payments that start out less than normal and increase gradually over two to eight years. For more information, call Fannie Mae at 800-732-6643, or see www.fanniemae.com.

2. **Consider Federal Housing Administration–insured mortgages made through banks or other lenders.** FHA loans typically require a 3% down payment, but you must pay a fee equal to 3% of the loan—that's $3,000 on a $100,000 mortgage. FHA-insured loans are usually limited to $67,500, but can go up to $151,572 in high-cost areas like New York City and Los Angeles.

3. **Borrow from family members for the down payment.** If your relatives have deep pockets and big hearts consider Fannie Mae's so-called **3/2 loan**. You put down 3%; Mom, Dad, or any relative contributes the other 2%. Anytime you borrow from your parents, treat the loan as a business transaction. There should be a note specifying an interest rate and repayment schedule. Interest should be set according to market rates. If a family member offers to cover part of the down payment, be sure to get a note from that person stating that he or she is giving you the money as a gift. Otherwise, your lender will suspect that you received a loan and the debt may hinder your ability to borrow as much as you need.

PROBLEM: You don't have the cash for the up-front cost of mortgage insurance.

SOLUTION: Finance the insurance. Several mortgage insurers, including GE Capital Mortgage Insurance and Mortgage Guaranty Insurance, let you pay your first year's premiums in monthly installments—which would come to about $50 a month on a $100,000 home. Insurance with this feature costs a bit more, but if the lower up-front payment helps you afford the loan, the financing is worth the price.

PROBLEM: Your credit record is flawed.

SOLUTION: Come clean and offer a good explanation. Most lenders won't reject you because of two or three 30-days-late payments on your credit report. If you have had numerous 30-days-late payments, have been late 60 days or more on any payments, or have defaulted on a loan within the past two years, you'll have some serious explaining to do. By volunteering the information and a reasonable explanation, you may be able to convince a lender that you're actually a good risk. If that fails, a mortgage broker who specializes in helping bad credit risks might be a possibility. For a list of mortgage brokers in your area, contact the National Association of Mortgage Brokers (703-610-9009; www.namb.org).

Mortgage Loan Discrimination

Some mortgage seekers face a special hurdle: bias. According to studies by the Federal Reserve and others, minority mortgage applicants are turned down two to four times more often than whites. The Fed has also discovered that lenders sometimes discriminate against single women and young people. Discrimination can be tough to spot. It may take the form of an unhelpful loan officer or one who tries to steer you to another bank. For a rundown of your rights, look for the Federal Reserve's information, *Home Mortgages: Understanding the Process and Your Right to Fair Lending,* on the Federal Reserve Web site (www.federalreserve.gov; for ordering assistance, telephone 202-452-3244 or fax 202-728-5886).

If you feel you have been treated unjustly, call the discrimination hotline at the U.S. Department of Housing and Urban Development (800-669-9777; www.hud.gov). There are several other steps you can take to protect yourself:

- **When you apply, find out how long you can expect to wait for a decision.** Then call the lender if you haven't heard by the promised date. Some banks may simply delay action, hoping you'll give up. Demonstrating that you intend to stand up for your rights may improve your chances of qualifying for a loan.
- **If the bank turns down your loan request, ask for an explanation of its underwriting standards.** This information may help you learn whether the institution rejects all loan applicants with credentials like yours.
- **Watch out for lowball appraisals.** If the stated reason for your rejection is that the home you want to buy is worth less than the purchase price, ask to see a copy of the lender's appraisal report. Then, if the appraisal seems unreasonably low, take it to a fair-lending expert such as one at the U.S. Department of Housing and Urban Development. This kind of pro may be able to spot evidence of bias in the subjective information that's often part of an appraisal—comments about the quality of neighboring houses, for example. By law, you are allowed to obtain a copy of your appraisal, although you must request this in writing.

Working with a Mortgage Lender

Once you have been approved for a loan, take a shot at predicting which way mortgage rates are headed over the next few months. If you think rates will rise, lock in a rate at application. Some lenders let you lock in for 60 days or longer at no charge. Others require a deposit, often equal to 1% of the loan's amount. Be sure you'll be able to close before the lock-in period ends. Otherwise, if rates have risen, the lender can boost your rate, too.

You can chop weeks off the loan-processing period by dealing with a lender who follows alternative documentation guidelines. This procedure streamlines the mortgage application routine. For example, instead of requiring a letter from your employer confirming that you have a job, the lender will accept W-2 forms from the past two years and a current payroll stub.

Another way to close on a house more quickly is to get your loan application preapproved. Even before you've found the house you plan to buy, many lenders will approve you for a mortgage of a specific amount. Then, all a lender has to do after you find a house is have it appraised and ensure that the seller can legally transfer title to you.

Lenders typically charge fees known as **points** for granting mortgages. One point equals 1% of the loan amount. Often a lender will charge one to two points; that works out to $1,000 to $3,000 on a $100,000 mortgage. With most lenders you can lower your interest rate by agreeing to pay more in points. For instance, you may be offered an 8% rate with no points, 7.7% with one point, and 7.6% with two points. How do you decide which is best? By figuring out how long you plan to stay in your home.

Let's say you can get a $100,000 fixed-rate 30-year mortgage at the terms just described. The monthly payment on the no-point loan would be $734; on the two-point loan, it would be $706. It would take you 72 months, or six years, before the $28-a-month savings would fully offset the two points ($2,000/$28 = 72). So, in this example, paying points now in exchange for a lower rate would make sense if you plan to stay in your home at least six years. If you expect to move again sooner, it won't be worth it to pay the points.

In addition to points, borrowers may be asked to come up with numerous other costs at the closing, not to mention the price of hiring a mover. For a list and description of these assorted expenses, see the following table:

YOUR MORTGAGE FEES

Type of Cost	Charge
Application fee A lender's charge to cover the initial costs of processing your loan request and checking your credit report. Generally not refundable.	$75–$300
Appraisal An estimate of the property's value.	$150–$400
Survey An inspection of the boundaries of a property and any improvements on it.	$125–$300
Homeowners insurance Protection against loss from fire and other natural hazards. You may be required to carry flood insurance, too.	$300–$600
Lender's attorney's review fee What the lender pays the lawyer or company conducting the closing on its behalf.	$75–$200
Title search and title insurance An examination to confirm ownership of the real estate plus insurance against any loss caused by discrepancies to property's title.	$450–$600
Home inspection A written review of the structure.	$175–$350
Loan origination fee Charge for the lender's work evaluating and preparing your mortgage.	1% of loan
Mortgage insurance Protection for the lender in case you default. Generally required only when you make a down payment of less than 20%.	0.5%–1% of loan

Type of Cost	Charge
Points Prepaid interest charged by the lender.	1–2% of loan
Your attorney's fee The cost of hiring a lawyer to look out for you when negotiating a contract to buy a home.	$500–$1,500

Always attempt to negotiate a lender's fees. This is easiest to do when your local housing market is in the dumps and lenders have trouble bringing in mortgage borrowers. Consider the savings scored by one man who took out a several-hundred-thousand-dollar mortgage at a New York City area thrift in 2000. The bank offered to lock in its 4.85% rate on a one-year ARM for 60 days. He asked the bank to extend its lock to 90 days free of charge and got it. That saved him roughly $1,250. In addition, he avoided having to borrow at a higher 7.35% when interest rates rose. By insisting that the bank waive all fees except those that he was legally required to pay, he was also able to get the bank to cover its own attorney's fee ($350), the mortgage underwriting fee ($207), the application fee ($273), and the appraisal fee ($187).

Chances are your lender will one day sell your loan to another lender while you are still paying it off. Before that happens, you should get a letter from your lender, known as a **sign-off letter**, explaining its plans, and a **sign-on letter** from your new lender. If you get only one such letter, or something looks fishy, call your original lender to verify the information and make sure that the letter wasn't written by a scamster who got his hands on your name and address. Never send your mortgage payment to another firm if you haven't both the sign-off and the sign-on letters. When you get the first statement from the new lender, review it carefully to be sure the institution got everything right.

Homeowners with adjustable-rate mortgages, unfortunately, need to check to see that their lenders aren't overcharging them. Lenders could come up with the wrong figures when they recalculate ARM payments—either by honest goofs or by unscrupulous greed.

Should You Refinance Your Mortgage?

If you already have a mortgage, you might want to **refinance** it—swap the loan for a different one—to get a lower interest rate, snag a lower monthly payment, unload the loan faster, or pull some money out. Refinancing also is sometimes a smart idea for homeowners who want to get out of an ARM and into a fixed-rate loan in order to know exactly what the mortgage payment will be for the life of the loan. You will encounter the same procedure and often the same types of costs as you did when you got your first mortgage. Don't forget to find out if your lender will waive any refinancing fees. Although some lenders waive points for refinances, you could spend up to 5% of the outstanding principal in refinancing costs, plus any prepayment penalties on your first mortgage.

For many years the general rule of thumb was that you should refinance only if the interest rate on your current mortgage was at least two percentage points higher than the prevailing market rate; now, it's as little as one percentage point. Say, for example, you had a five-year-old fixed-rate loan with an 8% rate and $105,000 balance. If interest rates on new 30-year fixed-rate loans had dropped to 6.75%, you could refinance and lower your monthly payments from $774.12 to $650.53. Instead you might choose to refinance with a 15-year fixed-rate loan at, say, 6.25%. Your monthly payments would be $859.98—higher than they were before the refinance—but you'd pay off the entire mortgage in just 15 years. You'd also save a bundle: You'd pay just $54,498.35 in interest on the new 15-year loan, compared with $133,894.04 had you chosen to refinance with a 30-year fixed loan.

In many ways, however, this one-percentage-point rule is too simplistic. Lowering your interest rate by as little as a quarter of a point can save you money in the long run. What's more, the rule was invented at a time when lenders charged a lot to refinance. In slow housing markets, some lenders waive their application fees and pay your closing costs. The crucial question for anyone considering a refinancing is: How long will I stay in my home? If you plan to remain well beyond the time it would take to recoup your closing costs through lower monthly payments, it makes sense to refinance.

When balancing the cost of refinancing against your savings, you'll need to figure out this break-even point. To do this, subtract the monthly payment on your current mortgage. Then add up the costs of refinancing, including points, closing fees, and taxes. Then divide your costs by your monthly savings. For instance, if your current loan is 10% and you can refinance to a 9% mortgage with $1,500 in assorted expenses, it will take 21 months before you start saving. Some lenders, however, levy no points or closing costs to refinance but charge an interest rate that is higher (say three-quarters of a point or so) than if you had paid the points up front. With a no-closing-cost, no-point loan, you break even immediately as long as your new rate is lower than your old one.

Shop the deals offered by a half dozen or so lenders before applying for a mortgage refinance (see box on page 131 for Web sites that will help). Be sure to check with the lender who holds your current mortgage. The firm may be willing to waive some of the closing costs to keep your business.

Shopping for a Home-Equity Loan or Credit Line

Home-equity loans (or **second mortgages**) and **home-equity lines of credit** let you borrow against the value of the equity you've accrued. They're hot—with rates that easily consign such rival sources of cash as credit cards to their rightful place in credit inferno. Factor in the deductibility of home-equity interest payments on loans up to $100,000 and the deal gets even better. To figure the after-tax cost of a home-equity loan, subtract your marginal tax rate from 1 (to find your tax rate, see Chapter 4); multiply the result by the loan's interest rate. So for someone in the 30% bracket, the after-tax rate on an 11% home-equity loan is 7.7% (0.70 x 11%).

A home-equity loan can be taken all at once; a credit line lets you draw against it over time. With both home-equity lines and loans, the maximum amount you can borrow depends on the value of your home, as determined by the lender's appraisal. You frequently can borrow as much as 75% to 90% of the house's value, minus the balance on your mortgage. You must typically repay a lump-sum loan within 10 to 20 years. Credit lines generally must be paid off within two to 15 years. Just remember: If you default, you could lose your home.

Home-equity loans typically have fixed rates. Home-equity credit lines generally have interest rates that fluctuate monthly. In most cases, the variable-rate lines are set at zero to two percentage points above prime. When shopping for a variable-rate home-equity deal, look for interest rate limitations such as **floors** and **ceilings** (minimum interest rates and maximum interest rates). Lower ceilings are better.

Which is better, a home-equity loan or a line? Go with a line if you'll be using the debt for recurring expenses like a child's college tuition or if you're not sure how much you'll need to borrow. Just avoid borrowing more money than you can pay back in three to four years—a hedge against an unexpected zoom in interest rates. A fixed-rate loan is best if you don't want to be faced with the prospect of rising payments due to rising rates.

These days it's fairly easy to find a lender willing to waive part or all of a home-equity's up-front points and fees, saving you $200 to $1,500 in closing costs. But beware: Some lenders are pushing home-equity loans hard, with deceptive come-ons or exorbitant costs. Don't sign up unless you clearly understand the loan agreement.

For example, be sure your monthly payments will cover a portion of both your loan's interest and principal. Some home-equity loans look inexpensive because you pay only the interest each month. Their true cost is clear, however, when the loan is due and you must come up with the balance to pay off the principal.

To be safe, follow these tips:

- **Reserve your home-equity debt for big-ticket bills such as college tuition or home renovation.** Believe it or not, a growing number of banks are encouraging their customers to use home-equity loans to cover ordinary expenses. Many lenders now issue credit cards that let cardholders draw on the equity in their home, even permitting customers to draw on their home equity via their ATMs. Prudence argues against using these cards.
- **Shun any home-equity deal that can sap all—or even more than all—your equity.** A home-equity loan or line that lets you borrow more than 80% of the value of your home minus outstanding debt carries a big potential pitfall: Should home prices fall and you wish to sell, you might have to come up with more money than you can get from the sale to repay the mortgage and home-equity debt. Today, some lenders even let you borrow as much as 25% more than your home is worth. The money that you borrow above the worth of your home, however, is not tax-deductible.
- **Don't borrow more than $100,000.** Interest is deductible on home-equity loans over $100,000 only if the money is used for home improvements, business expenses, and income-generating investments. If you use your loans for other purchases beyond the $100,000 limit, you won't get any tax breaks.

Shopping for a Personal Loan

A personal loan from a bank, S&L, or credit union is about the most expensive way you can borrow, short of a cash advance on a credit card or going to a loan shark. Typically, such **unsecured personal debt**—so named because the loans are not backed by an asset such as a home or a car—comes in the form of a loan with a term of one to five years or a line of credit that you draw upon as you need it. Personal loans come with a rate that is typically pegged to the prime rate—way above the prime rate. The average rate at banks and S&Ls recently: 14.53%, less than 10 percentage points above prime, when the prime rate was at a 40-year low, at the end of 2001. Typically, credit unions have the lowest rates on unsecured personal loans.

Student Loans

For answers to questions about federal student loan availability, eligibility, and where to get student loans, contact the U.S. Department of Education at 800-433-3243; www.ed.gov; or Sallie Mae (Student Loan Marketing Association) at 800-891-1410 or 800-239-4269; www.salliemae.com. See Chapter 10 for details on loans for students.

Sources of Emergency Cash

If you're in a bind and need to borrow cash fast, check out the following:

• **Retirement plans at work.** The tax law prohibits withdrawals from 401(k)-type plans except in narrowly defined emergencies. However, most employers will let you borrow from your 401(k), 403(b), profit-sharing, or thrift plan. The interest is not deductible, however. These loans generally have a maximum term of five years (sometimes up to 10 years if you use the funds to buy or renovate your home), a rate that is often as low as the prime rate or prime plus one percentage point, and a fixed-repayment schedule through payroll deduction. The most you can borrow is 50% of your account's value, up to $50,000. You usually can get your loan in a matter of days, and you won't be subjected to a credit check.

One of the seeming advantages of borrowing this way is that you are paying interest to yourself on the amount that you borrow. In other words, the interest you pay goes right back into your plan's account. In truth, however, that's not as terrific as it seems. After all, the money in your account would be growing tax-deferred along with its investments if you didn't take it out for a loan. One clear drawback with these loans: If you're fired or quit your job and have an outstanding balance on one, you will have to repay it quickly. Otherwise you'll owe taxes on the amount still due plus a 10%

early withdrawal penalty if you're younger than age 59½. The bottom line: Don't borrow against your 401(k) or other employer plan until you've exhausted other alternatives such as student loans and home-equity loans.

- **Margin loans.** Getting this kind of loan from your stockbroker by putting up stocks, bonds, and mutual funds as collateral is fairly popular these days. That's understandable, considering that a margin loan lets you borrow at a rate near or below prime; the rate is roughly the same as the home-equity rate. When you take out a margin loan, the interest you owe accumulates in your account, so you can repay whenever you want or wait until you sell the securities you've put up as collateral.

  Before you call your broker for a loan, make sure you understand these three main drawbacks:

  1. **Interest on margin loans is tax-deductible—but only if you invest the money and not if you borrow to buy tax-free bonds or municipal bond funds.** There is another tax limitation. You can generally deduct margin interest only up to the amount of interest and dividend income you receive in a year.

  2. **Your broker may have to sell your securities.** If the value of your stocks and bonds drops, you can get a **margin call** requiring you to put up more cash or securities as collateral. If you don't ante up, the broker may have to sell some of your investments to reduce your balance. To play it safe, avoid borrowing more than 20% of your portfolio.

  3. **A margin loan creates leverage, making your investments riskier.** Borrowing to buy stocks and bonds magnifies your losses if the value of your securities declines.

- **Cash-value life insurance loans.** Borrowing against your life insurance policy can sometimes provide easy money at low rates. But pay it back quickly or you will diminish the value of the policy for your survivors. That's because if you die with a loan outstanding, the death benefit of your policy will be reduced by the loan's balance.

Seven Ways to Be a Smart Borrower

Now that you're familiar with the borrowing basics, you're ready to follow these seven strategies:

1. **Borrow for long-term goals, not short-term pleasures.** Try to take out loans only for purchases that will pay long-term returns, like a house, a home remodeling, a college education, or a car, and not for a better wardrobe or a European vacation. One

useful rule of thumb: Never take out a loan that will last longer than what you're buying.

2. **Apply for the shortest-term loan you can afford.** Stretch to make the larger monthly payments that come with shortening a loan's term. By doing so, you'll pay less in interest over the life of the loan. Consider your choices for a $20,000 car loan at 9.5%. If you select a five-year loan, you'd pay just $420 a month but spend $5,200 on interest, bringing your total payments to $25,200. Opt for a three-year term, however, and although your monthly payments would rise to about $640, you'd pay just $3,060 in total interest or $23,060 in total over three years. By biting the bullet and taking on the higher monthly payment, you could save $2,140 in interest costs.

3. **Pay as much as you can up front.** When you finance a purchase, put down as much as you can—and don't go by lenders' guidelines. Double or triple the minimum down payment the lender demands, if possible. If you can make one or two large payments during the loan's first months without incurring a prepayment penalty, do it. This strategy, known as **front-loading**, can shave months off your loan.

4. **Consolidate high-rate credit-card debts with a lower-rate card or home-equity loan.** If you carry a balance on several credit cards, you may be able to merge them into one balance on a single low-rate card. Many credit cards will send you a balance transfer form or so-called convenience checks that you can use to pay off your balances on other cards. Be sure to ask your issuer to describe its terms on a balance transfer first: Some treat transfers as cash advances and thus may impose a transaction fee of up to $10 or charge higher interest on the amount you transfer. If your debt is large enough and the rate is low enough, however, you can still come out ahead. For example, if you transfer your $5,000 balance from a card that charges 18% interest to a card that charges 13% interest, you could save $125 in interest over just the first six months.

   Another option is to scoop up debts into a home-equity loan, assuming you're a homeowner. Say you're in the 30% federal income tax bracket and transfer $10,000 from credit cards that charge 18% interest into a 9% home-equity loan. You'll save about $4,340 in interest payments over five years, plus another $1,300 or so in federal income taxes, since the home-equity interest is tax-deductible.

5. **Shop around for the best borrowing deal.** The most recent issue of MONEY or perhaps your local newspaper is a good place to start. You can find lists of the best credit cards, as well as the best deals on mortgages, home-equity loans, and car loans in your area.

   Be sure to call at least half a dozen lenders before taking out a new loan. Two options you should always check out: credit unions and the bank where you have your savings. On average, credit unions offer loan rates that are one to two and a half percentage points lower than those available at banks and S&Ls. What's more, they have become increasingly flexible about their membership; call the Credit Union National Association (800-358-5710; www.cuna.org) to find out if there is one in your area that you can join. Also, ask a loan officer where you keep your checking and savings accounts whether depositors get special breaks on loans. You can sometimes get a half-point discount on the interest rate on short-term loans by having payments deducted automatically from your account each month.

6. **Review your credit report before applying for a loan.** Credit-reporting agencies keep data on your debt payment history and the amount of credit you already have. They then sell this information to lenders, merchants, and other credit issuers, who use it to target you as a potential borrower and to decide whether to grant you more credit. You can get a copy of your credit report by calling each of the major agencies: You can order a copy for no more than $8 from TransUnion (www.transunion. com; 800-888-4213), Experian (www.experian.com; 888-397-3742), or Equifax (www.equifax.com; 800-997-2493).

7. **Negotiate rates and fees.** Though lenders don't like to admit it, with a little arm twisting many today will cut their credit-card interest rates and fees, as well as lower costs on all kinds of loans. You can score potential savings simply by asking for a better deal and, if necessary, threatening to take your business elsewhere.

You can also save beaucoup bucks by asking lenders for lower interest rates and fees on car loans, home-equity loans, and mortgages. Most banks have an official rate for each type of loan they make. But if you are an existing customer or have a good credit rating, it's not difficult to convince the bank to lend to you at a lower rate.

How can you cut yourself such a deal? First, get a copy of your credit report two months before you plan to borrow money, so you can correct any errors before you meet with lenders. Second, compare rates and fees from a bunch of institutions and ask the two or three with the best deals to beat each other's offers. Finally, prepare to offer the lender something in return for its largesse: Many banks will shave as much as one-half percentage point off the interest rate on your car loan, for example, if you arrange to have your loan payments deducted automatically from your checking account.

What to Do When You've Been Turned Down

If you apply for a loan or a credit card and get turned down, demand a copy of your credit report from the three big credit bureaus: Equifax, TransUnion, and Experian (toll-free numbers and Web sites are listed above). Carefully review your reports for mistakes. According to one recent survey, about 30% of would-be borrowers said they were denied credit because of an error in their credit reports, and close to half who checked their credit reports reported finding errors.

Here are some other common causes for credit rejection and how to avoid them:

- **A recent move.** Credit-card issuers prefer people who have lived at the same address and had the same job for at least a year or two. Attach an explanatory note to your application if you've moved or changed jobs within the past two years.
- **Too many credit inquiries.** Every time a lender checks your credit history, that inquiry shows up on your record. Trouble is, several recent inquiries—and shopping for a car loan might generate half a dozen—can make a credit-card issuer worry that you are about to take on too much debt. If you think your credit report will show more than five inquiries in the past six months, attach a letter that explains the reason.
- **Too much debt.** Card issuers want evidence that you can handle credit, such as having made prompt payments for at least a year on one or two credit cards, store accounts, or car loans. You risk rejection, however, if you owe 80% of your credit limits on two or more cards or if you owe anything at all on four or more cards. This rule can snag credit-card gamers who transfer their balances from card to card in search of super-low rates. If you don't cancel your old accounts, you'll risk being hamstrung by credit overload when you apply for a loan or a new card.

Even people with pristine credit histories who pay their balances in full each month can be rejected because of a pocketful of plastic. Prospective lenders almost always scrutinize the amount of unsecured credit available to you as shown in your credit report. If they notice that you have, say, five credit cards with a credit limit of $5,000 each, they may be reluctant to lend to you. When canceling a card, scissors don't cut it. You'll need to write or notify your card issuer and ask that it notify the credit bureaus that your account has been "in good standing and closed by the borrower." Insist, too, that the card company send you a copy of this letter.

Maybe there was a legitimate reason for your credit problems—a job loss or a serious illness, for instance. Then, send a letter of explanation to each credit bureau and let each know that those problems are behind you. This way, prospective creditors will be able to read that letter in your file, making them perhaps more understanding than they would have been.

If your credit-card issuers have taken away all your cards, apply for a secured card. This will help you establish your creditworthiness. You'll automatically qualify for the card, as long as you agree to keep a savings account with the card issuer and keep an amount equal to your credit line in the account. You are likely to find that after a year and a half of paying your secured-card bills on time, you can switch to an unsecured card with a lower rate.

Credit Counseling and Bankruptcy

If you're unable to pay lenders on time, be up front with them. Tell your creditors what the problem is and the amount you think you can pay per month to get rid of the debts. Each creditor probably has repayment guidelines for customers in distress. So if you lose your job, for example, you might be able to negotiate a breathing spell that will temporarily cut monthly charge-card payments by 25%. Some lenders let you waive paying interest charges for up to six months if you can demonstrate that you'll have no problem paying your bills in full when that time is up. One other possibility: See if your lender will let you refinance your loan at a lower interest rate. It's a long shot, but your lender may go along if it appears that this move can prevent the institution from taking more drastic action against you and get some money back, too.

When a creditor refuses to negotiate further, seek outside help. Head for the nearest nonprofit **credit counseling service**, which you can find by calling the National Foundation for Credit Counseling (800-388-2227; www.nfcc.org). A credit counselor will first review your debts and your ability to pay them, then set up a supervised payment plan. The initial consultation is often free. After that, you'll be charged according to your ability to pay. The average fee is $10 a month, but some people aren't charged at all.

Credit counselors typically create a two-year or three-year schedule for liquidating your debts. Then they notify your lenders to get them off your back. Each month you write a check to the counseling agency for the specified payment amount, and counselors mail out separate checks to your creditors. About 60% of the people who go to the NFCC for assistance find that within three and a half years, they've wiped their debt clean.

Do not confuse these legitimate counseling programs with so-called **credit repair services**, a/k/a credit doctors or credit clinics. These operators promise to remove adverse data from your credit report and even get you a credit card for a fee of as much as $500. Although some of these firms are legit, most charge excessive fees and do nothing that you can't do yourself or with the help of a less expensive nonprofit counseling service.

If all else fails, you may have to file for **bankruptcy**. The time to weigh this desperate measure is when creditors threaten to seize part of your wages through a court process called **garnishment**. Bankruptcy stops creditors from hounding you by putting you under the protection of U.S. Bankruptcy Court. Of course bankruptcy has its price. First, you'll have to liquidate most of your assets, but not your retirement accounts such as IRAs and pensions. This could possibly include your house if you have one. Then, a record of the bankruptcy will show up on your credit bureau files for seven to 10 years, making it tough to get credit and borrow money. You may be sentenced to a long term of paying cash for practically everything.

CHAPTER 7

Smart Strategies for Buying a House, Condo, or Co-op

Home ownership isn't merely the American dream, it's really the American way. More than 60 million Americans own their own homes, and nearly nine out of 10 persons who've yet to buy a home say attaining ownership status is their top financial goal. That ringing endorsement for owning a home is well founded. Beyond the personal satisfaction of owning your own property—which no one can really put a value on—there are two compelling financial reasons to own a home.

First, over long periods of five to 10 years, home values on average appreciate at a rate that has outpaced the annual inflation rate. While housing experts and economists don't expect rapid home price appreciation in the future, there is near unanimous agreement that home values will continue to appreciate at a rate that at least matches inflation or exceeds it by a percentage point or so a year. In 2000 home prices rose 4.3% on average, while inflation increased by 3.4%. Of course, what happens in your neighborhood depends on your local economy.

In addition to the fact that it's an asset that will grow in value, your home is the best tax deduction you've got. That's because the federal government has (so far, at least) left intact the deductibility of mortgage interest, while it has gutted other write-offs such as interest paid on consumer loans and credit cards. Currently, homeowners can deduct

100% of their mortgage interest payments—up to a $1 million maximum—provided the loan is used to finance either a primary residence or a vacation home. Property taxes are also deductible. Your home can also be a source of tax-advantaged lending to yourself: As Chapter 6 explained in detail, you can use your equity in a home (the appraised value of the home minus the outstanding balance of the mortgage) as collateral to get a home-equity line or loan. Rates on these loans are generally five percentage points below what you would pay for a general personal loan, and the first $100,000 of interest is tax-deductible.

While the financial and personal reasons for owning your own home are no doubt compelling, it is critical for any potential home buyer—whether a first-timer or a repeat buyer—to develop an astute strategy. The main reason is pretty simple: Homes are expensive. According to the National Association of Realtors, the national median-priced home in 2001 cost $147,300, up 6% from 2000; in high-priced metropolitan areas such as San Francisco and New York City, typical prices can be double that amount. Unless you plan on acquiring a stable of Ferraris, buying a home will undoubtedly be the single biggest purchase of your life. What's more, with home prices likely to appreciate at an annual rate that exceeds the rate of inflation by 1% to 2% a year, if you overpay by 10% or more when you purchase your house, it will take at least a few years to recoup the cost of that misstep. Then, when you sell your home, you may pay a real estate sales commission of anywhere from 4% to 10%, which would work out to a few years' worth of appreciation that you won't be able to pocket. So any chance of breaking even will probably take at least five years if you overpay and at least two years even if you pay a fair price.

To make sure you get the most house, condo, or co-op for your money, this chapter covers the rules and tools you need to construct a winning game plan. Follow this step-by-step guide to maneuvering through the home-buying process and you'll emerge with a place you love that's also a solid financial investment. One quick note to potential first-time buyers who haven't been able to save enough for the down payment on a home: Get smart! Flip back to Chapter 5 and read up on how to construct a painless savings plan. You'll be surprised how quickly you can amass the $10,000 or so you'll need for the down payment.

Renting Versus Buying

While owning a home is a wise financial move for the vast majority of Americans, there are a few scenarios where it is probably better to rent than own. For instance, if you plan on moving within three to five years, it's smarter to rent. That's especially true if you anticipate slow appreciation and then tack on the costs of selling a home. If you have the bad luck of buying right before your part of the country downshifts into an economic slowdown, home prices in your area could slide or stagnate for a couple of years. Once you add in the cost of the real estate agent's sales commission and your moving expenses, you could easily be out by more than 10% if you try to sell your home a few years after moving in.

You might also consider renting rather than owning if rents in your community are too cheap to pass up. As a rule of thumb, consider being a tenant if the rent on a place you like equals about 65% or less of the monthly mortgage costs—including property taxes and homeowners insurance—that you would pay to own a comparable dwelling. Visit www.homefair.com and select the "Rent vs. Buy" financial calculator to receive a detailed analysis that compares the after-tax costs of owning and renting.

Keep in mind, however, that even though renting can cost less now, the long-term cost of renting could soon outstrip today's cost of a fixed-rate mortgage. For example, let's say you set out to purchase a house with a price tag at the national median of $147,300. At a 7% interest rate, a 30-year fixed-rate loan with a 10% down payment will cost about $980 a month. Annual property taxes and homeowners insurance vary, but let's say they add up to about 3% of the purchase price. So in this example, your total monthly cost of home ownership would come to about $1,350. Remember, though, that you can deduct both the mortgage interest and your property taxes on your tax return. So for someone in the 30% federal tax bracket, the after-tax cost drops to $930. While the tax benefits will decline in the latter stages of your loan as your mortgage payments are earmarked to pay down more principal than interest, your property taxes will remain fully deductible.

Now consider what happens if you decided to rent at a cost of just $900 a month, including the annual premium for a renters insurance policy. That's $450 less a month out of pocket than if you had bought, and still about $30 cheaper on an after-tax basis. Unless you have a landlord who moonlights as an angel, however, the rent will undoubtedly rise. Let's say the rent increases at a rate of 4% a year on average, which is about in line with the historical long-term rate of inflation. After five years the rent will hit $1,094, and in the 10th year you'll be forking over $1,332 a month to the landlord.

In the 20th year your rent will be in the neighborhood of $1,972. Some expensive neighborhood! Now, remember that 30-year fixed-rate mortgage? It doesn't budge. So after 20 years you'll still be paying just $980 a month. Sure, your taxes and insurance premiums will probably increase. However, the bulk of your housing cost—the mortgage—won't rise one penny, and those property taxes will remain fully deductible (unless Congress changes the law). Most important, while you get nothing in return for your rent apart from the right to live there for another month, your mortgage payments are helping you build up equity and your net worth. Eventually you can tap that equity to take out a loan or, when you sell, either keep the cash or use it to buy a more expensive residence.

Of course, there are other costs of ownership that renters don't have to worry about, such as maintenance. Fortunately, major outlays that are actually improvements—say, replacing the heating system—can be added to the original price you paid for the home, thereby increasing what's known as your **cost basis**. That means when you sell the home, any taxable gain (your sales price minus your cost basis) will be lower than it would otherwise be. For a full description of the tax angles when you sell your home, turn to Chapter 8.

Scoping Out the Right Home for You

Everyone's heard that the key to a successful real estate deal is location, location, location. Even more important to home buyers is plan, plan, plan. Think of your job—finding and buying a home—as though you are an architect. The success of your project will come from all the time and effort you put into building and executing a solid strategy. Much of your important planning work should occur before you even meet a real estate agent.

The key to the home-buying process is knowing what you can afford to buy. More precisely, it's knowing what a mortgage lender says you can afford to buy. So the first step is to turn to Chapter 6 and read up on how lenders compute the amount of money they are willing to lend to you for a mortgage. In addition, you can log onto one of the many Web sites that cater to buyers. On sites such as www.ourfamilyplace.com or Yahoo! Real Estate, you will find helpful tools that will estimate what price range you can afford. You'll need to come up with quite a bit of cash just to get the loan—the down payment plus a bushelful of closing costs. When you get a mortgage, your lender will give you a helpful brochure called *Settlement Costs*, produced by the U.S. Department of Housing and Urban Development (HUD), that estimates the up-front costs you'll have to pay when you buy the home. Note, too, that Web sites including www.ziprealty.com provide a plethora of tips for buyers.

This is a good time to get your down payment squared away. You'll generally need to make a 10% down payment, though anything under 20% will require buying private mortgage insurance that, for homes in the $100,000 price range, can add about a quarter of a point to the loan payment. Some lenders will pay the premiums in return for a slightly higher interest rate.

If you have the down payment money stashed away, great. You may instead plan on supplementing your down payment savings with a gift from family members. In that case, ask them to transfer the money to you now, rather than waiting until you're ready to take out the loan. Here's why: Lenders won't give you the loan—or will give you only a smaller loan amount—if the bulk of your down payment is a gift or loan from your parents or in-laws. However, if that money is deposited in your bank account months before you begin shopping for the mortgage, the lender will consider it as your personal asset, not a gift or loan.

You know what you can afford to buy. Now you need to determine what you want to get with that money. If you will be buying the house with a companion or spouse, you need to be sure you're both in agreement on what you're looking for in shelter. Equally important, you'll want to decide which items you would be willing to compromise on, since no home will have everything you want in exactly the way you dreamed it would. The following checklist will help you sort out your housing "needs" from your housing "prefers."

Once you've created your imaginary home in your mind, you next want to research the local housing market. A real estate agent will certainly be able to help you understand the market (more about agents in a moment), but there's no substitute for doing your own legwork. It will give you firsthand knowledge of what's happening in your area. Plus, when you are ready to hook up with an agent, your market knowledge will prove that you mean business and will let you get a quick lead on whether the agent's pitch about market conditions sounds accurate.

If you are moving to a new and unfamiliar area, log onto town and county Web sites or head to the library of the town (or towns) you are interested in. Almost every local paper will have a real estate section where you can get an idea of recent sales. Also, some newspapers are available online. In addition to listing the sales prices of recent home deals, many of these newspapers also list how long the homes were on the market

YOUR HOME-HUNTING CHECKLIST

Mark in the checklist below which attributes are absolute necessities (CRUCIAL), potential deal breakers (IMPORTANT), ones you can be flexible about (WOULD BE NICE), and ones you can pass on (NOT IMPORTANT):

STYLE	CRUCIAL	IMPORTANT	WOULD BE NICE	NOT IMPORTANT
Spanking new				
Less than 50 years old				
More than 50 years old				
Colonial				
Split-level				
Ranch				
EXTERIOR				
Stucco				
Brick				
Wood				
Siding				
Yard				
Garden				
INTERIOR SPACE				
1 bedroom				
2 bedrooms				
3 bedrooms				
4 bedrooms				

(INTERIOR SPACE)	CRUCIAL	IMPORTANT	WOULD BE NICE	NOT IMPORTANT
More than 4 bedrooms				
1 full bathroom				
2 full bathrooms				
3 full bathrooms				
More than 3 bathrooms				
Master bed/bath				
Family room/den				
First-floor family room				
Eat-in kitchen				
Separate dining room				
Home-office space				
Attic/basement storage				
Central air-conditioning				
Gas heat				
Oil heat				
Electric heat				
Fireplace				
More than 1 fireplace				
1-car garage				
2-car garage				
3-car garage				

LOCATION

	CRUCIAL	IMPORTANT	WOULD BE NICE	NOT IMPORTANT
Neighborhood with children				
Can walk to school				
Can walk to town				
Can walk to transportation				

and the owners' original asking price. Quite often you will also find a table that lists the typical or average sales price from a year or two ago. (Or, go to www.domania.com for selling histories of particular towns, streets, and even houses.) This will help you get a feel for whether homes are selling quickly at a price very close to the asking price (a hot housing market) or if they are sitting on the market for more than, say, three months and selling for more than 10% below the asking price (a cold housing market). If the local paper does not furnish this information, call the local Board of Realtors; many publish a monthly or quarterly report on market activity.

While you are researching, check out the recent economic activity in the area. Specifically, you want to know if the local job growth rate is rising or falling. A handy guideline: If the rate of growth has fallen by more than 50% in one year—say, from 2% to 1%—home prices are likely to remain stagnant in the near future. Where there is no job growth—that is, the rate has turned negative—prices are likely to decline. Conversely, if the job growth rate is increasing, you can expect home prices to follow suit. You can find job growth statistics for nearly 300 metropolitan areas in *Employment and Earnings*, a monthly publication of the U.S. Bureau of Labor Statistics. Go to www.bls.gov to view most of the stats or to order the publication. Even if an area has strong job growth, be mindful if most of that growth is in one industry or if the entire economic base of the region is dependent on one industry.

Working with a Top-Notch Real Estate Agent

Now it's time to hire a real estate agent to help you on your hunt—probably. While there's no law that says you must work with a real estate pro, you may put yourself at a disadvantage if you try to house hunt on your own. True, you could go on your own from house to house advertised in the paper or online. You might even pay to join a realty Web site (such as Century 21's site, www.century21.com) that can direct you to homes for sale in your area. And, by 2003, 80% to 90% of the listings on the **Multiple Listing Service (MLS)**, a compendium of all the homes in a local region that are for sale, will be available online for anyone to view. However, keep this in mind: Though the Internet provides virtually everything you may want to know, it's you who will have to do the legwork if you choose not to hire a professional.

A real estate agent is also a great time-saver: It's up to her to make all the arrangements with the seller and the seller's agent for you to visit a home. A savvy real estate pro provides valuable advice on the attributes and drawbacks of certain neighborhoods (the schools aren't so hot; it's a quiet complex; traffic is a problem . . .), as well as information on recent market sales. Finally, a real estate agent can also help you determine both how much home you can afford and which mortgage lender to use. Increasingly, real estate brokers are hooking up to online services that let them scan mortgage terms of a variety of lenders in the area. (You can do this yourself by logging onto www.mortgageselect.com.) A brief clarification about job titles: Don't feel that you have to work with someone called a real estate "broker." The broker's employees—associate brokers or sales agents—are fine, as long as you are working with someone who is motivated and knowledgeable.

Finding the best real estate agent takes a bit of work. If you have friends who live in the area you're moving to, ask them for names of agents they or their friends have used. When you don't know anyone in the area, a trip online or to the library again will be helpful. You can check out recent advertisements and announcements of home sales in the newspaper (both online and print editions) to give you a lead on the names of the locally productive agents. If the newspaper lists only the name of the brokerage firm that handled the sale, call the firm and make an appointment to meet with the head of the office to discuss which employee is suited to your needs.

Meet with several agents or brokers and ask the following four questions to size them up:

1. **Do you work at this job full-time?** Your main job is finding out how dedicated the agent will be in finding you a home. Sure, that Broker of the Year plaque on the office wall looks impressive, but is it from 2001 or 1991? You want someone hungry and aggressive who is willing to push for you.
2. **How many homes have you listed and sold in the past year?** There's no magic number here, but once you interview a few agents, you'll get a pretty good idea which ones are the pluggers and which are the plodders.
3. **Which neighborhoods or towns or what price ranges of homes do you work in primarily?** Real estate agents tend to specialize in particular places or homes in certain price ranges. You want to find an agent who really knows the landscape in the area you're searching. If you want to live in East Platte and she says she really knows Platte, North Platte, and South Platte, keep on looking. It's also important to find an agent who specializes in homes within your price range. If you want a home costing about $150,000, you won't get much attention from an agent who specializes in luxury homes in the $500,000-and-up price category.
4. **How long have you lived in the area?** Newcomers aren't necessarily bad—they

often are the most motivated—but if you are new to an area, you're probably best off working with an agent who can really give you the inside scoop.

Theoretically you can work with as many agents as you want, but give serious thought to working with just one. If your agent knows you are working with other agents, she is probably going to lose a bit of enthusiasm in working with you since there's a good chance you won't be buying the house with her assistance. Of course, if you are unsatisfied with your agent after a few weeks, you can then branch out to your second and third choices.

No matter how much you like your agent—and she you—don't forget this is a business deal. And guess what? Real estate agents work for the seller, not you. After all, that's who pays the agent. Here's how the real estate brokerage compensation system works: The seller pays a percentage of the sales price, typically 4% to 10%, to his agent, who then shares that commission with the agent who was working with you, the buyer. You aren't going to pay the agent one penny, no matter how many hours the two of you work together. Because your agent's compensation will come from the seller, you've got a troubling conflict of interest when it comes to negotiating your asking price. If you bid $150,000, but tell your agent you are really willing to pay as much as $165,000, the agent must tell the seller that you will go to $165,000. You'll learn more about this arrangement later in the chapter, but for now just keep in the back of your head that your agent works for the seller, not you. At least most of the time . . .

Now here's the exception to that rule: You could also opt to hire a real estate pro known as a **buyer's broker** who will work exclusively for the buyer, not the seller. While buyer brokerage is still a small part of the industry, it is a rapidly growing specialty. You can find a buyer's broker by contacting the National Association of Real Estate Buyer's Brokers (888-286-8539; www.narebb.com).

Hiring a so-called buyer's broker or broker's agent can be a smart move if you are house hunting in an unfamiliar area or if you don't have the time or initiative to look at many homes. A good buyer's broker ought to conduct extensive research that will help you be a sharp bidder and price negotiator. For example, a seller's broker will give you a list of recent comparable sales and sales prices in the area, but a buyer's broker will provide you with more important information, such as when the current owners bought the home and the price they paid. The buyer's broker will also spend time researching recent property tax issues. That way you won't be unpleasantly surprised later to learn that the property taxes will jump to $6,000 when the home is sold and the tax assessor then reevaluates the home.

Because the sole fiduciary responsibility of the buyer's broker is to you and not the seller, you can also expect to have some frank discussions on the pros and cons of one home versus another or one neighborhood over another. Agents who work for sellers often are extremely discreet. Finally, buyer's brokers can be a godsend for folks who loathe negotiating; the broker can literally do all your bidding and negotiating. You can also arrange for the broker to help you shop for a mortgage and your homeowners insurance.

Of course, there's a catch: Unlike other buyers who work with conventional real estate brokers, you'll need to pay for this service. Even after paying the buyer's broker, however, your net cost to buy a home may wind up lower than if you had opted for the traditional arrangement where the agent works for the seller. That's possible because the buyer's broker should be able to negotiate a lower sales price than if you did the negotiating yourself. In fact, one national firm found that when it used buyer's brokers to assist more than 250 of its relocating employees, the brokers nailed down sales prices that were generally 9% below the initial offer price, compared with a typical 4% discount for buyers who worked with seller's agents. In dollar terms that's a saving of $7,500 on a house listed at $150,000.

Unfortunately, there's no industry standard for how buyer's brokers get paid, so you'll have to discuss the particulars of your arrangement with the brokers you interview. If you can, try to strike a compensation agreement in which you'll pay the buyer's broker a commission equal to 2% to 3% of your target price range. However, if the house you end up buying was found through the Multiple Listing Service, then a buyer's broker shouldn't cost you anything; the broker agrees to split the price in order to participate in MLS. Ask for at least three recent clients you can speak with to see if they were pleased with the agent's service and the compensation agreement.

Home buyers who want negotiating help and nothing more might consider hiring a buyer's broker on an hourly basis. Figure on paying between $60 and $125 per hour. Make sure your real estate agreement includes an upper limit on how much you will ultimately pay. You can arrange for a cap that is equal to 2% or 3% of the sale price or set a specific dollar limit.

To find a competent buyer's broker, nothing beats a word-of-mouth referral. Otherwise call the local Board of Realtors and ask if they have a list of local agents who either work part-time or exclusively as buyer reps. Online sites such as www.homegain.com and www.narebb.com also provide referrals. If you strike out these ways, check the local Yellow Pages for listings of buyer's agents.

Once you choose a buyer's broker, give her a reasonable period of time to help you; an agreement that covers two to three months is sufficient. Don't sign an **exclusive rights agreement**, forcing you to pay the agent an agreed-upon fee or commission even if she doesn't help you find the house you eventually buy. Instead, ask for an **open agreement**, in which you'll pay the agent only if she helps you land the house.

Add a Lawyer to Your Home-Buying Team

In most parts of the country, you've got one last job before you start to actually look for homes: Hire a lawyer. You'll want the lawyer to make any necessary changes to the real estate purchase contract and help you through the closing process, to be sure all the legal mumbo-jumbo is completed. Once again, word of mouth is the best way to shop. Check with friends; in addition, your agent will surely have names of two or three local lawyers who either specialize in residential real estate transactions or spend a sizable amount of time working on these deals. Be sure to stick with a lawyer who knows local real estate customs and has experience in reviewing and drawing up real estate contracts. While your cousin Ned's brother-in-law may be a terrific lawyer, he isn't going to be all that helpful if he specializes in corporate takeovers.

You'll want to meet with the lawyer now—or at least have a short phone conversation—to tell him you're about to launch into a house hunt and that you expect you'll need his assistance sometime within the next few months. By taking this step early, you'll ensure quick access to your lawyer when you're ready to make a bid on a home. If you wait until that point to find a lawyer to review your offer to purchase, you will waste a crucial day or two—which could mean losing out to a more organized bidder. Plan on paying the lawyer an hourly fee of anywhere from $75 and up. Depending on where you live and the complexity of your contract, the lawyer's charge could run between $1,000 and $2,000 or so.

Shopping for Your Home (Finally!)

Now on to the real job: finding your future house, condo, or co-op. There are always homes on the market, so you can house hunt any time of the year. If you can be flexible, though, consider shopping during the off-season; that's wintertime in many parts of the country. (The most active house-buying season is typically spring.) By shopping during the off-season, chances are you'll find an agent who isn't very busy and can devote plenty of time to you. You also might have the good luck to be the only interested buyer a home seller has seen in weeks—or months. While that doesn't mean the seller will be desperate, you may find he's quite amenable to negotiations.

No matter how good a memory you've got, after a few hours of house hunting, you'll be hard-pressed to remember if the master bedroom with the skylight and Jacuzzi was in the three-bedroom contemporary ranch or in the 75-year-old farmhouse with the new addition. To help you keep it all straight, bring along a camera. Ideally you want to pack a Polaroid so you can make any notations right on the back of the photo. You might also want to bring along a video camera. The idea is to have a record of what you saw so you'll have a visual reference later on when reviewing all your potential future homes. An etiquette tip: Make sure you ask the agent to check if the homeowners object to having you take a few shots.

You will also need a notebook to mark down any particulars of the house. While your agent should give you an information sheet on the house that includes the price the owners are asking, the lot size, and a current property tax assessment, you'll want to jot down additional information.

You'll also want to bring along your poker face. The goal, after all, is to negotiate the best deal you can get. So even if you've just walked into your dream house and your heart is pumping, look as dispassionate as possible. One item you want to leave at home: the kids. Regardless of how well behaved or cute they are, house hunting is serious business; you want to spend all your time checking out the house, not chasing after your kid.

While surveying a house, see if you can get any information from the agent—or the homeowners if they're present—about why the home is on the market. If it's part of an estate sale or if the owners have to move across the country to a new job in a month, you may be dealing with a very motivated seller. That could mean a steal for you. Or your antennae might pick up that the sellers have been living in the house for 20-odd years. If that's the case, they're probably in the position of selling the home for a lot more than they originally paid. A longtime owner may not be as reticent to shave a few thousand dollars off the sales price as someone who moved in just a few years ago. Ask the agent, too, if any appliances or furnishings are included in the sale price. Try to limit your search to four houses a day. Otherwise you'll find yourself dazed, confused, and exhausted. Don't forget to check out the **for sale by owner (FSBO)** listings online and in newspapers. In these instances the seller isn't using an agent. While you can find some great deals in so-called FIZBO, be sure to use a lawyer to handle the transaction.

Tips for New Home, Co-op, and Condo Shoppers

No doubt about it: New homes can be enticing. Not only is everything bright, shiny, and in great condition, but you can probably even get to customize the home. It's essential, however, to make sure the builder has a reputation for doing quality work; these days builders sometimes cut corners to finish the jobs more quickly and build in more profit. Ask for the names of three buyers who moved into one of the builder's homes within the past three years or so. Talk to these homeowners about how well the builder finished the customizing work and if they have had any major problems with the structure since they moved in.

Be cautious about buying a home that's part of a large project still in its early development stages. If less than 50% or so of the development has been sold, you run the risk of moving into a lemon: Unless most of the homes in the development eventually sell, your home's value will have little chance of appreciating. Plus, many developments advertise common areas, such as tennis courts or a swimming pool facility. These areas are typically the last part of a development to be completed, though. If the housing complex is not successful, the builder may never finish constructing the amenities that enticed you in the first place.

Value-conscious shoppers who are attracted to new homes shouldn't automatically give the cold shoulder to existing homes. According to the National Association of Home Builders, the median price for a new home is just over $147,300, somewhat more than the cost of the median-priced existing home. You'll also have a tough time negotiating price concessions with the builder. That tactic works best during economic recessions, when demand is low and builders are more inclined to bend a bit to get their homes sold.

Condominiums can be a terrific opportunity for first-time buyers or anyone shopping for a home in an expensive housing market, since condo prices can be lower than a comparable single-family detached home. However, the location and amenities at the condo can certainly drive up the price. Condos are either apartments or town houses; while each owner has absolute control over his own unit, all the condominium owners share some common areas. Each condominium owner must make a periodic payment— usually monthly—to cover common charges for the upkeep of areas such as hallways and lobbies and for maintenance of the roof and grounds.

If you're looking at a condo in a new development, make sure you do all the research mentioned above for new homes. One added risk is that you have no idea if the common charge is actually enough to cover costs or if the actual costs will cause a hike in the common charge. Home buyers looking at existing condo developments, however, can learn if the development has been able to maintain the property without frequently imposing big increases in the common charge. Ask your real estate agent to get information on the amount of the common charge for the past five years or so.

The best way to nail down value in a condominium is to concentrate on developments where most units serve as the primary residence for the owner, rather than as rental real estate investments. The live-in owners have a bigger stake in the upkeep and appreciation of their properties. Also, be wary about buying if the condo development is near an area where a number of new complexes are being constructed. Overbuilding means there could soon be more supply than demand, and that will make it extremely tough for condominium values to rise.

Cooperatives, or **co-ops**, are a rather small and arcane corner of the residential real estate world. Generally limited to New York City and a few other large metro areas, co-op apartments and town houses are essentially corporations where each owner of a unit within the building or development is a shareholder. All the shareholders wield veto control over the corporation's activities: You can't buy, sell, or rent a co-op unit without the approval of a co-op board. You'll be interviewed by the board before you buy, so use that experience as an opportunity to size up your neighbors. Will they let you rent out the unit if you later decide to move and have trouble selling? How many units have been for sale in each of the past few years? How long were they on the market? Did the board deny any prospective buyers—and if so, why?

In addition to getting a feel for your fellow shareholders, prospective co-op owners need to assess the financial strength of the corporation. That's because the co-op owns one collective mortgage; if the couple in apartment 3B misses two months of payments, the rest of the co-op's shareholders will need to cover the payments. Generally that comes out of the co-op's cash reserves. Your lawyer can help you determine the health of the co-op's reserves and find out whether shareholders have been hit with hefty special assessments to cover the cost of major repairs, such as replacing the heating system or roof.

What You Should Expect from the Seller

Will the seller tell you if something is wrong with his home? That all depends. **Seller disclosure** about significant defects in their homes is mandatory in 29 states: Alaska, California, Connecticut, Delaware, Hawaii, Idaho, Illinois, Indiana, Iowa, Kentucky, Maine, Maryland, Michigan, Mississippi, Nebraska, Nevada, New Hampshire, North Carolina, Ohio, Oklahoma, Oregon, Pennsylvania, Rhode Island, South Dakota, Tennessee, Texas, Virginia, Washington, and Wisconsin. While seller disclosure is voluntary in the other states, most real estate agents encourage—and even require—their clients to complete a disclosure form for prospective buyers. So in those states, always ask if there is a recently completed disclosure report; be wary of any homeowner or agent who says no.

Typically, the seller-disclosure form includes a laundry list of all the operating systems and amenities in the home, including items such as the air conditioner, sump pump, intercom, rain gutter, and garbage disposal. The seller is required to report if he is aware of any significant defects or malfunctions in those items and must also note any problems with the electrical or plumbing systems. Where forms are mandatory, sellers must also let prospective buyers know of any environmental hazards, such as the presence of radon or lead paint in the house. Many disclosure forms also demand the seller report if he made any alterations or additions to the house without obtaining the proper permits.

While you will eventually hire a professional home inspector to assess the condition of any home you intend to buy, obtaining a seller-disclosure form is a helpful first step in learning the state of the house. The information on the form can also be useful during your negotiations; if you know ahead of time that there's asbestos in the basement, you may ask that your purchase be contingent on the asbestos being removed before you make a deal.

Making a Bid on a Home

Once you find the home you want, it's time to make a bid. If you are working with a buyer's broker, you'll get all the help you need in determining the best initial offer and overall negotiating strategy. However, if you are working with the seller's agent, you need to bear down and be a smart player. The seller's agent should give you data on at least three comparable homes that have sold within the past few months. You'll want to compare the original list price and final sales price of the homes. Then pull out the calculator and see the difference. If the final sales price is 5% lower than the asking price, you can make your bid at least 5% less than the asking price. In fact, you'll want to give yourself some negotiating room, so consider a bid that is 8% to 10% below the list price. It's essential, however, to be sure you're assessing the pace of recent home sales and prices. If homes are selling 5% below list today, but were selling 10% below a few months ago, that's a sign that the market is improving for sellers. Conversely, if homes that now sell at a 5% discount were selling right at their asking price a few months ago, that's a tip-off that the market is improving for buyers.

While you don't want to overpay for your home, you also want to avoid committing the big mistake of getting greedy and making a lowball bid. If homes are generally selling at 5% below list and you have determined that the house you want is fairly priced, offer 8% to 10% below the list price, not 20%. While you may think that a 20% bid is a smart opening salvo that will help you negotiate a lower price, the seller will more than likely interpret it as an insult—and may refuse to negotiate with you at all.

Once you choose the amount of your initial offer price, the agent will write up the **offer to purchase**, which your lawyer should review. In addition to the price, your offer will also include a closing date (generally 45 to 60 days from the time you and the seller agree to the deal), plus a few contingency clauses that your lawyer will work out with you. Typically, you want the deal to be contingent on (1) your obtaining a mortgage; (2) a home inspection that shows the house has no significant defects; and (3) a guarantee that you may conduct a walk-through inspection 24 hours before the official closing. Don't write down a specific date, since the actual closing date may need to be changed. This last clause is important: You want to make sure everything is up to snuff before you become the owner. If the sellers have already started packing and tore out a light fixture that created a gaping hole in the ceiling, you'll want to agree about repair costs before buying the house.

You'll also need to offer the seller a **good-faith deposit**, which is also known as **earnest money**. Basically you're making a deposit on the purchase of the house; the typical deposit amount ranges between 1% and 3% of the purchase price. Ask your agent or lawyer to deposit the earnest money in an escrow account; the seller will get the cash upon the successful completion of the deal. You don't want to test the good faith of the seller by giving him the check directly before any deal has been closed.

Negotiating with the Seller

If you use a real estate agent, she will pass along your initial bid to the seller. After that, you need to stay near a phone as the negotiation begins. Expect the seller to give the agent a counteroffer that will be somewhere between his original price and your bid. You can make a counter to his counter, but if his offer is what you had set in your mind as a fair price to pay, tell the agent you've got a deal. However, if it's still too steep a price, you can make a second bid.

By all means, consider other negotiating tactics. For instance, you could tell the seller you'll agree to his counteroffer if the washer and dryer are thrown into the deal. Be creative: If you learned during your house hunt that the sellers are having trouble finding their next house, tell them you're willing to delay the closing date for an additional month if the price comes down. The seller may want that extra breathing room enough to cut the sale price by the $2,000 you had been anticipating. Keep in mind that the amount of room you'll have to negotiate will depend a lot on the pace of your local housing market. You have far more leverage if homes aren't selling than if you're competing with other bidders for the same house.

After Your Offer Is Accepted

Once the seller has agreed to take your offer, you've got some more chores to take care of before he'll hand over the keys. Your biggest job is landing an acceptable mortgage. If you have a buyer's agent, you can enlist her help scouring local lenders for deals. Whether you use an agent or not, make sure you do some of your own legwork, including checking out mortgage calculators, rates, and loan products on the Web. The mortgage business has become extremely competitive, so lenders will offer very different deals. See Chapter 6 for advice on how to shop for the best deal on or off the Web.

To help you with your mortgage shopping, consider hiring a **mortgage broker** to do the searching for you. This expert is a kind of intermediary between lenders and consumers. The mortgage broker has access to many different lenders and their mortgages and may be able to help you find the kind of loan you want. If you haven't been in the mortgage market for a while, you might be thinking that mortgage brokers are just for desperate folks who get turned down at banks. Well, mortgage brokers can be especially helpful if you are less than a stellar candidate for a loan—for instance, you can afford to make only a 5% down payment or you were out of work within the past year. In such cases a mortgage broker can help find you a lender who is willing to work with your unconventional situation. You can also find mortgage broker Web sites, such as www.mortgageit.com, www.mortgagebot.com, and www.homeadvisor.com.

You won't really pay more out of pocket by using a mortgage broker, since generally the mortgage he obtains for you will be a wholesale price that doesn't include origination fees and closing costs, which typically can add up to 2% of the loan amount. A mortgage broker makes his living by adding on such fees for his services, but the fees can be built into the loan product.

To find a worthy mortgage broker, ask your agent or lawyer for recommendations; state licensing is pretty worthless. In addition to word of mouth, contact the National Association of Mortgage Brokers (703-610-9009; www.namb.org) for a list of mortgage brokers in your area. You're looking for a broker who can cast his net wide and let you select a loan from a variety of lenders. So when you interview several mortgage brokers, ask them how many mortgage lenders they deal with and the range of options available. You want to be sure that the broker doesn't have a sweetheart deal with one lender who'll wind up charging you a higher mortgage rate or fees than the competition. If you're really diligent, you'll also ask for three recent clients you can contact to see if they were satisfied with the broker's service.

You'll need to get a **homeowners insurance policy**, of course. Don't slough off this job. Buy a lemon and you'll be stuck without sufficient coverage to pay for costs of repairing or rebuilding your home in the event it is damaged or destroyed. (For details about shopping for the right homeowners policy, see Chapter 2.) Plan on spending between $500 and $1,000 a year for a $150,000 house, depending on coverage and where you live. If you currently own a home, you obviously already have a relationship with an insurance agent. If not, ask your real estate agent, friends, or lawyer for recommendations, or go to the Web. Some insurance agents represent just one insurer, while others, called independent agents, can sell policies of different companies. The bottom line: You want your policy to be with an insurer on solid financial footing. The last thing you need is an insurance company that could be stretched beyond its financial limits.

Your lender will require you to pay for a professional **home appraisal** to make sure the house is worth what you are paying (or, more to the point, the amount the lender is loaning you). In addition to the appraisal, you want to hire a professional **home inspector**. Again, your real estate agent or your lawyer can give you some names of local inspectors; so can friends who have bought homes in the area recently. Be sure to talk to clients of inspectors before you agree to hire one of these pros. The home inspection business is something of a racket; just about anyone can call himself an inspector, and just about anyone does. At the very least, work with an inspector who has been trained and certified according to the standards of the American Society of Home Inspectors (800-743-2744; www.ashi.org). That's no guarantee that your inspector won't turn out to be an Inspector Clouseau, but it will help you weed out the fly-by-nighters.

The home inspection will cost about $175 to $350 and takes an hour or two to complete. Schedule the inspection so you can tag along; you'll be amazed what you can learn about the house. Not only will the inspector point out whether, say, the electrical system or gutters need to be repaired or upgraded, but you'll also learn about the overall condition of the house and the quality of its construction materials. If you're new to the area, the inspector can recommend local contractors for future repair work. If the inspector discovers a major problem—like the gutters need replacing—have your lawyer discuss the matter with the seller. You'll want the seller to either fix the problem before you move in or deduct the cost of the repair from the final sales price. For a full list of mortgage and closing fees, see page 140.

Closing on the Home

The actual process of taking possession of the house, condo, or co-op from the seller is a ritual with some regional differences. Some areas refer to it as **settlement**; others call it **close of escrow**. The players also vary. In some markets the lawyers handle the festivities, while escrow companies are in charge in other regions. Regardless of how it works in your neck of the woods—and your agent will tell you what's common if you are new to the area—all closings have the same outcome: The buyer takes possession of the deed to the house.

To get to this happy moment, you will first need to sign a slew of checks to cover all sorts of closing costs. At least 24 hours before the actual closing ceremonies, the lender will give you a final U.S. Department of Housing and Urban Development **Settlement Statement** that will list all the charges you will be expected to pay at the closing. Review this statement carefully with your lawyer. The two big-ticket items in the statement will be the **loan origination fee** and the **loan discount cost**—more commonly known as **points**. (For more information on points and other closing fees see Chapter 6.)

You'll also find a charge of $75 to $300 or so for an application fee (includes initial costs of processing your loan request and checking your credit report). An **appraisal** charge of $150 to $400 is also standard. Ask the lender for a copy of the appraisal. It contains detailed information on the particulars of your home's structure as well as the appraiser's evaluation of its market value based on comparable homes that have recently been sold. Since you pay for the appraisal, you are entitled to a copy. However, you may have to make the request in writing since some lenders don't like sharing this info.

Title insurance is another expense you'll incur. While your lawyer will conduct a title search to make sure no one else has a claim to your home or property, the lender will want to protect itself from any future title concerns by making you buy a policy that will protect you and the lender in case any questions arise in the future. Plan on paying about $450 to $600 for the title search and insurance.

The lender will probably also require you to establish an **escrow account** that it can tap if you fall behind on your mortgage and property tax payments. (If you're borrowing less than 80% of the home's value, the lender may let you get away without an escrow account. You'll have to ask for this waiver, though.) Thanks to regulations introduced by HUD in late 1994, the lender can now ask for an escrow deposit that covers only two months' worth of payments. In the past, lenders made borrowers deposit up to six or even eight months of mortgage costs.

Make sure your up-front settlement fees don't include a charge for hazard insurance; your own insurance policy will cover that, so there's no reason to pay the lender. To avoid any confusion, ask the lender what specific documentation it will require at the closing to confirm that you have secured the necessary homeowners insurance.

Once you pay all the settlement charges—including a **transfer tax** and **deed recording fee** charged by the county or municipality—your lender will have you sign a bond or note that commits you to repaying your loan. Next the lender will have you sign the mortgage. Then the lender will write you a check for the amount of the loan (you'll be very rich for about 60 seconds), which you will quickly endorse and pass to the seller. Once the seller accepts the check, he'll hand over the deed to the house along with the keys. You now own your home. One last bit of work before you begin celebrating: Make sure whoever oversees the closing takes the deed to the county clerk's office to be recorded.

Taxes and Home Ownership

As mentioned earlier in the chapter, your home is a great tax haven. The biggest break is the deductibility of mortgage interest payments made for a primary or second home, up to a maximum of $1 million. At the end of each year, your lender or the mortgage service firm that handles your loan will send you Form 1098, which lists the amount of interest you paid for the year.

Uncle Sam also gives you a nice homewarming gift the year you buy your home: The points you pay on your mortgage are fully deductible, as long as you can deduct all of the interest on your mortgage and claim the deduction in the year you paid the points. In fact, even if the seller pays your points, you can deduct them. The same Form 1098 will include an accounting of your point costs. Other home-buying fees, including the cost of an appraisal, title insurance, attorney's fees, and transfer taxes, aren't deductible, but they'll save you on taxes in the future. You'll wind up adding them to the cost of your home, which will reduce any taxes you'll pay on the eventual gain after you sell the place someday. Go to www.irs.gov and reference Tax Topic 504 for more details.

The 1997 tax law also gave welcome relief to home sellers, since you don't have to pay tax on gains of up to $250,000 if you're single or up to $500,000 if you're married and filing jointly. But you must have owned the home as your principal residence for two out of the last five years. You can keep taking this exclusion as many times as you want so long as you meet the two-year ownership rule. If your home sale profits top the exclusions—lucky you!—taxes will be due on the excess gain.

If you move to take a new job, you may be eligible for a handful of tax deductions available by filing IRS Form 3903. The general rule is that your new job must be full-time (at least 39 weeks in the first year, or 78 weeks over the first two years for self-employed individuals), and the job must have spurred a move that is at least 50 miles from your current home. If you meet those stipulations, go ahead and deduct the entire cost of moving your belongings and your family to the new house. You don't have to itemize to get these write-offs; they show up as an adjustment to income on your 1040 long form. One caveat: The cost of meals during your family's trek to the new home is no longer deductible, thanks to a 1994 change in the federal tax code.

Buying a Vacation Home

The aging baby boomer brigade is stimulating strong demand for second homes right now. This is because most boomers are moving into (or are in) their peak earning years, when they begin to contemplate buying and owning a vacation home. Consequently, the values for vacation homes have risen sharply and will continue to rise steadily in the coming years. The last time boomers made a concerted housing move was during the mid- and late '70s, when their rush for first homes set off a surge in residential real estate prices around the country. The growth in the number of telecommuting workers also buoys vacation home prices. Second homes once relegated to weekends are now increasingly used as offices one or two days a week, as online capabilities make it possible to work away from the traditional office.

While the prospects for vacation home appreciation are strong, prospective second-home buyers need to be extremely careful when hunting for their Shangri-las. In addition to following the strategies outlined in this chapter and understanding the tax rules for vacation homeowners (see Chapter 17), you'll increase your chances of landing a great second-home deal by following a few additional rules:

- **Rent for at least one season before buying.** Get familiar with the area before committing to a home purchase there. While you're renting you can investigate different neighborhoods or sections of a development and decide where you would like to live.

- **Shop during the off-season.** It's best to do your house hunting when the area isn't at the peak of popularity. You'll get more attention from agents during the off-season, when they aren't dealing with the usual deluge of in-season renters who are considering making a purchase. There's a good chance you'll get a better price in the off-season, too, since you'll be talking to sellers who won't have many prospects and will be more open to negotiating. You may also find it easier to be more businesslike during the off-season; shopping for a beach house when it's 30° and a storm is brewing off the coast is a lot different from house hunting when the area looks like a picture postcard.

- **Make sure the vacation home is within three hours of a major city.** The demand for vacation homes near a major metropolis will likely remain strong, since there is a built-in pool of prospective buyers to tap into when you decide to sell. City folk will continue to clamor for getaways within weekend commuting distance. If you plan on renting out the home, the same pool of urbanites will provide a strong supply of prospective tenants. The more remote the location, the harder it will be for you to find a buyer when you want to sell someday.

- **Look for a two-, three-, or four-season home if you plan to rent out the place.** You can generate far more rental income if your vacation home is attractive to renters during different seasons. While a beach house may be ideal for summer, a home that attracts renters in two or more seasons will increase your rental opportunities.

- **Plan on paying more for a vacation home mortgage.** Lenders get a bit nervous when offering mortgages for a second home. After all, if you run into financial trouble, chances are you'll unload your second home—and pay off the loan—before you consider selling your primary residence. So expect a hefty down payment requirement of at least 20%. You'll also be charged a mortgage interest rate that is as much as a quarter of a percentage point higher than if the mortgage was for a primary residence.

- **Factor in all maintenance costs.** Many vacation home developments include a homeowners association that levies annual fees. Before you buy, find out what costs the association usually covers and ask for a five-year record of how the fee has increased. You may also need to hire a local contractor to keep an eye on the house during the seasons you're not using the property. Your real estate agent will be able to estimate the typical fees for this out-of-season service.

- **Deal with the issue of homeowners insurance before you buy the house.**
Make sure you understand the availability and cost of insurance for vacation homes in the area. This advice is especially important in areas where flood and storm damage are frequent threats. Talk to an insurance agent familiar with the area in advance of your house hunt. You'll get an idea of what typical premiums are for local vacation homes, and the agent may be able to tip you off to certain spots that are especially prone to flooding or storm damage. This crucial information will keep you from buying a property that could get clobbered—both by the elements and financially.

- **Find a good accountant.** The Internal Revenue Service has complicated rules for part-time landlords, so renting out your vacation home is likely to get complicated. If you rent your house 14 or fewer days a year, it's considered a standard residence. Mortgage interest is deductible on up to a combined $1.1 million in principal, and you don't have to report the income. If you rent more than 14 days a year but also use the house yourself more than 14 days (or 10% of the time it's rented, whichever is longer), it's still considered a residence. But you do have to report the income, and deducted expenses can't exceed rental income. Finally, if you rent more than 14 days a year and use the house yourself for 14 or fewer days (or less than 10% of the rental period, whichever is longer), it's considered a pure rental property. The expenses you can deduct depend on how involved you are in managing the property—so talk to your accountant.

CHAPTER 8

How to Get the Most Out of Your House, Condo, or Co-op

House-itis. It can strike at any time, regardless of whether you moved into your home two years or two decades ago. There's just no predicting when a once happy homeowner suddenly gets that itch for a bigger, better, or simply different home. Maybe it's the imminent arrival of another child that's got you contemplating adding on an extra room or moving to more spacious digs. Conversely, once all the kids have moved out (finally!), the house could simply seem too big. Or a job relocation could be the culprit. Alternatively, if you are now part of the growing contingent of work-at-home types, altering your quarters may be necessary to make room for office space. In this chapter you'll get all the information you need to cure your house-itis.

First you'll see whether some remodeling or renovations might be the antidote to your house problems. If you plan to become one of the millions of homeowners who annually spend a total of more than $100 billion to upgrade their homes, you'll find advice on how to spend your remodeling money wisely. If you need to make a move, you'll learn how to make yourself a successful home seller. These days a smart sales strategy is crucial. With over three million homes on the market each year, there's plenty of competition among homeowners. So you need to equip yourself with the competitive edge that will distinguish your home from all the others.

What to Know about Remodeling

Just because your current house doesn't provide all the room and amenities you and your family want doesn't necessarily mean you should move—renovating and remodeling your home may be the best way to deal with that discontentment. And the best method is approaching the task with a well-thought-out plan—a financial blueprint.

Your first job is to be realistic. The day will eventually arrive when you or your heirs will want to sell the house. When this time comes, the goal will be to recoup as much of the cost of your renovation projects as possible in the sale price of the home. That will be especially difficult if your previous remodeling and renovations have upgraded your house far beyond the value of other homes in your neighborhood. As a general rule, then, you'll want to avoid upgrading your home to a level that exceeds the median price of neighborhood homes by 15% to 20%. Of course, there's no law against improving your house to make it the standout gem of the neighborhood. But just go into the project knowing that you can't expect to fully recoup the cost of the upgrade.

It's a good idea to understand the types of remodeling projects that tend to offer the best paybacks when you eventually sell your home. That may help you decide which type of project to undertake or which to do first. According to *Remodeling* magazine's (www.remodeling.hw.net) annual survey, adding a bathroom and upgrading a kitchen offer the best payback potential. On average, homeowners are able to recoup about 98% of the cost of adding a second bathroom and 102% of renovating a kitchen when they sell their house. (These percentages assume you have a contractor do the work and sell the home within a year of completing the job.) Adding a master bedroom and bath is also a high-payback undertaking, with an average recoup rate of 91%. But if your plan is to just build a deck, the payback rate will be about 73¢ for every dollar spent on the upgrade. And adding a home office only gets you 69% back, on average.

When you choose to remodel or renovate, you can tap into a rare tax break offered by Uncle Sam. To finance your project, you can borrow against the equity in your home and deduct 100% of the interest payments on this home-equity line or loan, up to a maximum value of $100,000. In today's competitive bank-lending environment, these loans are available at rates typically well below the typical rates charged for personal loans. (For details on how to shop for the best home-equity deal, see Chapter 6.)

Labor costs account for about two-thirds of the price of any renovation project. To reduce the bills for your remodeling job, you could do a lot of the work yourself, but that assumes you have both the expertise and time. Therefore you'll probably need to hire a professional contractor to do much of the work.

If you are working with an architect or designer, this pro can provide you with names of reliable contractors who've done a good job on other projects. Alternatively, you can check in with friends who have had work done that you admire. No matter how highly an architect or friend may recommend a general contractor, make sure you ask for additional references. You want to get a few different opinions on the quality of the contractor's work, how well he stuck to the timetable, and his willingness to repair or alter any parts of the project that didn't meet your expectations. You should also contact the local Better Business Bureau (www.bbb.org; www.bbbonline.org) or your local government's consumer affairs department (many have Web sites; simply type in "consumer affairs department" and the name of the town) to make sure there are no outstanding complaints against the contractor. For a large project, ask prospective contractors whether they have their own crew to perform all the jobs or whether subcontractors will be hired. If you will be dealing with subcontractors, you'll need to go see their work to check that it's also up to your standards.

Tell all the contractors that you will only consider written bids and that all bids must include a breakdown of all costs as well as a detailed description of the materials that will be used on the project. Once you have a bid, do not fall for any pressure tactics such as being told that this offer is good only for 48 hours. Simply tell the contractor that you will call him within a week. If you decide to accept the bid, all the specifics need to be spelled out in a written contract. Include the date when the project will begin, the materials that will be used, and what sort of guarantee the contractor will give on his work. A decent contractor should have no problem with a one-year guarantee.

You also need to work out a payment schedule and have it spelled out in the contract. This is the trickiest step. Pay too much up front and you may be left in the lurch. Pay nothing and you may never see him again. The ideal arrangement is to have as many payments as possible. If the project will last eight weeks, pay 20% at the end of every two weeks, with the stipulation that the final payment will not be made until 30 days after the work is completed. This will insure that the work is completed, and it also allows you some time to live with the new construction and see if any problems need to be ironed out. One final job before you sign the contract: Make sure the contractor has a workers' compensation insurance policy that covers his employees, as well as a liability insurance policy to cover himself and his crew while they are on the job. Ask that a copy of these insurance policies be attached to the contract.

Keep in mind that hassles may be minimized if you use the Internet to find a contractor. Web sites such as www.improvenet.com and www.servicemagic.com provide free membership and access to hundreds of thousands of contractors throughout the United States. Additionally, these sites evaluate and screen their contractors so that you can be sure any potential hire is both licensed and insured. Internet sites such as these also list answers to common questions, answer your specific questions, provide free online estimates, and schedule repairs. When valuable information such as this is just a few keystrokes away, it's hard not to try it out.

When You Want to Sell Your Home

You've decided that rather than fix up your house, you'd rather just move into a different one. Or you want to relocate for work. Although you can put your house up for sale any time of the year, if you're not in a terrific rush, try a bit of strategic timing. That is, put it on the market when you will be competing with a smaller pool of homes. In most regions of the country this means wintertime. Not only will you probably find agents clamoring to represent you, but any prospective buyers will give your home more attention than usual since it may be one of just a handful on the market. That's quite an advantage compared with the spring and summer markets, when dozens or even hundreds of homes are for sale. Be prepared for your home to stay on the market for between three and six months. Of course this varies with market conditions. If there is plenty of buyer demand in your town and you have set a fair price (more on both later in the chapter), you'll probably be able to make a deal quickly. However, if sales are sluggish, you'll need to be patient. And strategic . . .

To sell your house wisely, you need to devise a strategy that takes into account the current market conditions, the competition from other seller wanna-bes, and the general economic outlook in your area. Get started on scripting your winning plan by spending some time studying local real estate in the newspaper and online (Yahoo! Real Estate; www.ziprealty.com; www.domania.com). Keep an eye on these for a month or so to get a feel for prices in various neighborhoods. Many real estate sources now print both the selling price and the original list price. Calculate the difference between the two and keep a ledger of the typical gap.

If you've got the time and initiative, head to the library or go online and pull out newspaper and real estate listings from six months and 12 months ago and do the same calculation. This will give you an idea of the trend of home sale prices—whether they are going up or down and if there is a pattern about how close the sales prices are to the original asking prices. All this data will be crucial to help you set the price for your home and even later when you begin negotiating with a potential buyer. For instance, if you found that most homes were selling at 10% below list price a year ago, but are now typically selling at list price or just 3% below list, that's a great sign for you. It indicates that sellers aren't having to take low bids from buyers. In other words, you are in the enviable position of putting your home on the market during a seller's market. Another positive sign: If homes were taking an average of, say, nine weeks to sell a year ago but now are on the market for less than six weeks, you've got more confirmation that sellers are gaining momentum. Conversely, if either the gap between list and sales prices or the time on market is getting larger, then you must prepare for a tough sales environment.

Before getting to the next logical step—hiring a real estate agent—it's worth discussing the most enticing but most misunderstood part of the home sale process: selling your home without professional assistance. Trying to go the **for sale by owner** (**FSBO** or, as it's sometimes called, **FIZBO**) route is no doubt attractive, since you'll avoid paying an agent's commission, which typically runs anywhere from 4% to 10% of the sale price of the home. With the median-priced existing home now selling for roughly $147,300, that commission can be anywhere from $5,892 to $14,730. And given that you are lucky if your housing market is appreciating at a 3% clip, the commission can be the equivalent of anywhere from one and a half to three and a half years' worth of appreciation.

Be careful, though. The FIZBO route can be a great example of being penny-wise and pound-foolish, especially in a slow housing market. Here's the big problem with going it alone when homes in your area aren't moving: At a time when others are struggling to get their homes sold, you will have a better shot at getting a lot of buyer attention if you have a pro hustling for you. If you don't hire an agent, your home will not be included in the **Multiple Listing Service (MLS)** run by the local Board of Realtors. And that MLS is the single greatest marketing tool available to homeowners who want to become home sellers. All agents (and by 2003, all Internet users) can tap into this computerized listing (Internet users will only be able to view 80% to 90% of the listings) of prospective homes to produce a roster of homes that fit the specifications of their home-buying clients. Shut yourself out of the MLS and making the sale can become one tough challenge. However, there is always the Internet. Online realty sites such as www.ziprealty.com are becoming more and more common. These sites give sellers the opportunity to list their houses for a much lower cost. In addition, the Internet almost certainly expands the potential buyer audience.

Time is another major consideration for those trying to sell FIZBO. You'll need to spend time writing and placing ads online and in newspapers, screening all callers, and arranging times when you will be available to show the house. In today's world of two-income households, that's a lot to ask of yourself or your spouse. But if you think you have the time and gumption to pull off a FIZBO, make sure you position yourself as ideally as possible.

Your first job as a FIZBO is to hire a lawyer. This is crucial. Since you won't have a real estate agent helping you deal with bidding and contracts, you need a lawyer to represent you from the get-go. And just because you're going it on your own, don't slam the door or phone on any broker who inquires about the house. You haven't signed any listing agreement, so you have no financial obligation to the broker. Just listen to what the broker has to offer. It could be that she is working as a buyer's broker and being paid by the buyer, so you won't lose any money by having her show your house. Or you can just tell the broker that she is welcome to let her clients see your house, but that you have no intention of paying her one penny. Remember: If you ultimately find that selling your home is too difficult, you may eventually want to hire one of the brokers you've met.

Any seller who tries FIZBO must work very hard to establish credibility with prospective buyers. So it's essential to establish that your price is fair. Hire an appraiser (cost: $250 or so) to get a fair value for your home. You will base your asking price on this appraisal and can also show the document to prospective buyers as proof that you are being reasonable.

Working with a Real Estate Agent

There are plenty of compelling reasons to hire a real estate agent and get professional assistance. Since hiring an agent is the only way to gain complete access to the Multiple Listing Service, you'll effectively open your home's doors to more prospects. In addition to getting your house in the MLS, a skillful agent will provide a variety of other services, such as making sure that only financially qualified buyers are shown your home, helping you get the best price, and ushering you through the closing process.

The real estate agent's first job is to help you determine the price you will ask prospective buyers to pay. This is called the **original list price**, or **asking price.** To determine this price, the agent ought to present you with at least three recent sales in your area to show how long the homes were on the market, their original list price, and the final sales price for each. This market analysis will also include the agent's assessment of whether recent activity is improving or slowing down.

Agents are also responsible for placing ads on the Internet, in newspapers, and in local real estate inserts distributed at grocery stores and shopping malls. The agent may also arrange for one or more open houses, in which other agents will be invited to see your home before it goes on the market. This technique serves as a pre-market screening to generate enthusiasm among local real estate agents for the new listing. Prospective buyers who want to see your house will be filtered through your agent's office to make sure they have enough income to purchase your home. Your agent will also assist you during the negotiating process when you and the buyer try to work out a deal. Home buyers don't always remember, but you should: When a real estate agent shows your house to someone shopping for a home, the agent is working for you and trying to get you the best price.

Choosing the right real estate agent may be the most important decision you make when selling your home. If the agent who initially sold you the house is still in business and you were pleased with that deal, by all means ask the same agent to help you sell the house. The next-best idea: Ask for references from friends who've sold their homes recently. Otherwise, check the newspaper for firms that seem to be most prominent not just in advertising, but also in the listings of homes that have recently sold. Make an appointment with the head broker at a few of these agencies. Tell each broker your specific needs and then ask which agent in the office is best qualified to sell your house. Don't simply accept anyone who is offered up. You want to make sure the agent is successful and motivated. Ask how many sales the agent completed during the past year, whether the agent works full-time or part-time, and if the agent has expertise in selling homes in your price range. The idea here is pretty simple. You want an agent who has already proven to be successful at getting homes like yours sold. And don't be shy about asking the agent for a few references—then calling them.

Once you find an agent, the next step is to formalize your relationship by signing a **listing agreement**. This document lays out the specifics of your arrangement, including how long you will let the agent represent you to prospective sellers as well as the amount of the agent's compensation when she engineers a sale. In most cases you will need to sign an **exclusive listing**, in which you agree that the agent will receive a commission regardless of whether she is actually responsible for finding the person who ultimately buys your house. The common commission fee for exclusive listings is 4% to 10% of the final sale price of the home. (Just so you know how this works: Your agent doesn't pocket the entire amount; typically the agent's firm keeps half, and the other half belongs to the firm whose agent brought you your buyer.) The only time exclusives aren't required is when there is no MLS, which usually occurs only in rural areas. In these situations the buyer doesn't sign up with any one agent. Rather, all interested agents take a shot at making the sale, and the agent and the firm that get the deal done receive the entire commission. Because the real estate agent in a nonexclusive listing won't be splitting the commission, the seller using her should not agree to a commission above 5% or so.

When you sign on with an agent, be willing to commit to a three-month hitch, but no longer. If your house is still unsold after 90 days but you are pleased with the agent's efforts, you can simply renew the agreement. What you don't want is to be locked into a four-, five-, or six-month agreement and find out after the first two months that your agent isn't terribly motivated. Then you're stuck.

At the point when you and the agent are reviewing the listing agreement, ask about some peripheral issues. If you are uncomfortable with a For Sale sign being posted in your front lawn, tell the agent now. You should also alert the agent to any stipulations that are important to you. The agent should be amenable to what you want, but it's only fair to lay out your requirements up front rather than run into difficulties once the agent gets down to work. For example, if you don't want the agent bringing strangers into the house when you are at work and the kids are home with a sitter, just lay out your schedule ahead of time.

A tip: While the 4% to 10% commission is common, it is not written in indelible ink. The exact percentage depends upon state, city, and the house's price range. All commissions are negotiable. So if you have a very expensive home, talk to the agent about reducing the commission. After all, a 10% commission on a $100,000 home is $10,000 while a 5% commission for a $400,000 home is a stunning $20,000. When you bring up the idea of a lower commission, ask the agent how it will affect the marketing of the home. A hungry agent probably won't flinch, since she is still in line to make a tidy sum when the house sells. But if you have an agent who tells you a lower commission won't work because she'll be able to offer the buyer's agent only 2.5% rather than 5%, then you've got a big decision to make. One option is to talk to some other agents. Another is to work out a deal with the agent by agreeing to a higher commission if the home sells at least for its original list price, but 5% if the final sale is at least 5% or more beneath your original asking price.

A bit of counterintuitive thinking will pay off if you are about to put your home up for sale in a tough selling market. Rather than scrimp on the commission, offer a bonus of one percentage point or so for any agent who pulls off the sale within 95% of your list price. That incentive will certainly keep your house in the thoughts of all agents in the area, who will no doubt be interested in the possibility of bringing in an extra .5% commission.

One big red light that needs flashing: Do not agree to a **net listing**, in which the seller agrees to hand the agent all proceeds that exceed a pre-determined sale price. For example, if you set a $100,000 price and the home sells for $115,000, the agent would keep the $15,000, or a whopping 13%. These setups are illegal in half the states. If you live in a state in the other half, just say "No, thank you."

Between the world of FIZBOs and full-service agents, there is a viable middle ground known as **discount brokers**. You can find these fee-for-service real estate agents in the Yellow Pages or on the Internet. They operate sort of like self-service gas stations. A discount agent will supply you with what you need, but you have to get out and do some of the work yourself. For instance, you can hire a discount broker for a flat rate or a commission of 2% or so. Because you are getting a cut rate, you won't get all the help of a full-service agent. So you will have to work out with the discounter what jobs you will take on, such as placing ads or showing the home to prospective buyers. One warning here: By working with a discount broker, you won't be listed in the MLS system, since the agent isn't about to split such a low flat fee or commission. That may not be a terrible problem if you are in a hot housing market. But in slower markets, ask the discount agent what you can do if the discount route doesn't work after, say, three months or so. In most cases your discounter is a member of the local Board of Realtors. So if you ultimately decide you need to have your house listed on the MLS, you can agree to pay a 2% to 3% commission to a buyer's broker who finds your house via the MLS.

Once you've chosen an agent or decided to sell your house yourself, it's time to check in with your lawyer to tell him you're getting ready to put the house on the market. All you want to do at this point is effectively put the lawyer on notice that you'll need his assistance within the next few weeks or months to review all bids and contracts. The reason for this preliminary call is so you will be assured of quick access to your lawyer once you finally receive a written bid. If you wait until then to call, you may have to wait a few days before the lawyer gets moving on your request. And don't think you can save a few bucks by working without a lawyer. An attorney familiar with real estate contracts will be invaluable in reviewing the buyer's request for contingency clauses in the contract, as well as in doing the research and paperwork to prove you have full title to the house.

Preparing the House for Sale

You wouldn't wear a rumpled and dirty shirt to an important job interview, right? Well, consider putting your home up for sale the equivalent of a very important job interview. You've got to make a good first impression. In this case you want to impress buyers, so you need to dress up your house in the most impressive way possible. That means sprucing up the exterior. So if the house is in dire need of painting, do it. It may cost a couple of thousand dollars, but the first impression is crucial and a neat exterior can be the difference between getting the home sold and having it sit on the market for a few more months. Also, weather permitting, fill the front yard with shrubs and flowers. At the very least, purchase a few planters and fill them with inviting colorful plants at the front door and by the driveway. If your lawn and garden area is looking, well, a bit mangy, consider hiring a gardener for a one- or two-day massive cleanup job: Give the lawn a professional mowing, trim the shrubs, and remove any dead and ungainly plants.

Go through each room and remove as much clutter as possible. You also don't want the place to be full of religious symbols, personal artifacts, or imposing artworks that may not be in the buyer's taste.

Caveat emptor is a goner when it comes to selling a home. Now, over half the states require that all sellers complete a disclosure form that lists all known structural and operational problems, from a leaky roof to a garbage disposal that is on the fritz. And in the states that still don't mandate disclosure, wise real estate agents require their sellers to present prospective buyers with a rundown of the condition of the home's structure and operational systems.

Savvy sellers won't see disclosure as just a necessary evil. Rather, you can turn it into a nifty selling tool. Add as much detail as you can think of, such as the year you had major systems repaired or overhauled. And provide the name of the contractor who did the work. A detailed—and honest—rundown of every aspect of the house will impress all home shoppers. You can also go a step farther and make available copies of your utility bills in each season, as well as a copy of your most recent property tax bill. If you live in a condominium or cooperative apartment, make sure all shoppers are presented right off the bat with the documents listing the maintenance fee and common charges; don't make the prospective buyer ask for the detailed information. That sort of candor telegraphs how eager you are to make a deal and what a decent person you are. You'd be surprised how many people buy homes these days just because they like the sellers.

How to Set a Price That's Right

Select an asking price that is too low and you'll undoubtedly get a buyer, but also needlessly forfeit thousands of dollars. Set the price too high and you will live the seller's nightmare of spending months on the market without many buyers stopping by, let alone making a bid on your home. To get the best price for your house, condo, or co-op and sell it promptly, you need to make sure you settle on a competitive and alluring initial list price. Here's where your agent starts to really earn her commission. She should automatically present you with a detailed market analysis that shows the key elements of recent sales in the neighborhood that are most like your place. That includes a breakdown of the original asking prices, the final sale prices, and the number of weeks or months the houses were on the market. The Internet site www.domania.com provides similar services for free. These **comparables** are really the only factors you should use in determining the general price range for your home. Accept the fact that the price you paid when you bought the home is irrelevant. That's right: irrelevant. Just because you paid $150,000 for your home at the market peak a few years ago doesn't mean a prospective buyer will automatically match or exceed that amount. If comparable homes now sell for $140,000, that's what you can expect to receive for your home.

A renovation or remodeling job will no doubt affect the value of your house, but you won't receive a 100% payback. For example, the fact that you added a third bathroom may well increase the value of the home, and your agent will be careful to use three-bathroom homes for your comparables. But at no time will the actual cost of your project come into play. Just because you paid $25,000 for the renovation project doesn't mean you can increase your asking price by $25,000. Fortunately, you'll be able to get some additional payback on the project after you've sold the house. That's because the IRS lets you add the cost of all actual improvements to the price you originally paid for the house. This **adjusted cost basis** is the base amount that you will then use to calculate the taxable capital gain. Because you have effectively raised the purchase price, you will therefore have a smaller taxable gain to report.

Once your agent has provided the market analysis of comparable sales in the area and you know the ballpark you'll be playing in, your job is to pull out the research you did at the library and sit down with the agent to talk pricing strategy. If you determine that the recent trend is that homes are taking longer to sell and that the gap between list price and sale price is widening, you are in a slowing sales market. So should you need to make a move quickly, you'll have to make the price of your home extra enticing to attract attention. Consider setting the asking price of your home 5% or so below its market value. Advertising that sort of value will get you the kind of buyer action you need.

You should also consider a strategic approach to putting your house on the MLS system. Most of these real estate listing systems segregate homes into price categories of $10,000. Therefore, if you set your asking price at $151,000, your home will be included in the $150,000-and-above screens. But if you instead set the asking price at $149,000, you will also capture all the prospective buyers whose upper limit is the $140,000 to $149,000 level. So while you've started $2,000 lower, you've greatly increased your number of possible buyers, which is a savvy move in slow sales markets.

If you are in the enviable position of selling your home during a local real estate boom—lucky you!—then you can afford to add a bit to your home's current market value when setting an asking price. For example, let's say $150,000 is the market value, but you and your agent have determined that homes are selling within just a couple of weeks of landing on the market and are getting snapped up right at the asking price. If your comparables are from a month or two ago, they may slightly understate the strength of the market since those sales occurred. With your agent's input, think about adding 2% or so to the market value. But be careful about getting greedy. If you set the price at too high a premium, your home will not get enough attention from shoppers. Then, chances are, no one will make you a reasonable offer.

Don't assume you can simply lower the price in a few weeks if you aren't getting any serious buyer attention. It's tough to shift the focus on your home once the agents and buyers have moved on. The critical time for any home is the first few weeks it arrives on the market. That's when agents and buyers will give it their closest attention. You can't be assured the buzz will return in a month when you lower the price. By then, some other houses have come on the market and they're drawing the interest of agents and buyers.

Consider taking what might be called the Goldilocks approach: If the housing market is neither too hot nor too cold where you live, be realistic and set the price in line with the comparables. But leave yourself a bit of negotiating room; that means tacking on a bit to the market value. Everybody does it. Remember your research that showed homes were selling 3% below their original list price? Well, then add that 3% or so to your list price. This becomes your negotiating cushion. If a potential buyer makes a bid that's 5% below list price, you can then make a counteroffer that is 3% lower. That may mollify the buyer and you've got a deal—right at the price you determined was the home's true market value. Of course, the process of determining your home's asking price is far from a science, so talk to your agent about how the bidding process usually works in your area and where a comfortable cushion would be for your list price.

Showing Your House

This is another area where the agent earns her commission. Your best bet is to leave this job completely to the agent and not be present when a prospective buyer comes by to see your home. If you happen to be at home, try to be as invisible as possible. You don't want to be drawn into a conversation with the buyer that tips your hand too much.

If you are present and a buyer makes an oral bid, do not show any emotion. Simply tell the buyer you will consider any written bid. Once you have a written bid, your agent and your lawyer can review the offer.

Renting Out Your Home

If you live in a very slow market and can't make a sale but must make a move, don't resign yourself to being house stuck. You can at least cover your mortgage costs by renting out the house temporarily. If you can find renters who are interested in buying when they have more savings, you may be able to work out a deal where you lease the house to the renters and give them the option of buying the home within a specific period—say, two years. To help sweeten the deal, you can agree to credit 10% or so of their rent payments toward the purchase price of the house. While this arrangement can be a lifesaver if you must relocate to a new area, it does have a few drawbacks. You will not only still own the home and be responsible for its upkeep, you'll also become a landlord. Plus, you probably won't be able to qualify for a mortgage to buy a home in your new town until you are able to sell this home and pay back the loan. So if you are renting out your home, chances are you'll become a renter, too, temporarily.

If the renters ultimately decide not to buy the house, you can either extend your rental agreement with them or put the house back on the market. With luck, the local economy will have improved enough so that you can now find a buyer willing to pay a fair price for the home. But if the market is still sluggish, you may be able to take advantage of an IRS rule that will let you deduct the loss from the sale if you have rented out the property for the two years prior to the sale.

Negotiating with a Potential Buyer

Congratulations, you have a bid on your home. Even if it's lower than you expected, do not be discouraged. At least the ball is in play. Now huddle with your agent and figure out your next move. If the bid is just 5% below your asking price, it looks like you'll be able to make a deal. Make a counteroffer that gives back the cushion you worked in—say 3%—and tell the prospective buyer you've got a deal, but no more negotiating. Chances are very good that the home shopper wants this process to be over with, too.

However, if you get a bid that is 10% or more below your asking price, you have a few choices. Ask your agent to help you assess the buyer's approach. It may be that the person making the bid just likes to negotiate. Some people do. If so, make a counteroffer that is 2% or 3% lower and see what offer you get next. Otherwise, you can just have your agent convey that you have set a fair asking price and that you will not entertain a bid that is so far below it. What you're doing here is forcing the buyer essentially to raise his initial bid before the negotiating begins. Of course, there's the risk that the buyer will simply refuse and walk away from the house. But if you are pretty confident that you've set a fair price and that the buyer is trying to take advantage of you, then you need to be willing to let such a lowball bidder walk.

Another approach is to give in a bit on the price and then add in some barter. For instance, if you have a terrific gardener and your landscaping is part of the home's charm, tell the bidder that you'll pay for the first six months of the gardener's bill when he moves in. Or if the dishwasher and other appliances weren't originally part of the sale, you can now offer to throw in one or two of the appliances.

In addition to deciding how to deal with the bidder's offer, you also need your lawyer to review the contingency clauses that the bidder has included in the bid. Unless you are totally desperate to make a sale, do not agree to a clause that states the deal goes through only if the buyer is able to sell his current home. That's his problem; don't make it yours. If you agree to that clause, you could be stuck waiting, while being unable to entertain offers from other buyers.

Your lawyer should also make sure that each acceptable contingency is given a specific time frame in which it must be completed. For example, it is perfectly reasonable for the buyer to make the deal contingent on the house passing a home inspection. But you want to make sure that the inspection is done within a week of signing the contract. The same is true of the closing date. Make the buyer commit to a reasonable date; don't leave it hanging in the air.

If you and the prospective buyer can't agree on the price and your bartering didn't help close the deal, you might consider helping the buyer by offering to pay some of his mortgage financing costs. **Seller financing** can be especially enticing to first-time buyers who are typically a bit cash strapped to come up with the down payment, let alone cover all the mortgage and closing costs.

If you have a government-insured loan, you may be sitting on your best marketing tool. All loans insured by the Federal Housing Administration before December 15,

1989, and all Veterans Administration loans issued before March 1988 are what's known as **fully assumable loans**. That means you can transfer the mortgage to the buyer, who then takes control of the payments without having to qualify for the loan. For all government loans issued after these dates, the buyer will have to meet the lender's qualifying criteria.

Another seller-financing tool is to buy down the buyer's mortgage rate by agreeing to pay an extra point or two in the closing costs. In general, every point the seller pays will reduce the interest rate on the buyer's mortgage by an eighth of a percentage point. That not only helps lower the buyer's monthly mortgage costs, but the new lower rate will also make it easier for him or her to pass the lender's financial qualification screen. In addition to helping get the deal done, you get a nice tax break, too. Uncle Sam lets you add the cost of these **buy-down points** to your cost basis, thereby reducing the size of the taxable gain you will have to report to the government. But don't get too excited. Unlike the points that you paid when you bought your house, these points can't be claimed as a deduction on your federal tax return.

Once you and the bidder have an agreement, you'll both sign the contract and the buyer will make an **earnest money deposit** with the agent or lawyer. This good faith financial gesture is typically equal to 1% to 3% of the sale price and will be credited to the down payment at the actual closing.

Speaking of the closing, your job is to show up—generally with your lawyer—and have the deed to the house ready to pass along to the new owner. One of the contingencies you probably agreed to was allowing the buyer a final walk-through inspection of the house a day before the closing. This should just be a formality, so the buyer can make sure there isn't any confusion about which appliances and fixtures stay with the house.

At the closing, you and the buyer will write each other a few checks to settle some shared payments. For instance, if you already paid the entire property tax bill for the year, but you're moving after just six months, then the buyer must reimburse you for half of the payment. Or if you haven't yet been billed for the property tax, you'll need to write the buyer a check for the six months you were the owner.

After the buyer writes a slew of checks to his lender, he will sign over a check to you for the agreed-upon sale price. You then write a check to your lender to cover the remaining principal balance on your mortgage. Then you give the buyer the deed to the house and the deal is done. You have officially sold your home. Now just remember to give the new owner the keys.

Taxes and Home Selling

If you sell your home at a taxable profit or a loss, the sale must be reported to the Internal Revenue Service. Your lender will report the transaction by filing Form 1099 with the IRS. And as the seller, you must report the sale by filing Form 2119 with the IRS and showing the gain or loss on Schedule D of your federal tax return; if the gain is tax-free, you need not file this form. To help you wade through these forms and procedures, contact the IRS (800-829-3676; www.irs.gov) to obtain a copy of Publication 523: *Tax Information on Selling Your House.*

While the federal government may be interested in taxing your capital gain on the house, you won't be expected simply to subtract the sale price from your original purchase price and consider that the taxable gain. Rather, the tax code lets you add to the original purchase price a bunch of costs you paid during the time you lived in the house. You can tack on only the costs for actual improvements, such as replacing the roof, installing central air-conditioning, or adding a bathroom. Basic maintenance and repairs such as cleaning the gutters or painting the exterior are not considered to be improvements. In addition to the cost of improvements, you'll also be able to add on a variety of fees you paid in the process of selling the home, such as the sales commission you paid to the agent. The sum of all additional costs is added to the original purchase price, and the total is called the **adjusted cost basis**. You subtract this final adjusted cost basis from the sale price to determine any capital gain. New rules in 2001 may allow you to exclude any gain from income up to a limit of $250,000 ($500,000 on a joint return). See IRS publication 523 for details.

CHAPTER 9

Getting the Most Out of Your Career and Benefits

Okay. You've got an office, a respectable paycheck, and a stack of engraved business cards. Are these the trappings of a hot-rod career or a plain old job? The answer depends on what you make of your own unique career journey. Savvy career climbers know that any single job may help them advance to the next rung on the ladder, but long term, a successful work life is much more complex than simply getting the next job. It's having and taking advantage of benefits from your employer. It's balancing your work life with your life away from work. It's parlaying your skills to get more money and more enjoyment from your job.

For better or worse, paternalistic corporations and the decades-long careers they fostered have disappeared from the corporate landscape. But even though the job-hopping "looking for a multimillion-dollar-dot-com-stock-option-payoff" career game plan in the late '90s helped people understand the value of portable skills and negotiating compensation packages, it was soon clear that the revolving-door approach to staffing was no better way to build a company than to always promote from within.

As a result, you probably will have many jobs at lots of places over your working years—but forget about changing jobs as the primary way to quickly climb your career ladder. Over the next decade or so, smart career planning will require some deft strategic moves. In 1953, the average American professional changed jobs just three times over the course of a career. Today that number is up to seven jobs—more than likely in different professions and different industries. Yeah, that may sound like more changes than you want to make, but think about it: For most of us that trek may cover a span of 40 years or more. Do the math, and ask yourself: Do you really want to stay at one job longer than 5.7 years (on average)? But all this moving will require some rather fancy career footwork to best the competition for the most attractive, high-paying gigs. Employers of the twenty-first century require their fast-trackers to be super-specialists—adaptable types equipped to juggle several skills and tasks.

While you may not be able to control your entries and exits through corporate America's doors as much as in the past, don't let news of layoffs or tight job markets discourage you. At the same time companies are slicing layers of management in one part of their business, they may be ushering in a new set of employees with a completely different set of skills in another.

Don't assume you're stuck in the field you've chosen, either. Thousands of people chuck one field for another every year, and plenty of others dream about doing it. In fact, when a MONEY survey asked respondents, "If you could start again, would you choose the same career?" a striking 42% said they'd take a different route today, with more women (50%) than men (35%) ready to choose a different path.

Four Keys to a Successful Career

Worried that you might not have what it takes to make it on the job in the future? Take it easy. This chapter will lay out the details of getting ahead in the workplace of today and tomorrow. Before zeroing in on the details, though, here are four broad themes to remember for improving your odds of on-the-job success:

1. **Further your education.** Consider these telling statistics: For every dollar earned by a college graduate, the average high school grad makes about 64¢. Holders of doctorate and professional degrees take home almost twice as much as those who have BAs. For every dollar earned by holders of professional degrees, bachelor degree holders earn 55¢. For every dollar earned by holders of doctorate degrees, bachelor degree holders earn 64¢.

   A fast-tracker's learning curve shouldn't end with any particular degree. By building up new skills at work, you stand to enhance both your career and salary. Among the abilities most sought after in corporate America today: computer know-how, for starters. Workers who use PCs to ply their trade, for instance, earn roughly

10% to 15% more than those who don't. Other top talents include technical writing ability and managerial wizardry. Regardless of your line of work, in our global economy foreign languages can give you added leverage. Luckily there are plenty of places that can help keep your skills competitive. Hundreds of colleges and universities nationwide offer executive education programs—from managing difficult people to accounting for nonfinancial managers—through seminars, career development programs on campus, in the workplace, and on the Web. Both new and seasoned managers might want to consider comprehensive training available through the American Management Association (AMA) in New York. For $225 per year, members have access to AMA publications, surveys, and 10% discounts on seminars, videos, and books. Held in New York, Chicago, San Francisco, Atlanta, and Washington, D.C., classes range in duration from one to five days and cost between $1,000 and $7,000. For more information, call the AMA at 212-586-8100 or 800-262-9699 or check out the Web site at www.amanet.org.

2. **Don't thumb your nose at lateral moves.** "Up" would seem the only logical career climber's destination. As corporations continue to strip away management layers, however, you can count on more job openings to be sideways moves. Plus, by testing out new opportunities in other departments and divisions at your current employer, you may gain valuable experience, not to mention great networking contacts and a better view of how the overall firm functions.

3. **Job-hop judiciously.** Recent college grads can afford to surf from post to post for the first two to four years out of school. It's a great way to find your way in the working world. In midcareer, though, you should carefully orchestrate your voluntary job switches. Don't make a switch before asking yourself the following three questions:
   • Would the new post move you in a career direction that's in keeping with your overall goals?
   • Are you thinking about accepting the new job not because you think it's a worthy one, but merely because your current job is a bummer?
   • If the new position is from an employer trying to lure you, would you be so eager to move if you weren't being hotly pursued?

   If your answers to these questions reveal that you're thinking of making a job hop just for convenience or because you're flattered to get an offer, stop! You're making a mistake.

4. **Feel free to make a career switch.** No matter how old you are, it's never too late to make a 180° turn and plunge into a new career. Just try to pick a new career that melds your passion with the skills you've aced in a previous one. To get help making

a radical move, see a **career counselor** or **career coach** for advice. A one-on-one could range from $60 to $75 per hour, but check out community colleges and universities in your area. They may offer these services for a much lower cost.

Another way to make the transition smooth is to find out what fast-growth fields have a need for your talents. You may be surprised by some of the categories in which the U.S. Bureau of Labor statistics predicts high growth. (See table below for details.)

THE 10 FASTEST GROWING OCCUPATIONS, 1998–2008

(Numbers in thousands of jobs)

Occupation	Employment		Change	
	1998	**2008**	**Number**	**Percent**
Computer engineers	299	622	323	108
Computer support specialists	429	869	439	102
Systems analysts	617	1,194	577	94
Database administrators	87	155	67	77
Desktop publishing specialists	26	44	19	73
Paralegals and legal assistants	136	220	84	62
Personal care and home health aides	746	1,179	433	58
Medical assistants	252	398	146	58
Social and human service assistants	268	410	141	53
Physician assistants	66	98	32	48

Source: U.S. Bureau of Labor Statistics, 2000 Employment Projections.

THE 10 INDUSTRIES WITH
THE FASTEST WAGE AND SALARY
EMPLOYMENT GROWTH, 1998–2008

(Numbers in thousands of jobs)

Occupation	Employment		Change	
	1998	2008	Number	Percent
Computer and data processing services	1,599	3,472	1,872	117
Health services, not elsewhere classified	1,209	2,018	809	67
Residential care	747	1,171	424	57
Management and public relations	1,034	1,500	466	45
Personnel supply services	3,230	4,623	1,393	43
Miscellaneous equipment rental and leasing	258	369	111	43
Museums; botanical and zoological gardens	93	131	39	42
Research and testing services	614	861	247	40
Miscellaneous transportation services	236	329	94	40
Security and commodity brokers	645	900	255	40

Source: U.S. Bureau of Labor Statistics, 2000 Employment Projections.

WHERE THE JOBS WILL BE

According to Woods & Poole, a respected economics research firm in Washington, D.C., the following 10 metropolitan areas (listed alphabetically) stand to offer some of the best job opportunities from 1998 to 2005:

1. Austin/San Marcos, Tex.	6. Phoenix/Mesa, Ariz.
2. Laredo, Tex.	7. Provo/Orem, Utah
3. Las Vegas, Nev.	8. Punta Gorda, Fla.
4. Naples, Fla.	9. Sarasota/Bradenton, Fla.
5. Orlando, Fla.	10. Wilmington, N.C.

REALITY CHECKLIST

The following 10 tips can certainly help you wade through the myriad options you face as you try to make critical career decisions:

1. Do what you enjoy and seek financial rewards later.
2. Define what job satisfaction means to you and apply the criteria in each job you land.
3. Always have a Plan B. If something doesn't work out where you are, know your next move.
4. When leaving a job, do so with as much grace as you can. Burning bridges is a bad idea.
5. Be flexible about your hours. Dolly Parton's song about working nine to five won't cut it anymore. In this techno age, you may be on call around the clock via cell phone, e-mail, pager, or fax.
6. Spot the smartest-working person where you work and use him or her as the standard to outperform.
7. Look for new challenges. Ask your boss for high-profile project-type assignments that will highlight a full range of your skills.

8. Don't be afraid of failure. Risk takers usually reap rich rewards.

9. Take time to appraise what you've learned or could have learned from each job.

10. Turn workplace changes to your advantage. For instance, a streamlined department in your office could give you a greater chance to excel.

How to Search for a Job

You know the old saying "Look before you leap." Oddly, many people don't heed this crucial advice when seeking a new job. Make sure you do. Just think: Many employers hiring today are likely to put job candidates through interview paces not once, but three or four times—which may include online and telephone interviews. Why shouldn't you check them out as thoroughly as they do you? A proper search takes time. Some experts say job hunters who've already been in the workforce can today count on spending an average of one month on the interview circuit for every $10,000 they formerly earned. Remember these tips the next time you're ready to survey the employment terrain:

- **Tap your network of friends and associates to meet people working at companies that interest you.** Reach out to everyone possible for "insider information" about the companies you're keen on. Career counselors figure that as many as 80% of all managerial or white-collar jobs are filled through the corporate grapevine, so it truly does pay to broadcast your situation to as many people as possible.

- **Do the research.** Curious about general job prospects in your field? Want referrals to organizations that can give you further job-seeking information? Maybe you're an unemployed recent college grad and are searching for detailed job descriptions in a particular field. No matter where you are in your work life, if you're looking for a job, head to your library's stacks and page through the thick *Occupational Outlook Handbook*, published annually by the U.S. Department of Labor (www.bls.gov). This publication contains job growth forecasts in hundreds of job categories through the year 2008.

- **Surf the Internet.** Increasingly, companies post job openings on the Web, too. In fact, there are more than 3,500 Web sites with job postings. Three comprehensive sites are Monster.com (www.monster.com), Headhunter.net (www.headhunter.net), and JobOptions (www.joboptions.com), which have between 10,000 and 50,000 listings apiece and are updated daily.

Once you've selected a potential company, visit its Web page. You can find it by entering the company's name in a search engine like Yahoo! (www.yahoo.com), Google (www.google.com), or Lycos (www.lycos.com). For a more critical look at employers, read the latest news reports on them at sites like Wall Street Research Net (www.wsrn.com) and Business Wire (www.businesswire.com). Use search engines or ask your librarian to help you cull newspaper and magazine stories about particular employers you're researching. Articles will tell you things like whether there have been layoffs lately and if so what kinds of severance packages were offered; who has been promoted recently; the quality of the top management; and if there have been any major scandals or success stories. Publicly traded companies will also have earnings reports and sales histories on record.

You can also find chat rooms and discussion groups on the Net where you can talk with current and former employees about the companies, including www.workforce. com and www.delphi.com.

• **Find out if you'll be entitled to an employment contract.** Recent corporate cutbacks have made professionals more wary—and more savvy—about jumping into new job situations. While there is no way to assure job security, you may be able to get a safety net in the form of an employment contract. Drawn up by your prospective employer, this document articulates your job title, duties, and salary as well as any benefits, such as vacation pay, bonuses, and severance arrangements. These contracts, usually reserved for executive types, specify a length of employment, anywhere from a year to three years.

Remember: Although employment contracts protect you in many ways, they also serve the needs of your employer. For this reason, be sure to review the contract language carefully, searching for any clauses that might be restrictive or nebulous. Once you have a firm offer in hand and an employment contract is presented, take your time with it. Ask your lawyer to review it to be certain it serves your interests.

Résumé Dos and Don'ts

It's no fun to draft a **résumé**—laying out your life history on a single sheet of paper or a Web page dedicated to you. Coming up with just the right résumé is tough, too. After all, this is a document that requires you to be assertive but not pleading, impressive yet not pompous, a calling card that can land you in the interview chair, not the reject pile. Highlight anything that distinguishes you as someone who gets results. For more help in crafting a winning résumé, heed these dos and don'ts of paper and electronic résumés:

PAPER RÉSUMÉS

Do
1. **Pay attention to presentation.** Avoid offbeat typefaces and use white or cream heavy bond paper. Be brief and use active words to describe your previous duties.
2. **Include all your educational credentials, including any courses or seminars you've taken recently to upgrade your skills.**
3. **Double- and triple-check for grammar and spelling errors.** Nothing irks a manager more than reading about someone's stint at General Mothors.

Don't
1. **Simply prepare a list of your past jobs or education.** Instead, flaunt your responsibilities and what you learned from each job.
2. **Include your salary history.** You may over- or underprice yourself before getting a foot in the door.
3. **Dust off an old résumé and slap your latest job on top.** Take the time to tailor your pitch to the work you're seeking.

ELECTRONIC RÉSUMÉS

Do
1. **Use keywords or labels, focusing on nouns, rather than verbs.** Searches are generally done by keywords or phrases that include essential characteristics needed to fill the job, such as: education, skills, knowledge, and abilities.

2. **Place the most important keywords toward the top of the résumé.** The employer's search program may have a limited number of items it can scan for—typically beginning at the top of the document.

3. **Keep your résumé and cover letter to no more than 65 characters per line** just in case those you are sending it to have a different e-mail program, computer format, or screen width. This makes your résumé easier to read and safe to print.

4. **Keep the design simple.** Use a lot of white space and limit design elements. For example, use asterisks and capital letters, rather than underlining or bolding. This is especially important when using plain text, for some elements (e.g. bullets, bold, italics) are not recognized in this format.

5. **Use common language.** Not all searches have synonym tables, so to maximize the number of "hits" between a position search and your résumé use words everyone knows.

Don't

1. **Assume that the person you are sending your résumé to has the same program or e-mailing capabilities as you.** While it is true that many e-mail systems can accommodate document attachments, it is not true that every person or group will be able to receive it in that format. Ask the employer what format he prefers or consider using plain text, which is universally accessible and in some cases required.

2. **Send your cover letter and résumé as two files.** Consolidate the two documents into one file, by cutting and pasting your cover letter in the space before your résumé. This limits the chances of items getting lost or mixed up.

From Résumé to Job

Once you've polished your résumé, you need to circulate it effectively. At first, you'll probably be best off narrowing your focus to the few employers suited to your search.

- **Job Web Sites.** You can post your résumé on one of several electronic databases seen by recruiters nationwide. Or, you can zap your vita over the wires via services such as Monster.com, HotJobs.com, and most of the online job sites listed in this chapter.
- **Executive recruiters.** If you're an unemployed manager who has either been looking for work for a while or is open to the idea of moving, you may want to let an **executive recruiting firm**—a/k/a **headhunter**—flaunt your credentials far and

wide. Approximately one in five midlevel managers land new positions with the help of headhunters. To locate reputable firms, check www.kennedyinfo.com or browse through *The Directory of Executive Recruiters* in your library. Make a note of those who specialize in your field plus local ones.

As a rule, you should bypass **retainer firms**. These firms are used for specific job searches (typically on the executive level), where there is an exclusive relationship between the client and the search firm. Final payment ranges from 27% to 35% of the total compensation package for the first year. Instead, check out **contingency search firms**. Because these are not exclusive firms and they make a buck only when their applicants land a job, they tend to be more motivated in locating and selling top talent.

Most contingency recruitment firms won't charge you a fee unless you get hired. Reputable ones that do, demand about 25% to 33% of your first year's salary, but only after you've started your new job. Should you wind up going with a fee-based firm, be sure to get a signed contract that clearly specifies all costs and services up front.

- **Temporary work.** When looking for a job, don't forget investigating temporary work. Over 11% of temporary employees are from professional occupations, including managers, computer systems analysts, scientists, and engineers.

  You may be surprised to learn just how rewarding temp work can be. For starters, the pay is often decent. Generally, temps earn hourly wages that are on par with full-time jobs in their fields. Some temp jobs even provide workers with health insurance and vacation pay. Even more encouraging: About 72% of temporary workers go on to permanent positions within one year. The best way to up the odds of getting hired is showing the company how it can save money. Aside from reading the classifieds, try calling personnel managers at companies where you'd like to work and ask for recommendations of the agency they use. Incidentally, you'll find temp agencies on the Web at www.business.com, www.careercity.com, www.tempz.com, and www.hruniverse.com or in the Yellow Pages under "Employment Contractors—Temporary Help."

- **Networking.** Serious networking requires careful orchestration. It's one thing to meet someone who may help advance your career. It's quite another to find ways of compelling that person to remember, you and help you when you need assistance getting a job. And remember, once you meet people, the Internet is a great way to stay in touch. There are several ways to network like a pro:

1. **Join professional associations on the local level.**
2. **Check out your college alumni network.** Check out the local chapter of your alma mater in your area. Call your school's alumni office to see what kind of job placement is available to alums and see if your college has a Web-based résumé service for its graduates.

3. **Sweat the details.** Keep in touch with your networking contacts with small gestures. Thank-you notes after a lunch date are de rigueur. You'll stand out even more by sending a new contact things like relevant newspaper clippings, the names of other people in the field, or reminders of upcoming events.

Acing a Job Interview

If you haven't been on a job interview in a while—or ever—you may be surprised at the kinds of questions being asked these days. For instance, you might be asked to write an essay on the spot about your past successes and failures. Or you could be asked for an example of something that would make you a useful addition to the staff during your first year on the job. You might even be given a psychological test to see if you're the kind of person that the hirer is looking for. Also note that the first round of interviews may be via e-mail or telephone, as companies continue to find ways to cut costs and save time.

So how do you sell yourself properly? The key is to show the potential employer that you know a great deal about what the firm needs, that you have what it takes to get the job done, and that you'll fit in well with the current workforce there. The wrong way is to just keep talking about what a terrific person you are and how people like you. Try to give at least one example of something you did at your last job that would be helpful at this job.

Also, show the interviewer that you've given a lot of thought to the job by asking dazzling questions of your own. Don't be shy about asking key questions such as how many people will report to you, how often you'll be expected to travel, how the retirement savings and pension plan is structured, what kind of health, life, and disability insurance coverage you would receive, and so on. But save the specific questions about your potential compensation package until later in the process.

Getting the Pay You Deserve

Before you go into the job interview, you should have a pretty good idea of what the job will pay and what the competition is paying. Salary sites on the Web and want ads in trade journals and local newspapers will help you establish this figure. Better still, a contact at the firm or a competitor could clue you in.

Try to get the company to make you an offer before you reveal your most recent salary. If you're asked first, however, take a few minutes to spout all the responsibilities the job entails. Then, put on a poker face and cite a figure that's in the high end of your range. You may wind up negotiating from there.

If the interviewer hits you with a pay offer that is downright chintzy, you have a few options:

- **Hedge.** Explain to your prospective boss that while the job sure feels like the right fit, you're still weighing a few other opportunities (even if you aren't).
- **Ask if part of the money you're requesting could come from a bonus pool or if you can get stock options.** Or see if you can get the firm to commit to giving you a raise of a specified amount of money in six months if you meet certain goals laid out in advance.
- **If you're in the upper rungs of management or know that you'd be quite a catch, ask for a signing bonus.** If so, you may want to negotiate further, say, taking a $5,000 signing bonus and tacking on another $5,000 to your salary vs. accepting a $10,000 up-front bonus. This way your annual pay increases are assured to be larger.
- **Walk away.** Granted, this strategy takes guts, especially if you've been offered an alluring job. One possible advantage here: By sticking to your guns, you'll be giving the employer a taste of your convictions. That may cause the firm to pony up the money you want after all.

SALARY WEB SITES

Ever wonder if you're being paid what you're worth? These sites help you figure out what you're really worth on the open market—and they take much of the guesswork out of salary negotiations. Following these guidelines will help you get the most from your research.

- **Start big.** General salary sites such as those run by Salary.com and the Economic Research Institute are the best places to begin. These portals give you instant access to surveys for hundreds of job titles and professions in many locations. Many of these inclusive sites also offer career advice and industry and job market overviews to help you put the salary statistics in context.
- **Use at least one niche site.** Look for resource links to niche sites that focus on your particular career and industry. These provide even more precise pay figures and in-depth counseling. For example, one niche site, Law.com (www.lawjobs.com), covers compensation for law school professors, public interest lawyers, law clerks, and public defenders, to name only a few. That kind of detail is likely to be more useful than a salary report for "attorneys" or "lawyers."
- **Read job descriptions, not just job titles.** After all, your experience as a sales manager may be very different from the sales manager jobs included in a survey.
- **Be honest about your skills.** Look for surveys that are based on skill levels and set realistic goals for yourself.
- **Know your industry.** Salaries for, say, an accountant or an office manager can vary widely from one industry to another.

Here are five sites to kick off your search:

- America's Career InfoNet (www.acinet.org)
- Economic Research Institute (www.erieri.com/doltrends)
- Korn/Ferry International (www.futurestep.com)
- Salary.com (www.salary.com)
- U.S. Department of Labor Bureau of Labor Statistics (www.bls.gov/oco)

Getting More Money from Your Boss

Although it can be tough to get extra cash from your boss, it's not impossible. The magic words are bonus and stock options. More and more, companies around the country are getting rid of annual raises and replacing them with these two options. Generally, **bonuses** range between 2% and 30% of your annual pay. And more and more companies are offering **employee stock options** to workers at all levels as an incentive to improve performance. To boost the size of your bonus or number of options, do whatever you can to show your boss just how useful you've been in making your employer more profitable, efficient, or both. The subject is no longer taboo. You need to raise the issue gingerly, however. If you can demonstrate to your superior that you're underpaid, simply ask for the money you think you deserve to receive. (See box earlier in chapter on salary sites to help determine that figure.) These guidelines can also help:

- **Enlist your boss in your efforts.** "One of the most successful tactics I've seen is to enlist the support of a manager," says Michael O'Malley, author of *Are You Paid What You're Worth?* "You can say, 'I think I've been a good performer over the years, and I see what other organizations are paying. My pay doesn't strike me as right. Could this be something we investigate?' Very often a manager will go to HR and argue that salaries are off. If you're a good performer, they'll want you to stay."
- **Time your request.** Most salary reviews occur after annual performance meetings, but that doesn't mean you have to wait to ask for a raise. Not surprisingly, the best time to request a pay hike is after you've accomplished a goal or achieved some notable success. "If you're having a good year, and you know that merit budgets aren't that big, it's sometimes good to politick ahead of time about your expectations," says O'Malley. "Then everyone will be aware that you expect more."
- **Don't be confrontational.** Approach salary negotiations as a cooperative dialogue. Despite using these negotiating strategies, sometimes the answer will be "Sorry, everybody gets the same raise this year." In that case, if there's a bonus pool where you work, ask your supervisor what it would take to either start swimming in it or get a larger bonus than you were promised. You might want to set target goals with your boss and then update the list periodically.

Getting the Most from
Your Benefits

The difference between a good job and a truly great one may be bundled in a package of perks. A decent **benefits package**—health coverage, life insurance, one or more retirement plans—may have a value of as much as a third of your pay or more, but many employers offer less. These days a generous benefits package is truly a gem to covet.

As corporate America has looked for ways to cut costs, many firms have either cut back on their benefit plans, required employees to pony up more cash for their perks, or both. Moreover, many companies are asking employees to pay larger sums to cover both health premiums and medical deductibles. Businesses are getting especially stingy, too, about giving their retirees health benefits; some are forcing their ex-employees to pick up the entire tab for coverage, while others are eliminating health benefits altogether for seniors.

It's up to you to keep abreast of how your benefits measure up. You ought to pore over the employer's benefits handbook as soon as you accept a job or even while you're interviewing for a position if you can get your hands on it. If you're a new hire, ask for a conference with your benefits counselor or personnel manager to ensure you understand everything you're entitled to receive and when you're eligible to start getting the benefits. At many companies, for instance, health coverage doesn't kick in until several months after you've started. (To assess how your benefits stack up against those offered by large U.S. corporations, see worksheet below.)

What follows is a guide to making the best use of the benefits you have at work:

MEDICAL COVERAGE

For a detailed discussion of health care insurance and how to size up the different plans, see Chapter 2. Assuming your employer offers a choice between a fee-for-service and a managed-care plan, take a hard look at the less expensive managed-care programs.

RATE YOUR COMPANY'S BENEFITS

Fill out the worksheet below to see how your employer's benefits package stacks up against those of America's largest corporations. To find the answers, grab your benefits policy manual or visit your company's Intranet. This worksheet and scoring system is roughly based on MONEY's Best Company Benefits survey. Both were developed in conjunction with international benefits consultation firm Milliman USA.

HEALTH CARE

1. How much do you contribute each month for medical coverage?

SINGLE COVERAGE	FAMILY COVERAGE	POINTS	SCORE
No coverage	No coverage	0	
$170 or more	$480 or more	3	
$125 to $169	$350 to $479	5	
$75 to $124	$220 to $349	8	
$20 to $74	$60 to $219	11	
$0 to $19	$0 to $59	13	

2. How many medical plans can you choose from?

NUMBER OF PLANS	POINTS	SCORE
0 to 1	0	
2	1	
3 or more	2	

3. Does your company:

	POINTS NO	YES	SCORE
Offer a dental plan?	0	0.5	
Pay 50% or more of dental plan?	0	0.5	
Offer a vision plan or a flexible spending account?	0	0.5	

4. If your company offers retirement medical coverage, when is an employee who is hired at age 30 first eligible to retire with benefits?

AGE	POINTS	%	SCORE
66 or older	4		
65	5		
63 to 64	6	Multiply by	
59 to 62	7	x percentage of =	
57 to 58	8	premium paid	
55 to 56	9	by employer.	
53 to 54	10		
51 to 52	11		
Age 50 or younger	12		

DEFINED-BENEFIT PENSION PLAN

5. What percentage of final pay does your company's pension plan provide after 20 years of service?

PERCENTAGE OF PAY	POINTS	SCORE
No plan	0	
Less than 10%	3	
10% to 19%	6	
20% to 29%	11	
30% to 39%	15	
40% to 49%	19	
50% or more	21	

6. Can you receive a lump-sum distribution from your pension plan?

	POINTS	SCORE
No	0	
Yes	4	

DEFINED-CONTRIBUTION SAVINGS PLAN

7. How much of your pay will your company contribute to your employee savings plan—for example, a 401(k) or 403(b)—in both matching contributions and profit-sharing contributions if you make the maximum allowable contribution to the plan?

PERCENTAGE OF PAY	POINTS	SCORE
No plan	0	
Less than 4%	3	
4% to 5%	7	
6% to 8%	9	
9% to 11%	13	
12% to 14%	17	
15% to 19%	24	
20% or more	30	

8. Can you do either of the following?

	POINTS	SCORE
Borrow from your plan	1	
Change investments daily	1	

STOCK OPTIONS

9. At what level is an employee eligible for stock options?

	POINTS	SCORE
No stock options offered	0	
Top management only	0.75	
Middle management and above	1.0	
Professional staff and above	1.25	
All full-time staff	1.5	

LONG-TERM DISABILITY

10. If you become disabled, how much is your long-term disability benefit?

PERCENTAGE OF PAY	POINTS	%	SCORE
No coverage	0	Multiply by	
49% of pay or less	0.5	x percentage of =	
50% to 59% of pay	0.75	premium paid	
60% of pay or more	1.0	by employer.	

LIFE INSURANCE

11. How much life insurance does your company provide?

ANSWER	POINTS	SCORE
No coverage	0	
Less than one times pay	0.5	
One times pay	0.75	
Two times pay or more	1.0	

Add up your points for questions 1 through 11 to calculate your total points.

	TOTAL SCORE

HOW DOES YOUR COMPANY RATE?

EXCELLENT COVERAGE   52 points or more: Lucky you. Most of the ingredients of a great benefits package are already in your plan.

GOOD COVERAGE   42 points to 51 points: Assess whether your package will provide enough retirement income for your lifestyle.

TYPICAL COVERAGE   32 points to 41 points: Meet with your benefits administrator to make sure you understand all the features in your plan.

Chances are, if you're married, both you and your spouse have access to health plans at work. Which one is best? To find out, you'll need to comb through the provisions of each to see how you can get the best features for the least amount of money. When scrutinizing plans, consider each of these important factors:

- **Deductibles.** Count on shelling out about $200 to $300 a year on employer plans. On individual plans, the deductible is personally selected. Remember the general rule about these deductibles, however: The higher the deductible, the higher your reimbursement and the lower the payment.
- **Out-of-pocket maximums.** If you anticipate high medical bills, compare the maximum amount each plan requires you to pay before it picks up 100% of the tab.
- **Choice of providers.** Just because one plan may have more doctors doesn't necessarily make it a better choice. You'll want to make sure that the doctor you'd use in any managed-care network is not oversubscribed. You can find out how harried physicians are by calling the provider or the doctor directly and asking how many patients he or she has. Don't forget to see which hospitals, labs, and pharmacies are affiliated with each plan. If your favorite pharmacy or the hospital you prefer isn't in the group, you may not want to join the managed-care plan.

Almost half of large U.S. companies now offer **flexible spending accounts (FSAs)**, which let you pay for certain unreimbursable medical costs, child care costs, and perhaps commuting costs with pretax dollars. Here's how they work: You decide how much you'd like to place in your FSA during the year (typically between $2,000 and $5,000), and the amount gets zapped from your paychecks in equal installments before taxes. When you need access to the funds (for such costs as health deductibles, prescription eyeglasses, even cab rides to your doctor's office), you simply fill out a claim form for reimbursement. Best of all, with an FSA you can withdraw the maximum amount pledged even before you've paid in the cash for it. Anyone with significant out-of-pocket medical bills—more than a few hundred dollars a year—definitely ought to consider enrolling in a tax-saving FSA, if one is available.

Now, here's the catch with an FSA: You lose any funds that you pledge but don't use during the year. So before signing up for an FSA, carefully gauge how much you think you'll incur in out-of-pocket medical, child care, or commuting costs during the year ahead.

LIFE AND DISABILITY INSURANCE

Most large corporations dole out free life insurance equal to each employee's annual pay. Anything more, say benefits counselors, is considered munificent indeed. Typical, too, is free long-term disability coverage, which pays you as much as 60% of your salary should you become incapacitated.

Is it wise to sign up for extra life and disability insurance, known as **supplemental coverage**, which is often available through your company? Perhaps. If you've determined that you do want to beef up your insurance, check the rates and coverage offered by insurers outside your employer, too. Your company's rates may not be the best. For instance, if you are in good health, are a nonsmoker, and are under the age of 45, you can probably buy term life insurance more cheaply from an agent or a low-load life insurer than through your employer.

RETIREMENT PLANS: IRAs, 401(k)s, 403(b)s, AND 457s

If you work for a company that will help finance your golden years, consider yourself lucky. That help could be in the form of a pension or a match on an employee's 401(k) contribution. Nonprofits often offer similar vehicles, known as 403(b) plans. Named for a section in the tax code, such **defined-contribution plans** let you stash away dollars, before they're taxed, through payroll deductions. The earnings grow in your account tax-deferred. By federal law, employers must offer several places for you to park your 401(k) dough, such as stock and bond funds, money-market funds, and company stock. As a bonus, most employers will match a portion of your contributions, usually 50¢ for every dollar you ante up. (For more detailed advice on the care and feeding of your 401(k), see Chapter 11.)

If your company offers a 401(k) plan, sign up as soon as you're eligible. This may sound about as obvious as "Eat your vegetables," but recent surveys report that about 20% of eligible employees don't participate in their plan. To help make your retirement comfortable, contribute as much as you can afford, as early as you can. Over the next few years, the allowable maximum will rise from $11,000 in 2002 to roughly $16,500 in 2010 (that's when the 2001 tax laws expire). Generally speaking, however, if your salary falls in the top 20% for all earners at your firm, you can probably contribute no more than 6% to 7% of your pretax salary to the plan. Some plans also let you salt away after-tax dollars.

However, the key to maximizing your retirement savings is to diversify the investments in your 401(k) account. Although it may be tempting to load up your 401(k) with company stock, don't! Remember that the employees of the energy giant Enron were gung ho about their company before it took a major dive into bankruptcy in 2001.

As you hopscotch from one job to the next, remember that unlike the assets of a traditional pension plan, the money in a 401(k), a 403(b), and a 457 is fully portable as long as you follow a few rules. In order to escape costly taxes and penalties when you leave company A for company B, you must **roll over** these accounts into an Individual Retirement Account or to your new company's retirement plan. Keep in mind, the clock is ticking. You have just 60 days to do this before the tax man cometh.

To transfer funds properly, do not request a check from your old employer. You'd be taking possession of your retirement assets, which is a sure way to get slapped with the dreaded 20% federal withholding tax. Instead you'll want to do a **trustee-to-trustee transfer**, in which funds go directly into the investment you've selected for your IRA (typically a mutual fund) or from the plan administrator at one job to the next. Before switching jobs, you'll want to discuss these moves with your benefits department to ensure the transfer goes smoothly. The process may take several months or even up to a year.

STOCK OPTIONS

In the last decade, **stock options** have been a boon to millions of Americans. Previously a perk solely for the rich and powerful, options have now gone mainstream and become a crucial part of compensation for many employees. In fact, some 10 million people now have them, according to the National Center for Employee Ownership, a tenfold increase since 1992. No wonder *Fortune* magazine called these lucrative and highly desirable perks "the next best thing to free money."

First, let's be clear about what a stock option really is. An employee stock option is the right given to you by your company to buy ("exercise") a certain number of shares of company stock at a preset price (the **grant, strike**, or **exercise price**) over a certain period of time (the **exercise period**, which typically is up to 10 years). You have two choices: (1) You can buy the stock with your own money at the reduced price and hold on to it. (2) You can buy and sell the stock immediately to reap the gains, which is the difference between your exercise price and the market value on the day you exercise. Either way, that gain is taxed as income. Whenever the stock's market value is greater than the option price, the option is said to be "in the money." Conversely, if the market value is less than the option price, the option is said to be "underwater."

Many people think about options as if they were shares of stock. We look at them a little differently. While the value of options fluctuates with the price of stocks, in other ways they are more akin to cash bonuses that vary in value depending on the future prospects of your employer. Unlike a regular bonus, however, you don't have to pay taxes when you're granted the options—only when you exercise them—which gives you the added benefit of tax deferral. Plus, with stock options you don't have to put up any of your own capital to generate income. (The longer you hold on to your options, the more likely the stock price will rise.)

For a minor fee, you can ask a broker to do a cashless transaction, in which you simultaneously exercise your options and sell the shares. This way you maximize the inherent leverage of options. You commit no capital, and you reap the windfall in cash.

Although you can keep the company stock when you exercise (instead of cashing out), we don't recommend that strategy. First, you will have to put up your own money to buy the stock. (Say good-bye to the "free money" concept of options.) Second, you may already be overweighted in company stock if, say, your employer uses stock for the company match portion of your 401(k) retirement savings plan.

DEFERRED COMPENSATION PLANS

Another form of forced savings, these plans are designed for highly paid executives who can afford to put aside a portion of their earnings. You make an election to defer a bonus or part of your salary until a stated time and you are not taxed on the income until you actually receive it. By deferring part of your compensation, you hope to avoid a current tax of, say, 35% or 38.6%, and ultimately pay tax at a lower rate on funds that have appreciated tax-free in the meantime. To set up a deferred compensation plan, you must enter a written arrangement with your employer.

OTHER CORPORATE GOODIES

In this age of diminishing corporate givebacks, there is some good news. More companies are willing to offer **family-friendly benefits**—perks that tend to be easy on the corporate coffers and, in turn, raise job satisfaction among employees. Some of these perks may be unwritten, and still others may be up for negotiating. So check out the ones below, and if your employer doesn't offer them, try politely to push for a change in policy:

- **Telecommuting.** These days, millions of workers perform some part of their job via a computer connected to their employer. Some telecommute employees work directly out of their home and others travel to technology telework centers, which have computers, fax, etc., but are much closer to home than the office.

- **Flextime.** Flextime lets workers forgo standard hours and put in ones best suited to them. Because flexible schedules demand increased efficiency of employees, many firms actually view these arrangements as a boon to productivity. If you have only a few years on the job, you probably won't be permitted to work flextime, since management may be skeptical of your ability to pull off such an arrangement. Once you have five or more years under your belt, though, you may be able to strike a deal.

- **Vacation and comp days.** It's common to start at a new company with two weeks of vacation, more for senior executives. What do you do if you get just two weeks or so but put in dozens of unpaid overtime hours on weekends and holidays? One way to get your due—and to potentially extend your vacation—is to keep a tally of those phantom hours and request time off for them. You've got nothing to lose by asking.

- **Employee Assistance Programs and referral services.** Need a good lawyer? Want help in sizing up college choices for your teen? Believe it or not, your company may be able to help. Roughly 55% of all Fortune 500 companies now boast referral services that assist employees with everything from finding a reliable babysitter to counseling about spousal abuse. Some firms even have the equivalent of a concierge on their premises, ready to help make your life outside work a little easier. Depending on where you work, these programs may be formal or informal, offered on or off site. Ask your benefits counselor whether such programs are available. Before spilling private secrets about your life to an employee assistance counselor, however, find out who could ultimately have access to that information. You may find that getting a little help at work isn't worth the invasion of your privacy.

- **Child care assistance.** According to a 1998 study conducted by the Families and Work Institute, 9% of companies with 100 employees or more reported they had child care available at or near the worksite. Nearly half offered **dependent-care assistance plans (DCAP)** that help employees pay for child care with pretax dollars. But only 5% offered vouchers or other subsidies for the payment of employee child care. Only 4% of the companies had backup or emergency care. If your regular sitter gets sick at the last minute, for instance, your child could spend the day (or before- and after-school hours) at an on-site company facility. Because these services are either free or low-cost for parents, they are wildly popular, making availability extremely limited.

Some employers also offer flexible spending accounts that let employees set aside a specified amount of money, pretax for child care expenses. A pretax child care FSA is a great deal, but you can't use it if you claim the child care credit on your tax return. So if you already take the credit, you may need to run some numbers to see if you'll save more on taxes with an FSA or with the credit.

If you feel that your company is below the curve on the child care score, speak up. Get together with other colleagues who would like to see some sort of child care plan and approach your manager or benefits counselor with a workable arrangement, such as a successful one in use by a nearby firm or competitor.

- **Financial planning and legal advice.** A fairly recent trend in the employee benefits field is the offering of financial and legal advice to employees. Often such seminars are free and quite useful. Just be careful that the speaker isn't there to hawk his or her own products or business. Unions sometimes provide such services to their members, too. Members of the United Auto Workers, for instance, are entitled to free legal services, such as the drafting of wills. So even if your boss doesn't pay you what you deserve, you might to able to use his office to learn how to make the dollars you do earn stretch farther.

CHAPTER 10

Paying for Your Child's College Education

Nobody needs to tell you that the cost of college is out of sight—and headed even higher. The College Board's Annual Survey of Colleges estimates that tuition, room, and fees these days average about $8,470 a year at a public college and $22,541 at a private one. And if your child has his eye on one of the elites, such as an Ivy League school, make the yearly average $39,310 (includes tuition, room, board, books, fees). Worse still, by 2011, the average price of a four-year college degree will range from $20,829 to $28,562 per year (range done by region, the first being the south, the least expensive, the latter being the northeast, the most pricey). Still thinking Ivy League? Then prepare to shell out $62,726 a year. In general, you can expect the cost of tuition and fees to rise about 5.5% a year over the next decade.

But don't throw up your hands just yet. Though sobering, the figures aren't quite as daunting as they sound. Don't forget that your income will be rising just as college costs increase. So that fatter paycheck will help cover some of the tuition bills. Also, your child will likely qualify for some financial aid in the form of grants, scholarships, loans, or campus jobs. On average, about 65% of traditional undergraduates (full-time, full-year students) have at least half their costs met by financial aid. The average amount of financial aid received: $8,295 a year (from all sources including federal, state, institutional, and private). Borrowers who get federal loans take out an average of $4,774 a year. Plus tax-sheltered college savings plans such as the 529 plan and Education Savings Account and tax initiatives like the Hope Scholarship Credit and the Lifelong Learning Credit can help soften the blow. Still, there's no question that a chunk of money for college will come directly out of your family budget. So to give your child the widest possible choice of schools when the time comes, you'll need to do two things: Start saving for college as early as you can and, as application time approaches, search out all possible sources of financial help.

Figuring How Much You Will Need

Until your child has actually been accepted to a college and secured a financial aid package, it's impossible to know exactly what costs you'll face. After all, your income, the financial aid formulas, and the inflation rate for tuition bills will change over time. As a result, the farther off college is for your child, the more tentative your estimates will have to be. Still, by making some preliminary calculations now—even if your son or daughter is just starting to crawl—you'll gain a firmer sense of the financial challenges that lie ahead.

Virtually every family can get some kind of financial help putting a child through college, if only through a government-guaranteed loan. At the same time, though, virtually every household sending a child to college is expected to kick in its share of college costs, known as the **family contribution**, based on its income, family size, and debts. Unfortunately, it will be up to the college and the federal or state government to determine the minimum size of that contribution, not you. As a result, the amount of aid your family qualifies for will be, at best, the difference between that designated contribution and the full cost of the college your child chooses. (A fuller description of negotiating an aid package appears later in this chapter.) If the college your child will go to is financially strapped, the size of his or her aid package may be even less than that. For a rough preview of how much your required family contribution might be today, go to the Web sites listed in the box "College Savings, Financial Aid, and Scholarship Web Sites" on page 224 to find online calculators. You can also check out the "How Small Savings Can Add Up" table in Chapter 5 to see how long it would take to save, say, $50,000 if you put away $20 a week in an account earning 7% interest. Answer: 20 years.

Once you have this approximate number in hand, you may be pleasantly surprised or shocked and appalled at the amount of saving it will take to pay for your son's or daughter's education. Armed with this information, however, you'll be ready to devise a strategy to meet—or at least approach—your goal.

Tax-Sheltered College Savings Plans

The good news on the college savings front comes in the form of two important tax-sheltered savings: the **529 college savings plans** and **Coverdell Education Savings Accounts** (formerly known as **Education IRAs**). In most cases, the tax breaks the plans offer make them preferable to other college savings vehicles, including custodial accounts.

529 COLLEGE SAVINGS PLANS

The **529 college savings plans** (www.collegesavings.org), named after the section of the tax code that governs them, allow anyone, regardless of income, to open an account and invest a hefty amount in stock and bond funds (more than $150,000 in many states). Most plans let you in with as little as $25 a month. The money can be used at any school in the country, and you keep control until the child goes to college. Best of all: The plan offers tax breaks of its own.

Given the generous tax advantages—plus the opportunity to shelter enough cash to actually make a dent in those six-figure tuition bills—529s are on their way to becoming the collegiate version of the 401(k), but even better. Though all 529 earnings are free of federal tax, some will be subject to minimal state taxes (though even these will not apply in most cases). Today most states operate 529 savings plans, plus many of them offer a tax deduction for 529 contributions. More good news: States are increasingly turning over the operation of their 529s to established money-management firms such as TIAA-CREF, Fidelity, Merrill Lynch, and Salomon Smith Barney. If your state does not offer a deduction, consider looking into another state's 529 plans, which are often available to residents of any state. However, before signing on with the state whose investment firm you prefer, investigate the fees involved.

Unlike 401(k)s, 529s may not be right for everyone. One major limitation is the lack of flexibility: Once you select an investment option, you can change it only once a year. If you need to tap the account for any reason other than education, you will pay a 10% penalty. Another flaw: A 529 account can end up hurting your chances of obtaining financial aid (as we'll explain further down).

So how do you know if a 529 is for you? Shortcomings and all, 529 plans are a hard-to-beat way to boost your college savings—provided you meet one of these four criteria:

- **You're in an above-average federal tax bracket, with time to save.** That would be the 30%, 35%, and 38.6% brackets. The critical advantage that 529 plans offer is tax-free compounding. Investors in lower tax brackets can benefit as well, but, as you'll see below, those parents need to focus on more than taxes.
- **You think you won't qualify for financial aid.** That's because the tax savings you get in a 529 plan blow up if you might qualify for financial aid—parents currently earning less than $100,000. Here's why. Under financial aid formulas, 529s are counted as the parents' asset until you withdraw the money. Gains from a 529 count as the student's income, up to 50% of which is considered available to pay tuition.
- **You live in New York, Michigan, or another high-tax state with significant 529 tax breaks.** If your state offers a generous tax deduction on 529 contributions, take a serious look at the plan even if you are in a lower tax bracket.
- **You're a grandparent looking to reduce your estate.** You can deposit up to $55,000 ($110,000 for a married couple) into a 529 plan without incurring the federal gift tax, making 529s an ideal way to move a big sum out of your estate quickly. A $55,000 contribution is counted against your $11,000 annual gift exclusion over five years, so you won't be able to make another tax-free gift to that beneficiary for six years.

Your first step should be to look at your own state's plan (if it has one). Some states also offer scholarships to participants of 529 plans. If your state taxes are high and your local plan offers generous tax benefits, you can stop reading here: Your best bet may be staying at home.

But what if you live in a state with low or no taxes—or with limited tax breaks? Then it's time to shop around for the best plan with a good manager and consider these points.

- **Stick with low-cost plans.** Expense ratios vary considerably. Some states' plans are sold by brokers, which layers on additional costs.
- **You could also pay other fees.** Some states charge to open an account; others tack on annual fees, although you can often get the up-front or annual fee waived if you sign up for an automatic investment program—or if you buy directly by phone or on the Web.
- **Look for the right investment choices, not the most.** The typical 529 menu is still fairly limited. In most plans, the key offering is an age-based portfolio, which gradually shifts the asset allocation as your child ages. For children under three, for example, some 80% of the portfolio may be stashed in stocks. As your child grows, the equity portion shrinks, so that by the time he or she is 18, the assets are held mainly in bonds or cash, ensuring that you can meet that first tuition bill.

Increasingly, states are adding conventional stock and bond funds to the original age-based portfolios. But because you can't switch your money around as freely as you can in a 401(k), having a vast number of choices isn't much of an advantage—and is potentially riskier. For most investors, the best choice is an age-based portfolio. You can also create your own stock and bond mix by opening more than one account in the child's name—one for each asset class—and controlling your own allocation by the amounts you invest in each.

In the past, these funds were criticized by financial advisers, as well as by **MONEY**, as being too heavily oriented toward fixed-income assets, even during the child's youngest years. However, even though more plans offer a wider range of asset allocation plans, a conservative strategy may be the most sensible. People forget that they usually have fewer years to save for college than for retirement—most often 10 years or less, since they tend to start late. If you lose a lot in the early years, it's very hard to make it up.

COVERDELL EDUCATION SAVINGS ACCOUNTS

As of 2002, you'll be able to invest $2,000 a year per child in an **Education Savings Account** and put the money toward the cost of kindergarten through high school, not just college. The phase-out range for married people filing jointly has been $190,000 to $220,000 of **adjusted gross income (AGI)**. (Your AGI is your wages, small-business profits, investment and pension income minus certain deductions such as unreimbursed business and medical expenses, IRA contributions, and alimony.) Contributions to these accounts are with after-tax dollars; however, withdrawals are tax-free if used to pay eligible education expenses. You can fund both a 529 and an Education Savings Account for the same student in the same year penalty-free. (Also, new legislation means those with education IRAs are now also eligible for Hope or Lifetime college tuition credit.) These accounts can be set up at most banks, brokerages, and some credit unions.

CUSTODIAL ACCOUNTS

Putting money in an account in your child's name can be a smart move—but only up to a certain point. Under the Uniform Gifts to Minors laws, you can pass along up to $10,000 a year to your child free of taxes (two parents can give $20,000). And that money can be invested however you wish.

The benefit: The IRS rules allow children under 14 to earn $750 a year tax-free; the next $750 will be taxed at his or her own rate, usually 10%. (Note: the amount increases each year. Assuming your investments earn 8% on average, the portfolio wouldn't throw off that much income until it tops $15,000.) But remember that once the portfolio is earning more than that, it will be taxed at your rate until your child is 14. What's more, money in your child's name may limit his financial aid down the road, because standard financial aid formulas require kids to fork over 35% of their assets before qualifying for help. You can retain control of the assets until your child is 18 (or 21 in some states) by investing in his or her name in a **Uniform Gifts to Minors Act (UGMA) custodial account** or by setting up a **2503(c) trust**. But after that point, the money in your child's name is his, not yours. If he uses it to spring for a souped-up Jeep Wrangler rather than college, there's nothing you can do about it. In short, the minor tax advantage of putting college savings in your child's name is almost certainly not worth the disadvantages.

So here's a reasonable compromise: Put a limited amount into a custodial account, just enough to qualify for the tax break. Then put the rest into a 529 plan.

The Best Investment Strategy for College Savings

Whether you choose a 529 or a Coverdell Education Savings Account, or decide to save in taxable accounts you manage yourself, the biggest factor in devising your college savings plan is the age of your kids. The younger they are, the more years you'll have to make your cash grow. If your children are very young, you have enough time to weather any short-term setbacks to your progress and can then invest heavily in higher-risk, higher-return securities. Meanwhile, however, inflation will be running alongside you all those years, pushing up the price of the education you're saving for. With older kids, your situation is reversed. A few more years of college inflation won't hurt you too much. But with fewer years to grow your cash, you'll need larger amounts of it to seed your college fund. So keeping your college stash safe will take priority over investing for the fattest returns. Here are the most sensible saving strategies, depending on the age of your child:

- **If college is eight or more years off.** Your biggest challenge is to out-race inflation, which can easily double current college costs before your child becomes a freshman. To stay ahead of inflation, you'll need an aggressive portfolio, and that means mostly—or exclusively—stocks. To lessen the odds that a slide in the U.S. stock market will crack your entire college saving nest egg, keep 80% or so of your money in stocks and the rest in bonds. (For a fuller description of portfolio diversification, see Chapter 13.)

- **If college is four to seven years off.** With college closing in, you need to back off a bit from full throttle and adjust your portfolio to the possibility that a big downturn in the stock market could badly crimp your savings efforts. So now is the time to start moving 10% to 15% of your aggressive stock holdings each year into more conservative investments, such as safe bond funds that buy short- to intermediate-term U.S. Treasury securities.
- **If college is only one to three years off.** For you, stocks are becoming way too risky to pay those looming tuition bills. So continue cashing out until no more than 10% of your portfolio is still in stocks—preferably in a conservative stock fund. Put the rest in short-term bond funds with maturities of four years or less and money-market funds. If your 529 savings are in an aggressive growth account (mostly stocks), see if you can open up another account using a more conservative allocation model to funnel new money into.
- **If college is less than a year away and your savings are in taxable accounts.** As your child begins packing for college, transfer enough cash to a money-market fund to see you through his freshman-year bills. Put the rest of your college savings in bank certificates of deposit timed to mature at the beginning of his sophomore, junior, and senior years. By staggering the investment lengths, you'll get maximum returns. If college is right around the corner and you haven't got the money you need, don't panic. But be sure to read "How to Borrow Wisely for College" and "Installment Plan for College" sections later in this chapter.

Tax Credits for College Students

While your student is in school, you can claim a **Hope Scholarship Credit** (up to $1,500) or a **Lifetime Learning Credit** up to $1,000 in 2002 and $2,000 in 2003 and beyond. You can't take a credit for expenses paid for with tax-free earnings from an Education Savings Account or 529 plan, so careful record keeping is a must. Nor will you be able to claim either credit if you take the new college costs deduction for the same student in the same year. If you face that choice—a possibility for a couple with an AGI under $100,000—calculate both options. A credit is generally more valuable, but taxpayers who qualify for just a partial credit may come out ahead with the deduction, which will go into effect in 2002 and will run through 2005.

If you are now paying off loans, you are more likely to be able to deduct up to $2,500 in student-loan interest in 2002. That's because the income cutoffs will be higher, and eligibility will extend for the life of the loan, not just the first 60 months of repayment.

Snagging the Best Financial Aid Package

There are three elements to most financial aid offers: **scholarships or grants, loans**, and a **campus job**. In name, at least, most packages are put together based on a family's financial need. If your income is $50,000 or less and you have few assets beyond your home, your child is certain to qualify for some form of help. Even with an income of $100,000 and few other assets, your family may still receive financial aid if you have two or more children attending college. If you qualify for aid, you can expect to receive between 65% and 100% of your need, according to standard aid formulas. The rest, however, must come from you.

In reality, though, how much aid your child actually receives and what form it takes depends partly on how well you and your student work the financial aid game.

HIRING AN INDEPENDENT COLLEGE COUNSELOR

If you don't think you're getting the best advice from your high school college placement office, you may want to consider hiring an **independent college counselor** to help you and your teen prepare and apply to college (including filling out the financial aid forms). Most of these pros are former admissions officers or high school advisers who now work on their own.

How can you tell if you should hire a personal college trainer to work with your child? Many public school advisers do a fine job with college planning and are respected by top colleges, so be sure to give your high school counselor a chance. A good public school adviser will start the college process during your child's junior year, offering advice and information on test preparation, college admissions, and financial aid deadlines. A good counselor should also be willing to talk about the admissions records of previous graduates. If you don't see this kind of activity, or if your child's counselor is notably unhelpful or too busy for one-on-one college meetings, then it's time to consider striking out on your own.

First, bear in mind that hiring a professional is not the only option. You can always carve out time to study colleges in guidebooks and on the Internet, looking for schools that offer a major in your child's main area of interest. Virtually all colleges have their own Web sites, and detailed information on financial aid and scholarships is available on such sites as www.finaid.org, www.fastweb.com, and www.collegeboard. org.

Of course, you may not have the time to spend researching colleges. Or perhaps you have to deal with divorce or another issue that can complicate your financial aid calculations. Or maybe you just want the comfort of expert guidance when faced with the prospect of spending $100,000 or more on college. In any of these cases, you may want to hire an independent adviser. Expect to pay a flat fee of $800 to $2,500, depending on where you live and the counselor's level of expertise; some will charge by the hour, typically $70 to $200.

To pick the best adviser, start looking early, since most college counselors prefer to begin planning during your child's sophomore or junior year of high school. Mark Sklarow, executive director of the Independent Educational Consultants Association (IECA), a Fairfax, Va., trade group, says that good advisers "should know which schools have generous financial aid policies and where [each] student might qualify for a package." Most counselors permit a free initial interview. Here's a quick checklist of what to look for:

- **Credentials.** Anyone can hang out a shingle as an educational consultant, including parents who got their kids into college and now consider themselves experts. Obviously, you want someone with years of experience. The IECA accepts only applicants who have worked several years as school-based counselors or college admissions officers; members must also regularly tour colleges and meet with admissions officers. Princeton Review and Kaplan, which are launching counseling services, may offer less experienced advisers supervised by veterans. (To get a list of IECA members in your area, call 800-808-4322 or go to www.educationalconsulting.org.)

  Keep in mind that advisers differ in background and training. Though most are knowledgeable on financial aid, some may also have expertise in assisting gifted students or those with learning disabilities. If you need specialized help, don't settle for a generalist.
- **References.** Any good counselor should be able to provide the names of several previous clients; be sure to call them to ask about their experiences. Also inquire about the prospective counselor's relationship with your public school adviser. Remember that your school adviser will be the one sending out references and transcripts. A testy relationship could be a problem.

- **No guarantees.** No reputable independent counselor will promise admission to a specific college or a guarantee of scholarship money; if they do, walk away. And steer clear of advisers who seem to push a particular school or boast of a close relationship with college admissions officers. As it happens, most counselors rarely contact college admissions or aid officers about individual students—and then only when a problem arises.

  Also avoid any adviser who recommends a wholesale financial makeover to maximize your chances of financial aid. Pouring money into annuities or dumping your stock portfolio could improve your aid prospects, but you'll be no better off if your finances are tied into knots.

- **Clear costs.** All charges should be stated up front and in writing. Unless the help you need takes only two or three hours—say, you want to review five or six schools that are interested in recruiting your star soccer-player daughter—you're better off arranging a flat fee.

  For instance, the Education Credit Corporation is a college financial aid counseling service that offers help to high school juniors and seniors looking for the best financial aid package to suit their needs. The service not only aids in finding the right financial aid package, it also helps students file the related paperwork and fill out the applications correctly. There is an initial consultation fee of $125 and costs thereafter can range depending on the services used, but on average fees hover around $500. For more information, call 800-477-4977.

  A package deal may include guidance over several years, including regularly scheduled meetings and phone access. Some independent counselors may even help your son or daughter choose high school courses and summer work opportunities that can burnish a college application.

  But the counselor should not offer to write a student's essay or prepare the applications. "The students have to take responsibility for themselves," says Steven Antonoff, a Denver educational consultant. After all, he says, "that's the point of going to college."

Ins and Outs of Financial Aid

To help boost the amount and quality of the financial aid package your child receives, keep the following in mind:

When asked why he robbed banks, Willie Sutton replied: "Because that's where the money is." State schools generally save their greatest subsidies for home-grown students. Private colleges generally have the richest endowment coffers. Before your child decides where he'll send his college applications, do a little homework on how much cash each of the colleges under consideration has to spread around. You can get such information by asking the college financial aid offices directly for the average percentage of costs covered by their aid packages and what portion of it is given in grants. Alternatively, you can check college guidebooks and Web sites (see box below) that contain data about financial aid and scholarships.

COLLEGE SAVINGS, FINANCIAL AID, AND SCHOLARSHIP WEB SITES

www.collegesavings.org The official 529 plan site, sponsored by the National Association of State Treasurers, where you can find links to plans in your state.

www.savingforcollege.com Run by 529 plan expert Joseph Hurley, this site provides regular updates on college savings plans. You can find details about each plan's strengths and weaknesses, as well as a lively message board.

www.finaid.org At this one-stop shop for college planning, you can find everything from aid-eligibility calculators to scholarship searches to detailed explanations of student loans.

www.collegeboard.org The purveyors of the dreaded SATs can help with the financial aid process. Their site offers calculators, scholarship searches, and useful facts.

www.fastweb.com Best known for its searchable database of 400,000 scholarships, this site also provides general financial aid info—including calculators—as well as tips on admission.

WORK THE FINANCIAL AID RULES TO YOUR BENEFIT

First, some background. When your child applies for financial aid, you must file the **Free Application for Federal Student Aid (FAFSA)**, which covers government aid and is used by most public colleges (800-4-FEDAID; www.fafsa.ed.gov). The application is available in public libraries, college financial aid offices, and high school guidance counselors' offices nationwide. The College Board's CSS/Financial Aid PROFILE (800-778-6888; www.collegeboard.com) is also used, but primarily by private colleges. The **PROFILE** is a customized form, involving a two-step process. The first step, the registration form, can be found in high school guidance counselors' offices, public libraries, or online. This form must be completed via the Internet or by phone, not by mail. Once the registration step is completed, the second step, the personalized PROFILE application (based on your registration data and college choices) will then be made available to you.

There are two formulas used to calculate your **Expected Family Contribution (EFC)**—the theoretical amount you and your child can finance each year toward college. Typically the **Federal Methodology (FM)** is used by public colleges and universities and the **College Board Institutional Methodology (IM)** is used by private institutions. If the EFC is less than the full cost of college, the school—again, in theory—will make up the difference with grants, student loans (which are often interest free while in college), and work-study jobs. The book *Paying for College Without Going Broke* (Kalman A. Chany and Geoff Martz, Random House, $18, 2002 edition) has the most up-to-date formulas. Read each line of the form carefully so you don't wind up shortchanging yourself.

Colleges use different variations of the PROFILE form. Depending on the schools selected when you register to apply on www.collegeboard.com, you will be asked different questions on the PROFILE application. In addition to the FAFSA and the PRO-FILE, some colleges may require you to fill out their own institutional admissions application. These are usually available at the colleges' financial aid offices or on their Web sites.

Review each college's financial aid literature to determine what forms are required and make sure you know each filing deadline. Tardiness can be costly, because most schools will consider a late financial aid form only after awarding aid to on-time applicants. By then, the majority of funds may be gone.

Filing procedures and forms change from year to year so be sure your information and paperwork relate to the academic year for which you are seeking aid. The following figures are based on the 2002–2003 academic year. According to the Federal

Methodology aid formula, students should contribute about 35% of their assets to pay for college. According to the College Board Institutional Methodology aid formula, which is used by many private colleges when awarding their own aid, students will be expected to contribute about 25% of their own assets.

Under the IM formula, up to 5% of parents' assets will be deemed available for college expenses, while up to 46% of their current income (after certain deductions) will be. Some assets are excluded; for example, 401(k) savings plans from employers or other retirement savings vehicles don't count as current assets. However, the amount contributed is considered untaxed in both aid formulas. (In the FM formula, home equity is also excluded.)

If you have two kids in college at the same time, you'll be expected to contribute 60% for each. With three, you'll pay 45%. And with four or more children in college during the same academic year, you'll pay 35%.

Under the FM formula used by public colleges, each additional dollar of asset will raise the expected family contribution a maximum of 5.65¢, while up to 46% of your current income (after certain deductions) could be accounted as available for college expenses. If you have more than one child in college during an academic year, the expected family contribution is divided by the number of dependent children in college.

By taking those assessment rules into account, be prepared to make some shrewd financial moves before you apply. But remember: The **base income year** (the one colleges use to make their financial aid decisions) is the tax year preceding the academic year for which you are seeking aid. For example, Jan. 1 of the child's junior year of high school to Dec. 31 of his senior year is the base income for the typical freshman starting college immediately after high school. So if you plan to make some changes, make them in time to possibly qualify for more aid. Here are some guidelines:

- **Don't overvalue your assets.** You have to disclose your income and assets—but you don't have to include retirement accounts like IRAs and 401(k)s or equity in your primary home.
- **Pay off consumer debt.** This debt is not considered in financial needs analysis, and paying it off will reduce your assets and boost your aid prospects.
- **Consider such moves as accelerating bonuses or taking capital gains before the base income year.** For instance, if you're planning to get rid of an appreciated asset to pay for college, do it more than a year before filling out the financial aid form. That way you will avoid having your gain counted as income just when your child is applying for tuition money and thus raise the size of any financial aid package.

- **Include the right people.** For divorced parents, figuring out whose financial information to report can be tricky. The short answer: If your child spends most of the year living with you, you need to disclose your own income and assets, but not your ex's. If you have remarried, you must include your new spouse's finances.
- **Ask questions.** Aside from counselors and financial aid offices, there are many places to get advice if you find the FAFSA confusing. Start with the free hotlines at Sallie Mae (800-891-4599) and the U.S. Department of Education (800-433-3243) or go to the Web sites listed earlier in the chapter.

Two more tips: First, a college may be stingy in allocating its financial resources to your child if its financial aid office feels you haven't explored all other opportunities, so make sure you've checked out all possible outside scholarships and grants. Second, send in the application forms as early as you can. The size of your total aid package won't change if you're a late applicant, but the best grants and most lucrative campus jobs may be gone as early as December.

SIX QUESTIONS YOU NEED TO ASK ABOUT FINANCIAL AID

Whether you choose to hire a counselor or do the work yourself, you still need to understand the tricky financial aid application process. Don't rely solely on college marketing brochures or the advice of experts; check all information and requirements, such as deadlines and required forms, with the college. To avoid some common pitfalls, here are six key questions to ask the financial aid officers:

1. **Do you always meet full financial need?** Don't be surprised if the answer is no. Today only a few dozen well-endowed colleges follow the traditional practice of providing enough financial aid to allow all students who are admitted to attend. So if a college claims that it meets full need, ask if that applies to everyone, including students admitted from the waiting list.

   To stretch their aid dollars, some colleges choose to **gap**—that is, meet only a portion of a student's financial need. Gapping can work in different ways: A college might meet the full need of only a portion of its students; other schools may aim to meet a percentage of assessed need across the board—say, 75% of need for all aid applicants. You may not know about the gapping policy unless you ask, since colleges rarely volunteer this information.

2. **How are your financial aid packages structured?** Ask your prospective college how the amount of grant money, which does not have to be repaid, compares with

loans or work-study jobs—obviously, the more grant money, the better. (Many schools employ what's called **preferential packaging**: The most desirable students get a bigger hunk of grant money and fewer loans or work-study requirements.) In addition, be sure to look past the first year's award. Even if the total aid package doesn't change after your son's or daughter's freshman year, be aware that the loan portion will probably increase and the grant percentage will shrink.

You should also ask about the average indebtedness of the college's graduates. Ending up with more than $15,000 in debt—not unusual at many private colleges— could be a big burden to a graduate who enters a low-paying career.

3. **Can I keep my outside scholarship?** For students who are academic or athletic stars, you will want to know how scholarship money from a source other than the college is treated. Until recently, many schools simply used such awards to replace the grant portion of the financial aid package, leaving the student no better off. But today, more colleges are allowing students to enjoy greater benefits from the awards. Ask about your prospective school's policy.

4. **Do you offer merit awards, and can my child qualify?** Apart from some highly selective schools, most colleges are dangling merit scholarship awards, and at times engaging in bidding wars, to get the best possible recruits. Even a B student may be highly sought after. Find out how your child's record compares with the SAT scores and grade-point average of the college's freshman class. If your child ranks in the top 20%, he or she is a good candidate for a merit-based scholarship at many schools.

5. **How does early decision affect the financial aid package?** An estimated 54,000 anxious students applied early decision in 2001—a jump of 30% from two years ago—in the belief that they would have a better shot at their first-choice college. The downside: They had far lower chances of getting the best possible financial aid deal. If you need aid, college counselors advise that you should not apply early decision. You can't be certain of the aid package you will get until April. Moreover, you won't have the ability to leverage competing offers, which can lead to a better aid package.

6. **What is your appeal process?** Nowadays colleges expect parents to negotiate aid packages. That doesn't mean you should automatically ask for more money. To persuade the financial aid officer to reconsider your package, you need to offer a specific reason, such as a higher award from an equally prestigious school or new information about your finances. Ask the aid officer what procedure you should follow to make an appeal and how quickly you need to deliver the information. And be polite, not demanding.

- **Negotiate from your strengths.** All schools want the brightest, most talented, and most interesting students they can find. Consequently, if your child is blessed with above average qualities academically, athletically, musically, socially, or otherwise, be sure he emphasizes them when filling out his college application.

- **Don't settle for the first offer you get.** Here's a little secret about financial aid: The package your child is offered isn't necessarily the best he can receive from that college. A bit of negotiating on your part can up the offer. So if your son is accepted at his first-choice school, but the financial aid offer is not to your liking, try testing the school's true interest in him. Call the financial aid office and explain that your child wants to attend the school but you simply can't swing it on the offered package. Mention any information you might have left out of the original application, such as support for your aging parents, high living costs in your area, or any new developments such as a job loss or a recent medical emergency. If another college, equally prestigious but less appealing to your child, offered a better package, use that as a bargaining chip, too.

- **Don't conclude your argument on the phone.** Tell the financial aid office that you'll be following up with a written statement that recapitulates all your points. Then do so. And keep a confident outlook. There are no guarantees, of course, but neither are there any penalties for asking. A college will not withdraw its acceptance or reduce your aid package simply because you challenge it.

Scholarships, Grants, and Other Freebies

The best kind of financial aid, of course, is an outright gift of money that you don't have to pay back. Depending on your family's economic circumstances, your child's brainpower, and your persistence in pursuing all possibilities, you may be able to secure more free cash than you think. Here's where to look:

Although you may be bombarded with offers, avoid pricey scholarship search services or books that promise to reveal "little known" sources of scholarship cash. The sad truth is that **portable scholarships**—the kind you can use at any school of your choice—are generally so small ($2,000 on average) that your child would need to earn a half dozen to make a real dent in college costs. Most scholarship awards of any real size come through individual colleges themselves. For online links to more than a thousand Web sites with scholarship information, visit the FinAid Web site (www.finaid.org).

You may be thinking that your family's income is too high to qualify for a scholarship. Not necessarily. Even if your family is well-off, your child may be able to snag an award if he's a good student. The definition of that will vary according to the academic standards of the college and the high school he graduates from. Generally, though, a good student is someone with a 3.5 average in high school and a score of 1200 or better on the **Scholastic Assessment Test (SAT)**. And don't rule out the possibility of other scholarships that aren't academics- or need-based, such as those given out for musical or athletic talent. Your child can improve his chances of getting a scholarship, however, if he targets a school where his academic standing makes him a star. Generally, this means choosing a less prestigious school than he could actually qualify for, a move worth considering only if the college is one that your child can be happy attending.

Your child may also be able to score a scholarship by gaining admission to one of the honors programs at state colleges. Most schools require above average grades and Scholastic Achievement Test scores; however, exact standards are set by each school. In addition to getting into special seminars and individual tutorials, plus meeting classmates as smart as he is, he'll become eligible for scholarships that are often the richest the school has to offer. For example, Ohio University's Honors Tutorial College looks for students who have an SAT score of at least 1300 and are in the top 10% of their high school graduating class. Most of the 230 students in the program get awards of $2,000 to full in-state tuition a year.

Many but not all colleges require students to file a second aid application form, in addition to the FAFSA, that may collect supplemental information or may be a separate, stand-alone form like the PROFILE, in order to be eligible for nonfederal (college-supplied) aid. Also, while need-based grants require "strong financial need," merit-based grants do not.

The federal government sponsors two programs for grants, whose money is provided outright and need not be repaid:

Pell grants (named after the senator who wrote the legislation creating them) are essentially guaranteed to every student who qualifies for the aid. The maximum amount of the grant changes every year, based on funding from Congress, but the average award in 2000–2001 was around $2,045. The amount awarded to a student is essentially equal to the maximum grant amount, $3,300 in 2000–2001, minus the student's expected family contribution.

Supplemental Educational Opportunity Grants (SEOGs) are not guaranteed, however. There is a statutory requirement that schools provide SEOGs first to students with exceptional financial need (defined as lowest expected family contribution) and give priority to Pell recipients. While the maximum SEOG is $4,000, the average is about $700. Also, whereas about one in four post-secondary undergraduates receives a Pell grant, only about one in 20 is granted a SEOG.

States, too, offer significant grant aid, though some require a student to use that aid at a public, state institution or provide service to the state after graduation. Not always, though. In Georgia, for instance, through the HOPE (Helping Outstanding Pupils Educationally) program, high school students with a 3.0 grade-point average can receive up to full tuition, books ($100 a quarter, $150 a semester), and fees to use at any Georgia public college or $3,000 a year for any Georgia private college. To find out what kinds of grants might be available in your state, call the state's department of education, generally in the state capital, or check the department's Web site.

What if your child is just not scholarship material and no grant money materializes? Is no-strings-attached cash out of the question? Not necessarily. Schools have their own quirky ways of rewarding loyalty. And if your first college kid can't get a grant, some colleges provide discounts for a sibling.

TWO SCHOLARSHIPS THAT REALLY PAY FOR COLLEGE

Most scholarships are more like scholar rafts—they pay only enough to keep you above water for a short while. But the two ocean liners listed below will really (or nearly) pay your child's way through college—if he can snare one. None is based on financial need, but competition to get these scholarships is extremely tough. And in the case of the Reserve Officers Training Corps scholarship, the payback may be more than he—or you—are up for. But both are worth a closer look:

1. **National Merit Scholarship Program.** Each year, students who score highest in the **Preliminary Scholastic Assessment Tests (PSAT)** are selected as semifinalists for a **Merit Scholarship** and invited to submit applications for awards ranging from a one-time scholarship of $2,500 to renewable corporate scholarships of $500 to $10,000. Final selection is based on academic excellence, test scores, community service, and recommendations. Roughly 8,000 of the 2 million students who take the PSATs each year get these scholarships; that's about one in 250. To get in the running, simply make sure your child takes the optional PSATs.

2. **Reserve Officers Training Corps (ROTC).**
   Army: For Army ROTC scholarships, your child must have a minimum GPA of 2.5, a minimum SAT of 920, or a minimum ACT of 19. (The ACT Assessment is a national college admission examination.) If your child earns this scholarship, he or she could receive up to $17,000 a year for tuition, fees, and books; and a stipend of up to $350 a month. In return, he or she must serve in the Army a minimum of four years.
   Air Force: For Air Force ROTC scholarships, a student must meet certain height

and weight requirements, pass a physical (push-ups, sit-ups, and a two-mile run), pass a medical physical, pass the Air Force Official Qualifying Test, be a full-time college student, and maintain a 2.5 cumulative GPA in high school. Test scores are looked at in combination with other academic material, but general scores should be around 1100 on the SAT or 24 on the ACT. The Air Force scholarships are three-tiered. The first tier, roughly 9% of the scholarships, covers any tuition. The second tier, around 16%, covers tuition up to $15,000 a year. The third tier, about 75% of the Air Force's scholarships, covers tuition up to $9,000 a year. All tiers offer monthly stipends ranging from $250 to $350 based on year in school and a yearly book allowance of $510. In return, students must serve a minimum of four years in the Air Force, starting duty within 30 days of college graduation.

Navy: The student must have a minimum SAT of 1050 or ACT of 22. He or she can receive up to full tuition, fees, a book allowance, uniforms, and a monthly stipend of up to $350. The student must be on active duty in the Navy for a minimum of four years in return.

How to Borrow Wisely for College

Despite your best efforts, there simply may not be enough money available through your savings, grants, scholarships, or on-campus work to meet the expenses of the school your child finally selects. If so, your only choices are for your child to trade down to a less costly school or for one or both of you to borrow the missing cash. Roughly half of all undergraduates borrow to pay for college.

While it's tempting to rush to the conclusion that your child must go to his first-choice school and the borrowing responsibility will be all yours, don't do it. Consider your own situation as well as your child's. For instance, you almost certainly should be setting aside cash for your retirement. If paying back more debt for college means that saving for retirement will become impossible, consider sending your child to a less expensive school or have him take out some loans himself. Be careful about your child's debt load, too. If you're not careful, your son or daughter could easily graduate from college owing an average of $10,000 to $15,000 in loans depending on the school. A student with $10,000 in debt (at 6% with a standard payment plan) will need to shell out over $111 a month to pay off the loan(s). That's a tough way to start out in the world.

Fortunately, reasonable college loans are available to both of you. For answers to questions about federal student loan availability, eligibility, and where to get such loans, contact the U.S. Department of Education at 800-433-3243; www.ed.gov or Sallie Mae at 800-891-1410 or 800-239-4269; www.salliemae.com.

To qualify for federal loans, you'll have to fill out the Free Application for Federal Student Aid (FAFSA) discussed earlier in this chapter.

Students with the greatest financial need are eligible for **Perkins loans**, available through colleges. These loans provide up to $4,000 per year of undergraduate study (maximum: $20,000) at a rock-bottom 5% interest rate. No interest accumulates while your child is in school, and he'll have up to 10 years to repay the loan, beginning nine months after he graduates (or leaves college). In certain situations the loan can even be forgiven—if your child becomes a teacher or a nurse working with disabled or low-income kids, for example.

If your family demonstrates financial need, your child can also receive a **federal subsidized Stafford loan**. This means he'll be able to borrow money at low rates with up to 10 years to repay and the federal government will pay the interest while he's in college. Both the maximum loan amounts and the interest rate are reset every few years. Recently, the largest subsidized Stafford loans ranged from $2,625 to $8,500 (depending on what year of college or grad school your child was in) and the interest rate was capped at 8.25%, with a 4% loan origination fee.

Even without demonstrating need, your son or daughter can get a **federal unsubsidized Stafford loan** directly from a bank, credit union, or other lender at the same low rate as a subsidized Stafford. With this type of loan, however, interest is not paid by the government while the student is in school.

If your lender sells your Stafford loan to the Student Loan Marketing Association (Sallie Mae), you're eligible for an even better interest rate. After you've paid 48 consecutive installments on time, Sallie Mae will shave two points off your rate (borrowers must continue to make payments on time to keep the benefit). So you might want to ask the financial aid office for lenders in your area that then sell their loans to Sallie Mae. Agree to a direct withdrawal from your bank account for loan repayments and Sallie Mae will knock off an additional quarter point.

Federal consolidation loans allow borrowers to refinance one or more federal education loans and significantly lower their monthly payment by extending the payback period. The original loans are paid in full, and a new loan for the combined balances is issued with new terms, including a new interest rate that is fixed for the life of the loan. Other participants in the Federal Family Education Loan Program generally offer loan consolidation as well.

When it comes time for your child to repay his loans, he'll have several options, including a graduated plan, in which the payments start out small but get bigger over time. For example, on a 10-year $10,000 Stafford loan with an interest rate of 6%, your child might pay just $50 a month for the first two years and $131 for the next eight. A similar plan pegs payments to a fixed percentage of his (hopefully rising) income.

Parents, rather than students, can also secure low-rate college loans through the federal government. As long as you have no loan delinquencies of more than 90 days and your child attends college at least half-time, you can take out a 10-year **Parent Loan to Undergraduate Students (PLUS)** for the difference between the full cost of your child's education and any financial aid he receives. The interest, at a rate that is reset every year, is currently capped at 9%. That's a few percentage points lower than what you'd pay for a personal loan from a bank or a home-equity loan. For more information call 800-891-1410 or go to the Sallie Mae Web site. PLUS loans, like unsubsidized Stafford loans, are available through most lenders.

HOW MUCH SHOULD PARENTS BORROW?

This worksheet projects the total college debt parents can afford without shorting their retirement plans. Take out your calculator or go to www.money.com/collegeloans.

1. Monthly after-tax income	$_____
2. Multiply line 1 by 0.35	$_____
3. Monthly mortgage or rent payment	$_____
4. Monthly home-equity loan/line of credit	$_____
5. Monthly auto loan/lease	$_____
6. Monthly credit-card payments	$_____
7. Other monthly debt payments	$_____
8. Add lines 3 through 7: Total monthly debt obligations	$_____
9. Subtract line 8 from line 2: Amount available for monthly college debt payments	$_____
10. Enter interest rate on loan (9% for PLUS)	%_____
11. Divide line 10 by 100 to get interest factor	$_____
12. Multiply line 9 by 12	$_____
13. Divide line 12 by line 11	$_____

Total you can borrow for college at your current income $_____

Source: Judy Miller, College Solutions, Alameda, Calif.

If you need to borrow more, see if your child is eligible for Bank of America's **Guaranteed Access to Education (GATE)** loan. The interest rate is 6.48% (quarterly rates are subject to change), with no cap. There are also no origination fees or prepayment penalties. Students can pay the principal and interest while in school, just the interest in school, or defer payment until six months after graduation. They have a maximum of 20 years for repayment, with a minimum monthly rate of $50.

Another possible solution is Sallie Mae's **Signature Student Loan**. If you've reached your loan limit for the federal Stafford loan, but you still need money for your education, the Signature Student Loan can help. You can apply for a Signature Student Loan if you're a student in good academic standing at an eligible undergraduate, graduate, or health profession school, and enrolled at least half-time. No income is required for student borrowers. Students with established credit may be eligible to borrow money without a co-borrower. Freshmen, foreign students, and those with low credit or no credit history will need a co-borrower. You can borrow up to the total cost of your education, including tuition, fees, room and board, computers, and other education-related expenses. (Lifetime maximum is $100,000.) Interest rates (APR—annual percentage rate) and loan fees are based on your credit history. Applying with a co-borrower may reduce the cost of your loan, as the co-borrower's credit history determines your interest and fees.

Three more low-cost sources of cash for college are your home, your company savings plan, and your cash-value life insurance policy.

- **With a home-equity line of credit**, you can borrow up to 80% of your equity, drawing out cash as needed for college bills. The rate generally fluctuates and is tied to the prime bank rate. But be careful. Typically, the home-equity line rate is a variable rate that ranges between 6% and 8% or prime plus zero to prime plus two. Since home-equity interest is tax-deductible, unlike most other types of interest, the after-tax cost of such loans makes them only a little higher than that of government-backed college loans. However, if you can't meet the payments, your house is at risk. What's more, some lenders and brokerage firms charge steep fees to take out home-equity lines, so be sure to compare the cost of the offerings before signing up for any. (For more information on home-equity loans and lines, see Chapter 6.)
- **Company savings plans**, such as 401(k)s, generally allow you to borrow an amount equal to up to half your account balance or $50,000 (whichever is less) at reasonable interest rates—often 1% or so over prime. The rate is fairly low because your loan is secured by the savings in your 401(k) account. However, if you don't pay the money back within the set time period—typically five years—it will be treated as a withdrawal and subject to income taxes and a 10% tax penalty.

- **Borrowing against the cash value in your life insurance policy might be worth looking into.** The insurer will charge annual interest of 6% to 8% and let you borrow up to the full cash value of your policy. Although you don't have to pay back the money, if you die and have a policy loan outstanding, your beneficiaries will suffer; they'll get just the insurance policy's face value minus the unpaid balance of the loan.

If you can't snag a low-interest loan, there are a handful of commercial lenders that offer college loans for all, or nearly all, college expenses (minus financial aid), with long repayment schedules at fairly attractive rates. Although students probably wouldn't use commercial lenders in place of federal low-interest loans (i.e. Stafford), if money is really tight, here's where else you can go:

- **Nellie Mae** will lend up to the entire cost of your child's education through its **EXCEL loan**. These loans can run as long as 20 years and are available at both monthly and annual variable interest rates. Cost: generally prime minus .75% to prime plus two, plus a onetime fee of typically 2% of the borrowed amount. For more information, contact Nellie Mae (800-634-9308; www.nelliemae.com).
- **The Education Resource Institute (TERI),** another private guarantor, lets you borrow up to the entire cost of education and stretch out loan payments as long as 25 years. The interest rate can be as low as prime minus .50%. Specific terms are set by the sponsors—primarily banks—that offer the program. For a list of guarantors in your area, call 800-255-8374; www.teri.org.

Installment Plans for College

Crisis time: The deadline for paying your child's college bills is looming, and despite all your best efforts, you simply don't have the needed cash. What to do? Look into loan programs made just for parents in your situation.

- **Academic Management Services (AMS) TuitionPay Monthly Plan** will charge you a fee ranging from $50 to $75 annually to set up a budget and installment schedule with your child's college that will let you pay the upcoming tuition money over a period of up to 10 months. But the college must be affiliated with AMS, as about 2,500 schools are. To find out more, call 800-635-0120 or 866-tuition; www.tuitionpay.com. Some schools have their own internal plans similar to this one, so contact your college to find out more.

Working for College Cash

You might want your son or daughter to help foot the college bills by working part-time during high school. After-school employment not only helps make college more affordable, but also teaches your child a little about the real working world. Plus, when your son or daughter puts at least some of the earnings in the bank or in a mutual fund, he or she will get an education in the world of personal finance. Just don't let your kid work so much that he won't have enough time to devote to his studies, causing his grades to suffer. For a fuller discussion about kids and money, see Chapter 20.

Your child's financial aid package may also include a college job, known as **work-study**, generally 10 or so hours a week of light work on campus for which he'll be paid roughly the minimum wage. Don't worry that limited part-time work during the school year will spoil your child's college experience or lower his grade-point average. Sebago Associates, commissioned by UPROMISE (an organization that promotes ways to boost college savings) published a study in August 2001 revealing that working a limited number of hours a week (e.g., 10 hours) at an on-campus job has a positive impact on student performance, while working a significant number of hours (35 hours or more per week) has the opposite effect. According to the study, on-campus jobs may build connections to academic departments or the college community in general, which may make students more likely to stay in school. So if your child must earn a large share of his college expenses, it's best for him to do so primarily through well-paid summer jobs. Here are some Web sites that may help: www.campuscareercenter.com; www.summerjobs. com; www.4internships.4anything.com; www.jobdirect.com.

Smart Ways to Cut College Costs

No matter how much you need to shell out for your child's college, chances are you wouldn't mind paying less. Here are four ways you or your son or daughter may be able to shave those tuition bills:

1. **Have your child zip through college.** Not only will you save a year's tuition if your son or daughter graduates in three years rather than four, your kid will get an extra year of lifetime earnings. But getting through college in three years requires more discipline than many kids have, so don't even think about it unless you believe

your child can pull it off. Most colleges let students take extra courses to graduate sooner, and some have formal three-year bachelor degree programs.

2. **Sacrifice selectivity for scholarship cash.** Increasingly, colleges other than those in the Ivy League and a few other hoity-toity institutions are giving out handsome merit scholarships to smart students, whether or not their parents can demonstrate financial need.

3. **Join the community.** Let's say your child goes to one of the nation's 1,014 or so community colleges for two years and then transfers to a four-year institution. Talk about savings! According to the College Board's Annual Survey of Colleges, community colleges charge an average of $1,705 a year for tuition and fees, far less than the cost at four-year schools.

4. **Stick around your home.** Nearly two dozen states dangle juicy financial incentives to good students who stay in-state for college. For instance, some states offer scholarships to students who have participated in the state-sponsored 529 plan. In some cases, however, you may have to demonstrate financial need and your child may have to keep up his grades in college. Your state's department of education can tell you if there are deals like this where you live.

CHAPTER 11

How to Retire
Comfortably

$\mathbf{N}$ow for the challenge to end all challenges. You don't even have time for a brief nap before this Everest starts staring you down: financing your retirement. This is the supreme test that will take more energy and attention than the other two peaks (buying your home and financing your children's education) combined. Proof: Most retirees today must plan to live for 30 years after the paychecks stop. Do a back-of-the-envelope computation on that one. The rule of thumb is that you'll need at least 80% of your final year's pay in retirement. (More likely that number could soar to 100% of your final pay or more if you plan several vacations a year and dining out at fancy restaurants a few times a week.) But for now, let's stick to 80% for this example. So if your income at the end will be, say, $80,000 a year, then you'll need $64,000 a year times 30, or $1,920,000. What?! A nest egg of nearly $2 million? How in the name of Bill Gates are you going to come up with that amount of change?

There are actually two answers to that question. They are the essential twin lessons of retirement planning that will be discussed in the rest of this chapter.

First, the frightening figure arrived at—$1,920,000—is grossly misleading. Feel tricked? Don't be angry, be instructed: You should have been aware that it doesn't take into account Social Security, which may be a more substantial part of your nest egg than you have been led to believe. Really. It also doesn't account for either the earnings you'll get on your investments or inflation. Lesson one: You must find out with reasonable precision the amount of money you'll need to accumulate by retirement, or you will not know how much you need to save. Later in this chapter you'll see how to do just that.

Second, you just have to do a few things right and the supersonic engine of compound interest will do the rest. For example, if starting at age 40 you put $8,000 a year in your 401(k) or other tax-deferred account and you earn an 8% annual return, you would accumulate $880,000 by age 62. But if you were to wait five years longer to start saving, your pot would be worth only $704,000. Lesson two: Your eventual success depends on how early you start building your nest egg, how well you fund it year in and year out, and how well you manage your portfolio over time.

The thread that runs through both of these lessons: you. Because of changes in law and corporate policy, employers and the government will be doing less and less to help you build your secure retirement. Consequently you will have to do more and more yourself. But if you do, the payoff will be spectacular: a comfortable, worry-free retirement.

Why It's All Up to You

For your parents and maybe even your grandparents, retirement was financed largely by Social Security and a company pension. The younger you are today, the more the retirement income scene will change from that traditional one. Take Social Security. As things now stand, it will replace about 40% of wages if you are like the average worker in the year 2000, who earned an average of about $32,000 a year throughout his career. But if your average salary is, say, $76,200 a year—the highest amount taxed by Social Security in 2000—only about 32% of that figure (or $24,384 a year) will be replaced by Social Security benefits. In addition, as your post-retirement income from other sources grows, count on more and more of your Social Security benefits being taxed. Right now, 85% of Social Security benefits are subject to federal income tax if your total income (including half of Social Security checks) exceeds $44,000 for married couples and $34,000 for singles.

You're increasingly on your own with employer-sponsored retirement benefits, too. About four out of 10 workers today are lucky enough to be accumulating traditional employer-paid pensions. These are the **defined-benefit plans** that pay out a fixed monthly amount for life after you retire. According to MONEY magazine's 2001 company benefits survey, retirees from major corporations tend to receive about 30% of their final salary if they have worked 20 years or more at the same company. Although these plans are still going strong at large companies, their years—if not their days—seem numbered. They are tremendously expensive to maintain, partly because the employer does all of the funding and partly because government reporting regulations are complicated and onerous. The number of small- and medium-size companies offering defined-benefit plans has been plummeting, and there's no reason to think that trend will reverse itself.

Some employers offering pensions have cut costs by switching to cheaper plans like the **cash-balance plan**. This plan accrues benefits more evenly over an employee's career and, therefore, tends to be a better deal for newer or younger employees or job hoppers. According to the MONEY survey, companies that offer these types of pensions typically replace 20% of final earnings (on average) for an employee who retires after 20 years.

Just as typewriters were swept away by computers, the defined-benefit plan is being replaced as the principal employer-sponsored retirement savings vehicle. Taking its place is what is called the **defined-contribution plan**, such as the 401(k) for private companies or the 403(b) for nonprofit organizations. The significant difference: You, the employee, do most of the funding and you take responsibility for deciding how to invest the money. Almost all large corporations that offer 401(k)s also match a portion of the employee's contributions.

In some ways, these 401(k)–type plans are a perfect match for the rootless work styles of Americans today. If you change jobs, you can take your retirement savings with you. That is a considerable improvement over traditional pensions, which are not typically portable and aren't worth much unless you stay for decades at one company. While you do become **vested** in a defined-benefit plan after three to six years of service at a company—that is, you become eligible to receive benefits—you usually have to wait until you're 65 to start receiving checks. So if you leave the company at, say, age 40 after 10 years there, the eventual payoff could be minuscule.

On the other hand, a 401(k) is far less secure than a traditional pension, which pays you that monthly check no matter how the stock and bond markets perform. You invest a 401(k) among a selection of investments. So your account's value when you retire is not guaranteed, but depends on how well you have managed it. All too often, employees invest their 401(k)s too conservatively, producing lower returns than those from old-fashioned pensions. Also, many employees either spend their 401(k) savings when they change jobs or borrow excessively from them, robbing their retirement years. On top of all this, companies generally contribute less to 401(k)s than they do to defined-benefit pensions.

It should be clear by now that the partnership of Uncle Sam (Social Security) and your employer (pension) isn't enough anymore to ensure a safe and sound retirement. Ask almost any retirement-planning expert and you will be told that the new configuration is a troika: Social Security; your company's contribution, which is more likely to be a 401(k)–type plan than a traditional pension; and your own savings and investments. Finding out just how big this third element needs to be is critical: The earlier you make some rough calculations, the easier it will be to amass what you'll need.

By completing the following worksheet or using retirement calculators listed in the box below, you'll know how much you'll need to invest to make your retirement comfortable. But what if you started saving too late or can't set aside such an amount in the years left before retirement? In that case you will have to make up the shortfall in the only other way possible: by working during retirement. The fact is, as many as half of all retirees take on less demanding jobs after they quit their full-time jobs. They do so not only to make up for a savings shortfall, but also to ease the emotional transition from work to full retirement.

RETIREMENT RESOURCES

If you are even marginally computer-literate and have Internet access, you can make the task of retirement planning considerably easier, a lot more accurate, and possibly even fun. Just visit some fine Web sites and spend an hour or two using the calculators and worksheets. For this small investment of time, you will gain considerable insight into the art of retirement planning and increased confidence in your ability to home in on how much you will need to finance your later years.

www.directadvice.com Online retirement planner lets you plug in goals and assets; then it customizes a printable savings and investment plan. Cost: $75 a year.

www.financenter.com Dozens of calculators figure expenses after retirement, the effects of inflation and more. Free.

www.financialengines.com Tells you the probability of reaching your goals. For a fee, the site recommends specific funds. Free/$14.95 for three months.

www.moneycentral.com Calculators forecast savings, income, Social Security, and more. Articles on topics like wills. Free.

www.money.com Track your portfolio's performance. A new feature lets you download holdings into the Financial Engines Web site for a free forecast. Free.

www.morningstar.com Portfolio-planning feature lets you input your current holdings, then tells you how much you have in stocks, bonds, and cash—and tracks day-to-day value. Free.

www.quicken.com/retirement Retirement Planner feature predicts your income in retirement, and whether your savings and investments will help you meet your goal. Information on retirement issues like taxes. Free.

WHAT'S YOUR NUMBER?

The moment you decide to get serious about retirement planning, your first act should be figuring out how much you'll need to retire well. This worksheet will help you calculate the rough amount you will need to retire comfortably, at age 65 or even before, in two different scenarios. One assumes that you want to leave money for heirs (line 3); the other is the more achievable goal of amassing assets that you will consume during your lifetime (line 4). To see where you are, add up all your retirement savings and the value of any lump-sum pension you may be eligible for and subtract that amount from line 3 or 4, depending on your goals. Our bare-bones calculations assume 3% inflation, an inflation-adjusted investment return of 5%, and a life expectancy of 90; they exclude Social Security benefits. You can also use the retirement calculators at www.money.com or the financial sites listed in the box on page 242.

Figuring out how much you need to retire

1. Enter your desired annual retirement income. (We recommend using 100% of pre-retirement income, less what you are setting aside for retirement savings.) $_____

2. Multiply line 1 by Factor A below, based on a target retirement date. This is your projected income need in the first year of retirement. $_____

3. Multiply line 2 by Factor B, based on your age at retirement. The result is the ideal retirement stake you would need: This lump sum should generate enough income to meet your needs without tapping your principal. $_____

or

4. Multiply line 2 by Factor C, based on your age at retirement. This is your minimum retirement stake. This lump sum should generate enough income to get you to age 90. After that, your assets will be exhausted. $_____

YEARS UNTIL RETIREMENT	INFLATION FACTOR A	AGE	FACTOR B	FACTOR C
0	1.00	50	24.2	20.7
1–5	1.09	55	21.8	18.6
6–10	1.27	60	19.9	16.2
11–15	1.47	62	19.0	15.5
16–20	1.70	65	18.1	14.1
21–25	1.97			

Source: Tarbox Equity.

Social Security—What You'll Get and When

Given the gloomy press Social Security has received in recent years, you may be wondering why this book includes a discussion of the subject at all. Why hold out false hope for a benefit that will likely not be around for our retirement anyway? After all, one survey showed that more adults under 34 believe UFOs exist than think they'll get Social Security.

What's really likely to happen to Social Security in the future? No one knows for sure, of course.

In all probability there will be some tinkering ahead—but not a wholesale junking of the Social Security system. One proposal on the table is the privatization of Social Security where workers will invest their own funds.

Here is what you can reasonably expect in the way of Social Security changes that would affect your retirement:

- **If you were born before 1938, you're home free.** The only blip on your Social Security screen is the fact that most of your benefits may be taxable now. Despite efforts to turn back the tide, it seems prudent to expect that if your retirement income will exceed $50,000 or $60,000, you will pay tax on your Social Security checks, perhaps even on every penny of them, in the coming years. Currently, as soon as your **provisional income** (your adjusted gross income plus tax-exempt interest and half of your Social Security benefits) inches past $35,000 on a joint return ($25,000 if you're single), 50% of your benefits are taxed. When your provisional income tops $44,000 on a joint return ($34,000 if you're single), up to 85% of your benefit is subject to federal income tax.

- **If you were born between 1938 and 1959, you are already heir to a slight delaying of your benefits and you're likely to be the first to see more of your benefits taxed.** The normal retirement age for Social Security, now 65, switches to age 66 for people born in 1943. It then gets pushed back a little more each year until it hits 67 in the year 2027 (people born in 1960). The fancy footwork with the retirement age also changes payouts for people who retire before 65. Today, if you retire at age 62, you receive 80% of your full Social Security benefits for the rest of your life. That percentage is scheduled to decline to 75% in 2009.

- **If you were born from 1960 on, you'll be fingered the most.** In fact, recent studies indicate that workers born after 1960 will get back less from Social Security than they have paid in taxes during their working years. You may wind up being able to keep only half of today's scheduled amount of Social Security benefits. The early retirement penalty will get stiffer for you, too. If you were born in 1960 or later, when your normal retirement age would be 67, retiring at 62 will mean you'll get only 70% of your full benefit, down from 80% today.

How much will your Social Security benefit check actually be, under today's rules? Finding out is one of the simplest matters in all of personal finance. Just call the Social Security Administration (800-772-1213; www.ssa.gov) and ask for a projection of your annual benefit, if you have not already been receiving this report. In a few weeks you will get a report laying out how much your check is likely to be, based on your income history and an estimate of your future income. (Every year such statements are sent automatically to anyone 25 years old and older, three months before their birthday.)

You will qualify for Social Security benefits under one of five categories:

- **Your own benefits**, based on your work record.
- **Spousal benefits**, based on your husband's or wife's work record (these benefits generally equal half of your spouse's full benefit).
- **Divorced spouse's benefits** (if you were married at least 10 years, your former spouse either is receiving Social Security or is older than 62, you are not remarried, and you have been divorced for at least two years).
- **Widow's or widower's benefits** (if you were married at least nine months and did not remarry before you were 60).
- **Divorced widow's or widower's benefits** (if you were married to your ex-husband or ex-wife at least 10 years, are 60 or older, and married your present spouse before age 60).

To give you a rough idea of the dollar amounts involved, the top monthly Social Security benefit for someone who retired in 2000 at age 65 was roughly $1,536 or about $18,432 a year. If these figures don't impress you, take another look. A couple, each of whom receives the top monthly benefit—and that will likely be more and more typical among two-profession households—would pull down close to $36,864 a year in Social Security at the 2000 pace. You'd need a stash of about $350,000 to generate that much income from assets earning an 8% return.

When should you start taking your Social Security benefits? That depends. If you can afford to delay getting the checks until age 70, you should. That's because you'll get a larger annual benefit by postponing the date the checks start arriving. For each year you hold off retiring past your 65th birthday (for those born before 1960) until you reach age 70, your Social Security check grows by 4.5%. Put another way, if you wait until 70, you'll get 22.5% more than at 65 and will keep getting that much more as long as you live. Conversely, you're penalized if you start receiving Social Security early;

retirement benefits are available beginning at age 62. Start taking Social Security at 62 and you'll get 20% less than you would have by waiting until 65—for the rest of your life. Even so, 62% of men and 73% of women start getting Social Security at age 62.

When you hit 60 or so, determine whether you expect to work after retirement. If you plan to keep working, estimate how much you would be earning. You may find that the amount you'll be pulling in will persuade you to delay getting Social Security checks until at least age 65 or until age 70. You may even find that it won't pay to work. The reason: Social Security benefits for people aged 62 to 64 are reduced by $1 for every $2 earned above $10,080. Good news: A recent law permits retirees who are working and who are older than 65, to receive 100% of their benefits.

Your Pension and Its Safety

Perhaps you're counting on getting a decent pension from your employer when you retire. Maybe you will. But keep in mind that two factors will greatly determine how big your employer's pension will be: how long you stay at the same employer and whether your employer is financially capable of making good on its pension promises.

The size of your pension checks will be based on your years of service and your salary over, typically, your three to five highest-paid years on the job. Traditional defined-benefit pensions rarely increase with inflation. Government workers, however, usually receive annual increases in their pension checks to offset inflation, known as **cost-of-living adjustments (COLAs)**. That may not be true much longer. Government budget balancers are eyeing COLAs closely, making them especially ripe for cutting.

Job hopping can sharply reduce the size of your defined-benefit pension, as shown by the following figures from the benefits consulting firm William M. Mercer. Take three people, each of whom has been working for 40 years, started with an initial salary of $14,900, got raises of 5% a year, and was earning $100,000 before retiring at age 65. The person who stayed at the same company for all 40 years might get an annual pension of $54,550. If he had two employers over those years, his total pension would shrink to $37,550. If he had worked at four employers, his pension would be cut to $30,300 per year. With eight employers, however, his pension would be cut to just $27,000—half the size of the one-employer employee.

The other consideration is the safety of your pension. Every year about 100 companies default on their pension plans. From 1975–2001, nearly 3,000 plans went under. That's a small percentage overall; indeed, about 72% of traditionally defined benefit pension plans are fully funded as of September 2002. But if you were an employee at one of the companies whose pension plans blew up, the effect on your retirement could be considerable. Fortunately, a federal agency known as the Pension Benefit Guaranty Corporation (PBGC) acts as something of a safety net for pensioners. The PBGC does not guarantee 401(k) or other employer-sponsored, defined-contribution savings plans, however. What's more, the PBGC won't necessarily guarantee that you'll receive your full pension even if your defined-pension plan tanks. By law the PBGC pays a maximum benefit—it is adjusted each year. The guarantee for persons retiring at age 65 in plans that terminated in 2001 is $3,392 a month or $40,704 a year. The amounts are adjusted for retirees at other ages. For example, if you take early retirement at age 55, the most PBGC will pay is $1,526 a month, or about $18,000 a year, for those who elect survivor benefits.

Pension reforms enacted in the Retirement Protection Act of 1994 set stiffer funding and information disclosure requirements for pension plans that do not have enough funds to pay all promised benefits. One of these reforms requires a pension plan with less than 90% of its necessary funding to notify participants and beneficiaries of the plan's funding status and the limits of the PBGC's guarantee. Anyone whose employer offers a pension plan, however, should do a little homework to learn how safe the plan really is. Ask your employee benefits office for a copy of Form 5500, which companies must file annually with the U.S. Department of Labor. Then read the actuary's report in the back of the form. That independent opinion will clue you in to the soundness of the plan.

Build Your Nest Egg Through Tax-Deferred Retirement Savings Plans

Now that you know what the government and your employer are likely to give you for retirement, you're ready to get cracking on what you can and should do for yourself. There is no surer way to a secure retirement than the tax-deferred compounding offered by 401(k) and 403(b) savings plans, IRAs, 457 plans (usually for government workers), and SEPs, Simple IRAs, and Keoghs (for self-employed individuals and small businesses). As we explained earlier, these plans will help you build your wealth faster due to the effects of tax-deferred or tax-free compounding. For instance, let's look at a comparison that was done for us by John Ziegelbauer from the accounting firm of Grant Thornton. Say a 35-year-old earning $80,000 routinely contributes 6% of his salary (or $4,800 before taxes) into a tax-deferred account such as a 401(k) plan. And just for comparison, let's say he also puts $4,800 of his salary into a taxable account

($3,360 after taxes, assuming that he is in the 30% tax bracket). Let's say that both accounts earn 8%. At age 65 his savings in the taxable account would total $263,398. Not bad. But in the 401(k) account, his savings would come to a hefty $604,522, and after taxes upon withdrawal, that would come to $423,165.

Traditional, Roth, and Nondeductible IRAs

There are three types of IRAs: traditional (deductible), Roth, and nondeductible IRAs. For all three, the 2002 maximum annual contribution of $3,000 will rise to $4,000 in 2005 and to $5,000 in 2008. For people age 50 or over, the limits will rise from $3,500 in 2002, to $4,500 in 2005, to $5,000 in 2006, and to $6,000 in 2008.

The contributions to **traditional (deductible) IRAs** are tax-deductible in the year that you make them. The earnings grow tax-deferred until you withdraw the money—then you pay taxes on what you take out, based on your tax bracket at that time. The basic rules on deductibility are as follows: If you have no retirement plan at work, you can write off your entire IRA contribution of up to the maximum annual contribution. If you are covered by a plan at work, however, the size of your deduction depends on your income. You can find this income phase-out schedule on the Internal Revenue Service Web site (www.irs.gov). If you're not covered by an employer's retirement plan but your spouse is, you can claim a full IRA deduction for 2002 as long as you meet certain income requirements. And if you pull money out of a traditional IRA before age 59½, you'll owe taxes plus a 10% tax penalty on the amount of the distribution. However, you must begin withdrawals by age 70½.

Roth contributions are never tax-deductible. However, earnings grow tax-deferred as long as you keep them in your account for at least five years and you are older than 59½ when you withdraw them. You'll be hit with the 10% tax penalty for withdrawals of your earnings before age 59½, but contributions may be withdrawn penalty-free at any time. One other key difference between a Roth IRA and the other two types: You don't have to start pulling money out at age 70½. Roth IRAs are a good choice for those who are not eligible for the tax-deductible feature of a traditional IRA. Roths also have income requirements that can be found on the IRS Web site.

A **nondeductible IRA** works the same as a traditional IRA, except you don't get the tax break at the time you invest. Like a deductible IRA, your earnings are taxed as ordinary income when you withdraw them, and you must begin withdrawals by age 70½.

Generally, you can pull money out of all three IRAs without penalty at any age, though, if the cash will be used for college expenses, to buy a first-time home ($10,000 limit), for medical expenses greater than 7.5% of your adjusted gross income, or for a disability.

So which type of IRA is best for you? In general, a Roth is great for people in their thirties and couples in their forties with kids (the account can be used as an estate-planning tool to give more money to your children). As a rule, the decision about whether to open a Roth IRA or another type depends on your age and what you expect will happen to your tax rate in retirement. These three rules will help you choose the most appropriate IRA:

- **A Roth IRA always beats a nondeductible IRA.** If you're married and your adjusted gross income is too high to qualify for a deductible IRA, a Roth is the better deal. Plus, the tax-free earnings on a Roth beat taxable earnings on a nondeductible IRA.
- **A Roth is better than a deductible IRA if you think your tax bracket will not drop after you retire.** Most people figure that their income will fall in retirement. If you're one of them, then a deductible IRA will probably be wiser than a Roth. But if you believe your income will rise in retirement because of, say, pension proceeds and Social Security benefits, a Roth will be better.
- **The longer you can wait to withdraw money from your IRA after retirement, the better a Roth looks.** If you're age 70 and earn 7% a year in a Roth IRA, you can double your money by age 80 by leaving it there instead of pulling it out and spending it. Of course, if you're over 70½, have earned income, and want to keep saving, a Roth IRA is your only choice.

You can also convert your old IRA into a Roth IRA if your household's income is $100,000 or less. Although you'll owe taxes on any deductible contributions plus the earnings in the account, all future earnings will be tax-free as long as you hold the account for more than five years and don't take distributions before age 59½. Converting to a Roth generally makes sense only if you think your tax rate will rise in retirement, you'll hold the money in the account for at least five years, you won't need to tap the IRA to pay the conversion taxes, and when converting to a Roth won't mean giving up some tax breaks limited by your income.

Employee Retirement Savings Plans

Americans on the job today are likely to find that by retirement, their 401(k), 403(b), or 457 account will have become their greatest single financial asset. These lucrative plans are among the best goodies employers have to offer, providing unparalleled opportunities to boost savings and defer taxes. The 401(k) plan is targeted to employees in the private sector—mostly at large and mid-sized corporations. The 403(b) is offered mostly to employees of educational and nonprofit institutions. Government agencies tend to offer their employees a 457 plan.

But no matter the title, all three plans allow you to invest a percentage of your pretax salary in stock, fixed-income, or money-market funds and your earnings grow tax-deferred until you withdraw them. The pretax angle is a beaut: for example, if you were in a 30% tax bracket in 2001 and contributed $5,000 of your pretax salary to a 401(k) account, you would have saved $1,500 in taxes for the year. Think of it as the equivalent of a $1,500 pay raise.

Perhaps the greatest plus for the participants of these programs is that most companies offering 401(k)s and some nonprofits offering 403(b)s match some or all of employee contributions, typically kicking in $1 for every $2 invested up to a certain percentage of pay. Your employer's matching contribution, if any, will produce an automatic return on your savings. A 401(k) contribution earning 9% a year with a 50% match will return a whopping 63.5% annually, after tax benefits are taken into account. For that reason, you should strain to invest as much of your pretax salary as the plan allows.

Another great feature of all three of these plans is that they are portable. In other words, when you change jobs, you usually can take your money with you to roll over into your new company's plan. You could also roll over the plan into your IRA, if you prefer a wider range of investment choices. However, if your current employer's plan offers a good selection of investments (and you vow never to tap your nest egg for a loan), you may want to keep the plan where it is until you're ready to retire. The contribution limit for 401(k)s, 403(b)s, and 457 plans is $11,000 in 2002, and will rise by $1,000 increments in each of the subsequent four years so that by 2006 the limit for each will be $15,000. After that, the limit increases in step with the rate of inflation. If you assumed an annual 3% rate, by 2010 the limit would be $16,500. (Take note: The ceiling on 401(k) contributions is also dictated by the particular rules of individual employers.)

For people aged 50 or older, the limits on these employer-sponsored plans are $12,000 in 2002 and will rise to $14,000 in 2003, $16,000 in 2004, $18,000 in 2005, and $20,000 in 2006. Assuming the same 3% annual inflation rate over the next four years, the limit for the 50-plus set will be $22,000 in 2010.

Retirement Plans for the Self-Employed

There are three basic types of tax-sheltered retirement plans for small-business owners and self-employed individuals: **Simple IRAs, Simplified Employee Pensions (SEP-IRAs), and Keoghs**. All three can be kept at almost any institution that offers qualified plans such as IRAs. For a Simple IRA, the $6,500 maximum contribution in 2002 will rise by $1,000 increments in each year to $10,000 by 2005. Limits will rise with inflation after that. Assuming a 3% rate, the limit will be $11,500 by 2010.

A SEP lets you deduct as much as 20% of your net self-employed income, up to $40,000 (whichever is smaller), and defer taxes on the earnings. Simples and SEPs are pretty easy to set up and require little record keeping.

A business owner can also set up a Keogh plan, which also allows you to contribute—and deduct from your taxable income—either as much as $40,000 a year or 20% of your net self-employment income, whichever is smaller. A Keogh can be designed so as to allow for loans, while a SEP plan cannot. To set up and maintain a Keogh plan, however, the record-keeping requirements are complicated. With a defined-benefit Keogh, you decide how much income you want to receive each year in retirement, within federal limits, and then you must hire an actuary to calculate the amount you must contribute each year to achieve that benefit. All of these plans require that you cover employees as well as yourself.

The Best Way to Build Your Nest Egg

The key words to remember: **asset allocation**. That's another way of saying diversification, but with one important added feature—you spread your money over just the right mix of stocks, bonds, and other investments. The extra touch is adjusting that mix according to your age so that your investment risks gradually diminish as you get closer to retirement. For most middle-income people, commonsense asset allocation means following two basic guidelines:

1. **Make stocks your central investment.** Fixed-income investments are the ballast of a portfolio, reducing its overall risk. But stocks are the long-term powerhouse and the only way to overcome the ravages of inflation. While stocks can certainly produce nerve-twisting losses in the short term, they have never lost money over every decade since World War II.

2. **Concentrate on mutual funds.** Asset allocation requires you to spread your investments over a number of categories. For example, you need to be in large-company stocks, mid-sized-company stocks, small-company stocks, and international stocks as well as bonds. Unless you have the time and skill to research and track many individual securities, stock mutual funds are your best option, offering low-cost diversification as well as professional management and convenience. You'll learn more about stocks, bonds, and mutual funds and how to build and manage a diversified portfolio in Chapters 13, 14, and 15. (For the best allocation depending on your age, see the pie charts that follow.) For advice about investing in annuities for retirement, see Chapter 16.

THE BEST PORTFOLIO MIX FOR YOU

The pie charts below provide a quick look at how best to divvy up your retirement portfolio, depending on your age. As you'll see, the older you get, the safer the investments become. **Small-cap** is short for small-capitalization stocks, which are companies whose total market value—the number of shares multiplied by the current stock price—is $1.5 billion or less. **Mid-cap** stocks are companies whose value is more than $1.5 billion but less than $10 billion. **Large-cap** stands for large-capitalization stocks, representing companies whose total market value exceeds $10 billion. **High-yield bonds** sometimes are known as junk bonds.

Here are the four model retirement portfolios—for those in their twenties to age 30; 30 to 40; 40 to 55; and 55 or older. Like many one-size-fits-all models, they're conservative, for the most part dividing up your stash into these categories: *stocks or stock funds*: large-cap, mid-caps, small-caps, and international; *bonds or bond funds*: investment-grade corporate, government, or high-yield bonds; and *cash*. (You may want to consider holding cash in another account to make better use of your tax deferral.)

• **Twenties to 30 years old:** Now is the time to put at least 80% of your retirement portfolio into stocks. With 30 to 45 or so years before retirement, there is plenty of time to make up for the sometimes sharp fluctuations that the stock market will inevitably endure. Based on past returns, a portfolio with 80% in stocks and 20% in bonds is likely to grow an average of 9% annually.

When you start out, you may not have enough money to break up your portfolio into the subcategories of stocks and bonds outlined above. In that case go for a single mutual fund that buys either **blue chips**, those large companies that offer solid capital appreciation with less volatility than small stocks, or an **index fund** that mirrors the S&P 500 index. If you're super-cautious, you might look for a balanced or **asset-allocation fund** instead. These all-in-one funds usually keep about 60% of their assets in stocks and the rest in bonds and other fixed-income investments.

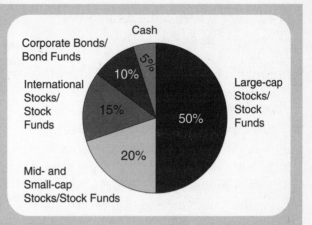

Once you have $10,000 or more to invest, begin putting together a diversified portfolio of funds. A recommended lineup: Invest 50% in large-company funds, 20% in mid- and small-cap funds, and 15% in international stock funds. To balance out your portfolio with fixed-income holdings, you might stash 10% of your money in high-quality corporate bonds with intermediate maturities of five to 10 years. About 5% of your investments could be in cash, if you feel the need. Steer clear of bond funds that carry loads or fees that total more than 1% of net assets; managers of such funds are generally unable to achieve performance good enough to overcome high expenses. (You'll find fees listed in every fund's prospectus.)

- **30 to 40 years old:** You may be inclined to turn down the risk level at this point, particularly if you have little children and big mortgages. Any such impulse should be honored, but not indulged. Since you still have about 25 to 35 years to go before retirement, you should stay with at least 70% of your money in stocks.

To do this, you can gradually trim your mid- and small-cap allocation to 10% and your international funds to 10% of your portfolio. Then transfer some of the proceeds to your intermediate-term corporate bond holdings, which should now be 15% of your stash, and the rest into high-yield corporate bond funds, which should now be 10% of your portfolio. And don't forget that 5% dash of cash.

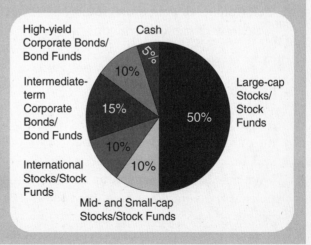

- **40 to 55 years old:** At this point in your life you have probably reached your peak earning years, but your savings may be held back by your kids' college bills. Considering these factors and the undeniable truth that you are beginning to close in on retirement, tone down your portfolio's risk level. You can do this while keeping a solid 70% of your portfolio in stocks. Simply put more money into large-cap and fixed-income funds, thus limiting your probable risk of loss.

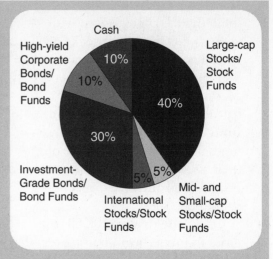

   Large-caps can expand to 40% of your holdings, and mid- and small-caps and international stakes can each drop to 5%. In the fixed-income portion of your portfolio, you might go for added security by upping your investment-grade bonds slice to 30% and cash to 10%, while keeping high-yields at 10%. You might want to switch some of your corporate bonds to U.S. government or tax-free issues. Instead of buying a mutual fund that buys U.S. Treasuries exclusively, you might do just as well by purchasing on your own Treasury notes that mature in two to 10 years. You can buy Treasuries directly from the Federal Reserve Bank (www.treasurydirect.com) with no fee or commission. For details, see Chapters 5 and 15.

- **55 years old or older:** Now that you've made it this far allocating your assets wisely, don't make the mistake so many people do as they approach retirement: Don't dump all your stock funds and settle in with safe CDs. In your fifties, you are looking forward to 30 or 40 more years of life, when inflation will be sucking the blood from your assets like the wealth vampire that it is. Even if inflation averages a tame 3% a year, the purchasing power of today's dollar will be cut in half in a dozen years. Your best bet is to keep your allocations at the same level as advised for people 40 to 55 years old.

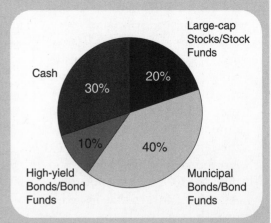

However, if you are terrified of taking on much risk at this point in your life (and you have set aside enough so that you don't have to), here's what you should consider. Stay with at least 20% of your money in large-caps and get rid of your mid- and small-cap funds. On the fixed-income side, you can increase your safety measurably by upping your investment-grade bonds (primarily U.S. government or municipal issues) to 40% of your holdings and keeping 10% in high-yield bonds. The rest, 30%, could be cash.

Three Critical Decisions About Your Retirement

Wise retirement planning is not all numbers. There is a huge emotional component to it, reflecting the fact that retiring involves one of life's most profound periods of change. No one really knows in advance how he or she will weather the process. That is why some people enter a period of prolonged depression, convinced that once a career ends, useful living stops, too. For others, the transition is so easy that anyone observing them might think such individuals were born to retire.

At any rate, three crucial decisions that many pre-retirees must make vividly display the mix of financial and emotional elements. They are (1) knowing when you should retire, (2) sizing up an early-out offer from your employer, and (3) deciding how to take your pension and 401(k) retirement account withdrawals.

DECISION 1:
KNOWING WHEN YOU SHOULD RETIRE

Recent studies indicate that about 25% of retirees are unhappy, primarily because they had not been ready to retire. For some, the decision had not been theirs to make. But in general, at the end of a long career most people think they are headed for freedom and do not stop to consider whether the free time they'll have will lie heavy on them or be the prolonged vacation they envision. Retirement planners say that six months or so after quitting work, reality sets in.

To make sure that retirement is a welcome reality, weigh carefully the decision to call it quits. Look for the two prime signals that you are ready to retire: (1) You find it harder and harder to keep your mind on your work; and (2) you view retirement not as a passive vacation, but as an active adventure.

Be honest with yourself and admit just how attached you might be to your life as it is at present. The more averse you are to change, the more you will have to work on making the transition bearable. If your employer provides retirement-planning seminars, take advantage of them. They are apt to address emotional as well as financial issues. If such seminars are not available, seek them elsewhere, perhaps through community groups. For more information, contact AARP (formerly American Association of Retired Persons) at 1-800-424-4310; www.aarp.org.

The following quiz, prepared by retirement specialist Helen Dennis at the University of Southern California in Los Angeles, can also help you decide if you are emotionally ready for early retirement. (The questions are designed for people who have worked 20 years or more; younger workers may get a false reading because, for example, they are confident of the availability of jobs.)

ARE YOU READY FOR RETIREMENT?

When completing this early-retirement quiz, circle as many answers to each question as apply to you:

1. The feeling that I make a difference at work is . . .
   a. extremely important to me.
   b. somewhat important to me.
   c. of little importance to me.
   d. not at all important to me.

2. My co-workers . . .
   a. are like my family.
   b. are my major social contacts.
   c. are rarely seen by me (and my spouse) outside work.
   d. are not very important to me.

3. At work, I feel . . .
   a. energized.
   b. extremely important.
   c. underutilized.
   d. overworked and underpaid.

4. To meet my financial obligations and responsibilities, I am counting on . . .
   a. my next pay raise.
   b. increasing my savings.
   c. winning the lottery.
   d. my spouse.

5. Retirement means . . .
   a. you're over the hill.
   b. you haven't yet peaked.
   c. you are old.
   d. you have new choices.

6. Power and influence . . .
   a. are aspects of my work that I thoroughly enjoy.
   b. are an essential part of my work.
   c. apply to others, not me.
   d. are almost impossible to achieve in retirement.

7. I plan to retire and live . . .
   a. alone.
   b. with my spouse.
   c. with a friend.
   d. with my mother.

8. I feel . . .
   a. attractive.
   b. unattractive.
   c. vigorous.
   d. mentally sharp.

9. I currently have . . .
   a. some wonderful hobbies.
   b. at least one volunteer commitment.
   c. few outside interests.
   d. some outside interests I would like to develop.

10. My spouse (or mate) . . .
    a. is eager for me to retire.
    b. dreads my retirement.
    c. has my chores planned.
    d. has packed our bags for a trip.

11. I consider myself . . .
    a. a good self-manager.
    b. a planner.
    c. a procrastinator.
    d. one who can advise others, but I have difficulty taking my own advice.

12. Knowing I will have free time in retirement . . .
    a. I have planned how I will use my time.
    b. I don't have a clue about what I will do.
    c. I have a plan, but I don't know if it will be fulfilling.
    d. I think that I am already over-committed.

13. Most of my friends . . .
    a. are working and plan to continue working.
    b. are retired.
    c. plan to retire soon.
    d. are split among all of the above.

14. I've recently thought about . . .
    a. the losses I might feel when I retire.
    b. how my spouse and I will get along in retirement.
    c. what gives meaning to my life.
    d. none of the above.

Score: Give yourself one point for checking each of the following: 1a, 2a, 2b, 3a, 3b, 4a, 4b, 5a, 5c, 6a, 6b, 6d, 7a, 8b, 9c, 10b, 11c, 11d, 12b, 12c, 13a, 14d. The higher the score, the less emotionally ready you are for early retirement. If you scored 15 to 22 points, either early retirement isn't right for you or you need to start preparing for it immediately; 9 to 14 points means you are a possible candidate for early retirement but need a little more emotional preparation; and 8 points or fewer suggests that you can retire happily tomorrow.

DECISION 2:
SIZING UP AN EARLY-OUT OFFER FROM YOUR EMPLOYER

The **RIF (reduction in force)** accompanied by a **package** or **early-retirement buyout** are becoming bywords of American corporate life. If one comes your way, you should be able to tell how generous the offer is and how much latitude you have in determining whether to accept it. You won't have much time, though. Employers typically demand that employees decide quickly whether to take early-out offers.

Compensation specialists report that such offers are becoming increasingly skimpier. Companies have shed the guilt they used to feel about downsizing their workforces and setting aside lifetime loyalties between them and many of their employees. Moral: If you are offered an early-retirement package, you may want to take it if only because the next one will likely be less generous—maybe a lot less.

Corporations generally use two types of buyouts. The first is the **early-retirement offer**, usually made to workers age 55 and over. It may include a better pension than you would normally have received retiring early; a bridge that pays you the equivalent of your reduced Social Security benefits until 62, when you can typically begin claiming the actual reduced benefits themselves; and a generous continuation of your medical coverage. Because formal early-retirement packages tend to be expensive, however, fewer than a third of corporations offer them. The second and more popular type of buyout is the so-called **voluntary-separation package**. It typically amounts to little more than enough to tide a family over for a year at most.

Here are the two considerations that should determine how to evaluate an early-out offer:

• **What choice you really have.** You can't be forced, under federal law, to take a package. Of course, you can be fired later for poor performance, demoted, or see your job eliminated—without any recourse. If you are inclined to turn down an offer, ascertain if your company wants you to stay. Let's say that your boss seems happy with your work and the offer is company-wide. Then, you can probably ignore it if you choose. However, if your boss is not pleased with your performance or the offer is restricted to a specific department, you might be wise to take the money and leave.

Perhaps the offer is generous but you don't feel pressure to accept it. Then turn it down. Remember that your pension rises with your salary and years of service. If you have been toiling at the same address for a couple of decades, it may be worth your while to carry on there for another few years.

• **What's in the offer.** The best elements in an early-retirement package: adding several years—from two to five—to your age, length of service, or both to fatten your pension payout; and a Social Security bridge. The best terms in a separation package: two or three weeks' salary for each year of your service, up to a maximum of a year's pay. A poor package, by contrast, might include only a week of salary for each year of service, or the offer might top out at 26 weeks and give you no health insurance.

Many early-retirement offers include lifetime health insurance, but voluntary-separation packages typically do not. The prospect of buying private insurance at a cost of several thousand dollars a year may be daunting. If you are not healthy, you may not even be able to obtain coverage. Since health care costs are sometimes the difference between comfort and poverty in retirement, this is no small consideration.

DECISION 3: DECIDING HOW TO TAKE YOUR PENSION AND 401(K) RETIREMENT ACCOUNT WITHDRAWALS

The first rule of making your money last is not to touch your retirement accounts until you have to—either to pay the bills or because the law requires you to do so. The reason? In a word: taxes. The longer you can continue to rack up tax-deferred returns, the better. An added bonus, especially if you're in a high tax bracket, is that sales from your taxable portfolio may count as long-term capital gains, at an 18% or 20% tax rate, while retirement plan withdrawals are taxed as ordinary income, at rates up to 38.6% through 2003; 37.6% through 2006.

An even bigger issue than minimizing taxes is figuring out how much money you can withdraw from your portfolio each year without running out of cash. Once you decide how much you need to cover expenses—and to what extent a pension, Social Security, or part-time work can fill the gap—you need to come up with a withdrawal strategy that doesn't deplete your account too quickly.

Retirement specialists warn that many retirees are too optimistic when they think they can withdraw 8% or more from their portfolios each year. Part of the problem is inflation. The other is basing plans on average returns and ignoring the sequence of annual returns. If a bear market occurs soon after you start taking withdrawals, you could run out of money much faster than you expected.

The best policy is to keep withdrawals to between 3% and 5% during the first year, and then adjust for inflation. If a withdrawal rate of 5% sounds too low—on a $500,000 portfolio, it amounts to just $1,500 a month after taxes if you're in the 28% tax bracket when you want to retire, in, say, 2006—consider taking a part-time job after you've retired. Or postpone retirement and keep stashing money in your retirement accounts. Even a short delay can mean a substantial increase in your retirement savings.

By law, you must start making mandatory withdrawals from your 401(k) and traditional and nondeductible IRAs, 403(b), Keogh, and SEP plans by April 1 of the year following the year you turn 70½. (If you have a Roth, of course, you never have to tap the account.) The federal penalty for not taking out at least the minimum is stiff: a full 50% of the amount you should have withdrawn. And you—or your financial advisers—are responsible for figuring out that number. To do that you'll need to use a uniform life expectancy table. (To see the new life expectancy tables, go to www.irahelp.com, the site run by tax expert Ed Slott.) The age of your beneficiary no longer figures into the calculation (unless, in the one remaining exception, your spouse is your beneficiary and is more than 10 years younger than you are).

Taking Your Pension: To Lump or Not to Lump

If an old-fashioned defined-benefit pension is in your future, you probably will be offered a choice when you retire. Take the pension as an **annuity** and get a monthly check for the rest of your life or take the money in **one lump sum** and invest it yourself. To lump or not to lump, that is the question.

Many pre-retirees warm to the idea of having a large lump sum. It makes them feel more secure about their future and lets them fantasize about spending it and possibly leaving a big chunk to their children or grandchildren. This kind of daydreaming, however, can lead you to turn one of the most important moves of your retirement planning into a long-term nightmare.

That's why many retirement planners who have much experience and their clients' interest at heart often recommend the annuity route for pensions. They see it as the safer way to go if the client is not ready or able to take on the responsibility for investing such a large amount of money—which could be as much as $1 million or more for many professionals and middle managers who have been at the same company for decades.

What if you are capable of guiding your investments and see it as an interesting way to spend some of your time in retirement? Then, taking the lump may be a smart move. With this choice, you can dip into principal if necessary to meet emergencies—an annuity can never give you more than the monthly allowance. In addition, while the value of the fixed annuity will inevitably decline because of inflation, you can protect a lump sum against rising prices by putting part of it in blue-chip growth stocks.

The best advice for anyone facing the lump versus annuity decision: Hire a competent tax accountant or a financial adviser or planner who specializes in retirement to help run the numbers and explain the pros and cons of both choices. This is one financial decision you don't want to make alone. You will be dealing with complicated actuarial assumptions, intricate tax regulations, and probably the largest pile of money you've ever had. Here are just a few questions you should discuss with your adviser:

1. Should you take the lump and pay tax on it at a favorable rate through 10-year averaging?

2. Should you roll the money over into an IRA, delaying taxation until you withdraw cash while letting the principal grow untaxed; how long are you likely to live; what rate of return can you expect on your investments?

3. Do you think inflation will erode your savings?

Here is a rare gift from the IRS, for those born before 1936: 10-year averaging. This special deal can lessen the tax blow, but you must take the money out in a lump sum.

Ten-year averaging is best for accounts worth around, say, $150,000 or so. The reason: The tax is calculated using 1986 rates, which are more generous to a moderate-size portfolio than today's are. This option requires you to pay income tax on your entire distribution in the year you take it, but you'll be taxed as if you were taking just 10% of the money, 10 times. So if you had, say, $150,000, you'd be taxed as if you were receiving 10 payments of $15,000—which adds up to less than the tax on one $150,000 chunk. Ask your accountant or plan administrator whether you qualify. If you qualify for 10-year averaging, use Form 4972 to figure your tax both ways and choose the one that results in the lower bill. And note: If you choose 10-year averaging, and if your pension distribution is less than $70,000, part of it is tax-free, thanks to what is called the minimum-distribution allowance.

You can use averaging only once. If you expect a bigger lump-sum distribution from another qualified plan in the future, you might want to postpone taking advantage of averaging. For instance, maybe you're taking early retirement from your current job and are going to work for another employer with a better savings plan and plenty of years before your next retirement. Odds are you'll do better by using averaging when you retire from your next position. Also read the next section to learn more about rollovers.

When you compare taking a lump sum through tax averaging with rolling over the whole caboodle into an IRA, the IRA is typically the winner. One exception: If you are going to be in a higher tax bracket when you draw money out of the IRA than you are when you retire, the rollover could be more costly than averaging. In general, however, the rollover wins not only because you are likely to be in a lower bracket later on, but also because the money will continue to compound tax-deferred inside the rollover IRA—a powerful force that often enlarges a nest egg measurably during the early years of retirement. Have your financial adviser or tax pro calculate how you would fare with each option.

What You Need to Know About 401(k) Rollovers

When you change jobs or retire, you'll likely get a five-, six-, or seven-figure lump sum from your 401(k)—probably the biggest pile of money you'll ever handle. Managed wisely, this payment can be a VIP pass to your retirement security.

Ideally, a lump-sum distribution should be funneled into either an IRA or another employer's plan, where you invest it to last a lifetime. But beware: Making a bad rollover decision could easily cost you more than half your nest egg in unnecessary taxes, penalties, and poor investments. Therefore, when making any rollover, you'll want to mind these points:

- **Be sure to do a direct, or trustee-to-trustee, transfer to the financial institution that will hold your IRA or manage your new 401(k).** If your old employer ends up writing a check in your name, 20% of the money will be withheld for taxes; therefore, in order to roll over the full amount, you will have to come up with the extra 20% yourself. If you do receive a check directly, you have 60 days to make the transfer. If you miss the deadline, the IRS will deem the amount a withdrawal and will impose an additional 10% penalty tax.
- **If you're rolling over into an IRA, the money must go into a regular IRA.** You can convert later to a Roth, if you wish to take advantage of its post-retirement tax benefits. If you want to retain the option of transferring your money from the IRA into a new employer's 401(k), keep the IRA separate from your other savings accounts and avoid mixing contributions. More on that particular rollover tactic in a bit.

Since your moves should fit into a comprehensive retirement-planning and tax strategy, you may need to work with a financial adviser, especially if you have a big bundle or are hoping to retire soon. Even if you hire a pro, however, you still need to understand the basics. We've broken them into three life stages for managing your rollover:

STAGE 1: CHANGING JOBS

Many employees who change jobs choose a cash payment rather than a rollover. But cashing out carries a price. You'll owe income taxes plus a 10% penalty if you're under age 59½, and you'll lose the opportunity for future tax-deferred growth.

- **Keeping the money in a 401(k).** If you like the investments in your former employer's 401(k) plan or don't want to go through the trouble of choosing new ones, there's little downside to staying put. It also may make sense to stick with the plan if you've made a significant amount of after-tax contributions. Why? You can't roll over dollars that have already been taxed (although you can roll over the earnings on those contributions).

- **Moving the money to your new 401(k).** This makes sense if your new plan has more or better options, or lower fees, than your previous one. Old plan or new, a 401(k) can be helpful if you'll ever need to borrow against the assets during an emergency. You can't do that with an IRA. Also consider a 401(k) if your job involves a high risk of lawsuits or if you fear bankruptcy: Company plans are federally regulated, so they're exempt from creditors; IRA assets, by contrast, are subject to state law, which may not protect them from creditors.

- **Rolling over into an IRA.** With all the benefits of 401(k)s, why would you opt for an IRA rollover? There are several reasons. First, an IRA lets you select virtually any investment option. It also provides more flexibility in choosing your beneficiary and (if you are retiring early) taking distributions. Another reason might be that your former employer won't let you keep your money in the company's 401(k) plan since most employers don't want to keep track of their ex-employees and all their descendants. Finally, today's good 401(k) plan might morph into tomorrow's bad one, especially if your old company merges or goes through a bout of cost cutting. In fact, most financial advisers prefer IRA rollovers to 401(k)s for their clients.

STAGE 2: APPROACHING RETIREMENT

The clock is ticking: It's time to decide what to do with your retirement plan money—keep it where it is or make the final rollover that will serve you throughout your retirement. You first need to determine when you will start making withdrawals. The payout procedures can differ significantly between 401(k)s and IRAs, but if there's one universal rule, it is this: You should draw first from your taxable accounts, so that your IRAs and 401(k)s can compound tax-deferred as long as possible. After all, your retirement could last 30 years or more, so you need to maximize growth.

Before making any rollover choice, check the rules of your company plan—details can vary widely from company to company. And consider these key rollover options for pre-retirees:

- **An early withdrawal from your 401(k).** If you have a sizable 401(k) but little money in your taxable accounts, you may want to stick with your company plan. That's because at many companies you can retire between 55 and 59½ and make regular withdrawals from your 401(k) without paying a penalty. (Your distribution schedule can continue if you later return to the work world—or even rejoin the same employer.) Of course, once you turn 59½ at any company, you're free to take out your 401(k) money at will without penalty if you're retired. But how you take advantage of the 401(k)'s early-withdrawal opening depends on your particular plan's policies. In most cases, you can choose only among the regular retirement withdrawal schedules set by the plan or take a lump-sum distribution. Simply pulling out your money may, in fact, end up being the best choice, since it offers the greatest flexibility. You could set aside what you need to spend in the next few years—taking the income tax hit— and roll over the rest tax-deferred into an IRA.

- **Turning your IRA into a 401(k).** This could be an intriguing option if you have little in a 401(k) but a lot in an IRA rollover. Moving that IRA money into a 401(k)—if the plan rules allow such a switch—will let you tap into your nest egg while avoiding the more restrictive early-withdrawal schedule of IRAs, which we note below. Bear in mind, though, that you'll need paperwork to prove your IRA is a rollover from a company plan and has not been mixed with other IRA money. (That's why we noted in the last stage to be careful in this area.) And the move may not be worth the hassle if you intend to roll out of your 401(k) in a few years.

  401(k) limitations. If you're older than 59½ and retiring, there's little reason to stick with your 401(k). Many company savings plans simply aren't that accommodating to retirees, and some plans force workers to take out all their money by the official retirement age, typically 65. If you don't make prior arrangements, such as a direct rollover into an IRA, you could be automatically mailed a check for the distribution—minus the 20% withholding tax.

  IRA limitations. If you really need to make withdrawals from your nest egg before age 59½, think twice about an IRA rollover. Generally, the only way to avoid paying an early-withdrawal penalty on an IRA is by taking periodic payments based on your life expectancy. (This rule for determining payment schedules applies to all IRA owners regardless of age.) The younger you are, the smaller your income stream will be. Plus, once you start taking withdrawals, you must continue for at least five years or until you turn 59, whichever is later.

- **A chance to unload company stock.** If you own a big helping of company shares in your retirement plan and you can't touch your company stock while you're still working, use an IRA rollover as an opportunity to diversify. Retiring workers with a bigger chunk may want to consider taking an in-kind distribution, which can sub-stantially lower your tax bill. Here's how it works: If you keep your company stock in your 401(k), you'll pay regular income taxes on it as you withdraw money. But before you roll over the money into an IRA (or take a lump sum), you can choose to with-draw some or all of your company stock separately. At that point, you'll pay tax not on the full value of the stock but only on the cost basis, which is what the shares were worth when they went into your account. When you sell the stock, you'll owe taxes only at capital-gains rates on your long-term profits. This strategy is a no-brainer if your stock has zoomed in value. But if gains have been modest, you may do better paying ordinary income taxes. Check with an accountant. Of course, if you can diver-sify out of company stock while you're still working, so much the better.

STAGE 3: IN RETIREMENT

Okay, you're no longer working. Time to chill out. Your chief task these days is man-aging your rollover and other retirement accounts. If you haven't already rolled out of your former company's 401(k) plan, consider doing so now, since IRAs generally offer the widest investment options for keeping your portfolio on track, as well as the best alternatives for distributions and estate planning. Here's what you need to consider:

- **Staying with stocks.** If you have a hefty nest egg, you will need to be well diversi-fied among stocks, funds, and other assets. Clearly, an IRA rollover to a good brokerage firm or other money-management outfit offers more choice than the typical 401(k) plan. But even though you may be changing your account, don't assume you all of a sudden need to make major changes in your asset allocation. In the early stages of retirement, you usually need as much growth as you did when you were working.
- **Updating your beneficiaries.** If you wish to pass money on to your heirs, IRAs are the more flexible choice. For example, nearly all 401(k) plans require that your spouse be listed as the primary beneficiary of your account, unless he or she signs a waiver. That makes it more difficult to pass money to your children or other heirs. By con-trast, major brokerage and mutual fund companies generally offer plenty of beneficiary options on IRAs. (If yours doesn't, attach a customized form that spells out your wishes—or move your money to a firm that offers more flexibility.) Always double-check your beneficiary forms, and update if necessary. To pass your IRAs to desired heirs, the people must be specifically named on the forms—stating your wishes in your will does not override the account documents.

• **Watching your withdrawals.** When it comes to mandatory withdrawals, IRAs rule, since they offer more options than company plans do for setting withdrawal schedules. Bear in mind, though, that by April 1 of the year following the year you turn 70½ you must begin withdrawing the required minimum distributions from your tax-deferred accounts, be they IRAs or 401(k)s. As we indicated earlier, the federal penalty for not taking out at least the minimum is stiff: a full 50% of the amount you should have withdrawn. And you are the one who is responsible for figuring out the number. As you've no doubt guessed, calculating the precise amount of that minimum distribution is no easy task, since the rates are based on your life expectancy and, in one specific instance (see page 261) those of a beneficiary.

Choosing Where You Want to Retire

While most retirees don't move out of their communities, each year about 500,000 Americans in their sixties do. What do they look for? According to experts interviewed by **MONEY**, retirees look for these attributes when they relocate, in descending order from most important to least: low crime, mild climate, affordable housing, attractive environment, proximity to cultural and educational activities, strong economic outlook, and excellent health care. (For places that score well in those departments, see the "Best Places to Retire" feature on www.money.com.)

Your priorities, of course, may differ. When you have chosen a place that seems right, spend six months to a year visiting the area—in as many seasons as possible—before you take the big step of buying a house there. During that time, soak up as much information as you can about the area. Find out about the best neighborhoods, activities for retired people, offerings by local colleges, the quality of municipal services, the cost of living, and so on. This is the only way to make sure that you and the community make a good fit.

One factor in choosing where to live in retirement is the amount of state taxes you'll owe. As it turns out, although every state has special provisions to lower tax liabilities for people age 65 and older, your tax bill can differ dramatically just by crossing state lines. Major differences:

• **Seven states have no personal income tax:** Alaska, Florida, Nevada, South Dakota, Texas, Washington, and Wyoming. Tennessee and New Hampshire impose individual income tax, but only on interest and dividend income.

- **Five states have no state sales tax:** Alaska, Delaware, Montana, New Hampshire, and Oregon.

- **Five states completely exclude Social Security benefits from their personal income tax bases,** and do not base their personal income tax on federal adjusted gross income (AGI) or federal taxable income (also called piggybacking): Alabama, Arkansas, Mississippi, New Jersey, and Pennsylvania.

- **Twenty-two states, plus the District of Columbia, allow taxpayers to deduct Social Security benefits that are included in federal AGI.** So in the following states, the Social Security benefits that are taxed at the federal level are not taxed at the state level: Arizona, California, Delaware, Georgia, Hawaii, Idaho, Illinois, Indiana, Kentucky, Louisiana, Maine, Maryland, Massachusetts, Michigan, New York, North Carolina, Ohio, Oklahoma, Oregon, South Carolina, Virginia, and Wisconsin.

- **Six states do impose tax on Social Security benefits that are taxed at the federal level** but either exempt a portion of the benefits or provide deductions for lower- to middle-income taxpayers: Colorado, Connecticut, Iowa, Missouri, Montana, and Utah.

- **Seven states tax all Social Security benefits that are taxed federally:** Kansas, Minnesota, Nebraska, New Mexico, North Dakota, Rhode Island, and West Virginia.

- **Vermont** is the only state that calculates personal income tax as a percentage of the federal income tax, including the federal income tax on Social Security benefits.

- **Most states that have an income tax exempt at least part of pension income from taxable income.** Different types of pension income (private, military, federal civil service, and state or local) are often treated differently for tax purposes. Only three states—Illinois, Mississippi, and Pennsylvania—fully exempt all pensions, both private and public, from taxation.

- **Seven states fully exempt public pensions** (federal, military, state, and local) but do not fully exempt private pensions. These states are: Alabama, Hawaii, Kansas, Louisiana, Massachusetts, Michigan, and New York.

CHAPTER 12

How to Manage Your Estate

More than any other chapter in this book, the one you're starting now deserves to be launched with a sermonette. Sorry about that, but there's no other way. Estate planning is the one personal finance topic that has a chilling effect on most people. And it shouldn't. When you're in your twenties, you tell yourself it's too early to think about such a grim subject as how to dispose of the worldly goods you haven't even accumulated yet. But that starts a process of putting it off until, ripe and maybe even a bit rich, you find yourself pushing 60. You know you should have looked into estate planning earlier, but the habit of procrastinating is almost as old as you are. Or perhaps you've never done any estate planning because you didn't want to pay a lawyer to draw up a will or trusts.

Here's the truth, short and bittersweet: Everyone—from the moment they are on their own financially—needs to think about estate planning and then do something about it—especially since Congress changed some key estate-law rules in the 2001 tax law. So don't wait a day longer. Strong words? Yes, but the argument behind them is just as powerful. There are six reasons to embark on estate planning: (1) to make sure that each of your assets goes to precisely the person you want to have it; (2) to prevent estate and death taxes from taking a huge bite out of your assets, leaving a diminished legacy for your heirs (see page 274 for a quick summary of estate tax limits); (3) to be sure your children are in good hands after you die; (4) to be prepared in case you can't take care of yourself any longer; (5) to have enough cash available for your heirs after you die in order to cover taxes due and pay your burial expenses; and (6) to be sure your loved ones know what you want them to do if you become incapacitated or die. Here are two examples of why estate planning can really matter.

A freak auto accident ends your life at age 29. You and your live-in lover have been accumulating stuff—furniture, a CD player, silverware—for four years. You may even own a house, condo, or co-op. Together, you've talked about wanting most of these possessions to go to the other in case one of you died. You've also made it clear that certain items of jewelry or art are to go to a brother or sister for sentimental reasons. But since you never bothered to make a will, under the laws of your state everything that you own goes to your parents.

Cancer claims your husband at 59, just as he is about to retire. You've been blessed over the years. The house you bought 33 years ago for $35,000 is now mortgage free and worth $450,000. You and your husband have retirement accounts, savings, investments, and personal property that push your net worth to $1.8 million. It turns out that your husband has kept all the assets in his name, however, and also died intestate, or without a will. Under the laws of the state where you live, his 90-year-old mother gets one-third of the $1.8 million, you get a third, and your two children split the other third. The fact that you and your husband had agreed that you were supposed to get it all doesn't matter to the state. Due to the spousal exemption, your third (or $600,000) will not be taxed, but if he died in 2002, the federal government would take $54,800 in estate taxes from the rest of the taxable estate since your husband's estate would have fallen into the 32% federal estate tax bracket. It could have been worse, because estate tax rates run as high as 50%. But it could have been much better: If you and your husband had done your estate planning, you could have eliminated the tax entirely.

End of sermonette.

Drafting a Letter of Instruction

Perhaps the most important estate-planning move you can make is the one that is easiest to ignore: drafting a **letter of instruction** to your loved ones. By putting down on paper the key things that should be done after you die, you will avoid many possible errors of judgment by your family and also help make the process of handling your final affairs a bit easier. You don't have to hire a lawyer to write this document. Just be sure you include the following: who should be contacted after you die; what kind of burial and funeral you prefer; how to take care of immediate financial matters; where your key financial documents are located; and any views you have about such important personal issues as how you'd like your children to be raised and what to do with your home. Of course, be sure that your family and key financial advisers know where to find this letter of instruction.

How to Own Your Property

Every time you take legal possession of a sizable asset—a house, a mutual fund, a bank account, jewelry, a car—you create a situation that determines how your estate will be distributed and taxed. So here's the first rule of estate planning: Decide how you want to own each important piece of property you acquire. You have a number of choices: fee simple or sole ownership, joint ownership (also known as joint tenancy with right of survivorship), tenancy in entirety, tenancy in common, and, in some states, community property. Many couples think that holding all their property jointly is always the best way to go. In fact, it isn't.

When confronted with the legal terms below, most Americans tend to become instantly befuddled. In fact, most people don't have the vaguest idea how they own their prime possessions. So here's the short of it: If yours is the only name attached to the asset's title, you own it individually ("fee simple"). If your name and one or more others appear on the title, then you all own the property either "in common" or as "joint tenants," depending on the laws of your state. Your best bet is to ask a lawyer in your state whose judgment you trust and then make sure that from then on you take ownership in the way that best meets your needs. Here are the detailed descriptions:

- **Fee simple** means that a piece of property is individually owned. You decide who will get it after you die. If, say, a husband's name is the only one that appears on the deed and other documents related to buying the house, he owns it outright and his wife has no part of that ownership. While this arrangement might simplify things if the couple eventually divorce or if his wife's work makes her vulnerable to being sued, it would considerably complicate any surviving spouse's life. That's because the house would have to go through **probate**, a costly and time-consuming court process discussed later in this chapter. (Attorney's fees and probate court costs cut at least 5% off an estate.) So if you're part of a couple, hold property as fee simple only when an estate attorney whom you trust advances a powerful reason for doing so.

- **Joint ownership** or **joint tenancy with right of survivorship** is designed for couples, married or otherwise. It means that two people share title to an asset and upon the death of one of them the survivor automatically becomes the sole owner. On the other hand, one partner has the right while alive to sell or give away his or her share without consulting the other. Joint tenancy is the easiest way to avoid the legal process of going through probate court. It makes a lot of sense if the value of your estate in 2002 is less than $1 million—this figure will rise each year before hitting $3.5 million in 2009. Joint ownership isn't necessarily the smartest way to hold assets if your estate's value exceeds the federal tax exemption amount set for that year, since a surviving spouse's estate worth more than, say, $3.5 million in 2009 would be vulnerable to federal estate tax. (Refer to estate tax law table on page 274 to see how much individuals can pass on to beneficiaries tax free until 2011, the year the current estate tax law bill expires.)

  In addition, if both spouses die simultaneously, the whole estate will immediately become subject to taxes. Another drawback of joint ownership: If one of you becomes incapacitated, the other may need to get permission from a court to sell jointly held assets.

- **Tenancy by the entirety** is a form of joint ownership recognized in some states. It differs from joint tenancy with right of survivorship in one important respect: Tenancy by the entirety requires a partner, who must be a spouse, to secure the permission of the other before disposing of his or her share in the asset. This provision avoids such unpleasant surprises as when, say, a husband gives valuable assets to his children from an earlier marriage without informing his wife. One drawback: If a couple die with the entire estate in tenancy by the entirety, one spouse might be wasting his or her federal estate tax exemption.

  This would be true in a situation where a husband dies before the wife, and all of the deceased husband's property went to the wife under protection of the unlimited marital deduction. In that case, estate tax would be deferred completely at the husband's death, but the estate would be taxed at the wife's death. And at her death, she would be then entitled to only *her* lifetime exclusion and effectively the husband's would have been "wasted." To take advantage of both exclusions, a portion of the assets (up to the exclusion amount, which would be $1 million in 2002) should go to the children or to a trust for their benefit and the rest of the property to pass under the marital deduction.

- **Tenancy in common** is when two or more people share ownership in property with the right to bequeath their shares to whomever they wish. In other words, the surviving spouse won't necessarily get all the assets in the estate when his or her spouse dies. Also, tenants in common don't have to have equal interests in an asset, unlike joint tenants and tenants by the entirety. You could have a 55% interest and the other tenant could have a 45% interest, for example. Tenancy in common often is used by business partners and spouses who plan to leave their valuables to somebody else— say, children from a former marriage.

• **Community property** is the rule for couples who are residents of Arizona, California, Idaho, Louisiana, Nevada, New Mexico, Texas, Washington, and Wisconsin. In those states all property acquired after a couple gets married is considered to be owned equally by the two partners. All assets owned by one of the partners before the marriage continue to be owned separately. If you live in a community property state, you'll need a prenuptial agreement artfully crafted by a first-rate estate attorney in order to keep separate ownership of property that was acquired after the nuptials.

The Basics of Estate Taxes

To understand estate planning, you need to understand the rules of federal estate tax. (State death taxes vary tremendously depending on where you live; talk with an estate attorney to find out what you can do now to lower the death taxes when the time comes. For example, if you're about to retire, you might want to move to a state with low death taxes.)

Up to 2004, the unified estate and gift tax maximum is combined in one number (that would be $1 million in 2002 through 2003). The federal estate exemption represents the maximum amount of your estate that you can pass on free of federal estate taxes during your life or after you die. Beyond that, any individual may give to any other individual up to $11,000 (in 2002) a year without incurring any gift tax ($20,000 for couples). Starting in 2004, your estate tax and gift tax exemption are no longer unified. The lifetime gift tax exemption will be $1 million until 2010. And the estate tax exemption will rise incrementally from $1 million in 2004 to $3.5 million in 2009. (IRS Publication 448 provides more details on federal estate and gift taxes; go to www.irs.gov for contact information or to download. The rules are different and complicated for family-owned businesses, so talk to your estate-planning advisers for more information.)

The federal tax exemption amount set each year (see table) is actually more generous than it sounds. First, it is calculated after deductions for charitable gifts, debts, funeral expenses, and executor's and attorney's fees. Far more important, all property left to a surviving spouse goes directly to the spouse without tax, thanks to the unlimited marital deduction. So, no matter how large an estate is, it isn't taxed by Uncle Sam upon the death of a married individual as long as the assets are left to a surviving spouse who is a U.S. citizen.

If the surviving spouse is not a U.S. citizen, he or she receives no such special treatment under the law. The only way to get around this provision is to set up what's known as a **qualified domestic trust** for the survivor. The unlimited deduction is restored, but there may be no distribution of assets to that noncitizen spouse without incurring estate tax. On the other hand, he or she may draw all the income from the trust free of estate tax.

Taxable estates over the exemption amount, however, are severely whacked by the IRS. For details check out the federal tax rate schedule below.

ESTATE TAX SCHEDULE

The 2001 tax law slowly increases the amount you can leave to heirs tax-free and repeals estate taxes altogether for one year (in 2010); the breaks vanish in 2011. At that time, estates exceeding $1 million will be subject to the so-called death tax once again.

Estate Taxes	Exemption	Top Rate for Estate and Gift Tax
2002	$1 million	50%
2003	$1 million	49%
2004	$1.5 million	48%
2005	$1.5 million	47%
2006	$2 million	46%
2007	$2 million	45%
2008	$2 million	45%
2009	$3.5 million	45%
2010	Unlimited	35% on gifts/No tax on estates[1]
2011	$1 million	55%

[1]Modified cost-basis rules in effect for one year.

Sources: Economic Growth and Tax Relief Reconciliation Act of 2001, CCH, Joint Committee on Taxation, Research Institute of America.

It's easy to see from this table how quickly a middle-class family's legacy can become depleted. A house bought decades ago for five figures could easily be worth $500,000 today. Add savings, investments, life insurance, and retirement accounts and a couple's net worth can top $1 million with no problem at all. An estate of that size would trigger estate tax of hundreds of thousands of dollars, without savvy planning.

How big an estate do you have? To find out, scribble down on a sheet of paper the totals for all of your assets—your bank accounts and CDs, mutual funds, stocks, bonds, real estate, personal property, and the eventual death benefit of your life insurance policy. The sum of these figures gives you the total value of your gross estate. Then, add up your estate's liabilities: the amount left on your mortgage, other loans and debts still outstanding, the estimated cost of your funeral and burial costs, and the cost of settling your estate (figure 5% to 10% of the gross value of the estate). Subtract those liabilities from your gross estate and you'll have a rough idea of the value of your estate, before taxes. Fortunately there are a multitude of offsetting estate-planning techniques, including two that don't require hiring lawyers or drawing up fancy documents:

- **Making gifts while you are alive.** The annual $11,000-per-person (this limit is subject to change from year to year) gift tax exclusion can be a great way to reduce estate taxes. Let's say you have two children and three grandchildren, a beloved sibling, and a cousin who has not been as fortunate financially as you have been. In a single year you and your spouse could give $20,000 to each of these seven people tax-free, thereby reducing your estate by $140,000 in that year alone. You might also add some bequests to an institution such as your alma mater and to a few favorite charities, moving even more out of the grasp of estate taxes. When making a gift to someone under 18 (or 21 in California), you should put it in a custodial account at a bank, brokerage, or mutual fund. Name a custodian other than yourself. That's because if you don't, the IRS will treat the gift as part of your taxable estate should you die before the child reaches the age of majority.
- **Leaving your heirs investments that have appreciated.** Another way to substantially decrease the size of your taxable estate is what amounts to perhaps the largest loophole left in federal tax law. Some mordantly call it the "angel of death" provision. It is more formally known as **tax-free step-up in basis**. Translation: Your heirs pay no taxes on any capital gains on investments you leave them when you die. For instance, let's say you bought $10,000 of Berkshire Hathaway stock years ago and its market value is now $200,000. If you died tomorrow and left that stock to your daughter in your will, she would owe tax only on any capital gain between your death and the date she sold the stock. So your $190,000 in appreciation will not be taxed.

Reason: The basis for tax purposes of this asset was stepped up from $10,000 to $200,000 at your death.

The 2001 tax laws will do away with stepped-up cost basis after 2009. Also, this loophole, potentially huge in the case of appreciated stock, is somewhat less roomy when it comes to mutual funds. That's because funds typically make periodic capital-gains distributions and you must pay capital-gains tax on those distributions at the time. So from an estate tax point of view, it may be best to invest in stock mutual funds that have minimal capital-gains distributions. These could be index funds and other stock funds whose managers don't sell shares very often; a fund with a portfolio turnover rate of less than 50% would qualify. One cautionary note: Variable annuities and IRAs, a popular way of investing in stock mutual funds and deferring income tax, do not qualify for a tax-free step-up in basis.

Why You Need a Will—and Possibly Some Trusts

This chapter began with a sermon. Now here's an order: If you are an adult and have any assets, get a will! Without one, you will die intestate and upon your death the distribution of your property will be made according to the laws of the state you lived in. Chances are these laws will not correspond to whatever plans you had in mind for giving away what you've got. For instance, in most states a married parent's assets are apportioned among his or her spouse and children, often with half to two-thirds going to the kids. Then there is the matter of taxes. Writing a will alone will not free your estate from getting taxed. But a will is the proper repository for any trusts you might want to set up to minimize taxes.

In addition, a will lets you name a person or persons who will manage your affairs or take care of your children after you die. You'll want to name an **executor**, the person to carry out your instructions for disposing of your property. This way you'll avoid the need for a court-appointed administrator, who not only would likely be expensive, but would not have your best interests at heart, since he or she would not know you or your interests. If you have children, you'll also want to appoint a **guardian**. This person would be responsible for raising your kids and managing their inheritances if they were minors when you died—or, if you're married, when both you and your spouse died. If you fail to name caretakers for your kids, a probate court judge will appoint guardians of his or her own choosing for the children and their assets.

If you're thinking of relying on joint ownership as a worthy substitute for a will, think again. Here's why: Take a childless couple without a will who are in an auto accident in which the wife is killed while the husband survives for a day or so. The wife's half of the couple's joint property would automatically pass to the husband. Because there is no will, however, all of the couple's assets would go to the husband's relatives after his death, leaving her family with nothing.

If you're convinced that you need a will, here's your next order: Get it right! Otherwise the will may not do what you want it to do. For instance, if you have heirs who are very young, disabled, or simply disinclined to manage their money well, you will shortchange them if you write only a rudimentary will. What if you and your spouse die and you have left all your assets to your minor children in your will? The guardian of their property named in that will must then report expenditures and investments on the children's behalf to a judge. This gives a judge who is unfamiliar with your financial goals and investment philosophy power over how your legacy is managed and spent.

Be sure your will contains the following: your name, the date, your assets and the names of the beneficiaries you have chosen, provisions for any trusts (more about them shortly), the names of any guardians, executors, and trustees, and your signature. You'll need two witnesses who watch you sign the document. If you have changed the will, you'll be adding a **codicil**. Your original will and any codicils must be witnessed and signed. You'll want to update the will at least every three years, and certainly after any momentous event in your life such as the birth of a child, the death of a loved one, your marriage, or your divorce. In addition, it's important to have an estate attorney review your will after Congress or your state passes any major legislation affecting estate or death taxes.

You may have thought that trusts are exclusively a way for the rich to pass on money to their kids and save some taxes to boot. If so, it's time to jettison that notion. Actually, trusts are a financial device that anyone can use to own assets, to buy or sell them, or to transfer them. In some cases trusts can save on income taxes or estate taxes. In some cases they help speed up the processing of an estate after the person setting up the trust dies. Depending on the trust, you may or may not have to give up legal ownership of the assets you put into it.

To clear up some confusion about trusts, here are three myths about them that should be exploded right now:

Myth 1: Trusts are expensive. They actually can cost as little as $250 each.

Myth 2: Trusts are for old people. In truth, their primary function is to protect children and preserve their inheritances. It's wise to create a trust in your will to hold your children's inheritances. Among their other advantages, trusts keep money out of children's hands until you think the kids will be mature enough to manage the cash.

If you simply leave assets to your kids in your will, they can claim their inheritances when they reach the age of majority, which is 18 in most states.

Myth 3: Trusts are too complicated to understand. (The following short course on trusts will show that this is not so.)

It's true that trusts, like any legal documents, have their own jargon. Once you understand the different types of trusts and what they can do, however, you'll see that the world of trusts isn't really all that complicated after all.

The best way to make sense of the different types of trusts is by seeing how they fit into the answers to two key questions:

1. **When does the trust kick in?** That depends on which of the two types of trusts you're talking about. A **testamentary trust** is part of your will and takes effect upon your death; most trusts are testamentary. This kind of trust can save estate taxes for a married couple after the second spouse dies. However, a testamentary trust will go through probate. A **living trust** isn't part of your will, and it starts to operate during your lifetime. Another useful benefit of a living trust: The assets inside it escape probate.

2. **Can you change a trust if you change your mind?** Here again, it depends on which of two types of trusts you're talking about. A **revocable trust** means you can change its provisions or even terminate it while you are alive. Property in a revocable trust is part of your taxable estate because you controlled it during your lifetime. So there are no estate tax advantages to setting up a revocable trust. A revocable trust won't go through probate, however, and its contents will thus forever remain private. An **irrevocable trust** is one you can't change or alter. Nor can you control its assets. An irrevocable trust can dramatically cut your estate tax since all property in this kind of trust is not included in your estate for the purpose of calculating estate taxes. Confining? Yes! But a real money-saver for your heirs. You'll want to put appreciating investments in an irrevocable trust, since their growth in value won't be hit with gift or estate taxes.

There are eight basic types of trusts that you might want to consider, depending on your needs and wishes. Here's what they are and how they work:

• **Bypass trust.** (A living or testamentary, revocable estate tax cutter. Sometimes called an **A/B trust**, a **unified credit trust**, or **credit-shelter trust**.) A bypass trust is the most important trust in estate planning. Couples use reciprocal bypass trusts in order to leave double the standard exclusion to their heirs free of estate tax—for 2002 and

2003, that would be $2 million. In other words, a bypass trust can raise the amount your heirs will get from you.

Each spouse would set up a separate bypass trust. It can be either testamentary or living; most are now of the living variety, which do not involve the expense and inconvenience of probate court filings, as is the case with testamentary trusts. Say the husband dies or becomes unable to manage his financial affairs in 2002. At that point, up to $1 million of his assets gets placed in his trust. The wife then starts receiving income from the trust and is also entitled to as much as 5% or $5,000 of the principal each year, whichever is greater. In addition, the trustee has the right to give the wife whatever part of the principal she needs for general support or to pay her medical bills. If she were to die in, say, 2003, she could pass on to her heirs $1 million tax-free, thanks to her right to exclude that amount from her taxable estate. On top of that, the $1 million from the trust goes to the beneficiaries and no estate tax is due on that amount, either. (If the wife dies first, of course, her trust is funded similarly for the husband's benefit.) So the beneficiaries wind up with $2 million free and clear.

• **Life insurance trust.** (A testamentary, irrevocable estate tax cutter.) The death benefits from life insurance policies are often a major part of an estate. Not always, though. With this type of trust, your life insurance proceeds go into the trust instead of into your taxable estate, which reduces the amount of potential estate tax. So if you think your estate will be taxable, you might want to put your life insurance policy into one of these trusts. Typically, your spouse also gets income from the trust for life and can even tap its principal if necessary. After he or she dies, the remaining assets go to the heirs named in your trust agreement.

Two catches: First, once you put a cash-value life insurance policy in a trust, you give up the ability to borrow against it. (However, the transfer of a policy with cash surrender value constitutes a gift to the beneficiary. Unless you give your beneficiary a right of withdrawal of a certain amount of money, none of the transfer qualifies for the $11,000 annual gift tax exclusion.) Second, if you die within three years of establishing a life insurance trust, the benefits are included in your taxable estate. That's why attorneys often include a clause in this kind of trust agreement stating that should you die within three years, the insurance proceeds would go directly to your spouse or into a trust for his or her benefit. That trust, in turn, is included in his or her estate.

• **Qualified Personal Residence Trust (QPRT).** If your most valuable asset is your home—or if you're concerned about squabbling heirs—QPRTs allow you to give away your home at a deeply discounted value (that's great if you're betting that estate taxes won't get wiped out); live in the home after you've given it to the trust; and avoid probate and minimize chances that family members or others will contest your wishes.

QPRTs are established to last for a set amount of time before your home passes to your heirs. During the QPRT, you must use the home as your primary residence or for vacations. When the trust is established, the IRS discounts the value of the home. For example, if a 55-year-old man put his $1 million house in a 20-year QPRT, the IRS would value it at $202,450. The keys to getting a steep discount are the QPRT's term (longer is better) and your age (older is better). Creating a QPRT runs about $2,000 to $4,000. The trusts are irrevocable, so be sure you want one before you sign.

What's the catch? If you want to continue living in the home when the QPRT ends, you must pay your heirs fair market rent. Also, your heirs don't get a step-up in cost basis, as they would if they inherited the house via a will, so they may face extra capital-gains taxes if they sell the property rather than live in it themselves for at least two years.

- **Qualified Terminable Interest Property (QTIP).** Tax avoidance isn't the only reason to set up a trust. For instance, what happens if your surviving spouse remarries and her new husband spends the money you hoped would go to your kids? A **credit-shelter or bypass trust** helps to safeguard your assets for your heirs. But remember, you can't put in more than the estate tax exclusion. Put the remaining property in a QTIP trust.

  Here's how a QTIP works: In brief, a spouse—say, the husband—puts property intended for the wife in a QTIP. When the husband dies, the wife is entitled to all of the trust income. After her death, however, the trust principal passes to beneficiaries who were named by the husband when the trust was established. Assume, for example, that the husband dies first. Upon his death, assets intended for his wife go into the QTIP. His wife will receive the trust income during her lifetime, but she can withdraw trust principal only if she has no other means to pay for her health care, education, maintenance, or support. When the wife dies, whatever is left in the QTIP goes to the beneficiaries named by the husband. If the wife dies first, the QTIP will operate the same way, but with the trust income going to her husband before the principal is divided among her beneficiaries.

- **Charitable remainder unitrust.** (A living or testamentary, irrevocable income tax cutter that can also provide income for life.) This type of trust does a variety of useful things: It lets you give assets to a charity while you're alive, for example, and receive tax deductions when you make the donations, and it gives you or members of your family all the trust's income for life. After a specified time period, often upon the death of your surviving spouse, the trust terminates and the charity gets outright ownership of the assets. But, one hurdle for these trusts is that at creation, they must be set up legally so that the remainder interest for the charity will eventually be at least 10% of the initial fair market value of the trust. A charitable remainder unitrust is either living or testamentary because you can create one while you're alive or write it into your will. In the latter case, the donated property is still considered part of your estate, but a portion of its value is deductible before estate taxes are taken out. If you start a charitable remainder unitrust while you are alive, you'll probably get an income tax deduction in the first year equal to the value of the remainder interest, an amount that your lawyer or accountant can calculate using special IRS guidelines. Despite the irrevocability of the unitrust, you can drop the charity you originally named as beneficiary and name another later. Most charitable remainder trusts require at least $50,000.

- **Charitable lead trust.** (A living or testamentary, irrevocable income tax cutter that preserves assets for your heirs.) This variation on a charitable remainder unitrust assumes a level of affluence beyond that of most middle-class people. That's because the charity gets all the income from the donated assets until you die. Then your heirs receive the assets. In exchange for giving the trust's income, you get larger tax write-offs—in some cases up to the full value of your contribution. IRS tables compute the size of your estate tax deduction for a charitable lead trust based on the amount you contribute, the investment's projected rate of return, and the trust's specified life. For example, let's say you set up a 20-year charitable lead trust with a principal value of $100,000 and a payout rate of 6.5%. The charity gets $6,500 a year for the term of the trust and you get an estate tax deduction of $71,842. The value of the payout is deductible from your income tax only for the year you place the property in the trust. But since in future years the payout is taxed to the giver—you—many people decide not to claim any income tax deduction at all; then none of the payout is taxed to you.
- **Charitable remainder annuity trust.** (A living or testamentary, irrevocable income tax cutter that provides income.) This works much like a charitable remainder unitrust, but the charity pays the donor a fixed amount each year, usually 7% to 9% of principal. Appreciated property producing little or no income makes the best gift for this type of trust. The reason: If you sold the property and reinvested the proceeds for higher income, you would incur a taxable capital gain. If a charitable trust sells the property and then replaces it with an annuity, no capital-gains tax is due, however.
- **Grantor retained trust.** (A living, irrevocable estate tax cutter that lets you transfer property to your heirs.) There are three types: **GRITs** (for **grantor retained income trusts**), **GRATs** (**grantor retained annuity trusts**), and **GRUTs** (**grantor retained unitrusts**). If you are looking for ways to transfer major assets to your heirs while reducing your exposure to estate tax, one or more of these may be for you—after you have a serious discussion about them with your estate attorney. After you create a GRIT, you keep getting any income from it for a specified period. And a

house included in a GRIT would be yours to live in for a specified number of years. After the trust's term elapses, ownership of the property goes to the beneficiary, removing it from your estate. If you die before the trust expires, however, its assets are taxable in your estate.

Many wealthy people use GRITs to avoid estate taxes on such significant assets as houses, artworks, or antiques. GRATs and GRUTs differ from GRITs because the grantor—you—must get a fixed payment from the trustee, even if the trust does not generate enough income. In such a case, the trustee can either sell trust assets to cover the shortfall or borrow the funds.

A Trust Apart: The Living Trust

The **living trust** entered American folklore back in the '60s with the enormously successful publication of Norman Dacey's *How to Avoid Probate!* This volume, a large portion of which consisted of **inter vivos** (Latin for "among the living") trust forms waiting to be filled out, promoted the living trust as the ideal way to keep your estate out of probate court. All you did was set up an inter vivos or living trust and transfer your assets to it, and the property could pass unimpeded to your chosen heirs. What's more, since a living trust is revocable, you can alter it or even end it while you are alive. The popularity of Dacey's book has since spawned a hard-sell living trust industry hawking seminars, books, do-it-yourself kits, and direct advice from what some scornful lawyers dismiss as "trust mills."

As you might suspect, there's more to estate planning than just setting up a living trust. As a matter of fact, a living trust is not advisable for many people. What's more, a living trust doesn't do everything some of its hard-charging advocates claim. Before putting your signature on a living trust document, you'll want to discuss the matter with a first-rate estate attorney, but here are the things you should know before you even start his or her fee clock ticking.

The case for avoiding probate is compelling. As noted in the previous discussion of bypass trusts, not only is the court process expensive, it can be time-consuming. Probate courts often take from a few months to two or three years from the time of death until they are finally done with a case, although some states have streamlined the process. Still another plus: By avoiding probate court, living trusts ensure that your affairs are kept private after you die. Wills and trusts that pass through probate become part of the public record.

On the other hand, since a living trust is revocable, its contents are included in your taxable estate, a stark contrast to the essential function of most of the trusts named above—keeping assets safe from estate taxation. In exchange for taxes, the living trust offers vast flexibility. For instance, you can retain any or all income a living trust produces, act as the trustee, change the trust's provisions, or even terminate it.

Many middle-class people find themselves in just the right niche to benefit from a living trust because their estates are not large enough to be subject to federal estate tax; the value of assets in the estate does not exceed the federal estate exemption. If you think your estate may exceed the federal exemption when you die, you may want to set up a living trust to maintain control of the assets you place in it during your lifetime. When you die, the trust can remain intact for the benefit of your heirs or it can terminate, with its assets distributed to those same beneficiaries.

Another advantage of the living trust is that it accommodates what for many people is the best form of trusteeship. First, you can act as your own trustee while you are in good health. Should your doctor certify that you are no longer able to handle your own affairs, a successor trustee named by you takes over trust management. The far less pleasant alternative is for your family or friends to ask a judge to declare you incapacitated and name a **conservator** to handle your investments and pay your bills. A conservatorship's annual fees can equal three-quarters of 1% of your assets. Conservatorships also have an ugly history of political patronage and corruption.

Besides exposure to estate taxes, the biggest disadvantage of a living trust is the inconvenience involved in transferring your assets to it. Title must be meticulously changed on all documents for your stocks, mutual funds, life insurance, bank accounts, and real estate to show that the trust, not you, owns the assets. This is almost always far more tedious and time-consuming than you expect. Do it wrong (or forget to do it, as many people with living trusts have) and the assets will be subject to probate.

If you decide to set up a living trust, have your attorney write a so-called **pour-over will**, in which you can bequeath personal property of limited or sentimental value and, if you wish, name a guardian for your minor children. This is also the place to stipulate that any items that you neglected to put in your living trust should go there after your death. As a result, all of your property will be administered in one place for the security of your beneficiaries. Any such forgotten items will become subject to probate, though.

Your particular situation may have a bearing on whether a living trust is appropriate for you. For instance, gay partners may be particularly well suited for a living trust. Their relationship often is not legally recognized, and their wishes set down in a will may be more easily challenged in court than if they had set up living trusts. A gay partner can be trustee, co-trustee, or successor trustee and take over managing the assets immediately if the other partner is incapacitated. A co-trustee can be one of two people serving in a joint trustee capacity or a person who is appointed to oversee the acts of a bank or brokerage firm serving as a trustee. A successor trustee is named to take over in the event the initial trustee dies or is removed or resigns from the position.

Picking Executors, Trustees, and Guardians

As outlined earlier in this chapter, these are the three essential players who can carry out your wishes once you are no longer able to do so. An **executor** is the person you name in your will to wrap up your financial affairs and make sure your will is probated. A **trustee** is the person you nominate at the time you set up a trust to administer it. A **guardian** is someone you name in your will to watch over the interests of your heirs—principally young children—once you are gone. Some details and advice for choosing these critical appointees:

The executor of your will sets the value of the assets that are part of your estate. This does not include trusts, life insurance policies, pension plans, and some kinds of jointly owned property, which pass directly to beneficiaries. The executor sometimes must hire an appraiser, lawyers, accountants, and other professionals to identify asset values. Fees for all these pros come out of your estate, as does the executor's fee, which typically can run from 3% to 5% of the estate. (If the executor is a family member or friend, the fee often is waived.) The executor sees that all your remaining debts get paid, files tax returns, and distributes whatever is left to your heirs. He or she must keep careful records and give the probate court a detailed account of all money received, spent, or held by your estate.

For estates of up to $2 million or so, with only a handful of beneficiaries and few complicated assets like a portfolio of volatile stocks, the best choice for an executor is often a spouse or best friend—in short, a beneficiary. For larger estates, two executors may be advisable: someone close to you who will be able to interpret your wishes and another person, perhaps an employee of a bank or another financial institution, who will make business or investment decisions, pay taxes, and keep records. You can spell out their specific responsibilities in your will; otherwise both executors are considered equally responsible for all aspects of the estate. Before you decide on an executor, make that person aware of your choice to ensure that he or she is willing to accept the responsibility. Some people won't want the responsibility that comes with being an executor; you and your heirs will be far better off finding this out before you die. Go over your will with your executor: Your intentions must be known so they can be carried out.

Choosing a trustee is even more critical if you have any trusts. While the executor's job lasts at most a year or two, the trustee's can drag on for decades and affect the disposition of most, if not all, of your assets. The trustee typically gets wide discretion to manage your property and distribution income and even principal. That's why a trustee ought to know enough about personal finance to be able to make sound investment judgments either on his own or based on the advice of reliable advisers.

Just as with an executor, it is wise to base the selection of a trustee largely on how tough a job he or she will face. If the trust provides for mandatory distribution of income or trustee discretion regarding just one or two beneficiaries, the task will not be too challenging. But if the trustee will have discretion to distribute income and principal in unequal amounts among several heirs, the job can become hellishly complicated. Just consider all the deliciously gossipy books and magazine articles relating the fights among beneficiaries and the suits brought by heirs against trustees charging mismanagement. If you think that kind of thing can happen only to the Rockefellers of the world, you're wrong.

More and more, in fact, middle-class families are turning to independent trustees, for reasons far more mundane and practical than internecine jealousy. In the past, when trusts were used primarily for large estates, the trustee's main role was to preserve assets. That's how the comic-book caricature of the sleepy bank trust department presided over by a dreamy octogenarian came into the culture. Increasingly, as middle-class estates have become the order of the day, the demand is growing for trustees who will preserve purchasing power for trusts that may last many years. So the emphasis is moving toward counteracting the effects of inflation.

To find this kind of expertise, you might want to hire a professional trustee, usually a trust company that may be independent or a subsidiary of a bank or investment house. Interview at least three or four trust companies to make sure that you'll get the kind of service you want. Ask about their fees (usually an annual charge of 1% to 1.5% of the value of the assets under management) and their investment philosophy, so you can see if you are comfortable with it. Many families name a **co-trustee**—a friend or relative who will be able to work with the pros, to make sure your wishes are fulfilled.

If you have minor children, you'll want to name a guardian for them in your will or trust. Choose this person extremely carefully. The best candidates for the job are friends or family members who are not only young enough to cope with children, but have the time and inclination to take up the responsibility. Sound out any prospects beforehand, to test both their will to perform the task and their values, which should be similar to yours. You may even want to appoint two guardians: one to take care of your children's well-being and the other, known as a **property guardian**, to manage their finances. Splitting the duties is especially worth considering if you don't think the guardian who will be raising your children has enough knowledge to handle your finances well.

Living Wills and Powers of Attorney

Just as trusts may be underused because of the mistaken impression that they are only for the rich, living wills are often not in place when they should be; however, attitudes seem to be changing.

A living will typically consists of two parts. One states exactly what kind of medical treatment you want—and/or do not want—in case you have a terminal illness or one from which recovery is deemed medically impossible. Depending on the state in which you live, you may need one medical directive or you may need two. Let's talk about them separately first. A **durable power of attorney for health care** (also known as a **health care power of attorney**) gives another individual you choose the right to make medical decisions for you if you can't make them for yourself. A **living will** tells your loved ones (and the staff of a hospital) how you wish to be cared for in case you become terminally ill and includes instructions about whether you wish to be placed on life support. In some states both of these have been replaced by a single document called a **medical directive**. Hospitals and nursing homes often hand out forms, but it's better to have handled these matters beforehand. You can get copies from estate-planning attorneys, or at stores that sell legal documents, or for free by contacting the Partnership for Caring, a national nonprofit organization that works to improve the quality of care at the end of life (800-989-9455; www.partnershipforcaring.org). Other helpful Web sites for elder-care resources: Children of Aging Parents (800-227-7294; www.caps4caregivers.org), Eldercare Locator (800-677-1116; www.aoa.gov/elderpage/locator.html), and the National Academy of Elder Law Attorneys (520-881-4005; www.naela.org).

Just as with a guardian, you should ask the person you want to designate as your proxy whether he or she will agree to take on this role, if necessary. Usually this person will be a close friend, your spouse, or one of your children. It's also essential to be sure that your designated proxy, family, financial advisers, and doctor have a copy of your living will. Bring a copy to a hospital whenever you are admitted, too.

Before moving on to the next section, a word or two about **durable power of**

attorney for finances. A durable power of attorney for finances is a document that gives another person the ability to make financial decisions for you if you become incapacitated and can't do so for yourself. That person can access your accounts and sign your checks if necessary. Many estate planners will include a durable power of attorney in a basic estate package.

It's well worth having. Say your father, long widowed, falls ill and as a result his financial life starts to unravel. Bills are going unpaid. Creditors are calling. Without power of attorney, you'd have to go to court and ask to be named his legal guardian. You'd have to report to the court frequently, filing documents on how assets are performing and how much money is being spent. People who've been through this process say it's a nightmare. Having power of attorney is the way to avoid it.

Whom should you give this important power to? Most people give it to their spouse or an adult child, a sibling, or a trusted friend. It should be someone who is comfortable enough with his or her own finances to be able to handle yours. If you have no family members or friends whom you trust to make sound financial decisions, you can give power of attorney to your longtime accountant or attorney.

You will want to talk to your estate lawyer about all of these issues because they are complex, require precise execution, and vary from state to state. Also, your lawyer can often tailor aspects of your estate plan to your exact desires. For instance, a power of attorney can be made as broad or narrow as you like, deferred (as with a living will), or otherwise. That is just one reason why selecting a lawyer for your estate plan is critically important.

Choosing and Using an Estate Attorney

Here is a rule that is easy to follow and that, if ignored, could cause catastrophe: All but the simplest estate documents should be drawn up by a competent lawyer. For a simple will, go ahead and spend the $250 or so that a lawyer will typically charge. You could, of course, save a few bucks by drawing up the will yourself with the help of a software package like Quicken Lawyer 2002 Personal Deluxe, which you can buy online at www.nolopress.com, or by calling 1-800-992-6656 ($41.97). Trouble is, you might think the issues of law are simpler than they actually are, glossing over a legal thicket that could expose your will to challenge when it is probated. A will program may also not be as precise as you'd like. For instance, the software might give so much discretion to trustees that you can wind up letting the trustee favor one of your children over another. A will needs to be reviewed periodically, and on occasions such as the passage of a major tax law, software is no substitute for a knowledgeable attorney. Even more important, each state has a different set of persnickety formalities you must follow to the letter in order to make a will valid. Get any of them wrong and your heirs could face the horror of watching as a court declares your do-it-yourself will invalid and you intestate. Then the laws of intestacy kick in and distribute your assets according to their provisions, not your desires.

One safe use of a will-writing program: Draw up the document with the software and then take it to a lawyer. By putting so many of the details in order ahead of time, you will incur fewer billable hours of the attorney's time.

When you move beyond a will into the more complicated territory of trusts, it's imperative to find a competent estate attorney. A savvy lawyer will also be an essential ally if you own property in more than one state or have a stepfamily; in both instances estate planning can get tricky. As with any professional, word-of-mouth referrals are the usual way of locating a lawyer. A reliable way to check out any lawyer referral is to go to the public library or a law library and look him or her up in the *Martindale-Hubbell Law Directory* (www.lawyers.com). It lists attorneys throughout the United States and features a rating system based on the judgments of other lawyers in the same community. The two top ratings: **a v** (for excellent legal ability and adherence to ethical standards) and **b v** (for high to very high legal ability and adherence to ethical standards). If the attorney you're vetting has either of these designations, you can be pretty sure of his or her competence. Being absent from *Martindale-Hubbell* or lacking one of its top ratings is not necessarily a negative mark, however, particularly for younger lawyers.

When interviewing estate lawyers, you'll want to find out about their fees and their judgment. Attorneys usually charge by the hour, but that information is of no use to you unless you know how many hours will be involved. As a rough guide, you should expect a simple will and a marital trust to cost you at least $1,000 and a pair of living trusts from $1,500 to $3,000. (Of course costs will vary, depending on where you live.) Since your estate attorney will likely be with you for years, through significant changes in your life and those of your loved ones, the advice you get may go far beyond trusts to family relationships. For instance, you may need to rely on your estate lawyer for advice on what to do about a disabled child or your elderly parents. A rule of thumb: If you can say that you have real faith in your attorney's honesty and common sense, you can be reasonably sure that you've chosen well.

SECTION THREE

INVESTING YOUR MONEY

CHAPTER 13

How to Invest Wisely

Why should you bother investing when the times are so unpredictable? After all, as investors repeatedly discover, the market can take some terrifying dives. The answer: inflation and taxes. If your savings, after taxes, don't grow faster than the cost of living, their purchasing power will steadily erode. Put another way, if you don't find a way to put your money to work for you effectively, you'll never be able to reach the financial goals you cherish. In short, after you begin taking care of your emergency savings fund, you need to start investing in stocks, bonds, and mutual funds.

The following example, which doesn't even account for the take of taxes, will show you why. Had your grandmother stashed $90 under her mattress 50 years ago—the price of a decent-quality, three-piece bedroom set in 1945—that money today would buy little more than a set of sheets. If she had invested that $90 in a bank savings account that kept even with inflation, she could still afford that roomful of furniture. But if she had put her 90 bucks in the stock market, it would have grown to more than $63,771 today: enough not only for that bedroom set, but for a down payment on a second home to put it in. If that story doesn't impress you, here's a scarier one: Investing wisely can mean the difference between retiring to a cushy house on the 18th green or retiring to a state-run oldsters' home.

Saving, while extremely important, is essentially just putting money away for safe-keeping. Investing, by contrast, is using your money to produce more money. Are you thinking that you need a lot of money to invest? You don't. Many equity mutual funds,

which pool money from small investors and use it to buy stocks, accept initial investments as low as $500 or even $250. Generally, you get a break on the initial investment
minimum when you open an IRA. Most funds let you invest as little as $50 or $100 a
month through their automatic investing programs. You can also see what it's like to be
a stock investor by purchasing a single share of a company for, say, $30.

The truth is, it isn't hard to learn how to invest and by investing defensively, you can
protect yourself from losing money. Winning as an investor means using your brains.

Measuring Your Risk Tolerance

Before putting a penny into any investment, you need to come to grips with your risk
tolerance—how you'd feel about the possibility of losing money on your investments.
Let's say you decide to put some cash into a stock that involves more risk than you're
truly comfortable taking. If the stock tanks, you may well lose your nerve and sell. That's
usually exactly the wrong move, however. Selling at a low point means not only that
you've lost money, but that you will miss any gain that occurs if the investment
rebounds. Conversely, if a zigzag-shaped line charting your investment performance
won't make you lose any sleep, you may be hobbling your portfolio by stashing all of
your cash in investments that are too safe.

How much risk is too much for you? How much is not enough? The answer
depends largely upon two things:

1. **Your temperament**, or your own psychological appetite for taking risks.
2. **Your time horizon**, or the number of years you have to build your investment
   before you need to cash out.

First, take your temperament's temperature. To pin down your investing risk
threshold, take the following quiz, developed with the help of psychologist John
O'Leary, co-director of Lifecycle Testing in New York City:

MEASURING YOUR TEMPERAMENT FOR
TAKING INVESTMENT RISKS

1. When it comes to investing, my luck has been
   a. rotten.
   b. average.
   c. better than average.
   d. terrific.
2. Most of the good things that have happened to me have been because
   a. I planned them.
   b. I was able to exploit opportunities that arose.
   c. I was in the right place at the right time.
   d. God looks out for me.
3. If a stock doubled in price five months after I bought it, I would
   a. sell all my shares.
   b. sell half my shares.
   c. sit tight.
   d. buy more shares.
4. Making investment decisions on my own is something that I
   a. never do.
   b. do occasionally.
   c. often do.
   d. almost always do.
5. At work, when my boss tells me to do something that I know is a bad idea, I usually
   a. tell him or her that I think it is a mistake.
   b. get co-workers to join me in opposing the idea.
   c. do nothing unless the boss brings it up again.
   d. do it anyway.
6. In order for me to invest 10% of my net worth in a venture that has at least a 75% chance of success, the potential profit would have to be at least
   a. the same as the amount invested.
   b. three times the amount invested.
   c. five times the amount invested.
   d. no amount would be worth the risk.
7. When I watch television and see people involved in such sports as hang gliding or bungee jumping
   a. I think they are idiots.
   b. I admire them but would never participate.
   c. I wish I could try such sports once just to see what they are like.
   d. I think seriously about participating myself.

8. If I held a finalist ticket in a lottery with a one-in-three chance of winning a $50,000 prize, the smallest amount I would be willing to sell my ticket for before the drawing is
   a. $30,000.
   b. $17,000.
   c. $13,000.
   d. $10,000.
9. In the past, I have spent $100 on one or more of the following activities: gambling in a casino; betting on my own recreational activities, such as golf or poker; betting on professional sports. (Circle the statement that best applies.)
   a. I have done two or more of these in the past year.
   b. I have done one of these in the past year.
   c. I have done one of these a few times in my life.
   d. I have never done any of these.
10. If I had to make a critical decision that involved a large amount of money, I would probably do one or more of the following things. (Circle all that apply.)
   a. Delay the decision.
   b. Delegate the decision to someone else.
   c. Ask others to share in the decision.
   d. Plan strategies that would minimize any loss.

Scoring:
For questions 1, 3, and 4: If you answered A, give yourself one point; B, two points; C, three points; and D, four points.
For questions 2, 6, 8, and 9: If you answered A, give yourself four points; B, three points; C, two points; and D, one point.
For questions 5 and 7: No matter what you chose, don't give yourself any points. Moral courage and physical bravery don't have anything to do with your tolerance for investment risk.
For question 10: Subtract from five the number of answers you circled and give yourself the rest.

What Your Score Means:
8–16: You're a conservative investor, willing to take few risks.
17–24: You're a moderate investor, willing to take moderate risks.
25–32: You're an aggressive investor, willing to take greater-than-average risks.

Now that you know your temperament for investment risk, consider your time horizon. Remember this rule: The longer you can keep your money invested, the more risk you should take with it. If you plan to use a chunk of money within a few years to buy a house, for example, you can't afford to take a chance that the stock market will fall during that time period. So you should keep your down payment money in a safe place, such as a money-market fund, a bank CD, or Treasury bills. However, if you won't need the money for a decade or more—say, you're investing for retirement at age 65 and you're now 55—you face a significant risk if you don't invest at least some of it in stocks. The risk is that inflation will eat away at the earnings on your money in the bank. Moreover, a long time period helps compensate for short-term dips in the stock market.

While this rule generally means that older people should play it safer than younger ones—after all, younger people have a longer lifespan and therefore more time to recover from any bad investment—the truth is more subtle. Even 60-year-olds can expect to live at least another 20 years or so. So they need to keep in stocks a portion of the money they'll live on during retirement. Conversely, a 45-year-old couple with teenage kids shouldn't keep all their spare cash in the stock market. After all, they'll probably need to be sure they have some money salted away safely for college tuition in a couple of years.

The Five Major Investment Risks

There are more types of investment risks than you probably realize. Here is a guide to the five major ones:

- **Inflation risk.** The risk that your investments will lose out to inflation is actually the greatest threat to your wealth. Fixed-income investments such as CDs and bonds carry the most inflation risk because their yields are locked in and won't rise even if inflation does. Stocks are the best way to overcome the ravages of inflation. While inflation has averaged more than 3% per year since 1926, stocks have racked up average annual gains of 11.1% through 2001. During the same period, bonds rose just about 5.4% a year, on average, and cash equivalents like money-market accounts were up only 3.8%, according to Ibbotson Associates, a Chicago investment consulting firm.
- **Market risk.** The most obvious type of risk, market risk, is the chance that the value of your investment will fall and you might have to sell your holding for less than you paid. Stocks put you at greater market risk than bonds, bank CDs, or money-market

funds since they are more volatile. While you can count on your CD to chug along, paying you, say, 3% or 4% a year, a stock may lose 10% in that year—or gain 20%. In a worst-case scenario, if the company whose stock you own goes bust, you may lose the entire value of your investment. (But, as many investors in Internet stocks learned the hard way, you can lose well over 90% in an individual stock even if the company remains in business.) Federally insured bank CDs of under $100,000, by contrast, have no market risk, because you are guaranteed to get your principal back.

- **Default risk.** This type of risk is one that bond investors need to worry about. Default risk is the chance that the issuer of the bond won't be able to make interest payments. One way you can skirt default risk is by purchasing U.S. Treasury bonds or mutual funds that hold such bonds. Because the U.S. government backs these bonds, they're essentially free from the risk of default. But they're still vulnerable to an often more pernicious and less understood risk . . .

- **Interest rate risk.** When interest rates rise, bonds and bond funds fall in value because bond buyers are less willing to purchase the securities with the lower rates than new issues with current, higher rates (for more on this, see Chapter 15). The longer the duration of a bond, the farther it will fall in value if rates go up. That's why long-term, 10-year bonds are somewhat riskier—from the standpoint of interest rate risk—than, say, short-term, three-year bonds. Just ask any investor who bought long-term bonds in the late '70s and sold them after rates had risen in the early '80s. Their principal fell by roughly 45%. In a sense, you're taking on interest rate risk whenever you buy a bank certificate of deposit, too. By investing in, say, a five-year CD at 5%, you're taking a risk that interest rates won't rise during the five years you hold the CD. If rates go up, you'll be locked into a lower interest rate than the prevailing rate. In fact, you might one day find that your CD is yielding less than the inflation rate.

- **Currency risk.** This is one type of risk that you may not encounter, at least not until you become a more experienced investor. Currency risk crops up when you invest in foreign stocks or bonds or the mutual funds that invest in them. Simply put, it's the chance that your investments can lose value thanks to fluctuations in foreign currency. For instance, foreign stocks can lose value if the dollar rises against local currencies. Fortunately, over periods of five years or more, currency swings tend to balance out. (For the five-year period ending in mid-2001, however, the U.S. dollar rose substantially against most major foreign currencies.) If you plan to hold an international investment for decades, though, currency risk shouldn't have a significant impact on your portfolio's performance.

Why Diversification Pays

Diversifying is probably the single best way to reduce the risks of investing. It means, simply, spreading out your money among several investments. That way, if one of them suffers a loss, your entire portfolio won't fall as far as it would if all your money were devoted to that one investment. Not convinced? Remember the wipeout many Enron employees experienced when the company's stock plummeted at the end of 2001. Many of the biggest losers had 100% of their 401(k) holdings invested in Enron stock. Diversifying won't guarantee that you'll make money, however. In 1994, for instance, many people lost money in both stocks and bonds. Most bond investors made money in 2000, but those profits were often exceeded by their stock market losses. To diversify properly, take the following steps:

- **Split your money among the three basic asset classes: stocks (or stock funds), bonds (or bond funds), and cash investments such as money-market funds, money-market bank accounts, and Treasury bills.** Stocks let you profit by becoming a part owner of a company. If the company prospers, your shares typically increase and you'll make money, too. Stocks also are known as **equity investments** because they represent a share, or a piece of equity, in a company. Bonds, which are IOUs issued by corporations, governments, and federal agencies, produce income for you from their regular interest payments. You can also score profits from bonds if you sell them after their prices have risen. Cash investments are supersafe, highly stable, and liquid (which means they can be cashed in easily). Stocks power your portfolio's value forward, bonds provide income and typically a higher return than cash, and cash moderates the volatility of stocks and bonds.

- **Invest in mutual funds.** This is the easiest way to spread your investments around the asset classes. A mutual fund offers instant diversification since the fund manager pools money from many people like you and invests it in a variety of stocks, bonds, or money-market securities. Mutual funds are also a low-cost way to diversify. That's because it would probably cost an individual investor tens of thousands of dollars to buy as many securities as one mutual fund holds.

There are two main types of mutual funds: **open-end funds**, whose shares are sold directly by the fund companies, stockbrokers, and financial planners; and **closed-end funds**, which are far less common, have a fixed number of shares, trade on stock exchanges, and are sold by brokers. About 80% of open-end funds are **load funds**. They carry a commission (or a **load**, typically equal to a few percentage points of the amount you invest) and are the kind sold by brokers. By contrast, a **no-load fund** does not have an up-front fee. You buy this type of fund directly from the mutual fund company or from a fee-only financial planner, who makes his or her living by charging clients by the hour for advice. Unless you want professional fund-picking advice, you can save a chunk of money by buying only no-loads. The savings can be substantial: fully $500 on $10,000 invested in a no-load rather than a fund with a 5% initial sales fee. You can diversify even further by buying several different types of mutual funds with different investing styles. For more on diversifying in mutual funds, see Chapters 14 and 15.

Asset Allocation

Proper diversification gives you what's known as **asset allocation**. This investing term is based on the fact that each type of investment offers its own trade-off between risk and reward. Stocks, for example, deliver the highest returns over extended periods of time but are subject to occasional swoons. Between mid-March 2000 and early April 2001, for example, the Nasdaq composite lost an eye-popping 68% of its value. Bonds, by contrast, typically return less than stocks but provide steadier income and often rise in value when stocks are falling.

Here's how asset allocation works. Let's say you want to allocate assets based solely on your appetite for risk. If the quiz you took in the previous section told you that you're a **conservative investor**, an appropriate portfolio mix for you might be 50% stocks, 20% bonds, 30% cash. Assuming that markets perform in line with their historical norms, such a portfolio will usually show a loss of no more than 4% in its worst year.

If you're a **moderate investor** with an average appetite for risk, consider a portfolio of 60% stocks, 20% bonds, 20% cash. That mix figures to return about 7.5% annually, usually with a worst-year loss of 6%.

If you're an **aggressive investor**, consider 80% stocks, 10% bonds, 10% cash. That mix is likely to grow an average of 9% annually, usually with a worst-year loss of 15%.

When choosing your asset allocation, be sure to factor in your investing time horizon. If your primary financial goals are coming up within a few years, invest more than you might otherwise in safe choices such as money-market funds and short-term bonds. If you plan to let your investments ride for more than 10 years, go more heavily in stocks. The longer your investment horizon, the more aggressive you can afford to be in selecting investments.

As you grow older, start a family, and move closer to retirement, your investment goals and taste for risk will change. As a result, your asset allocation should change along with you. Younger people, for example, can aim for high returns with aggressive portfolios, since they have many years to recover from market slumps. As you get closer to retirement, however, you need to shift to a more cautious allocation that will preserve your gains.

When allocating assets, be sure to review your entire portfolio. That includes money you hold in employer-provided savings plans such as 401(k) or 403(b) plans, profit-sharing plans, Individual Retirement Accounts (IRAs), and Keogh plans. A large chunk of that cash may be in your employer's stock, so you already may be more heavily invested in stocks than you think. (See Chapter 11 for asset allocations based on years to retirement.)

How and When to Diversify

You shouldn't think of diversifying, much less investing in the stock and bond markets at all, until you've begun putting away some emergency money. Conventional wisdom says you need an emergency fund equal to at least three to six months' worth of living expenses, but we disagree. We think you should get in the investing habit as soon as possible. Suggested strategy: Earmark half your monthly savings for the emergency fund and half for investing. Once you're set for emergencies, all your savings can go toward investments. Here's what to do:

- **If you have less than $5,000 to invest,** the typical mutual fund minimum investment of $1,000 to $5,000 means that you may be limited to investing in just one to three funds. No problem. You can be well diversified with just one fund—as long as that fund is itself widely diversified. Your best choice: a **balanced fund** that holds a variety of both stocks and bonds.
- **As your portfolio grows to $10,000** or so, put the stock and bond portions in separate mutual funds—a strategy that lets you control exactly how much of your portfolio will go to each asset class. If you have enough cash for three different mutual funds, pick one bond fund and two stock funds. The two stock funds should have different investing styles, too.
- **With $20,000 to invest,** aim to own about four or five mutual funds. Now, you can afford to add to your portfolio a fund that buys small-company stocks. An interna-

tional stock fund would be another smart choice. If you're looking to beef up your income investments, consider adding a safe bond fund, perhaps a municipal bond fund that buys tax-free securities if you're in one of the higher tax brackets.

- **With more than $20,000, you can branch out to 10 funds,** if you're so inclined, although you're probably better off limiting yourself to no more than six or seven. If you own a lot more, you won't be able to keep track of them (let alone remember their names). Record keeping would be a nightmare, unless you take advantage of the tracking programs offered by financial Web sites such as www.quicken.com, www.microsoft.com/money, www.money.com, and others offered throughout this chapter. The more funds you own, the more specialized your new holdings should be. In this way you'll avoid duplicating investments you already own. You might, for example, add funds that buy mid-cap stocks (those with market values between $1.5 billion and $10 billion). The Fund X-Rays tool on Morningstar.com will help you identify overlaps in your fund investments.

For some people, mutual funds eliminate the gambling-like thrill of picking individual stocks. But individual stock issues carry risks that pertain to their particular companies, making them potentially more volatile than diversified mutual funds. The solution: If you are just starting to invest or don't want to spend time keeping track of lots of stocks, build up a portfolio of mostly funds, but set aside a small chunk of your equity allocation to devote to individual shares. Consider limiting your individual stockholdings to 10% of your overall portfolio and no more than 20% of the equity portion. Here again, don't buy more stocks than you can reasonably follow. You can be adequately diversified with just a dozen issues in different industries, which could cost as little as $25,000.

How and Where to Invest

Now that you know about the importance of proper diversification and asset allocation, you're ready to start following these six golden rules of investing to stay on track:

1. **Never invest in anything you don't understand.** If a stockbroker talks you into an investment you don't truly comprehend, how will you know if the investment goes sour or if the broker is taking you for a ride? Steer clear of the latest newfangled investment and put your money in stocks, bonds, and mutual funds.

2. **Invest automatically.** Thanks to the power of compounding, earnings on regular, periodic investments can grow rapidly. For example, if you put $100 every month into a mutual fund that earns 6% a year, you can accumulate $16,326 in 10 years or

$28,830 in 15 years—enough for a down payment on the average home. Better returns can bring bountiful rewards. Invest just $25 a week earning 10%, on average, for 25 years and you'll wind up with a wad worth $103,028. If you put $25 away for 30 years and earned 12% a year, you'd wind up with $378,621.

Automatic investing has another huge advantage: It forces you to **dollar-cost average**, a proven winning technique. This strategy calls for you to invest a fixed dollar amount in a stock or a stock mutual fund at regular intervals whether the market is rising or falling. Consequently, you end up purchasing fewer shares when the price of the stock or fund is high and more shares when it's low. A $100 investment in a no-load mutual fund, for example, will buy 10 shares when the fund sells for $10 a share. If the fund declines to $8, your next $100 buys 12.5 shares. Thus, without ever deliberately timing your purchases, you automatically stuff your portfolio with less costly shares.

Sticking to the methodical approach of dollar-cost averaging in both rising and falling markets boosts your eventual gain and, equally important, keeps you from being driven by your emotions during market swings. Best of all, you buy fewer shares when they are up and therefore pricey and more when they are down and therefore cheap.

There are three ways you can invest automatically and painlessly:

- **Employee-sponsored retirement savings plans** such as 401(k)s at private companies, 403(b)s at nonprofits, and 457 plans at government agencies let you invest a percentage of your pretax salary in an assortment of funds that grow tax-deferred until you withdraw the money after retirement. Once you sign up, the money comes straight out of every paycheck. For more on the unparalleled benefits of tax-advantaged retirement savings plans, see Chapters 5 and 11.

- **Mutual fund savings and reinvestment plans** are offered by nearly all fund companies. Here, every month the fund management firm automatically withdraws the amount of money you specify (usually a minimum of $50 or $100) from your checking account or even your paycheck or Social Security check and transfers it into the fund you select. To enroll, you simply fill out a form authorizing the fund to siphon a set amount at regular intervals. You can switch off the flow at any time without penalty by calling the fund. You can also automatically reinvest the dividends and capital gains paid by the fund. Another bonus: Fund companies often waive minimum investment levels for customers who sign up for automatic investing plans.

- **Stock dividend-reinvestment plans** (known as **DRIPs**) offer a great way to make more money and keep you from running to the bank to deposit that $12.50 dividend check from your stock. You can also buy shares in stocks from hundreds of companies directly, through their dividend-reinvestment plans, or DRIPs. Sites such as BuyandHold.com, ShareBuilder.com, and NetstockDirect.com function as DRIP clearinghouses, allowing you to choose from a large number of stocks at commissions of $5 or less. Most of the companies with DRIPs reinvest your dividends for free.

3. **Go for consistency rather than flashy returns.** Too often, last year's success story is this year's also-ran. People who bought Internet and technology funds near the Nasdaq peak in 2000 suffered enormous losses the following year. Instead of stuffing money into the latest top-performing mutual fund, choose funds that have regularly outperformed competitors with similar objectives for three to five years. You can find this kind of information at Morningstar.com or in mutual fund rankings tables in publications such as **MONEY**, *Barron's*, *Business Week*, *Forbes*, and the *Wall Street Journal*.

4. **Adopt a buy-and-hold strategy.** Some investors—often those who fancy themselves so smart that they can predict market movements with great accuracy—indulge in a practice called "timing the market." These market timers move up to 100% of their dough back and forth between stocks and cash in an effort to dodge downturns and profit from market rallies. Over the short term, bright market timers can beat buy-and-hold investors. The truth is, though, that a simple buy-and-hold strategy is the better bet over multiple market cycles.

5. **Monitor the performance of each of your investments.** The best way to figure out how any of your investments is doing is by calculating its **total return**: a performance measure that combines dividends, interest, distributed capital gains, and price changes in a stock or mutual fund. Total return is expressed as a percentage gain or loss in the investment's value. To figure yours, use the worksheet on page 303.

6. **Rejigger your holdings annually.** The best asset-allocation strategies produce investment recipes you can leave in place for years. However, even a well-constructed portfolio requires periodic readjustment as rising and falling markets gradually alter your mix of assets. Once a year, rebalance your holdings by transferring profits from the parts of your portfolio that have done well to those that haven't. This will bring your portfolio back to your chosen risk level. As a bonus, it forces you to sell overvalued investments and buy undervalued ones. For example, in 1999 high P/E growth stocks trounced value stocks. As a result, an investor who wanted an equal weighting in the two groups would, by the end of the year, have had a portfolio that was out of whack. To rebalance a portfolio, you'd sell some profitable stock holdings—saying good-bye to some of your high-fliers—and then use the proceeds to buy more value stocks. It would have been a good move. From the beginning of 2000 to the summer of 2001, value stocks enjoyed significant gains while growth stocks fell sharply.

YOUR INVESTMENT'S TOTAL RETURN

A. Enter the value of your investment at the beginning
of the period you are examining.   _____

B. Add up any additional money you put into the investment
during the period. From that total, subtract any withdrawals
you made. (If you took out more than you put in, the figure
will be negative.) Enter the result.   _____

C. Multiply line B by 0.5 and add the result to the figure on line A.
(If the figure on line B is negative, you will subtract it.) Enter the result.   _____

D. Enter the value of the investment at the end of the period, plus
any interest, dividends, or capital gains that you have taken as cash,
rather than reinvested.   _____

E. Multiply line B by 0.5 and subtract the result from line D.
(If the figure on line B is negative, you will add it.) Enter the result.   _____

F. Divide line E by line C, then subtract 1 from the result. (If the result
is less than 1, your return is negative.) Multiply that number by 100.
This is your total return.   _____%

International Investing

More and more Americans are investing their money overseas—not just in foreign stocks, but in foreign bonds, too. Many experts believe that many people with a significant investment portfolio should keep 10% to 20% of it in foreign stocks or stock funds; foreign bond funds are a dicier proposition, as you'll see later. International investing gives you two arrows for your portfolio's quiver: added diversification and the potential for better returns.

The basic rationale for investing overseas is that while your U.S. shares are zigging downward, your foreign holdings could be zagging to big gains. As a result, investing in overseas stocks or stock funds was considered a way to lower the volatility of your portfolio. But lately, as trade barriers began falling and nations increasingly coordinated economic policies and currencies—à la the euro—the world's economies have become more tightly linked, and U.S. and foreign stocks have begun moving more in tandem. Plus, you'll face some complications that you needn't worry about with domestic investments. Currency risk, for example. And the chance that a particular country's economy will collapse, as happened in Korea in 1997 and Russia in 1998. It's also more difficult to get reliable information about many foreign companies than for U.S. companies because few countries require as much disclosure to investors as ours does.

For most small investors, it makes far more sense to invest in international mutual funds rather than in individual foreign issues. After all, think how hard it is to keep up with developments in foreign companies, let alone understand them. Another advantage of mutual funds: Many use hedging strategies that (in theory, at least) work to lower currency risk.

The first thing a fledgling international investor needs to learn is the difference between **international stock funds** and **global stock funds**. International funds hold only foreign stocks. Global funds, however, can invest in the United States as well as overseas. Here's the problem for investors who don't know the difference. Let's say you want to keep 10% of your overall allocation in foreign stocks. You put 10% of your portfolio into a global fund without realizing that its holdings happen to be 50% in the United States and 50% abroad. Your foreign exposure, then, is far less than you wanted: It's really 5%, not 10%.

When reviewing mutual fund performance tables, you may be intrigued with certain single-region or single-country funds. These are specialized mutual funds that invest only in one region of the world (say, the Pacific Rim) or in only one country (such as Mexico). Watch out! Single-region funds are more volatile than diversified international funds, and single-country funds are more volatile still. The reason: If one region or country suffers a crisis or an economic blow, many of its stocks are likely to suffer. (The converse is also true, of course.) To lessen the risk of investing around the world, make your first international foray a diversified international fund—that is, one that invests in a broad range of foreign countries but not the U.S.—since this allows investors to more finely tune their foreign exposure. The diversification benefits to this approach may be limited, however. Since most international funds stick to large multinational foreign firms that respond to the same forces as big U.S. companies, they have had fairly high correlations with U.S. stock funds in recent years.

You can easily get more diversification by adding a foreign fund that specializes in small-company stocks, since small firms that cater mostly to the locals are driven more by domestic economic forces than by global trends.

If you would rather buy individual foreign stocks, you'll most likely do so by buying what are called **American Depositary Receipts** or **ADRs**, sold on major U.S. stock exchanges. A bank owns the foreign shares and issues ADR certificates that trade in their stead. (Two good Web sites to check: J. P. Morgan's www.adr.com and Bank of New York's www.adrbny.com.) Stick with the ADRs sponsored by the foreign companies that issue the stock. That means you'll get accounting and disclosure comparable to that of U.S. firms. Without such sponsorship, you probably won't get as much information. (More on ADRs in Chapter 14.)

If you prefer individual stocks to stock mutual funds but don't want to mess with ADRs, consider investing in U.S. companies that do a lot of business overseas. As global trade increases, many cost-efficient U.S. companies enjoy greater international sales opportunities every year. Ask your broker for help identifying such stocks or use stock-screening tools on investing Web sites to ferret out this information for yourself.

International bond funds invest in foreign bonds. However, many experts doubt whether foreign bond funds make sense for the average investor. While bonds have a much lower potential for big gains than stocks do, they say, foreign bonds are just as vulnerable as foreign stocks to currency risk and the unpredictable swings in value that accompany that risk.

One more thing: Before investing in any foreign stock or bond fund, check the holdings of any U.S. mutual funds you already own. Many domestic funds invest quite a bit in foreign issues, so you may have more foreign exposure than you think.

Socially Conscious Investing

Some people shy away from investing because they think it means they'll have to turn their backs on their social and political ideals to make a profit. That's no longer true. In the past decade, socially responsible investing has boomed, led by mutual fund companies looking for stocks of companies that, for example, aim to reduce pollution or employment discrimination and steer clear of companies connected with businesses such as tobacco, gambling, and weapons manufacturing. There are now at least 142 mutual funds that profess to be socially or ethically responsible. Will you have to give up some potential profits to invest with a conscience?

Maybe not. The granddaddy of these funds is Domini Social Equity, which returned an average of 16% a year between 1991 and 2000. It holds about 400 mostly large companies with solid growth rates. In 2000, Vanguard launched a rival index fund, Vanguard Calvert Social Index, which invests in about 620 stocks. Another choice: TIAA-Cref Social Choice Equity.

The argument for socially responsible investing is that those companies that are not socially or ethically responsible are the very companies likely to run into financial problems that can drag down their stocks' price. Tobacco companies risk costly lawsuits from former smokers and their families, for example. And companies that don't encourage promotion of women and lack flexible family-leave policies risk losing valuable employees who could be improving the firm's bottom line.

There's one fairly significant drawback to investing in socially conscious mutual funds: The way the funds screen stocks can inadvertently increase your risk. Some sectors are partially or entirely excluded: alcohol, tobacco, oil, and defense, for example, which hampers diversification. And, as it happens, technology companies seem particularly adept at passing social screens. By mid-2001, the Domini Social Equity Fund had 28.3% of its assets in technology, far more than the sector's 17.5% weighting in the S&P 500. But that was nothing compared to the Parnassus Fund, which had 44.1% of its assets in technology at the same time. So a socially conscious investor might be making a big bet on tech without even knowing it.

The tricky part about investing in socially conscious stocks or funds is defining "socially conscious." Your idea of what's ethical and what isn't may differ from your next-door neighbor's. For example, some investors prefer buying shares only in companies with at least two women among their directors—a test passed by a minority of S&P 500 stocks. Other investors who favor stringent bans on animal testing avoid all drug companies and nearly all consumer-products companies.

Furthermore, even the socially conscious mutual funds don't agree with each other on the definition. Before investing in a socially conscious fund, read the prospectus and see whether its fund manager's ethics match yours. Is environmental responsibility, such as pollution control, hazardous-waste reduction, and energy conservation, most important to you? How about progressive employee policies, such as promotion of women and minorities, action on child care and AIDS, commitment to on-the-job safety, and fair bargaining with unions? Maybe your concern is good corporate citizenship, such as community involvement and charitable giving. Or you might feel strongly about excluding companies involved in nuclear power, animal testing, or alcohol production.

Of course, it's not impossible to invest in stocks of individual companies known for their commitment to socially responsible causes. One advantage of picking individual issues is that you can create and follow your own definition of socially responsible companies. These days, many large brokerages offer research or money-management services geared especially to socially responsible investors. You may want guidance, though, from an independent money manager or a newsletter whose views are similar to your own. The Social Investment Research Service (202-872-5319; www.socialinvest.com), a clearinghouse of this kind of information, can be a big help. The group's Web site has a complete listing of socially conscious mutual funds and, for $2 in shipping and handling, the group will send you a directory of socially conscious money managers around the country.

CHAPTER 14

How to Make Money in the Market with Stocks and Mutual Funds

When Americans talk about investing, more often than not they mean buying and selling stocks. Almost every TV news program dutifully reports the daily perambulations of the Dow Jones Industrial Average or Standard & Poor's 500-stock index, a courtesy they don't pay to price changes in municipal bonds, Miami Beach condos, baseball card collections, certificates of deposit, or the dozens of other investments people own. For all the exposure it gets, however, the principles of investing remain a mystery to most people—even veteran investors need to brush up on the fundamentals from time to time.

In a poll conducted by the investment management firm CIBC Oppenheimer, more than half the respondents wrongly believed that most stock investors are wiped out at one point in their life. (True, some investors were wiped out in 2000 and 2001, but many of them had invested imprudently by buying Internet stocks with borrowed money—or **buying on margin** as it is called on Wall Street—or **day-traded** [bought and sold the same shares of stock within one day's trading] until their stake vanished.)

Whether or not you, too, find the stock market intimidating—or perhaps merely inscrutable—you will need to learn more about it if you are serious about reaching your long-term financial goals. The reason is simple: Over periods of a decade or more, a broad selection of stocks or stock mutual funds are odds-on favorites to provide higher returns than any other investment open to the public. That has been the case for the better part of two centuries, and there's no reason to think it will change anytime soon.

On the whole, American corporations have been astoundingly successful at generating wealth for the shareholders who own the corporations. From 1982 through 2000, for instance, the average annual return on stocks has been 16.9%.

An easy way to invest in the stock market is through mutual funds rather than individual stocks. One or more funds will give you instant diversification, plus professional management. What follows is a quick overview of the stock market and how to analyze stocks, followed by sections that will help you as an investor in mutual funds.

Making Sense of Stocks

When a corporation needs to raise money, it has three alternatives: It can borrow the funds from a bank or from private investors such as insurance companies; it can borrow from the investing public by issuing bonds; or it can sell ownership interests in the company by issuing stock. When you purchase stock, you become, literally, part owner of a business. You are entitled to a proportionate share of any **dividends** the company generates—and, if the firm liquidates, to a proportionate share of any assets remaining after other creditors have been paid. In short, you participate in the fortunes of the business. You share in the risk that it may not succeed and in the potentially unlimited rewards if it does.

Not every dollar you invest in stock goes straight to the company's treasury, of course. Stock investors only really add funds to corporate coffers when they purchase shares at the **initial public offering** (an **IPO** is when the company issues stock for the first time) or at a **secondary offering** (a new issuance of shares by a company that already has stock outstanding). In the vast majority of trades, a current shareholder simply sells his stock to another investor who wants to buy it.

A company can issue two types of stock: **common stock** or **preferred stock**. Common stock is the type most investors buy and sell. Sometimes the stock pays a dividend, sometimes it doesn't. A company that has already issued common stock may choose to issue preferred stock, which in many ways is more like a bond than a stock. The dividends are usually considerably higher per dollar invested on preferred shares than on common shares. Also, if the company goes out of business and there is any money to distribute to investors, you'll be paid off before common-stock owners. In addition, your preferred-stock dividends are fixed, just as a bond's interest rate is set by the issuer. So even if your company prospers, your dividends won't rise. They won't fall if the company stumbles, either. A preferred stock is designated **pf** in a newspaper's stock tables.

Every so often, a company may choose to split its stock. In a 2-for-1 **stock split**, for instance, instead of owning, say, 100 shares at one price, you suddenly own 200, each worth half as much as before. (As a result, a stock split doesn't make your investment any more or less valuable than it was before.) A company splits its stock when the management thinks the share price has risen so high that it now discourages some potential investors. By splitting a $100 stock into, say, a $50 stock, the company thinks small investors may be more tempted to buy shares and thus help bid up the price even higher. Over the years, Wall Street has concluded—usually correctly—that the decision by a company's board of directors to split the stock indicates confidence in the company's future. (Legendary investor Warren Buffett, however, will have none of this. He has vowed never to split the shares of his company, Berkshire Hathaway. By fourth quarter 2001, it cost about $74,000 to buy a single class-A Berkshire Hathaway share.) A company can split its stock in any combination—2 for 1, 5 for 1, 3 for 2, whatever. (In fact, a company whose share price has fallen significantly can even engineer a **reverse split**. In the case of a 1-for-20 reverse split, the holder of 100 shares of a 50¢ stock would emerge with five shares of a $10 stock. Generally, companies that need to resort to reverse splits underperform the market.) You can determine if a stock has split within the past 52 weeks by looking for an **S** in the newspaper stock listings.

Can you make money off of stock splits? Yes and no. Studies have shown that stocks that split have beaten the market by five percentage points a year for decades. However, to capture those returns, you would have had to buy shares in every single one of the thousands of stocks that have ever split and hold them for one year. Many experts advise against buying stocks solely on the basis of splits. However, if you're already thinking of buying a stock, and it splits, you can take that as a good signal that the stock may be a good buy. And if you're considering two similar stocks, and one of them splits, that's probably the one you should go with.

Making Sense of Stock Mutual Funds

A stock or equity mutual fund is a kind of corporation whose sole business is to pool its shareholders' money and invest it in stocks. (Other kinds of mutual funds invest strictly in short-term money-market securities or in bonds; you can read more about them in Chapters 5 and 15.) The fund's investment strategy is designed and carried out by a professional money-management firm, which spares individual investors the time and effort of researching, selecting, and keeping track of a portfolio of stocks. The money managers charge generally between 0.2% and 2.5% of the fund's assets per year for their efforts, but millions of investors have clearly decided that the convenience of leaving the investment work to professional managers is worth the cost. According to a 2001 study by Investment Company Institute, about 52% of the nation's households own mutual funds. On average, equity funds account for 65% of a shareholder's mutual fund portfolio.

The Historical Return of Stocks

You've probably seen the disclaimer in mutual fund advertisements: "Past performance is no guarantee of future results." That's a good thing to keep in mind when evaluating any individual stock or stock mutual fund, and it's also worth remembering when looking at the historical returns of stocks in general. Nevertheless, three basic truths about the performance of stocks are worth remembering:

• Over the long term, stocks outperform other financial assets.
• The short-term performance of stocks is a complete toss-up.
• The long-term performance of stocks is quite consistent.

The figures most often cited in discussing historical stock market performance are those compiled by the Chicago investment research firm Ibbotson Associates: From 1926 to 2001, the return on stocks worked out to an average of about 11% a year, compounded annually. That is far superior to the returns on bonds and Treasury bills, which returned only 5.3% and 3.8%, respectively. The difference is stark enough on an annual basis, but get this: Over 30 years through 2001, stocks earning 11% annually would have turned a $10,000 investment into $228,305. By contrast, a $10,000 stake in bonds would have grown to just $44,982, and the same $10,000 invested in Treasury bills would have given you only $30,183. Don't forget, the period since 1926 includes a fair number of rough patches for stock investors, including one Great Depression, three major wars, the hyperinflation of the '70s, the biggest stock market crash of the 20th century in 1987, and the tech-stock calamity of 2000–2001.

How to Size Up a Stock

Your objective in searching for stocks should be the same as it would be in any kind of shopping: to find the best merchandise at the lowest price. Simple enough. The only problem is that the stock market is reasonably efficient. In other words, the best merchandise rarely trades at the lowest prices. Conversely, any stock trading at a cheap price is likely to be, in some way, damaged goods.

A stock's price represents the sum of all information known about a company, from news, company reports, analysts' opinions, and so on, filtered through the judgment of thousands of investors.

You don't have to outdo Wall Street's wizards to succeed as a stock investor—you just have to match the market's average. After all, doing just that well historically would have given you a better return than nearly any competing investment. Follow the prudent stock selection techniques outlined below, avoid paying inflated prices for stocks, and diversify your holdings so that one stock's unforeseen misfortunes don't ruin you, and you'll do fine. There is one other requirement, though: patience. Stocks pay off reliably only in the long run. If you panic and sell when things look bleak, you'll constantly be selling when prices are lowest—exactly the time you should be buying.

WHAT MAKES A STOCK CHEAP

There are two ways to size up a stock: **fundamental analysis** and **technical analysis**. Fundamental analysis is what most amateur and professional investors do. It simply means analyzing the vital signs of a company—its financial shape, the quality of its management, its prospects for the future. When doing fundamental analysis of a stock, you're taking a close look at the company's balance sheet, its debt, and how much its earnings are likely to grow in the future. Technical analysis, by contrast, means studying the historical trends of the price of a company's stock or, more broadly, the price trends of stocks in an entire industry or the stock market overall. Technical analysts love to use charts with fever lines that track the performance of stocks. They think past trends can help predict whether a stock or a variety of stocks will rise in the near future. (Some people think they are full of beans.)

Determining whether a stock is a bargain or overpriced is not simply a matter of comparing the cost of its shares with that of another stock. An unprofitable company with high debt and no growth prospects is no bargain at $5 a share. Conversely, a stock that trades for $100 may be a steal.

Instead, the way to judge value in a stock is to compare its trading price to the economic value you derive as a shareholder. These benefits come from the dividends the company generates, growth in the company's assets (which you as an owner have a claim on), and the profits the company earns. These comparisons are expressed in the key **price-to-earnings**, **price-to-dividend**, **price-to-book**, and **price-to-earnings-growth ratios**:

• The **price-to-earnings ratio** measures the stock's price against a year's worth of the company's earnings (or profits) per share of stock. **Price/earnings** or **P/E** is the most closely watched and widely cited measure of any stock's inherent value. Profits, after all, are the reason a company is in business, and all the benefits that make a company a worthy investment flow from its earnings. (Since a stock's share price is always several times larger than its earnings per share, the P/E ratio is often referred to as the price/earnings multiple or, to those in the know, simply the multiple.) The higher a stock's P/E, the riskier it is.

You can measure P/E ratios several ways. The ratios printed in stock tables in newspapers and on Web sites are based on the current stock price and the company's earnings as reported over the previous four quarters. While a P/E based on these **trailing earnings** eliminates guesswork, investors should be most concerned with their stock's price in relation to what analysts expect to happen to the company's earnings over the next 12 months. A P/E based on **projected earnings** gives you an insight into whether the stock's potential is factored into its current price. For example, in the summer of 2001, generic drug maker Barr Laboratories traded at a P/E of 54 based on trailing earnings; on that basis it was quite expensive, compared with the 500 stocks in the Standard & Poor's index, which carried an average trailing P/E of 24 at the time. But because analysts expected Barr Labs to earn 144% more in fiscal 2002 than in 2001 (it introduced generic Prozac in the summer of 2001), its P/E on its estimated 2002 earnings worked out to a much more reasonable value of 21.5 times earnings, a multiple actually below that of the overall market. Of course, this assumes the earnings estimates turn out to be right, or conservative.

Since, as a rule, the lower the stock's P/E, the better the value, it's not surprising that studies have shown that low P/E stocks tend to outperform their high P/E counterparts in the aggregate. Unfortunately it's not all that simple in particular cases. A fast-growing company like General Electric may be reasonably priced at 27 times next year's earnings, while General Motors may be no bargain at seven times earnings if it turns out that worldwide auto sales are about to slip.

Thus, a stock's P/E alone doesn't tell you what you need to know about its prospects. You also have to compare its current P/E against the overall stock market and its particular industry. Historically, the average P/E of stocks has been 15%; from 1990 through 2001, it averaged about 22.1%. If a stock that interests you has a P/E much higher than that of the market, you should ask yourself: Do the stock's prospects warrant it? If the P/E is lower, could the bad news about the stock be overblown? You should also weigh the P/E against the company's projected growth rate. A company growing at 20% a year whose stock is trading at a P/E of 15 is a steal; a company growing by just 8% with a P/E of 15 may not be. Interest rates also influence the general level of P/E multiples. P/Es tend to rise when interest rates fall, since when rates are low, bonds offer weak competition with stocks for investors' dollars.

• The **price-to-dividend ratio** of a stock and its even more often cited inverse, the stock's **dividend yield**, measure the share price in relation to the annual cash payout to shareholders. A $50 stock that pays an annual dividend of $2 per share has a price-to-dividend ratio of 25 to 1, or a yield of 4%.

In recent years, companies on the whole have reduced the percentage of earnings that they pay out in dividends. The reason: Most investors would prefer their profits come in the form of long-term capital gains (which are taxed at a maximum rate of 20%) rather than dividends (which are taxed as ordinary income at rates as high as 38.6% through 2003 and 37.6% in 2004 and 2005).

Many excellent companies pay little or no dividends at all, preferring to reinvest profits back in the business rather than pay out a sizable portion of them to shareholders. In such cases, a tiny or nonexistent yield is not necessarily a reason to rule out a stock. Similarly, an extremely high yield isn't always a sign that the stock is worth purchasing. When a stock has a dividend yield between 10% and 20%, this is often a sign that the market expects the company to reduce—or eliminate—its dividend shortly.

• The **price-to-book ratio** measures a stock against the value of its company's assets minus its liabilities (its net worth). When figuring a stock's price-to-book ratio, you divide its price by the book value per share. Here's an example: If a stock is selling for $20 a share and its book value per share is $10, its price-to-book ratio is two.

Unlike the P/E ratio, there's nothing prospective about the price-to-book ratio. It values companies as they are, without asking the investor to make any prognostications about their future performance. That doesn't mean, however, that savvy investors accept a company's stated book value as gospel. Often, the value assigned to some assets on the company's books understates or overstates their true worth. Companies frequently carry real estate, for example, at its acquisition cost decades after acquiring it. As a result, a real estate–rich company such as a railroad may have a true net worth far in excess of its stated book value. Book value can also mislead on the high side: Inventory may be valued at its wholesale price, even if it's unsellable. That can then make an apparent book-value bargain an expensive mirage.

Such caveats aside, buying stocks with low price-to-book values has proven to be a smart long-term strategy. The reason for the low price-to-book strategy's success? Since stocks trade at a low price-to-book because most investors are down on their prospects, low price-to-book stocks may have a greater chance of catching a favorable shift in Wall Street opinion than do high price-to-book stocks.

Be careful, though, about using book value as an absolute yardstick. For financial companies, book value is extremely important. It's significant for thriving industrial companies, but almost irrelevant for smokestack businesses that are in trouble. Steel stocks have had low price-to-book values for decades, but they have been dreadful investments during that period. Why? Because steelmaking in the U.S. is a bad business. A steel plant that is carried on the books at $300 million is, in reality, nearly worthless if it can't be operated at a profit.

• The **price-to-earnings-growth (PEG)** ratio is an increasingly popular way to gauge whether a stock is reasonably priced and is likely to go up in price over time. You take the stock's P/E ratio and divide it by the company's expected earnings growth rate. So, for instance, a company growing 25% a year that sells for 25 times earnings has a PEG ratio of 1. These days, however, most high-quality companies with double-digit growth rates command P/Es that are at least 1.5 times their growth rates. Rules of thumb: Avoid buying stocks that sell for more than twice their growth rates—no matter how great you think the business is. When a company with a high PEG ratio has problems, its shares can fall off a cliff. When the PEG for a solid grower is less than 1.5—or, better still, less than 1—that's a pretty good clue that the stock may be a buy.

For stocks that pay significant dividends, a more refined valuation approach uses the **PEGY ratio**. With PEGY you divide the stock's P/E plus its dividend yield by the expected earnings growth rate. (After all, what really matters—especially in tax-deferred accounts—is a stock's total return to shareholders, which includes price appreciation and the dividends it pays.) A stock with a 10% growth rate and a 3% yield might be a fine purchase if you could buy it at a P/E of 18.5 or less.

You can find PEG ratios at many financial Web sites.

OTHER VALUATION TERMS YOU SHOULD KNOW

- **Market capitalization:** the current stock market value of a company, which is calculated as the share price multiplied by the number of shares outstanding: **large-cap stock** (generally more than $10 billion in market cap); **mid-cap stock** ($1.5 billion to $10 billion); **small-cap stock** (less than $1.5 billion).

- **Profit margin:** income divided by revenues. When gauging a company's profit margin, be sure to compare it with that of other companies in the same industry. For instance, good margins for a software company might be 25%, while 2% is considered fabulous for a grocery chain.

- **Return on equity (ROE):** net income divided by shareholders' equity, or, literally, how much a company is earning on its money. This ratio can be used to show how a company's earnings measure up to those of the competition, as well as how they compare with past performance. A rising return on equity is a good sign.

- **Yield:** the percentage rate of return paid on a stock in the form of annual dividends or the effective rate of interest paid on a bond or note.

Where to Research a Stock

While divining the hidden meaning (if any) in a company's P/E multiple or price-to-book ratio may take a bit of work, laying your hands on the information is remarkably easy. Whatever the shortcomings of the U.S. stock markets, lack of data isn't one of them. Securities laws require companies traded in the United States to reveal more about their finances than stocks traded virtually anywhere else, and hundreds of companies compete to make that information available to investors.

The power of the Internet at both delivering and crunching financial data makes computers the ideal tool for stock picking. It's now a snap to get real-time online stock quotes, financial data, company news, earnings estimates, and research reports on thousands of stocks almost instantaneously. The Net also offers easy-to-use portfolio-tracking and screening tools, alerts for key events like earnings announcements and analyst upgrades and downgrades. Start your research at the supersites—the best all-around financial destinations on the Web.

TOP INVESTMENT WEB SITES

Supersites: MoneyCentral (www.moneycentral.com); Quicken.com (www.quicken.com); Yahoo! Finance (http://finance.yahoo.com); CNN/Money.com (www.money.com).

Financial News: CBS MarketWatch (www.cbsmarketwatch.com).

Stock Quotes and Data: Market Guide (www.marketguide.com).

Company Research: 10K Wizard (www.10kwizard.com); BestCalls.com (www.bestcalls.com).

Stock Analysis: Multex Investor (www.multex.com).

Direct Investing: Netstock Direct (www.netstockdirect.com).

Mutual Funds: Morningstar.com (www.morningstar.com).

International: Worldlyinvestor.com (www.worldlyinvestor.com).

IPO: IPO Central (www.ipocentral.com).

Two library and online data sources that are required reading for stock pickers are the *Value Line Investment Survey* and *Standard & Poor's Stock Reports*. Both offer comprehensive financial data on thousands of companies. Both include an analysis of the company's prospects and a wealth of financial data—including P/Es, yields, and book value—going back a decade in S&P's case or 15 years in Value Line's. If you prefer, you can subscribe to Value Line at a cost of $525 a year or go to www.valueline.com. *Standard & Poor's Stock Reports* are considerably more expensive, but you can order detailed reports on individual stocks for as little as $2 at www.standardandpoors.com. You also can buy analysts' research reports at www.multex.com.

Although the tools on the financial site scan let you track the day-to-day, or minute-to-minute, progress of your portfolio, many experts say you'll do better as an individual investor if you check prices less frequently, such as once a week or a few times a month. (That way, you're less likely to turn into a trigger-happy day trader rather than a long-term investor.)

Perhaps the biggest value in online investing is the ability to sort through a large database for the stocks you really want to own. Perhaps you want to focus on stocks with yields above 2%, projected earnings growth over the next five years of more than 10% a year, and P/Es under 15. This process is known as doing a **stock screen**. Once you have your screen, you can then subject the stocks that pass it to a more detailed or rigorous analysis. (See box on page 317 on online portfolio-tracking tools.)

Your next step is to search the company Web site for a company profile, financial reports, and up-to-date news on management, product launches, press releases, and other company developments. You can find the Web site through the search engines on www.yahoo.com or www.google.com.

Growth, Value, and Income Stocks

In shopping for any kind of merchandise, some people believe that quality is the best value in the long run and don't mind paying carriage-trade prices to get it. Others argue that at some price, buyers are paying for reputation and that settling for a less exalted brand name is wiser. Still others identify a specific benefit that they get from a certain brand and will continue to stand by the product as long as it meets their needs.

With only a little stretching of that metaphor, stock investors fall into roughly the same categories. **Growth stock investors** are the quality chasers: In their minds, com-

ONLINE TUNE-UP TOOLS FOR
YOUR PORTFOLIO

Anybody can use the Internet to make cheap trades, but smart investors explore the Web's wondrous selection of sites and tools (many of which are described elsewhere in this chapter) that analyze and track your investment portfolio. Our step-by-step plan will help you monitor your holdings, track investments you're eyeing, analyze your assets, and consider ways you might want to tinker with your allocations.

Step 1: Set up your portfolio tracker. Your first assignment is to enter all of your stocks and mutual funds in a **portfolio tracker**—sorry, but finding a reliable bond tracker has been tough. The best trackers are on sites that not only update your portfolio throughout the day, but also help you track stocks that you want to watch. Some will alert you by e-mail when there are big moves or major news on your investments. The most worthwhile portfolio trackers can follow a stable of stocks from the date and price at which they were purchased, adjust for splits and dividends, and point out holes in your portfolio.

We recommend MSN MoneyCentral (moneycentral.msn.com), which lets you view your portfolio in terms of prices, valuations, and fundamentals. The tracker also lets you customize your view so you can include 52-week highs and lows, news, or other details (for details see complete profile earlier in the chapter). If you want something even savvier (though more difficult to master), try SellSignal (www.sellsignal.com), a tax-smart tracker that lets you know when to consider shedding a stock for maximum tax advantage.

Step 2: Look at the big picture. Once you get a handle on your holdings, it's time to determine how diversified you really are and how your investments interact to form a sound portfolio. Enter your stocks and funds into the Portfolio X-Rays tool at Morningstar (portfolio.morningstar.com) for a snapshot overview of your assets. Say you own a big slug of Intel and, unbeknown to you, so does one of your funds. X-Rays will tip you off to the fact that you may not be as diversified as you think. X-Rays assesses up to 50 stocks and mutual funds based on eight criteria such as asset allocation, sector, fees and expenses, and geographical diversity. (The site doesn't provide individualized advice unless you cough up a small monthly fee.) An added bonus: Morningstar lets you import your portfolio from the tracker at MSN MoneyCentral, as well as from AOL, Yahoo!, Quicken.com, and the CD-ROM versions of Quicken and Microsoft Money; Morningstar also allows you to export your data directly onto your PC's hard drive.

Step 3: Assess risk. Now check out just how volatile your holdings are and decide whether you can stomach their potential gyrations. Of all the gizmos purporting to analyze risk, we prefer PortfolioScience (www.portfolioscience.com) for its simplicity and flexibility. Just enter the ticker symbol of a stock or a portfolio of holdings and the Web site expresses risk as the dollar amount or percentage by which that security or portfolio could fluctuate daily, weekly, monthly, or annually. A share of Ford, for example, may typically go up or down $1 on a given day or $9.20 over the course of a year, according to the site. RiskGrades (www.riskgrades.com) is a similar but more complicated tool; it factors in variables such as market and sector conditions, plus one-time events like earnings surprises. It then assigns individual stocks or entire portfolios a risk score, ranging from zero for cash to beyond 1,000 for the most wildly speculative plays.

Step 4: Check on valuations. Finally, it's time to see if any of your holdings are ripe for thinning based on how they are priced relative to their historical levels. The security evaluation tool at Quicken (www.quicken.com) is an excellent starting point.

panies with high, sustainable profit growth are the ones that will serve their shareholders best in the end, almost regardless of how their price stands in relation to their earnings, dividends, or book value. **Value investors,** by contrast, look for companies whose prospects are ambiguous. A cloudy outlook lets their stocks trade relatively inexpensively in relation to their earnings, assets, and dividends. The value investors ultimately make money when the companies improve and other investors bid up their stock prices. Finally, there are **income investors**. They look for stocks with relatively high (or at least rising) dividends that can keep those checks coming and presumably rising for years to come.

While value, growth, and income investors may never agree with each other about a stock, each can make money. Growth stocks typically do better when the economy is slow and investors are willing to pay a premium for the relatively few companies that can sustain solid earnings growth rates. Value investors tend to prosper most during the early stages of a recovery, when stocks that had been ignored often come to life. Income investors often shine when the overall market is flat or falling and a generous dividend can help soothe the pain for shareholders.

HOW TO BUY GROWTH STOCKS

Growth stocks often make for more exciting stories than value or income stocks. Companies that almost invariably increase earnings faster than the market include classic stalwarts such as General Electric, Microsoft, Wal-Mart, and many other household names. But even faster growers can usually be found in rising, glamorous businesses. Since investor expectations toward such stocks are already fairly high, the shares tend to trade at P/E ratios that are considerably steeper than the market's. A stock whose earnings grow 20% a year, however, should appreciate in value 20% annually as well, as long as the P/E ratio remains constant.

The problem is that few companies can really grow 20% a year indefinitely. Trees don't grow to the sky, and profitable lines of business almost invariably attract competition, squeezing profit margins. If investors lose faith that a stock can grow faster than the market, the stock may tumble back to a P/E more in line with the market average or even lower. The result isn't pretty for shareholders, especially if investors have projected past growth trends to impossible lengths—as they have a tendency to do. In the late '90s, the fiber-optic components business was growing at a phenomenal rate and stocks in the sector were soaring. But in 2000 the sector crashed and most of the fiber-optic stocks fell catastrophically. The leader of the pack, JDS Uniphase, collapsed by 95% in just 17 months.

A similar rout occurred during the terrible bear market of 1973 and 1974. Before that smash-up, the so-called Nifty Fifty blue-chip growth companies also sold at outlandish P/Es. The favored Fifty were deemed "one-decision" stocks because you only had to decide to buy them. Since they were supposed to grow forever, you'd never have to think of selling them, right? In 1972 McDonald's sported a P/E of 83 and Polaroid traded at an amazing 90. By 1980 McDonald's P/E was just 9 and Polaroid's was 16. By 2001, according to the *Wall Street Journal*, Polaroid was contemplating bankruptcy. We guess it was a two-decision stock after all.

The upshot? Growth investors must answer two questions: Is the company's past growth rate sustainable? Is the stock's current P/E reasonable, given the firm's likely growth path? The ideal growth company operates in a market where demand is rising, few serious competitors are on the horizon, and its products are so popular that the company can boost profits without losing customers. Home Depot, a classic growth company and one of the best performing stocks of the past two decades, prospered not only because it increased sales by building more stores. As sales got larger, it could buy goods in even bigger bulk at lower prices, either boosting profit margins or squeezing out competitors—or both. Now that Home Depot is expanding into many of the nation's major markets, analysts contend that its future growth rate will be considerably lower than in the past. Although in 2002 it was still considered a growth stock, the Wall Street consensus was that it merited a lower P/E.

No stock, in fact, is an attractive investment if its P/E is too high. We already addressed the nightmares investors in Polaroid and JDS Uniphase endured. So do yourself a favor and always keep the PEG ratio in mind. Stocks of companies may be dangerously overvalued if their P/E is twice the projected annual growth rate, but they may be quite cheap if the P/E is below the growth rate. And never forget: Nothing is sexier on Wall Street than an explosive growth story. Spectacular growth stocks often get bid up to levels that defy rationality. In most cases, though, it's the steady mid-teens growers, such as the major pharmaceutical companies in late 2001, that produce the best long-term returns.

HOW TO BUY VALUE STOCKS

In contrast with growth investors, who select their stocks based mainly on what they believe will happen to corporate earnings in the near future, value investors tend to focus on the present. Trying to predict the future by projecting current trends, they argue, causes investors to be overly optimistic about hot stocks and too pessimistic about ones that are out of favor. Value investors look for basically sound companies that are temporarily on investors' blacklists. Value investing doesn't require you to make any educated guesses about the future except one: that eventually the market will recognize real value. Warren Buffett, one of the greatest value investors of the century, describes the value approach as the belief that "if I can buy a dollar for 50¢, something good might happen to me."

Value stocks come in two distinct flavors: turnarounds and stocks with relatively low P/Es. Turnaround stocks are depressed because something has happened, or is happening, to the underlying business. Earnings growth may have slowed, or turned negative, because a ballyhooed new product bombed, management made some errors, or an acquisition failed to meet expectations. But such companies can often regain their footing if they have strong franchises and healthy balance sheets.

In January 2000 the shares of Toys "R" Us, which sold for just $9.75, were justifiably depressed. The company's new online venture had been a very public flop, and it had failed to promptly deliver holiday gifts ordered online. In addition, its stores looked grim and it was losing market share to Wal-Mart. As it happened, though, the huge toy retailer was in no danger of going under. It brought in a new CEO, renovated stores, and fixed the online fiasco (through a joint venture with Amazon.com). In May of 2001, Toys "R" Us shares hit $31.

Low P/E stocks don't necessarily need a complete overhaul but they may need a slight positive development to get them rolling. In 2000 H&R Block saw its earnings growth slow following its acquisition of the Olde brokerage firm. The stock fell from a high of $29.75 in July 1999 to $13.50 in June 2000. At that time, the company's PEG ratio was less than 1. But the company remained financially strong and it continued to enjoy one of the very best franchises in America (how many other nationwide tax preparers for individuals can you name?). H&R Block made progress in integrating its acquisition, and earnings growth reaccelerated. By August 2001, the stock had risen to $36.24, up 168% from its 2000 low. The risk in this kind of stock is that unrecognized value may remain unrecognized for a long time. Until then, the stock's price will remain flat, at best, and the value investor will make no profits. Nevertheless, value stocks tend to be safer than growth stocks in the long run. That's because big losses tend to occur when companies fall short of shareholders' expectations; however, value investors become interested in stocks mainly after the bad news has become widely known. Whatever surprises occur in value stocks tend to be positive ones.

HOW TO BUY INCOME STOCKS

For some investors, the most intriguing aspect of any stock isn't the prospect for appreciation, but rather the size of the stock's dividend and the prospects for growth in that dividend. Over time, such income stocks tend to have lower returns than growth or value stocks. For investors who need to supplement their income with investment earnings, however, these shares offer a fairly secure stream of income and considerably less risk of loss than other stocks. As a result, income stocks are ideal for retirees and for long-term-growth investors looking for a conservative investment to add balance to their portfolios. Why not just buy bonds, which pay steady interest until they mature? Simple. Income stocks can and often do increase their dividends gradually over the years, countering the effect of inflation.

Popular income stocks include utilities, although, because of deregulation and increased competition, these are far less stable investments than they used to be. Regional telephone companies and a few mature blue-chip stocks, such as tobacco king Philip Morris, are also popular with income investors who are willing to accept a lower yield than from utilities in return for a better shot at capital gains from an increase in their share prices. Another favorite income stock group: **real estate investment trusts (REITs)**, which buy, manage, and develop properties. (For more on REITs, see Chapter 17.)

The first thing to look for in an income stock is evidence that the dividend can at least be sustained and ideally increased by its company over the years. Financial soundness is key: The chance that business problems could force a company to cut its dividend is much higher if the company has a large amount of debt and hence a large interest cost burden. Look for a **financial strength rating** of at least B+ from Standard & Poor's or a rating of 1 for financial strength from Value Line.

Another key factor for income stock investors is the **dividend payout ratio**, or the **percentage of earnings (profits)** that the company is paying out in dividends each year. You get this percentage by dividing the dividends per share by the earnings per share. If a company is paying out $2 in dividends per share and has earnings per share of $4, it has a dividend payout ratio of 50%. Less is more here, since a low ratio gives a company plenty of room to absorb a decline in earnings without threatening its dividend. A high dividend payout ratio suggests the company may have to cut its dividend. A payout ratio below 70% is healthy for a utility; below 40% is a promising ratio for an industrial stock.

If you're planning to use income stocks as ballast in a growth portfolio rather than as a source of income, you'll want to reinvest your dividends as they are paid. These days, many traditional brokers will do this automatically for you, but not many online brokers. If this is an important part of your investment strategy, you should choose your broker accordingly.

Another solution: Invest in stocks with dividend-reinvestment plans (DRIPs). In the previous chapter you can find a fuller description of DRIPs and Web sites that provide this service.

Risky Business in the Stock Market

By their nature, stocks carry risks.

However, some variations on traditional stock investing multiply the risks in the pursuit of higher profits. For instance, buying stock options gives you the chance to make—or lose—a bundle by speculating on the future price of a stock. In general, the four types of investments and strategies about to be discussed are for sophisticated investors who have money to gamble:

- **American Depositary Receipts (ADRs).** Of the four investments discussed here, ADRs are the most like ordinary stocks. Basically, ADRs are chits representing claims on shares of a foreign stock held in trust by the foreign subsidiary of a U.S. bank. They trade on U.S. exchanges just like domestic shares, subject to the same disclosure requirements as any security registered with the SEC. The advantage to Americans is that it's much simpler and less expensive to buy ADRs than to try to buy the underlying shares on a foreign stock exchange.

   Many ADRs represent shares in very solid foreign companies. Sony, Hitachi, Nestlé, and Royal Dutch Shell, among others, all offer ADRs. However, any form of international investing exposes you to risks you don't face when you buy U.S. shares. Most important, ADRs leave you vulnerable to currency risk, the chance that the currency in which the underlying stock is denominated will depreciate against the dollar, making the shares represented by the ADR less valuable to Americans. (Two good Web sites to check: J. P. Morgan's www.adr.com and Bank of New York's www.adrbny.com.)

- **Initial public offerings (IPOs).** One of the most electrifying dramas on Wall Street plays out when a hot company first issues stock. The company's owners generally make millions by selling their stake to the public. The investment bankers putting together the issue also rake in the dough, as do their favored clients—usually big institutions like pension funds and mutual funds—who are able to reserve shares and quickly unload them at higher prices when the rest of the market gets a chance to buy. During the Internet mania that prevailed from 1998 to 2000, dozens of technology IPOs more than doubled on their first day of trading. In 1999, the average IPO was up 194%, reports Thomson Financial Securities Data. In 2000? The average offering lost 27%. In 2001? It was difficult for any company to come public at all.

Most IPOs are clubby affairs: Brokers reserve shares in their most promising IPOs for big-ticket customers or, in some cases, investment banking clients or *potential* investment banking clients. If your broker promises to get you shares in an IPO, chances are it's only because the smart money doesn't want any. For example, the company may have a lackluster operating history or the offering stock price may be too high. (To bone up on IPOs, check out www.ipocentral.com.)

If you nevertheless are interested in buying IPOs, make sure that before you invest you read the prospectus—the booklet describing the company, its management, and the risks to investors. Check how the company's P/E ratio at the estimated share prices given in the prospectus would stack up against the competition. If those P/Es are not in line with ones of similar companies, find out why not. Watch out, too, if the prospectus notes that insiders are planning to unload more than a small percentage of their privately held shares in the stock offering. This could be a sign that the IPO was designed largely to make its founders rich, not you.

Finally, if you are able to buy shares at the offering price or on the first day of trading, don't hold them too long. IPOs often skyrocket during the first week or month of trading and then start to backslide. This is one area of the market where patient investors sadly often get left holding the bag. Sure, Microsoft, Oracle, and Cisco Systems were all IPOs once, but the performance of these few long-term winners is overwhelmed by the disappointments of the many long-term also-rans.

Initial public offerings sometimes trade as **penny stocks**. A penny stock is one whose share price is typically less than $5 a share. The stock is usually that cheap for an excellent reason—its company's prospects are dicey at best. As a rule, the best advice for investing in penny stocks: Don't.

- **Trading on margin:** The idea of trading on borrowed money has long tempted investors, and three-quarters of a century ago it helped spur the great bull market of the '20s. Back then, an investor needed to put down only $100 to acquire $1,000 worth of General Electric stock. Margin requirements have since been raised and, today, a person must put down at least $500 to make that $1,000 investment in GE. But the temptation remains as great as ever.

The Internet makes trading on margin easier than in the past. During Nasdaq's wild 1998–2000 ride, many investors used margin debt to turbocharge their stock returns. But when the market turned down, thousands of investors discovered to their horror that margin could increase losses as well as gains.

All it takes to open a margin account is a $2,000 balance and a click of the mouse. There's usually a questionnaire in place of a credit check. Investors can then borrow up to 50% of the purchase price of a stock.

The attraction of margin trading is devilishly simple. Say you've got $10,000 to invest in XYZ Corp. Borrowing an equal amount from your broker, you buy $20,000 of the stock. Now say XYZ shoots up 50%. Suddenly, you have $30,000 in shares. When you pay back the $10,000 you borrowed, plus the loan rate, you wind up with nearly $10,000 in gains. Had you traded on your savings alone, your gains would amount to only $5,000.

But say XYZ tanks by 50%. The $20,000 investment drops to $10,000. After paying back your $10,000 loan, your initial investment is decimated. Had you declined to borrow money in the first place, you would have salvaged $5,000.

Trading on margin is risky not just for you but for the brokerages, too. If your bet goes sour, so might their loan. When a sinking stock approaches the level where selling it wouldn't raise enough money to repay your loan, brokers can issue what's known as a **margin call**. Here's how it works: In an investment made on margin, a drop in the stock's value eats into your contribution first. When the stock price falls so far that the amount you had to put up is less than 25% to 35% of the current value of the investment, the broker can order you to sell the stock at a loss to repay the loan (even if you still think the stock will go up) or deposit more cash into your account immediately. If you don't, the broker can liquidate your other stocks to cover the loan without your consent, without your input, and, in fact, without even bothering to tell you.

It has to be said: Trading stocks with money that isn't yours is not investing—it's speculating. But if you're thinking of giving it a try anyway, keep these five essentials in mind:

1. **Learn all your broker's rules before you take a loan.** Each firm has its own rules.
2. **Make sure you understand the consequences of a margin call.**
3. **Only borrow amounts you can afford to lose**—or be able to cover easily with cash from other accounts.
4. **Keep your holdings diversified.** If you concentrate all your margined stocks in one sector—especially a volatile one—then the stocks are likely to rise or fall in

tandem. If they all fall at once, there's an increased chance you'll get hit with a margin call.

   5. **Never buy an IPO (or newly issued stock) on margin.** Fortunately, many brokerages won't even let you.

• **Short selling.** Often called **shorting**, selling short is a way of profiting from a decline in a particular stock. To sell short, you must open a margin account with your stockbroker, which lets you borrow up to half the value of your account. The interest rate you pay is the broker's **call rate**, which is typically slightly less than the prime rate that banks charge. In short selling, you are borrowing shares from the accounts of other clients of your broker or other brokerages and then selling them in hopes of replacing them at a lower price. The difference between the price you get when you sell and the (lower, you hope) price when you buy is your profit or loss on the short position.

   Selling a stock short is actually riskier than owning it. If you misjudge the stock's prospects and the share price goes up, your losses are theoretically unlimited. (A stock you short, after all, can appreciate 100% or 200% or even more, while one you own can never lose more than 100% of its value. Imagine if you had shorted Microsoft when it went public.) Investors short only stocks that seem ripe for a fall—those with high P/E multiples, seemingly inflated expectations, and cloudy business prospects. Still, overpriced stocks sometimes only get more overpriced, and when that happens short sellers get pinched.

How to Read the Stock Tables

Trying to make sense of the stock-listing tables in the business pages of the newspaper for the first time can be a bit like visiting a foreign country where you don't speak the language. Once you know the lingo, however, it isn't tough at all. Here's what you need to know to read the stock tables like a pro, using a New York Stock Exchange listing for the stock of Philip Morris:

YTD	52 WEEK				YLD		VOL		NET
% CHG	HI	LO	STOCK (SYM)	DIV	%	PE	100s	CLOSE	CHG
+12.9	53.88	32.88	PhlpMor **MO**	2.32f	4.7	13	346.7	27.13	−19

- **YTD % CHG** (first column) shows you the percentage change of that stock over the calendar year to date, adjusting for stock splits and dividends over 10% (in this case +12.9%).
- **52 Week Hi and Lo** (two columns) show you the highest price of the stock over the past 52 weeks, but not the latest trading day (in this case $53.88 a share), and the lowest price (in this case $32.88). If the stock just hit a 52-week high or low, that will be marked by an arrow, pointing up or down. As you'll see when you read the rest of the row, Philip Morris's stock on this day was selling for a price that was fairly near its 52-week low. The bigger the variation between the Hi and Lo price, the more volatile the stock.
- **Stock** is, of course, the name of the stock. In many cases the actual name of the company is too long to fit into the stock table listing, so you'll see an abbreviated version of it (in this case PhlpMor). In the *Wall Street Journal*, the symbol will be in boldface if the stock's price changed by 5% or more in the previous trading day or its previous closing price was $2 or higher. In some instances the stock's name will be followed by a letter. These are the most common ones and what they mean: **A** or **B** (there are different classes of stock; shareholders of different classes have different voting rights); **dd** (the company showed a loss in the most recent four quarters); **n** (the stock was newly issued during the last 52 weeks); **pf** (a preferred stock—Note: Preferred stocks are now in a separate section of the *Journal*); **s** (there was a stock split, dividend, or cash distribution equal to 10% or more in the past 52 weeks); **vj** (the company is in bankruptcy, receivership, or is being reorganized); **wt** (a warrant—a security that entitles holdee to buy shares in the future at a specified price); **x** (the stock is trading ex-dividend; that means the company declared a dividend within the past four days and if you buy the stock now, you won't get its dividend until the next one is paid, typically in three months).
- **Sym** is the stock's ticker symbol, in this case MO. Often, the stock's symbol will be the name of the company or something close, such as an abbreviation. For instance, the symbol for General Motors is GM; for Sears, it's simply S. In other cases, however, the symbol will be something more clever (Tommy Hilfiger is TOM, Anheuser-Busch is BUD, Southwest Airlines is LUV).
- **Div** is the stock's dividend over the past four quarters. If the column is blank, that means the stock doesn't pay a dividend. In this case, Philip Morris is expected to pay a dividend of $2.32 a year on each share of its stock. Dividends are normally paid quarterly. The **f** here means that the $2.32 is an annual rate.
- **Yld %** represents the stock's dividends or other distributions paid on the company's securities, as a percentage of its stock price. In this case, Philip Morris's yield is 4.7%. If the column doesn't show a number, it means there is no dividend.

- **PE** is the price earnings multiple of the stock, based on the stock's trailing earnings. Here, Philip Morris sports a price earnings multiple of 13.
- **Vol 100s** tells you how many shares of the stock were bought and sold in the previous trading day. You generally have to multiply the figure by 100 to get the actual number. If the whole line is underlined, that means the stock had an unusually large change in trading volume in the previous trading day. Typically, this happens because there has been some news about the stock. In this case, 34,670 shares of Philip Morris changed hands in the previous trading day.
- **Hi, Lo, Close** (three columns) finally tell you what you really want to know: How did the stock do in the previous trading session? The **Hi** shows the most the stock sold for, **Lo** shows the least it sold for, and **Close** shows what it sold for in its last trade of the day. Philip Morris got as high as $27.50, as low as $27, and finished at $27.13.
- **NET CHG** (last column) gives you the bottom line: how much the stock rose or fell in the previous trading day, expressed in dollars and cents. Philip Morris lost 19¢ a share.

How to Choose a Broker

When you're looking for a broker, you have four distinct choices. From the most to the least expensive, they are: full-service brokers, discount brokers, deep discounters, and online brokers. What differentiates them is the advice they give and how much they charge. **Full-service brokers** (Merrill Lynch, UBS PaineWebber) will call with stock ideas, and back this advice with reports from their research department. They'll keep an eye on your picks and let you know when they think changes are necessary. **Discount brokers** (Charles Schwab, Fidelity, Quick & Reilly) do less of this. **Deep discounters** (Kennedy, Cabot, Pacific Brokerage Services) do nothing of the kind. And while there's typically plenty of research available on the best **online brokerage sites** (E-Trade, Ameritrade), it's up to you to dig for it.

You may want to choose different kinds of brokers for different purposes. We believe that full-service brokers should get paid for their stock ideas. That seems only fair. But if you've done your research yourself, we don't see any reason to pay a hefty commission—discounters probably are fine. The nice thing about the way the brokerage world is shaping up is that you may be able to have both of those things in one account at one firm. Traditional, discount, and deep discounters almost always offer online trading, so you can get the best of both worlds—market research and cheap trades.

Any traditional full-service broker who wants to sell you a stock should be willing to provide you with the company's financial statements, prospectuses, and proxies, as well as the Value Line or S&P report. It also pays to ask for a copy of a recent report on the stock by the brokerage's own research analysts. (Don't treat these reports as hot tips, however; by the time the brokerage firm makes its company reports available to retail clients such as you, the big institutional clients like pension funds may have known the analysts' opinion for months.) If, in the end, you also want to ask the broker's opinion, fine. But consider him or her to be just one of several sources of stock-picking advice.

If you decide to sign on with a full-service broker, you should make sure that person has nothing to hide. To get a report on any broker, contact the National Association of Securities Dealers (800-289-9999; www.nasd.com).

By far the biggest growth in the brokerage business these days is in online trading, which is hardly surprising. Online trading remains the most cost-efficient, convenient, and smart way for self-directed investors to trade. If you know exactly what you want to do, why pay any more than you have to for the privilege? In recent years you've been able to execute online trades for as little as $7.

Online investing is here to stay, but it is not problem-free. Some investors complain of online brokerage systems crashing and slow customer service. But at least one thing is clear from the annual surveys that MONEY magazine does of the best online brokers. Overall service is improving, and new features are being added at a rapid pace. Fidelity, for example, allows users to download gain and loss figures directly into most tax-preparation software programs. To make your online experience successful, you need to figure out what you want and then find the broker who offers it. Some online brokers are easier to use than others, others are known best for their low commissions, and others provide top-notch customer service. Over the past few years, MONEY has recommended Fidelity, Merrill Lynch Direct, and Charles Schwab for mainstream investors.

How to Buy or Sell Stocks

• **Placing an order.** When you place an order to buy or sell a stock with any kind of broker, you have two choices. You can ask for a **market order**, as most small investors do. This simply means that you want the broker to get you the best price to buy or sell the shares at the moment. Alternatively, you can place a **limit order**. In this case you're giving instructions to your broker about when to buy or sell shares for you. If, for instance, you believe the stock's current $50-a-share price will fall, you could place a limit order telling the broker not to buy the shares until the stock drops to, say, $45. Conversely, if you own a $50 stock, you could tell your broker to sell the shares whenever the price hits $75. One type of limit order, known as a **stop-loss order**, helps prevent you from losing too much money. With this technique, you instruct your broker to sell your shares if their price ever falls to a specific level; for instance, you could tell the broker to sell if your $50 stock sinks to $40.

- **DRIPs and direct investing.** Low online-brokerage commissions have stolen all the press in recent years, but many large companies have long offered an even better bargain to existing shareholders—the **dividend-reinvestment plan**, or DRIP. DRIPs let shareholders plow their quarterly payouts into additional shares without incurring commissions.

  Many firms also sponsor **direct-investing plans**, or **DIPs**, which allow you to buy shares directly from the company, with fees comparable to or lower than you would incur at an online brokerage. These programs, however, have advantages other than low or nonexistent transaction costs: You can purchase fractions of shares; often you can have a specific amount—say, $50—regularly deducted from your checking account and invested automatically; and you usually don't have to start with a large minimum investment. But even though transaction fees are low, buying stocks this way can be very expensive since you must pay a commission each time you make a purchase. Your best bet is to make less frequent larger purchases to dilute transaction costs.

  Thanks to the Web, finding which companies offer DRIPs, as well as learning the specifics about each one, is a snap. Below are five places on the Internet to go DRIP hunting:
  - Netstock Direct (www.netstockdirect.com)
  - Drip Central (www.dripcentral.com)
  - Drip Investor (www.dripinvestor.com)
  - BuyandHold.com (www.buyandhold.com)
  - ShareBuilder.com (www.sharebuilder.com)

- **Buying stocks through an investment club.** If you are intrigued by the idea of buying stocks routinely with a small group of people, you'll want to join or perhaps even form an investment club. There are now thousands of investment clubs in the country, many with fewer than 15 people in them. Typically, the members get together once a month or so and talk about stocks they think are worth purchasing, plus ones they own that might be worth unloading. As a rule, each member kicks in between $10 and $100 a month. To find out more about such clubs, contact the National Association of Investors Corporation (877-ASK-NAIC; www.better-investing.org). Once you pay the $39-a-year fee (in 2002) for an individual adult membership, you'll receive information on how to run a club, how to analyze stocks, when to sell stocks, and so forth.

Knowing When to Sell Your Stocks

Clearly, it takes a lot of skill to be an astute buyer of stocks, but buying is a snap compared to selling. Deciding when to dump your holdings is the toughest question you face as an investor. Individual investors routinely "sell winners too early and ride losers too long," wrote researchers Hersh M. Shefrin and Meir Statman in a 1985 *Journal of Finance* article. They concluded that investors often succumb to fears of loss and regret when making sell decisions. People who don't want to make paper losses "real" hold on to poor performers, and those who don't want to regret a missed opportunity for profits sell winners.

It's easy to understand why. The great bull market that lasted into 2000 elevated buy-and-hold from strategy to religion. The great tech inferno that ensued, however, reminded all market participants that, for many stocks, the ideal holding period may not be forever. Clearly, there are times when the most devout buy-and-hold practitioner should consider selling. Maybe you're near a goal—college tuition, retirement, a second home—and you need to trim risk or raise cash. Or you're wondering if this year's losers can rebound. Or you're just doing an annual, semiannual, or monthly portfolio review.

Whatever your reason for pondering a sale, don't look at a stock's price and ask simply whether you should unload it. Instead, take time to pose questions and search for answers about the stock's prospects. Below we discuss four familiar scenarios:

- **I've got an enormous winner.** Does it still offer me what it did a year ago? Is it too big a piece of my portfolio? This is the kind of sell dilemma we would all like to face, but it doesn't have a one-size-fits-all answer. Many money managers say you should always have in mind a target price you feel reflects the potential you saw when you bought the stock. Some managers swear by these sell targets: They hit one and get out. But that often leaves money on the table. Respected fund manager Bill Nygren sees the target "not so much as an absolute sell signal but as a benchmark when periodically reevaluating your investment rationale." If earnings come in better than expected, he says, "or if similar companies sell for more than expected in the private market, raise your target."

  If you have a stock that's risen, say, eightfold, it probably represents more of your holdings than prudence dictates. Most benefits of asset allocation can be gained with fewer than 15 stocks, and you likely don't have time to keep tabs on many more. So you should consider setting a limit of 3% to 10%.

  Or you could employ a strategy familiar to anyone who plays blackjack. Cut your position in half. That way, you lock in a profit and get to keep playing with house money.

Remember, though, that when you sell a winner, you're going to give up a big chunk of your gain in taxes (unless you're trading in a tax-deferred account). If you invest what's left in a new stock that you sell after three years, it must beat your old one by about 10% annually just to get you to where you would have been had you simply delayed the sale of the old stock.

- **My stock is plunging.** Is it temporary? Should I buy more? Or is there a long-lasting problem? Research suggests that the biggest mistake people make is hanging on to losers. But panic is an investor's enemy, and buying on dips to average down is a time-tested investing method. What do you do? Here are a couple of strategies to consider:

    Growth fund manager John McStay generally sells a stock if it declines 20%. If the market is falling, he'll cut his losers more slack, but in a strong market, even a 10% decline may prompt him to bail.

    Because you, unlike fund managers, don't have to chase short-term performance numbers, a rigid sell rule may not be a necessity. But be careful not to commit the sin of pride that McStay's dump rule is designed to avoid. That leads us to a second strategy: If a stock drops 15% or more in a flat or rising market, reevaluate. Do you have real doubt about its long-term prospects?

- **My stock is going nowhere.** Should I be doing something better with my money? The question of how long to wait for a stock to soar is especially relevant to investors who don't always have cash to invest in their next big idea. Many stock sales by professional money managers are prompted by their desire to buy something else.

    If you conclude you don't have a better idea, consider spreading the money tied up in your going-nowhere stock among your existing best ideas, if that won't overly concentrate your portfolio. Or just sit tight. An idea will come.

- **My stock has done okay, but some of the fundamentals have changed.** Which ones are noise, and which ones tell me something? Investors pay too much attention to news events that have little to do with a company's value, says fund manager Richard Howard. In particular, he thinks the significance of political events and changes in company management tends to get overblown. Likewise, Howard says, investors wrongly concentrate on price-to-earnings ratios. "Prices are not fundamentals. They reflect fundamentals."

    The key is to discriminate between meaningful developments and temporary distractions. Here are two fundamental shifts that you absolutely must heed: changes in a company's core business and a falloff in its market position.

    If a company has changed its focus or made a major acquisition that looks questionable, it isn't really the stock you bought. Is there still a reason for you to own it?

And even a well-run company can see its franchise threatened, says fund manager Tom Marsico. "When I buy stocks, I'm looking for ones that I never have to sell," he says. "But I'd be wrong to hold on just for the sake of holding on."

Investing in Stocks Through Mutual Funds

Stocks are a necessary part of every long-term investor's portfolio, but selecting and monitoring a collection of them can be daunting at first, even a burden. You may not have the money—$25,000 to $50,000 or so—that it takes to assemble a reasonably diversified portfolio of eight to 10 stocks. You may not be particularly confident in your ability to understand the subtleties of a company's financial statement. You may not feel you have the time to keep track of a company's fortunes, so that you know when to sell.

If any of those descriptions applies to you, then you ought to consider following the example of millions of other individual investors and do your stock market investing through shares of stock or equity mutual funds. When you buy shares in a fund, you become part owner of the fund's stock portfolio, which is likely to hold scores of stocks (if not more) worth tens of millions, if not billions, of dollars. The job of selecting and monitoring the stocks in the portfolio falls to a professional money-management firm. (Usually, but not always, the money manager is the company that sponsors the fund and whose brand—such as Fidelity, Vanguard, T. Rowe Price, or Janus—appears in the fund's name.) By owning a fund, you not only leave the hard work to pros, you also indirectly reap the advantages of investing large sums of money. A multimillion-dollar fund, for example, can buy stocks at a lower per-share commission than you can. A fund will also be more diversified than any portfolio you could easily construct on your own.

Investing through funds does not, of course, remove all the work from equity investing. For instance, there's the not so minor matter of choosing the best fund or funds for you. Today, there are more than 4,600 stock funds. They range from relatively safe, income-oriented funds to highly risky Internet and emerging technology funds. Many are managed competently, even brilliantly; others are run by undertrained, overworked, distracted, or simply not very bright money managers. Some hold their expenses low, to give fund shareholders every possible advantage. Others carry fees so high that if you invest in them, you're at a disadvantage right from the start. It's up to you to find the equity funds that will match your appetite for risk and give you a respectable return. No easy task.

Unlike stocks, which you usually have to buy through a stockbroker charging a commission, many funds are sold directly by their sponsors with no sales charge—or **load**, as it's known in the fund business. These commission-free funds, called **no-loads**, account for about one-third of the equity funds available to small investors. You buy a no-load fund either by sending a check in the mail, going to a discount or online brokerage such as Charles Schwab or Fidelity that sells the fund, or, in some cases, by going to the fund company's Web site. Some fund companies let you buy stocks online.

The remainder of mutual funds are load funds, which are sold by brokers and financial advisers and carry fees of one kind or another. A standard load fund might charge a fee between 0.5% and 8% of the amount you invest. How these commissions are charged has grown more complicated in recent years. You now often have a choice of whether to pay the commission up front all at once or parcel it out over the period you own the shares. (See the discussion of A-, B-, and C-shares on page 337.) The thing to remember, though, is that if you buy a load fund from a broker, you will pay for the privilege of having him or her help you select the fund. If you buy directly from a no-load sponsor, you will pay no sales charge (or only a relatively small one), but you will have to make your choice about whether to buy it and when to sell it without the benefit of a broker's advice. If you factor out the sales charges, no-load and load funds perform about equally over time. Translation: When you pay a sales load, you do not get a better product for the extra cost.

Where to Find Out About Mutual Funds

The growth in the number of mutual funds has been matched only by the growth in enterprises purporting to analyze, rank, and allegedly help you pick winning funds. What's more, the funds themselves publish useful descriptions of what they do and how they've done. In addition, dozens of Web sites can assist you. Getting adequate information about funds—at least the biggest and most widely available—is not hard at all. You just need to know where to look.

The best online source for mutual fund information is Morningstar.com. For no charge, the site provides a detailed report on each fund's investment style, the tenure of its manager, the fees it charges, and its historical performance (including how it has done vs. similar funds). You also get a breakdown of the fund's sector bets (the percentage of assets in health care, technology, financials, and other key market areas), plus a listing of the fund's 25 top holdings as of its most recent reporting date. Funds are required to

THE ABCs OF FUND SHARE CLASSES

If you buy a load fund, be sure to consider what share class you're getting. That's because different mutual fund share classes reflect different fee structures.

- **A-shares** charge a fee when you purchase the fund, called a **front-end load**. This fee, which is a percentage of your initial investment, compensates the broker who sold you the fund.

- **B-shares** charge **redemption** or **back-end loads**, which you don't pay until you pull out your money. The amount of the back-end load usually declines the longer you keep your money in the fund. You pay less up front, but you end up paying more each year in expenses.

- **C-shares** (or **level-load funds**) usually, but not always, charge front- and back-end loads, though less than you'd pay on A-shares or B-shares. Again, you pay higher expenses along the way.

    Whether one share class is better for you than another depends on your circumstances: how much money you are investing, how big the fund is, the annual expenses, and your time horizon. But in general, if you have to buy a load fund, you're better off with A-shares. There are many other share classes, but these are the most common.

report their holdings twice a year, but many do so quarterly or even monthly. Note: This means the Morningstar data on specific holdings could be hopelessly out of date or nearly up to the minute. In either case, you'll learn a lot about the manager's stock preferences at a particular time. The site's Fund Selector allows you to screen for funds using a broad range of criteria. Morningstar also offers a star-rating system that rates how funds stack up against their true peers—large-growth vs. large-growth, small-value vs. small-value, and so forth. So you get a sense of how a manager has performed vs. managers of similar funds.

Morningstar's Portfolio X-Rays feature tells you immediately how much overlap there is among the holdings of the funds you currently own, as well as those you are thinking of buying. For an annual fee, premium members also can access fund analyst reports, stock analyst reports, and other proprietary features.

Fund Alarm (www.fundalarm.com) not only gives you a gossipy inside look at the fund business, but also helps you avoid bad funds. The company keeps a list of funds that have underperformed their benchmarks for the past 12 months, three years, and five years.

To get a complete list of a fund's holdings, you should get the fund's annual or semi-annual shareholder report directly from the fund or from your broker. Most publications that include full, periodic listings of funds, such as MONEY, *Barron's*, *Business Week*, and the *Wall Street Journal*, list the 800 numbers of the funds that you'll need to get this information.

Two publications provide the kind of detailed analysis of mutual funds that the *Value Line Investment Survey* and *Standard & Poor's Stock Reports* provide for stocks: *Morningstar Mutual Funds* ($395 a year; $55 for a three-month trial subscription; 800-735-0700; www.morningstar.com) and the *Value Line Mutual Fund Survey* ($295 a year; $49 for a three-month trial subscription; 800-535-8760; www.valueline.com). Modeled on the Value Line stock reports, both provide a thorough look at the past performance and current portfolio holdings of more than 1,000 funds as well as a description of the fund manager's investing style. You can generally find one or both in large public libraries.

Understanding the Different Types of Funds

To help investors assess U.S. domestic funds, researchers at Morningstar developed a style box, which is a nine-box tic-tac-toe grid (three rows and three columns). This matrix displays both the fund's investment approach and the size of the companies in which it invests. According to Morningstar, combining these two variables offers a broad view of a fund's holdings and risk.

The rows denote the average size of a fund's stocks: large, medium, and small. The columns sort a fund's holdings by average price: cheap value stocks, more expensive growth stocks, or a mix of the two, blend stocks.

- **Growth funds:** These invest in the stock of companies whose profits are growing at a rapid pace. Such stocks typically rise more quickly than the overall market—and fall faster if they don't live up to investors' expectations.
- **Value funds:** Value-oriented fund managers buy companies that appear to be cheap,

relative to their earnings. In many cases, these are mature companies that send some of their earnings back to their shareholders in the form of dividends.

So every domestic stock fund falls into one of nine pigeonholes: small-cap value, blend, or growth; mid-cap value, blend, or growth, and large-cap value, blend, or growth. Large-cap value would be considered the safest investment; small-cap growth would be the riskiest.

Median Market Capitalization	Investment style		
	Value	Blend	Growth
Large	Large-cap value	Large-cap blend	Large-cap growth
Medium	Medium-cap value	Medium-cap blend	Medium-cap growth
Small	Small-cap value	Small-cap blend	Small-cap growth

LOW RISK (white)
Large-cap value, Large-cap blend, Medium-cap value
MODERATE RISK (light tint)
Small-cap value, Medium-cap blend, Large-cap growth
HIGH RISK (dark tint)
Medium-cap growth, Small-cap blend, Small-cap growth

Source: Morningstar.

• **Other funds:** Since there is a lot of overlap in the stocks held in each of these fund types, you'll need to branch out to get any kind of meaningful diversification. That's where the more aggressive funds, like **aggressive growth funds, capital appreciation funds, small-cap funds,** and **mid-cap funds,** among others, fit in. Typically, these funds, which tend to be more volatile than large-cap funds, pursue one or more of the following strategies:
  • Invest in smaller companies, where earnings aren't as reliable as at bigger firms but where the potential for gains (and losses) is higher.

- Invest in pricey, high-growth stocks.
- Invest in stocks that are in "hot" industries, such as technology or health care.
- Invest in just a handful of companies.
- **International or foreign funds,** which invest outside the U.S., come in three basic flavors. The first, **international funds**, typically buy stocks in larger companies from relatively stable regions like Europe and the Pacific Rim. **Global funds** do likewise, but they can also invest heavily in the U.S. And **emerging market funds** invest in riskier regions, like Latin America, Eastern Europe, and Asia.

Categorizing funds by their investment approach is especially useful in understanding their recent performance. Stock investors tend to favor either growth stocks or value stocks, and mutual fund portfolio managers are no different.

Although many investors expect a professional money manager to excel in every kind of market, even the best managers rarely do. Most stick to the investment approach they know best, regardless of the approach that happens to be in vogue. For that reason, a fund manager's success typically rises and falls with his or her particular investment discipline. Indeed, studies show that investment style accounts for at least 75% of a manager's return. For the ultimate diversified portfolio of mutual funds, therefore, you should own funds that represent all investment approaches—both growth and value, and large- and small-cap versions of each.

But there's a subtler message behind this essential truth. If you buy funds when they're hot and sell them when they're ice cold, you won't have much success as an investor. Always be on guard against investment fads.

Oddly enough, one type of fund—**index funds**—has achieved an outstanding long-term record by not trying to beat the market. The goal of an index fund is to equal a particular market benchmark. The fund manager buys a portfolio of stocks that mirror the ones in a popular index, such as the Standard & Poor's 500 index. There are now more than 192 index funds, and you can find one for just about every type of stock you like: small-cap, mid-cap, large-cap, or international. During most years in the 1990s, S&P 500 index funds handily beat the average U.S. stock fund and, in fact, outperformed 90% of them. The biggest reason: Index funds have much lower annual expenses.

Index funds are not exciting—by definition, you'll never be able to brag about your index fund creaming the market—but they're very powerful tools, especially considering that, over time, 75% of mutual fund managers underperform the overall stock market. You could have a portfolio consisting of nothing but index funds if you wished, although active managers arguably stand a greater chance of beating the small-cap and international indexes. Possible solution: Make an S&P 500 index fund the core of your portfolio and then try to find bright small-cap, value, and international fund managers who have indicated that they can beat the averages in the long run.

BENCHMARKS FOR INDEX FUNDS

When people talk about the long-term performance of stocks, they're usually talking about the Dow Jones Industrial Average or the Standard & Poor's 500 stock index. An index fund can be based on one of several different benchmarks used to track stocks and bonds. Four of the most used indexes:

- **Standard & Poor's 500 Stock Index** covers large U.S. companies.
- **Russell 2000 Stock Index** covers small U.S. companies.
- **Wilshire 5000 Stock Index** covers large, medium, and small U.S. companies.
- **Lehman Brothers Aggregate Bond Index** covers the total U.S. taxable bond market.

How to Pick a Stock Mutual Fund

Once you've identified the kind of mutual fund you want to buy, your next job is to find a fund that executes that approach with aplomb. Style may account for three-quarters of a typical fund's return, but that still leaves 25% for the individual manager's skill (or lack thereof). It's tempting to assume that the top performing fund over the previous year or five years will repeat in the future. Too bad it rarely works that way, however. Markets can change, a manager's luck can run out, a fund can change its manager, and funds at the top in one time period rarely stay there for long.

A more realistic goal is to try to find managers who are likely to outperform the average fund in their group in the future. That seemingly modest endeavor is more of an art than a science, but you'll improve your chances of success if you look for something more than simply a top performance ranking. Here's what to look for as well:

- **Consistency.** When checking out a fund's past performance, look for evidence that suggests the returns were consistent and steady year after year rather than erratic flashes of brilliance. A few hot stocks, after all, could propel a fund's performance for years, but when the stocks cool down, so might the fund.
- **Bearable risk.** Volatility goes with the territory when you invest in stock funds. But you want to make sure that the fund you choose doesn't dish out more pain during

market downturns than you can take. So in your analysis, look for the fund's worst annual return in any of the past five or 10 years and ask yourself whether you could sit through a loss of that magnitude without selling or getting sick to your stomach. Success with mutual funds takes patience and persistence. If a fund's periodic losses would overwhelm both virtues in you, look for one that you can live with, even if its returns are less Olympian. For instance, rather than buying an aggressive growth fund, invest instead in a more moderate equity-income fund. You can also match a fund to your risk tolerance by looking at its manager's investing style, often noted in mutual fund performance rankings. Style, in fund parlance, means whether the fund buys large-, medium-, or small-cap stocks and whether the manager prefers growth stocks, value stocks, or some combination.

- **Low expenses.** All else being equal, a no-load fund with annual expenses below the domestic equity fund average of 1.43% will outperform a more costly load fund. Investing in a high-expense fund is like betting on a horse that is carrying a heavier load than the rest of the field: The nag still might win, but the odds are against it. Similarly, shrewd stock picking by a fund manager can more than make up for the burden of extra expenses, but unless you are convinced that the fund really has more promise than its less expensive competition, there's no point in starting out with a handicap. You can find the fund's fees as a percentage of assets—listed as the **expense ratio**—through Morningstar, Value Line, or other services. Here, according to Morningstar, are the average expense ratios for the broad categories of funds that buy stocks: large-cap value (1.41%), large-cap growth (1.45%), mid-cap value (1.44%), mid-cap growth (1.53%), small-cap value (1.52%), small-cap growth (1.62%).

- **Manageable asset size.** Funds with superb returns that win accolades from the financial press can become so popular that they balloon by hundreds of millions of dollars in a few months. A flood of incoming cash can force a manager to modify his investing approach and may even distract the manager from a careful daily monitoring of the fund's stocks. The fund industry is littered with once hot performers that became media darlings, swelled in size, and promptly turned into mediocrities. As a rule, be wary of funds whose sales have more than doubled over the previous year; you can find this information by looking at the year-by-year asset size of the fund in its prospectus. This is especially true of funds that specialize in small-company stocks traded over-the-counter, where big trades are hard to execute quickly and inexpensively. If a small-cap fund has grown beyond that point and is still accepting new money, you should probably make sure that none of it is yours.

- **Tax efficiency.** Ever heard the expression "It's not how much you make, it's how much you keep"? This maxim is especially apt for stock fund investors, since a fund's income and capital-gains distributions are taxed by the IRS. You can find the tax efficiency of a fund at the Morningstar Web site. Increasingly, annual fund performance rankings in magazines, newspapers, and Web sites list the tax efficiency of the funds, which is the percentage of a fund's total return that an investor in the 38.6% federal tax bracket would have kept after paying taxes on the income and capital gains distributed by the fund over the past three years. This percentage gives you a truer explanation of how well you would actually have done had you invested in the fund. For instance, if a fund returned 12% on average over three years and its tax efficiency was 87%, your after-tax return in the 38.6% bracket would be 10.4% (or 87% of 12%).

While most fund managers don't concern themselves with their fund's tax efficiency (their bonuses depend on pretax performance), a few funds do expressly attempt to minimize a shareholder's tax burden.

If you want to be almost certain that a fund will make minimal distributions, stick with one specifically designed to do so. Tax-managed funds execute a careful balancing act, offsetting gains with losses whenever possible to minimize distributions to shareholders. Many also charge a redemption fee if you sell within a few years; that's to dissuade shareholders from active trading, which can force a manager to realize taxable gains. Tax-managed funds typically follow low-turnover, benchmarket strategies much like index funds.

So if you're comparing two otherwise identical funds and one has a stated policy of tax-efficient investing, that's the one to choose—if you'll be investing in a taxable account. If you're buying the fund for a tax-deferred account such as a 401(k) or IRA, you don't have to worry about tax efficiency.

How to Read the Fund Listings

The mutual fund listings in the daily newspaper are easier to comprehend than the stock listings, but not by a whole lot. Making things even trickier is that different newspapers list funds differently. The following guide to the fund listings in the *Wall Street Journal*, using Oakmark Select as an example, will help you see how your funds are doing:

NAME	NAV	NET CHG	YTD %RET
OAKMARK:			
SELECT	27.26	−0.10	+17.3

- The first column gives you the **fund's name** and, if it is part of a fund family, the fund family name in boldface. Generally, the name of the fund will be abbreviated for space. In this case the actual name of the fund, Oakmark Select, is shown in the table. If the fund has various classes of shares, the letter for the class (A, B, C, D) will follow its name. If you see a **p**, this means that the fund levies a so-called 12b-1 fee, which is an annual charge to shareholders for marketing and distribution. If you see an **r**, that means the fund has a redemption charge, which you may owe when you sell your shares.
- **NAV** tells you the net asset value of the fund, which is the price of one share of the fund. A fund computes its NAV by dividing the total value of the fund by the number of shares. Like stock prices, NAVs can vary enormously for stock funds.
- **NET CHG** shows how much the fund rose or fell from the previous trading day in the value of dollars and cents. Oakmark Select lost 10¢ a share.
- **YTD % RET** stands for the year-to-date return on that fund since January 1 of that year. Oakmark Select is up 17.3% since the start of the year.

How to Use a Broker or Financial Planner to Buy Mutual Funds

Mutual fund investing is straightforward enough that most enterprising investors can do it without a stockbroker. If you nevertheless feel that a broker's or planner's counsel is worth an extra fee, make sure that you get the service you're paying for. Your broker should be able to provide extensive research on any fund he or she recommends. You should also ask for the reports on competing funds and ask the broker to explain why his or her choice is best for you. Occasionally a fund company or brokerage firm will promote a particular fund by offering brokers a higher than normal commission. So ask whether the adviser stands to make a higher commission on the recommended fund than a comparable one. If so, he'd better have a persuasive case why his fund is better than the competition.

Buying Your Funds at the Bank

Buying your mutual funds at your bank is certainly a convenient way to invest. However, remember that the funds are not FDIC-insured. Also make sure the salesperson asks critical questions about your risk tolerance, income levels, investment goals, and objectives. Finally note that many banks pay the fund salespeople more to sell customers proprietary funds managed by the bank, which may not be as good as what you could buy elsewhere.

Before you buy, do every bit as much research checking out the fund as you would if you were buying the fund on your own or through your financial adviser or broker.

CHAPTER 15

Investing in Bonds and Bond Mutual Funds

There are three main reasons why you ought to give bonds and bond mutual funds a close look. First, bonds can provide a steady stream of income, delivering more than what you would earn if you kept your dollars in a bank account or money-market fund. Second, bonds can help cushion your portfolio against sharp drops in the stock market—as investors learned in 2000 and 2001. Third, some bonds provide tax-free income, often a big advantage if you're in the 30% tax bracket or higher.

To better understand how bonds can fit into your overall portfolio, it helps to take a look at their historic performance. Long-term Treasury bonds that **mature** (or come due) in 20 years returned an average of 9.3% from 1970 to 2000. That compares with 12.9% for large-company stocks, according to Ibbotson Associates, the Chicago investment research firm. From mid-1999 through mid-2000 investors in mutual funds that buy bonds, commonly called **bond funds**, earned an average of 7.5% a year, according to Morningstar, the Chicago mutual fund research firm. But as with the stock market, the bond market has bad years from time to time—generally when interest rates or inflation shoots up. For instance, bond prices crashed in 1994, saddling investors with an average loss of 4.8%.

While bonds are less lucrative than stocks over the long term, they also can be less volatile. Intermediate-term bonds, which mature in five to 10 years, have lost money for investors just twice since 1970, according to Ibbotson. That compares to six losing years for large-company stocks. When the S&P 500 sank by 9.1% in 2000, long-term U.S. government bonds gained 21.5%.

Small investors can buy bonds in three ways:

- **You can purchase individual bonds through a broker and, in some cases, directly from the federal government.** (You can buy U.S. Treasuries through the federal government's TreasuryDirect program.) Although you can buy U.S. Treasury securities with as little as $1,000, it's best to invest at least $75,000 if you want to buy individual issues offered by municipalities (**municipal bonds**) or corporations (**corporate bonds**). That way you'll be able to buy enough different bonds to own a diversified portfolio.
- **You can invest in bonds through a mutual fund.** This strategy makes sense for people who have less than $75,000 to invest in bonds or who don't want to worry about picking individual issues. When you purchase shares of a bond fund, your cash is pooled with money from other people and then professionally managed. Many bond funds require minimum initial investments of $500 to $1,000; some accept amounts as low as $100.
- **You can buy unit investment trusts (UITs) from stockbrokers.** These are basically baskets of bonds that are held for the trust's lifespan. UITs are usually sold in units of $1,000.

How the Bond Market Works

Before you invest any money in bonds, it will help to understand how the bond market works. Companies and governments issue bonds to finance their day-to-day operations or to fund special projects, like new construction. Because most bond issues are so large, involving hundreds of millions of dollars, issuers usually don't sell their bonds directly to the public. Instead the bonds are marketed through an investment bank known as an **underwriter**. When bonds are issued, they are sold on what is known as the **primary market**. Older bonds can be bought through brokers from other purchasers on what's called the **secondary market**.

Think of a bond as an IOU. When you buy a bond you're loaning money for a set period of time to the issuer—whether it's the city of Chicago, General Motors, or the U.S. Treasury. In exchange for your dough, the borrower promises to pay you interest each year and to return your principal at maturity. As a rule, the longer the term of your bond, the higher your yield.

BOND WEB SITES

BONE UP ON BONDS AT . . .

Site Web Address (www.)	Comment
BondResources bondresources.com	Bond market updates, bond index yields
Direct Access Notes directnotes.com	Details on low-minimum corporate bonds
Investing in Bonds investinginbonds.com	Prices on frequently traded munis and corporates

INVEST IN BONDS AT . . .

Site	Web Addresss (www.)
E-Trade	etrade.com
Fidelity	fidelity.com
MuniDirect	munidirect.com
Schwab	schwab.com
T. D. Waterhouse	tdwaterhouse.com
Tradebonds.com	tradebonds.com
TreasuryDirect	publicdebt.treas.gov/sec/sectrdir.htm
Vanguard	vanguard.com

Interest paid on a bond is known as its **coupon**, a name that dates back to the days when bond investors had to clip the coupons on their bonds and send them to a trustee who would mail out interest payments. Today, interest payments are sent automatically to the bond owner's bank or brokerage account. The **face value** of a bond—the price at the time it was issued—is known as its **par value**. So the **coupon rate** is the bond's percentage yield at par value. For instance, a bond with a $1,000 face value that pays out $70 a year in interest has a coupon rate of 7%. Because a bond's lifespan and the schedule of coupon payments are fixed when a bond is issued, bonds are known as **fixed-income investments**.

When you divide the bond's coupon rate by its current price, you come up with what's known as the bond's **current yield**. This is the amount you would earn if you bought the bond today. Bonds sell at a **discount** if their current market price is lower than their face value. As a discounted bond gets closer to maturity, the discount narrows. At maturity, it vanishes. (If you buy a bond at a discount, you pay taxes on any capital gains from the rise in its price when you sell.) Bonds that sell at a price higher than their face value trade at a **premium**. If the face value and current value are equal, the bond trades at **par**. Another type of bond yield is the **yield to maturity**. This percentage figure accounts for both the interest payments and any capital gain or loss you have when the bond is due.

Some investors mistakenly believe they can't lose money in bonds. But don't let the term "fixed income" fool you. Although the interest payments you'll get from owning a bond are fixed, the return you will earn as a bond investor is not. That's because of the primary rule for investing in bonds: Bond prices move in the opposite direction of interest rates. So when interest rates rise, bond prices fall. And when rates fall, bond prices rise. The reason? When rates go up, newer bonds are issued paying the requisite higher interest, which makes older bonds with their lower interest rates less attractive to investors. The prices of these older bonds then fall to make up the difference. Similarly, bond prices rise when interest rates fall because their higher payout becomes more attractive than the lower rates offered by new bonds.

That's why arguably the most important figure to look at when investing in bonds is **total return**: It represents a combination of the bond or bond fund's yield and any capital gains or losses.

To understand what interest rate shifts can mean to you as a bond investor, consider the following example. You pay $1,000 for a 10-year bond issued by Able Shoemaker that carries a 6% coupon. As an Able bondholder you'll get $60 a year in interest ($1,000 times 6%). Shortly after you make your purchase, however, inflation heats up and interest rates rise. Sunshine Utility decides it needs to raise money, so it starts selling bonds that pay 7%, or $70 on a $1,000 investment. Suddenly your Able bond with its $60 payout doesn't look very attractive. You decide to dump it and use the money to snap up a 7% Sunshine issue. The trouble is nobody wants to give you what you paid for the Able bond with its 6% yield. The only way you can find a buyer is to take a cut in the price of your Able bond.

Here's another, more pleasant example. Let's say that one year passes and interest rates have fallen by one percentage point. Your $1,000 Sunshine bond is paying 7%, while new issues now are paying just 6%. Your bond is now especially alluring to other investors. To see what happens to the value of bonds if interest rates rise or fall by different amounts, see the table that follows.

THE EFFECT OF INTEREST RATE MOVES ON BONDS

The table below will show you what would happen to the price of a $1,000 bond with a coupon rate of 6% if interest rates rise or fall by one or two percentage points. You'll see that the longer the bond's maturity, the more you can gain or lose on an interest rate move.

	—————— Interest Rate Moves ——————			
	Your $1,000 bond's price if interest rates rise by . . .		Your $1,000 bond's price if interest rates fall by . . .	
Term of Bond	**One Point**	**Two Points**	**One Point**	**Two Points**
1–year	$990.05	$980.11	$1,000.96	$1,010.94
5–year	$950.84	$910.89	$1,040.38	$1,080.98
10–year	$920.89	$860.41	$1,070.79	$1,160.35
30–year	$870.53	$770.38	$1,150.45	$1,340.76

Source: Thorndike Encyclopedia of Banking and Financial Tables.

Short-term price fluctuations due to shifting interest rates don't matter much if you plan to hold a bond until maturity. At that time, you'll be repaid the bond's full face value. You could see sharp gains or losses, however, if you decide to sell a bond early or you invest in a bond fund whose manager buys and sells issues routinely.

Even if you're a buy-and-hold bond investor, interest rates can throw a monkey wrench into your financial plans. Let's say you own a corporate bond that is paying 8% interest, but rates have plunged to 6%. In that case Sunshine may decide to **redeem** (or **call**) its bonds before they mature. The company might call in its bonds because it wants to reduce its interest costs and no longer wants to pay the old, higher rate to investors. Although falling rates have pushed the price of your $1,000 bond up a couple hundred dollars, Sunshine is required to pay you only the par value of $1,000 if it calls in the bond. Not only will you get less than the market price, you'll have to find a place to reinvest the money that's been returned to you. Chances are you'll wind up settling for a new bond that pays 6%, not the 8% you were getting. Calls can be particularly painful if you're planning to live off your bond income.

Find out whether a bond you're considering can be called before you buy it. Just ask your broker whether the bond contains a **call provision**. If it does, this provision will explain the conditions under which a company can buy back its bonds and what price it must pay. Because there's a risk that you won't get the income you expect, callable bonds usually pay a higher interest rate than comparable **noncallable** bonds. If the bond does have a call provision, ask your broker for the bond's **yield to call**—this is the yield on a bond assuming that the bond will be redeemed by the issuer when it can first be called. This figure is especially relevant when the bond is selling at a premium. When a bond is callable, the lower of the yield to call and the **yield to maturity** is the rate of return that you're more likely to get.

The Different Types of Bonds

You can choose from a wide array of bonds and bond funds (we will discuss these later in the chapter), which vary in both the potential return they offer and their potential risks. When weighing your alternatives, keep in mind that the highest-yielding issues typically carry the highest risks. The following descriptions will help you sort through the bond buffet:

- **U.S. Treasuries.** These issues are the safest of all because the payment of interest and principal is guaranteed by the full faith and credit of the U.S. government. Treasuries are sold by the federal government through auctions held weekly, monthly, quarterly, and semiannually. When you buy a Treasury, the interest you earn is exempt from state and local taxes, but not from federal tax. You can buy Treasuries either through a stockbroker or directly from the federal government at www.publicdebt.treas.gov/sec/sec-trdir.htm. There are four different types of Treasuries:

  Treasury bills are ultra-short-term investments issued in terms of 13 weeks, 26 weeks, and one year. You buy so-called T-bills at a discount and get their full face value when the bills come due. The difference between the price you pay and the amount you get back reflects the interest you've earned. To buy individual Treasury bills, you must invest at least $10,000. T-bills can't be called.

Treasury notes mature in two to 10 years. Interest is paid semiannually at a fixed rate and the minimum investment is $1,000. Treasury notes usually can't be called.

Treasury bonds have the longest maturities—from 10 to 20 years. (The 30-year bond was discontinued in 2001.) Like Treasury notes, they pay interest semiannually and usually can't be called. You can buy a Treasury bond for as little as $1,000.

Zero-coupon Treasuries are also known as **strips**. These securities, which cost a minimum of $1,000, are sold by brokers at a deep discount and redeemed at full face value when they mature in six months to 30 years. For instance, you might pay $460 for a $1,000 zero due in 10 years. Zeros pay interest only at maturity; until that point, all the interest your bond accrues is reinvested, letting you earn interest on your interest. Zeros can be especially attractive if you need a fixed amount of money at a certain date, such as the year that you plan to retire.

But zero prices can be highly volatile—25% more volatile than standard bonds— which means you could suffer a sharp loss if you have to redeem early. The reason: These bonds have no coupon (which means that the issuer does not pay interest during the life of the security), and the smaller a bond's coupon, the more sensitive the bond is to interest rate shifts. The volatility of zeros can work in your favor, too, though. If interest rates fall and you redeem your zeros early, you could profit from a run-up in the value of your bonds. For example, if long-term rates fell from 7.5% to 5.5% over two years, your 10-year zero could jump 30% in value. One other drawback with zeros: Even though you don't get their interest until maturity, you have to pay taxes on the interest you've earned each year. There's one exception to this rule. If you keep your zeros in a tax-deferred account such as a traditional IRA or Keogh, you postpone paying the taxes until you withdraw from your account.

- **Corporate bonds.** Interest is fully taxable on these bonds, which are issued by businesses ranging from automakers to utilities. Because their value depends on the creditworthiness of the company offering the bonds, they carry higher yields and higher risks than secure U.S. government issues. Maturities of corporates can range from a few weeks to 100 years, though most have terms of one to 20 years. Unlike Treasuries, these bonds are frequently callable. Most corporate bonds are issued in denominations of $1,000. You can buy zero-coupon corporate bonds, but it's not advisable since the market for those bonds isn't very active. As a result, it's tough to get a fair price when buying corporate zeros.

Top-quality corporate bonds are known as **investment-grade bonds**. Corporate bonds with less than great credit quality are known as **junk bonds**, or **high-yield bonds** in polite company. They are rated Ba, BB, or lower for financial soundness by Standard & Poor's or Moody's, the leading bond-rating agencies. (Read more about ratings later in this chapter.) Junk bonds typically pay higher yields than other corporate bonds and much higher yields than Treasuries.

- **Municipal (or muni) bonds.** Munis are issued by state and local governments and agencies, usually for $5,000 and up. Their interest is free from federal taxes. If you live in the state issuing the muni bond, the interest is exempt from federal, state, and possibly local taxes. Munis mature in one to 30 years; they're often callable. You can buy zero-coupon municipal bonds, but as with zero-coupon corporates, these issues don't trade much, so you may not want to buy them unless you're confident that you'll be able to hold the bonds to maturity. Because munis provide tax savings, they tend to offer lower yields than taxable bonds that are just as creditworthy. To determine whether a muni investment is the better deal, you'll need to compare the yields of munis with taxable bonds on an after-tax basis. You can find out whether munis are right for you once you have two pieces of information. The first is the muni's yield; the second is your tax bracket. Then plug those two numbers into the following simple formula:

$$\textbf{Tax-equivalent yield} = \frac{\textbf{muni bond yield}}{\textbf{(1 − your tax rate)}}$$

To see how this works in real life, let's say you're an investor in the 31% tax bracket and you want to compare a muni yielding 6.5% with a Treasury bond yielding 7.8%. You divide the 6.5% muni yield by one minus your 31% tax rate, or .69. The result: a tax-equivalent yield of 9.4%. In this case, since taxable bonds are yielding just 7.8%, the muni would be the better investment.

There are two basic types of munis. **General obligation bonds** (or **GOs**) are issued by states, cities, and counties to finance the building of roads, schools, and sewers and are backed by taxes collected by the issuing government. They have traditionally been considered relatively safe because they are backed by the full faith and credit of the government selling the bond. **Revenue bonds**, on the other hand, are issued by specific institutions, such as an electric utility, a hospital, or a nursing home. These bonds are riskier than general obligation bonds because their payments are secured only by the income of the specific project your money is financing.

Like corporate bonds, municipal issues are rated by Standard & Poor's and Moody's for their credit quality. The highest-quality munis are backed by a bond insurance company, which guarantees the payment of interest and principal regardless of the issuer's health. But you'll pay for the protection: Insured bonds and insured bond funds can yield 0.10 to 0.50 percentage points less than comparable bonds that don't carry this protection. However, insurance won't protect you against interest rate risk or the chance that panic selling will drive down your bond's market value.

Another option for municipal investors looking for maximum safety and high yields is to buy pre-refunded bonds backed by U.S. Treasuries. Here, the interest and principal you get is assured because marketable securities, usually Treasury bonds, have been set aside in a special escrow account to meet these payments.

- **Mortgage-backed bonds.** These bonds—whose minimum investment is usually $25,000—represent an ownership stake in a package of mortgage loans issued or guaranteed by government agencies such as Ginnie Mae, the Federal National Mortgage Association (Fannie Mae), and Freddie Mac. The interest on these bonds is not exempt from taxation, and with the exception of Ginnie Maes, these bonds are not backed by the full faith and credit of the U.S. government. They mature in as long as 20 years and are not callable by issuers.

   Interest rate shifts are a special concern for investors in mortgage-backed securities. If rates fall, for instance, homeowners may decide to refinance their mortgages, prepay their existing loans, and then take out new mortgages at a lower interest rate. In that case, you the mortgage-backed security owner will have to reinvest your money at a lower interest rate, leaving you with a lower return than you expected. As a result, mortgage-backed bonds don't get as much of a boost from falling rates as other types of issues; in some cases they lose value.

- **Foreign bonds.** Issued by governments outside the United States to meet their financing needs, these bonds are offered at varying minimums, often $25,000. Because foreign interest rates don't move in lockstep with U.S. rates, the bonds can provide diversification to your portfolio. Foreign bonds subject you to currency risk, however. A small increase or decline in the value of the currency behind the bond could boost or slice the value of your investment. Say you buy a U.K. bond yielding 8%. If the value of the dollar rises 5% against the British pound, you'll be left with just a 3% return. If the dollar falls by 5%, though, your total return could jump to 13%.

Bonds Can Be Risky

When you buy a bond, the issuer promises that it will repay you both the interest and principal you are due. But can you be sure the issuer will make good on that promise? The answer lies largely in the bond's **credit risk**—the chance that financial troubles will make the borrower late in its payments or unable to meet the payments at all. The level of credit risk you face depends on the type of bond you buy and the issuer's financial health. Bonds, bills, and notes issued by the U.S. government are considered to have no credit risk, since they are backed by the full faith and credit of the U.S. Treasury. Junk bonds have the highest credit risk.

It's easy to get a feel for the creditworthiness of a particular corporate or municipal bond, since rating agencies such as Standard & Poor's and Moody's evaluate most companies and municipalities. Bonds from the strongest issuers carry the rating of Aaa or AAA. The next step down the credit ladder is Aa or AA and then A; all are high-quality bonds. Issues rated below investment grade, Ba or BB or lower, are considered to be speculative investments. The lowest bond rating for a bond that's not in default is C. A slight difference in a bond rating can be quite meaningful.

There are several reasons why a bond might not be rated. The issuer might decide the underwriting is too small. Or the issuer could view getting a rating as too costly or time-consuming. Alternatively, the issuer might just figure that the rating it will get will be low so it would rather not have one.

Investors generally get rewarded for taking additional credit risk. As a rule, the lower the credit rating, the more the bond yields, since you're increasing the chance that the issuer won't be able to make good on its payments.

You can find out a bond's rating by checking with your broker or one of the ratings services. Contact Standard & Poor's (www.standardandpoors.com; 212-438-2400) or Moody's (www.moodys.com; 212-553-0377).

Keep in mind, however, that a high credit rating when you buy the bond isn't a guarantee that you'll never face any credit risk. For one thing, a bond's credit rating can drop if the issuer's financial health declines. Some money managers also say that rating agencies tend to be backward looking and do a poor job of anticipating potential problems. One comforting fact: Bond price drops that generally follow ratings downgrades aren't as sharp as those from rises in interest rates, unless there's a real chance that a bond will default.

Even if you own a high-quality bond, you can lose money if you want to sell that bond and no one wants to buy it at the price you think is reasonable. **Liquidity risk** is the chance that you or your bond fund won't be able to unload a bond quickly without a stiff penalty. You don't need to worry about liquidity if you buy an individual bond and plan to hold it until maturity, but you should be aware of this risk if you think you might need to draw on your bonds to meet a sudden expense. Liquidity risk is also a concern for bond fund investors, since fund managers regularly add and subtract bonds from their portfolios and may have to dump issues to raise cash if a flood of investors redeem their fund shares and want their money.

The amount of liquidity risk you'll face depends on the type of bond or bond fund you are buying. U.S. Treasury issues are highly liquid. Their pristine credit quality means there's always a ready market for them if you want to sell. By contrast, the markets for bonds sold by municipalities and financially distressed companies can be highly illiquid since many of these issues trade rarely, if at all.

Reading the Corporate Bond Tables

BONDS	CUR YLD.	VOL.	CLOSE	NET CHG.
IBM 8⅜19	8.1	8	102⅞	−1/4
IBM 7¼02	7.4	612	98⅝	−1/8
IBM 6⅜00	6.7	133	95⅞	——

If there's anything harder to read in the newspaper than the stock tables, it must be the bond tables. Here's a primer on reading corporate bond tables:

- **Bonds** (the first column) tells you first the name of the issuer, in this case IBM; then the bond's coupon rate (ranging here from 6⅜% to 8⅜%); and then the last two digits of the year the bond matures and the principal is paid off (00 means the year 2000). The interest rate is a percentage of the bond's par value, typically $1,000. In other words, the annual interest payment on the IBM 7¼02 bond is $72.50 ($70 for the 7% and $2.50 for the ¼). If you see the letters **zr**, that means the bond is a zero-coupon issue; an **s** means nothing more than a space between the rate and the term of the bond; a **vi** means the issuer is in bankruptcy, in receivership, or being reorganized.

- **Cur Yld.** (the second column) tells you what interest rate you would earn if you bought the bond today at its current price. When the price is less than par, the yield is higher than the coupon rate, but when the price is above par, the yield is lower than the rate. Here, the first IBM bond has a price above par (102⅞), which is why its current yield is less than the coupon rate. All of the other IBM bonds here are trading below par, so their yields exceed their rates.
- **Vol.** (the third column) is shorthand for the dollar value of the bonds traded in the previous day, shown in thousands of dollars. You'll see that the IBM 7¼02 had the highest volume, with $612,000 traded. The IBM 8⅜19 had a thin volume of $8,000, most likely because so few people want to lock in an interest rate for roughly 17 years.
- **Close** (the fourth column) shows you the price the bond sold for at the end of the previous business day, in $100 units. This price reveals whether the bond is trading at, above, or below par. You can calculate the value of the bond by multiplying this figure by ten.
- **Net Chg.** (the last column) is the bond's gain or loss in the previous trading day. For example, the first IBM bond, which lost ¼, fell in value by $2.50. While the price of this bond was falling, its yield was rising.

How to Read a Government Bond Table

Here's how to read the tax-exempt bond table:

RATE	MATURITY MO/YR	BID	ASKED	CHG.	ASK YLD.
4¾	Feb 06n	99:08	99:10	+2	5.64
9¼	Feb 16	118:02	118:04	+1	7.52

- **Rate** (the first column) in the government bond table is the coupon rate on the U.S. Treasury bond or note. Put another way, it's the percentage of par value that will be paid out as annual interest. So if this column reads 4¾ that means the security is paying bondholders 4.75% interest.

- **Maturity Mo/Yr** (the second column) shows you the month and the last two digits of the year the bond or note matures. For example, if the column reads Feb 16, the bond is due to mature February 2016. An **n** means it's a Treasury note, not a bond.
- **Bid and Asked** (the third and fourth columns) show you the latest market price for the issue. Treasuries are traded over-the-counter, so there are no closing prices per se for them. The **bid** is the highest price being offered by buyers, and the **asked** is the lowest price sellers are asking. The difference between the two prices is known as the spread. Here, the figures after the colon represent a fraction of a 32nd of a percentage point. So, 118:02 means $118^{02}/_{32}$.
- **Chg.** (the fifth column) is the difference between the current bid price and the bid price of the previous trading day. Here, the February 2016 Treasury note gained 1%, while the February 2006 bond gained 2%.
- **Ask Yld.** (the sixth column) tells you the bond's yield to maturity. That's a combination of the bond's current yield and the difference between its current price and its value at redemption when the bond matures. You'll see that in these examples the yield to maturity is lower than the coupon rate for both the Treasury note and the Treasury bond, because they are selling at a premium. But if the yield to maturity were higher than the coupon rate for either, then the bond or note would be selling at a discount.

How to Buy U.S Treasuries

The simplest and cheapest way to build your own bond portfolio is to buy U.S. Treasuries directly from the federal government through its TreasuryDirect program. For one thing, you don't have to worry about credit risk. And by signing up for TreasuryDirect, you can buy newly issued two-, five-, or 10-year bonds in amounts as small as $1,000. No need to write a check. Uncle Sam will deduct the purchase directly from your bank account, if you wish—and even automatically reinvest the proceeds of maturing bonds into new ones. The fee for all this: zilch, as long as your account balance is less than $100,000, at which point you'd owe just $25 a year.

When you buy through TreasuryDirect, you are bidding in a government auction along with huge bond dealers like Bear Stearns and Salomon Smith Barney. If you like the notion of duking it out with the big boys, you can submit a **competitive tender**, which means you specify the number of bonds you want and the yield you'll accept. I don't recommend this, though. If you aim for too high a yield, your bid won't be accepted. Aim too low and you'll get your bonds, all right, but they'll be paying a subpar yield. Your best bet is to submit a **noncompetitive tender**, which ensures that you get your bonds at the market clearing yield, or the highest yield at which competitive bids are accepted. For details on TreasuryDirect and a schedule of auctions, call 800-722-2678 or go to the TreasuryDirect Web site (see the box on bond Web sites on page 348).

Mining for Munis

As recently as a few years ago, your choice in municipal bonds was often limited to whatever issues your broker happened to have in inventory that day. But today a number of discount brokers and other online bond purveyors allow you to peruse hundreds, even thousands, of munis online, complete with their recent offering prices and yields.

Even better, you can usually search their databases using such criteria as the bonds' credit quality, number of years to maturity, and current yield. Most sites give you the option of customizing your search even more by, say, weeding out certain types of bonds. Many investors avoid **callable munis**, for example, because the issuer may call the bond, or repay its principal early, if interest rates have fallen since the bond was issued. Such calls force bondholders to reinvest their money at lower rates. So if you want to lock in an attractive yield for a bond's full term, you can specifically exclude callable bonds from your search.

Another neat feature of these search engines is that they can help you tell whether the price quote you've gotten at a particular site—or for that matter from a flesh-and-blood broker—is really a decent deal. For example, by going to the search engines at several sites and plugging in a bond's CUSIP (a unique ID tag carried by each bond issue), you'll be able to see whether other firms are selling the same bond and, if so, what price they're charging.

Be careful, though. In the bond world, even something as simple as comparing prices can get confusing. While some of the prices on these Web sites are "live and executable"—that is, you are assured of getting the bond at that quote—many are "subject" prices—subject, that is, to the bond's still being available from a dealer at the quoted price. So a super-low quote may reflect not a bargain but a price that hasn't been updated. There's another complication. Most bond prices include the broker's **markup**, or profit, which means the price you see is the price you pay. But that's not always the case. Vanguard Brokerage Services, for example, adds its markup to the prices on the site when you place an order. Similarly, discount brokers may add a commission to their prices. So you want to be sure the quotes you're comparing include all charges and, of course, represent the current price of the bond.

New Deals In Corporate Bonds

As with munis, you can screen for corporate issues at many sites. But the more compelling development is that a small but growing number of companies have launched programs to sell **direct notes**—that is, new bond issues marketed to individuals rather than to institutional investors. These bonds go by a variety of names—Bank of America InterNotes, Freddie Mac Freddie Notes, GMAC Smart Notes. But what all these notes have in common is that they take some of the complexity out of buying corporate bonds.

They do this in several ways. First, they allow you to buy individual issues with as little as $1,000. Second, the bonds are offered to the public during week-long **open order periods** during which every investor pays the same price—$1,000 per bond—and gets the same yield. There are no additional markups or commissions, so you don't have to worry that you could have gotten a better price by shopping around at several different brokerage firms. Once the open period ends, of course, the prices and yields of these bonds bounce up and down with interest rates, just like all bonds. Finally, while most corporate bonds make interest payments twice a year, many bonds in these programs pay interest quarterly or monthly—a real plus if you're counting on interest income for living expenses.

Ironically, despite the "direct" moniker, you don't buy these bonds directly from the company. They're sold through brokerage firms, including some discounters, such as Fidelity and Schwab. You can also sign up for e-mail alerts about upcoming issues at the Direct Access Notes Web site (www.directnotes.com).

Buying Bonds Through Mutual Funds

Most small investors buy their bonds through bond funds. The most important reason is diversification. On your own, you might be able to purchase a single bond or a handful of issues. But as a bond fund holder, you'll own a stake in dozens, or even hundreds, of bonds. That gives you greater protection against interest rate fluctuations and the changing financial health of any single issuer. You may also benefit from the expertise of a professional money manager who can anticipate and quickly respond to changes in the economy or in the financial health of bond issuers.

There are other advantages to buying bond funds rather than individual bonds. Funds pay dividends monthly, while individual bonds pay interest only semiannually. That makes funds a better deal if you need a steady stream of income. If you're planning to reinvest your earnings, you'll wind up ahead with a fund because your interest payments are reinvested more quickly, letting you earn interest on interest at a more rapid pace. Bond funds offer instant liquidity, too: You can get your money out any time you want, sometimes by writing a check. You can also add to your bond fund stake at any time.

The main drawback of bond funds is that they don't have a fixed life. Fund managers are constantly adding and subtracting bonds from their portfolios. So there's no such thing as holding to maturity with a bond fund. As a result, you can't count on getting a fixed interest rate or a preset price when you need your money. Instead you'll be paid the current share price of the fund, which is known as its **net asset value**, or **NAV**. A bond mutual fund's NAV varies from day to day, based on market conditions. Consequently, depending on when you decide to dump your fund, you may be blessed with a capital gain (if rates have fallen since you invested) or saddled with a loss (if rates have risen).

Like individual bonds, funds fall into a wide range of categories. These groupings can give you some insight into a fund's strategy and investment objectives. But a bond fund's name doesn't always give you a clear picture of its risk level or holdings. Government bond funds, for instance, may hold mostly low-risk U.S. Treasury securities or be loaded with Ginnie Maes, mortgage-backed bonds that are more vulnerable to interest rate shifts. Still, the following broad categories will get you started toward understanding your bond fund options:

- **Government bond funds** invest in securities issued by the U.S. Treasury and federal agencies. This group includes short-term U.S. government bond funds, which have an average maturity of two to four years, intermediate U.S. government bond funds, which have an average maturity of four to 10 years, and long-term U.S. government bond funds, with an average maturity of 10 years or more. While government bond funds can hold mostly Treasuries or Ginnie Maes, Treasury bond funds typically invest at least 80% of their assets in securities issued by the U.S. Treasury; they can keep the rest in bonds from other government agencies. Longer-term bond funds normally offer higher yields than funds that hold intermediate- or short-term securities. But your total return isn't always higher if you hold a long-term fund. That's because long-term government bond funds are particularly vulnerable to jumps in interest rates. Short-term U.S. Treasury funds are the safest bond funds you can buy and the least volatile in price.

- **Municipal bond funds** invest in tax-exempt securities. If you're thinking about buying a muni fund, you'll want first to calculate its tax-equivalent yield to see whether you'll earn more with a tax-exempt muni fund or a taxable fund. General muni funds invest in a diversified mix of municipals issued by various states and are exempt from federal taxation. Single-state funds buy issues just within a particular state, letting residents earn interest free from federal, state, and sometimes local taxes. However, these funds are less diversified than general muni funds, which makes them especially vulnerable to a natural disaster or a downturn in the state's or region's economy. What's more, single-state funds may need to buy bonds that are less credit-worthy than the ones purchased by general municipal bond funds, since the supply of issues they can choose from can be quite limited. As with other government bond funds, there are short-term, intermediate-term, and long-term muni bond funds. (Some companies also sell limited-term muni funds, a close cousin to intermediate-term funds.) Muni bond funds come sliced one other way: by **credit quality**. You can buy a fund that invests primarily in investment-grade bonds or a high-yield muni fund that buys lower-quality, often junk, muni bonds. The high-yield muni fund may yield more, but it can take you on more of a roller-coaster ride.

  You can reduce your risks investing in muni funds by sticking to highly diversified funds that own bonds with maturities of less than 10 years and funds whose cash reserves equal at least 5% of assets. Information about a fund's bond maturities, cash reserves, and credit quality is available at www.morningstar.com and www.valueline.com; it also appears in the prospectus. Because cash holdings don't pay as much income as bonds, however, a fund with a cash reserve of 5% or more will yield a few tenths of a percentage point less than one with less cash.

  Another way some investors try to reduce their risks with municipal bond funds is by purchasing **insured muni funds**. These are funds whose bonds have private insurance, protecting investors against the possibility of default. Don't bother with such funds, however. The insurance will clip your yield a bit, and you can protect yourself against default just as well by buying a diversified fund that invests in top-grade muni bonds.

- **Corporate bond funds** invest in securities of corporate issuers, which makes them slightly riskier than government bond funds. **Junk bond funds** or **high-yield funds** are corporate bond funds that invest primarily in the issues of financially troubled companies. Given the high risks of owning individual junk issues, buying a fund is the best way to invest in this sector. The safest junk funds will have at least 50% of their assets in the highest-quality tier of junk bonds: those rated BB or B. Safer junk funds also hold plenty of actively traded bonds, typically securities issued by companies whose names are easy to recognize. In addition, the best junk funds are well diversified, holding 100 or more securities.

- **Ginnie Mae funds** typically invest at least 80% of their assets in Ginnie Maes and other mortgage-backed securities. They yield more than Treasury funds, and since Ginnie Maes are backed by the full faith and credit of the U.S. government, you don't have to worry much about credit risk. But these funds aren't as risk-free as many investors would expect. Because Ginnie Maes are highly sensitive to changing interest rates, you could lose money if you need to get your cash out after interest rates have risen.

- **Foreign bond** or **world income funds** invest primarily in bonds issued by foreign governments. **Global bond funds** invest in bonds issued both in the United States and abroad. **International bond funds** hold only foreign securities. Short-term world income funds stick to bonds with maturities of one to two years, while most other foreign bond funds have average maturities of five to 10 years.

If you want the diversification that comes from investing abroad, foreign bond funds are a better bet than individual issues. Remember, though, that these funds not only carry interest rate risk and credit risk, but also are vulnerable to currency risk. Jittery exchange rates can cause gains of as much as 10% in a single month, although the ups and downs tend to even out over the years. Many managers of foreign bond funds try to protect themselves against currency shifts by buying futures and options, a practice known as **hedging**. Currency hedging is no panacea, though. It can cost 2.5% to 5% of the value of the assets being protected. And even seemingly foolproof hedges can sometimes backfire, socking investors with unexpected losses.

What to Know Before Buying a Bond Fund

You can take two different routes if you want to invest in a bond fund. The first is to buy your fund from a broker or financial planner who earns a commission for selling you the fund. The second is to purchase the fund directly from the fund company or through a financial planner who collects a flat fee for his services. As with stock funds sold this way, these bond funds are called **no-loads**.

Before you buy any bond fund, assess your investment needs and determine how much risk you are willing to accept. If you're a conservative investor with a low toler-ance for risk and a short time frame, go for a short-term bond fund. Investors looking for a steady stream of retirement income, on the other hand, might consider an inter-mediate fund. And if you're willing to take on more risk in exchange for a higher yield, you might put as much as 5% to 10% of your portfolio in junk bond funds.

Be wary of bond funds without at least a three-year track record behind them. Mutual fund companies are notorious for creating new and untested funds that promise bond investors high yields with little risk but then produce unexpected losses.

Selecting a bond fund wisely requires doing a bit of research into the fund's invest-ment style and performance. You can learn a lot about a bond fund and compare it with others by going to www.morningstar.com or www.valueline.com and getting a free online report. Or you can leaf through the fund's prospectus and annual financial report. Either way, you'll learn what the fund's expenses are and how much you'll pay in fees on your investment. Both sources provide historical returns, and the prospectus also tells you how much of those returns came from interest income and how much from price changes. If you have additional questions, you can call your broker or your fund company's toll-free number, listed in the fund's prospectus.

Other sources can help, too. Publications such as **MONEY**, the *Wall Street Journal, Business Week,* and *Barron's* run periodic listings of bond fund performance. (For tips on how to read mutual fund tables, see Chapter 14.) The major financial Web sites, such as MSN MoneyCentral (www.moneycentral.com) and Yahoo! Finance (http://finance.yahoo.com), also provide a great deal of useful bond fund data.

To assist you in sorting through the world of bond funds, here are key factors to assess:

- **Expenses.** If you buy a bond fund through a broker, you'll pay a **sales load** to cover the cost of his services. Loads come in three basic forms. A **front-end load**, which can run as high as 2.9% of your initial investment, is deducted from the value of your account at the time you make a purchase. A **back-end load** is collected only if you sell your fund before a preset period of time. This type of charge typically starts at 5% if you sell your fund the year you bought it and then declines by 1% annually, van-ishing after year five. Some bond funds charge a **level load**, which is up to 1% a year. These funds also can charge a **12b-1 fee** of 50 basis points (one-half percentage point) or more. Whether or not your fund levies a sales charge, you'll pay an annual fee to the sponsor for investment management, record keeping, and other services.

  When you divide a fund's costs by its total assets, you get a key figure: its **expense ratio**. This is the measure of how much you'll pay each year in fees. Expense ratios for taxable government and corporate bond funds average 1.01%, or $101 a year on a $10,000 investment, according to Morningstar. Investors who buy tax-exempt municipal bond funds pay a little less, about 0.85%, while harder-to-manage taxable international bond funds charge an average of 1.31%.

It's especially important to compare expenses among bond funds. That's because bond funds with similar investment strategies tend to hold similar types of securities. So, apart from taking on more or less risk, the one thing a fund manager can do to stand out from the pack is to keep expenses low. High expenses can also take an enormous bite out of your returns if you're not careful. Say intermediate-term bonds are yielding 6%. If your bond fund charges 0.75% in expenses, it will yield 5.25%, or 12.5% less than the market yield. Be extremely cautious if you find a bond fund yielding one or more percentage points or more than another fund holding similar bonds if low expenses don't explain the difference.

- **Yield.** As a bond fund investor, you're likely to come across two types of yield calculations. When bond funds advertise, they must use a figure known as the **SEC yield**, which measures the fund's yield as calculated according to a standard formula mandated by the federal Securities and Exchange Commission. This number is based on the fund's income for the preceding 30 days. It tells you how much you would earn if you stayed in the bond fund for a year and the fund kept paying out interest at its recent rate. It's the best figure to use when comparing bond funds head to head.

  If you look at newspapers, magazines, and Web sites that track mutual funds, you're likely to come across the fund's **12-month average yield**. This figure will tell you what the fund actually paid out to shareholders over the preceding 12 months. While it's no guarantee of future performance, the 12-month average yield is the best proxy for how much income you would have earned over the past year.

  Keep in mind that the highest-yielding fund, even within a fund category, may not be the best investment for you. That's because bond funds can boost their yields in only two ways: by lowering fund expenses or by taking on additional risks. Some top-yielding funds later turn out to be disasters for investors. One clue that your bond fund is taking big gambles: Its yield is at least one percentage point higher than the average fund in its category and the difference can't be explained by lower operating costs.

- **Total return.** Bond fund investors are often tempted to pick a fund based wholly on its yield. But yield is only part of the story, of course, since it doesn't reflect capital gains or losses. To find out a bond fund's true return, take a look at its **total return**. This measure combines the income paid out with any changes in the value of the fund's shares. Simply put, total return tells you whether you made or lost money in a fund. Bond fund investors saw this clearly in 1994. Although their funds paid decent yields of 5% to 8% or so, they lost money for investors overall because interest rate hikes produced bond fund price declines. In 2000, when rates were falling, bond fund investors profited royally, since the price gains added to their returns.

Paying attention to total return also helps you avoid funds that pay high yields at a long-term cost to investors. For instance, many bond funds boost yields by buying premium bonds—ones issued when interest rates were high and which now trade above their face value. The prices of these bonds decline as they get closer to maturity, however, causing the fund's net asset value to fall. In other words, shareholders get handed a little extra cash in one pocket but wind up paying more out of the other pocket.

In evaluating a fund's total return, don't look just at the preceding three or six months. Instead see how the fund's return has varied over the last one, three, and five years. These numbers will give you an idea of how the fund has weathered the ups and downs of the bond market.

- **Average maturity.** Because bond funds own a pool of bonds, they have no single maturity. Instead they have what's known as a **weighted average maturity**, a measure of the maturity of all the bonds a fund currently owns. A fund's weighted average maturity (which you can find in a Morningstar or Value Line report) will give you some idea of how sensitive the fund is to shifts in interest rates. The higher the average maturity, the riskier a fund is. That's because it's likely to experience bigger swings when interest rates rise or fall.

- **Duration.** The **duration** of a bond fund is another, somewhat more precise, indication of how sensitive it is to changes in interest rates. The formula for calculating duration is complicated, but the basic point is this: The sooner your investment is paid back, the less it will be hurt by changes in interest rates. Don't get put off by the complex mathematics—you can generally get a bond fund's duration from the fund company or a rating service such as Morningstar. Instead pay attention to what duration can tell you about your fund. For starters, duration lets you measure how your bond fund will react to a change in interest rates of one percentage point or less. Take two bond funds, one with a duration of four years and one with a duration of 10 years. Assume that interest rates rise by 1%. In that case, the share price of the fund with the four-year duration will fall by 4%, but the price of the 10-year-duration fund will drop by a full 10%.

Duration is an extremely useful yardstick for comparing different funds. A bond fund with a duration of six years, for instance, is twice as volatile as a fund whose duration is three years. If you think interest rates will rise, you'll be best off with a short-duration fund. Because a fund's duration can't be longer than its average maturity, duration can also give you a clue as to whether your fund is taking above average risks. A short-term fund with a duration of six years, for instance, might be boosting its yield through the use of higher-risk securities.

Buying Closed-End Bond Funds

Most bond funds are what's known as **open-end**. They have an unlimited number of shares. If new investors come along, the open-end fund manager just takes their money and buys more bonds. If the manager decides he or she doesn't want any more money, the fund is closed to new investors. Another type of bond fund, however, is known as **closed-end**. This type of fund is, in many ways, more like a stock than a mutual fund. That's because like a stock, a closed-end fund has a finite number of shares and trades on an exchange. You pay a brokerage commission to get in or out of a closed-end fund. Unlike a stock or an individual bond, however, a closed-end bond fund gives you diversification because it contains a basket of bonds. Two common types of closed-end bond funds are **closed-end municipal bond funds** and **closed-end foreign bond funds**.

Closed-end funds can trade at discounts or premiums to their net asset value. In fact, most trade at discounts. That can be a bargain for an investor, since you're buying bonds for less than the market value of their assets. If you invest in a fund with a discount and bond prices rise, that lifts the net asset value of the fund, which tends to close the discount. The combination of a higher net asset value, smaller discount, and yield can produce a terrific total return. New closed-end bond funds often start out trading at premiums to their net asset value and then wind up selling at discounts. That's why it is wise to avoid buying new closed-end bond fund issues—even if they're pushed heavily by your broker—and waiting until the shares trade at a discount. The *Wall Street Journal* and *Barron's* publish weekly performance lists of closed-end bond funds. In addition, Morningstar and Value Line publish data that will tell you about a closed-end fund's holdings, the size of its discount, if any, and how that compares with its historical average. Ideally you'll want to buy a closed-end bond fund when its discount is wider than its historical average.

Buying Unit Investment Trusts

If you like the idea of diversifying among bonds and want to lock in an interest rate and a fixed maturity date, you might want to invest in a **unit investment trust**. Sometimes called unit trusts or UITs, these investments are packages of eight to 15 bonds put together by brokerage firms and sold in lots of $1,000. Unlike bond funds, UITs are not actively managed. In other words, the trust sponsor usually doesn't buy or sell bonds during the trust's life. Instead, the bonds put into a UIT are left there until the bonds mature and the trust expires, typically in 20 to 30 years. In most cases you get your interest checks monthly, though some trusts pay out quarterly or twice a year. You can sell some or all of your units before the trust expires on the secondary market at the current market price. However, you may incur a capital gain or loss, depending on market values at the time.

These investments have several hitches, however. For one thing, commissions tend to average a hefty 4% of the sales price; there are also annual fees of roughly 0.2% to cover administrative costs. Because these portfolios aren't actively managed, there's no protection against interest rate risk. If interest rates rise, you're stuck with the rate you've got. Similarly, you have no protection against a decline in the credit quality of the bonds since the UIT manager will hang on to the bonds for the life of the trust. A bond fund manager, by contrast, can buy and sell bonds at will, grabbing new, higher-yielding bonds and unloading issues whose credit rating has slipped. It's not easy to keep an eye on the value of your unit trust, either. Unlike bond funds, whose ups and downs appear daily in the newspaper, unit trust performance is virtually impossible to monitor. One other problem: If any bonds held by your trust are called, you'll get the principal back and then must find somewhere else to invest the money. As a result, you won't earn the yield you thought you would. To learn whether any bonds in a particular UIT are subject to calls, ask your broker or check the trust's prospectus.

How to Reduce Your Risks

Whether you're buying individual bonds, bond funds, or unit trusts, the following investment strategies will help you trim your investment risks:

- **Stick to intermediates.** The simplest strategy is to invest only in intermediate-term bonds, which have maturities of four to 10 years. Intermediates yield more than short-term issues, which mature in two to four years. However, they are less volatile than long-term bonds, which have maturities of 10 years or more.
- **Diversify.** Because bond prices can tumble from rising interest rates or an issuer's financial trouble, it's risky to hold a single issue. Instead, diversify by investing in a variety of issues with different maturities. You can get this diversification automatically by buying a bond fund or unit trust. If you would rather own individual corporate or municipal bonds, purchase at least five of them. (You need not worry about diversification with Treasuries, since their credit quality is unmatched.)
- **Ladder your bonds.** Another way to protect yourself against sudden shifts in interest rates is to build what's known as a **bond ladder.** This means buying bonds with staggered maturities. For example, you might split your bond portfolio among two-year, three-year, five-year, seven-year, and 10-year maturities. By doing this, you get an average maturity of about five years without having to worry whether you timed interest rate moves in the bond market exactly right. Every time one of your bonds comes due, just add another rung to the ladder. So when the two-year bond matures, put the money into a new 10-year issue. By laddering, if rates rise, you'll have new money available to invest at higher rates. And if rates fall, you will have locked in the older, higher rates for a portion of your portfolio.
- **Don't get carried away by taxes.** While the lure of triple tax exemption may be great, you shouldn't put more than 50% of your bond portfolio in the issues of a single state or in a single-state bond fund. If you keep all your eggs in one basket, you'll be vulnerable to a regional economic decline or a natural disaster.

CHAPTER 16

How to Invest in Annuities

Like most life insurance industry products, **annuities** can be a bit confusing. Stripped down to its essentials, an annuity is a tax-sheltered investment sponsored by an insurance company that pays you earnings and also has a death benefit. Generally, when you buy an annuity you hand over a lump of money—ranging from $2,000 to $10,000— to a stockbroker, insurance agent, or financial planner. This salesman then passes the money along to a life insurance company, which in turn issues the annuity contract. Some insurers instead let you buy a **flexible-premium retirement annuity** through regular periodic payments, sometimes of as little as $25 a month. In either case, the insurer agrees to pay the holder of the annuity contract a certain amount of money at a certain date; if you die while owning the annuity, the beneficiary you name will receive a death benefit. Just as with an Individual Retirement Account, the income that your money earns grows tax-free until you make a withdrawal from the annuity. Unlike an IRA, though, your annuity contributions are unlimited.

When you're ready to withdraw your money, you have three options. You can (1) pull all your money out; (2) withdraw a little at a time; or (3) **annuitize**. This latter option simply means that you can convert the account's value into a monthly income stream that can run for a period you select, typically the rest of your life. Incidentally, you don't need to annuitize with the same insurance company that sponsored your annuity; you can switch to a different company offering a better deal. However you decide to receive your cash, you'll owe income tax on the earnings when you get them, at whatever tax bracket you happen to be in at the time. If you take the money out of the annuity before you reach age 59½ you'll also have to pay a tax penalty for early withdrawal—10% of the accrued earnings.

By and large, there are no front-end fees on annuities. The salesman's commission, which ranges from 6% to 9%, is factored into the annuity's interest rate and your payout. In other words, the commission is hidden by tucking it into—or, more accurately, taking it out of—your earnings. Annuities come with hidden annual fees, however, which average 2.1% a year. That's slightly more than half a percentage point higher than the fees on an average mutual fund bought through a tax-sheltered IRA or 401(k). (But beware, averages can be deceiving and many annuities' fees are far above the average 2.1%.) Most annuities also charge you sizable fees for substantial withdrawals. These **surrender charges** are as high as 15% of your accumulated earnings for a withdrawal made in the first year of the contract. After that, the charges drop by about one percentage point each year until they disappear, typically in about seven to 10 years. Many insurance companies, however, let you withdraw 10% of your account's value each year without incurring any penalty (although Uncle Sam will not be as forgiving if you're younger than 59½).

Once you get beyond those basics, things get thorny. For instance, deciding which annuity—if any—is right for you means choosing not only between two payout options—deferred and immediate—but also between two rates of return: fixed or variable. Before jumping in, realize that there are two very important reasons why you should use extreme caution before buying annuities. First, no annuities are federally insured, even those sold in banks. You might not realize this, given the aggressive marketing of annuities in bank lobbies. It's easy to assume that because an investment is hawked in a bank and because bank CDs have federal insurance, the investment must be insured, too. The second reason for approaching annuities with eyes wide open is that these products generally require a long-term commitment from you. Otherwise you'll wind up paying more in fees than you'll earn on the investment.

These caveats aside, annuities have their merits, and you may want to give them a look. A well-chosen annuity can sometimes be a sensible, tax-deferred way to save for retirement that's at least 10 years away. Alternatively, an annuity can help ensure a reliable, lifelong income stream once you've stopped working.

There are two basic types of annuities, each offering a different schedule of payouts:

- **Immediate-pay annuities**, sometimes called **lifetime annuities**, are purchased with a lump sum, typically by people in retirement who want to provide a guaranteed stream of income for themselves. You might get the lump sum from your pension plan distribution or from your IRA. As its name suggests, an immediate-pay annuity begins doling out regular payments as soon as you buy the contract—generally on a monthly basis. Part of the problem with immediate-pay annuities is that by locking in a set amount of income, your earnings can get eaten away by inflation. That is, although the cost of living will keep going up, the size of your monthly checks won't.

- **Deferred annuities**, which are the type most annuity investors choose, appeal mostly to people in their forties or fifties looking to postpone paying taxes on their investment earnings for years to come, typically until retirement. You don't start receiving their income until you either cash in the contract, make periodic withdrawals, or annuitize. (Consult a financial planner or tax adviser before making any withdrawals, since the rules are complicated.) Think of deferred annuities as tax-sheltered CDs or mutual funds—with higher fees. You can buy them either with a lump sum or on the installment plan.

The amount of income you'll receive depends in large part on a second choice you'll have to make when shopping for an annuity: fixed or variable. If you opt for a **fixed-rate annuity**, the insurer pays a specific, fixed interest rate usually for a year, though some companies lock in rates for as long as 10 years. The earnings are tax-deferred if you go with a deferred annuity. In recent years, fixed-rate annuities have paid 5% to 9% annually. Each year, the insurer announces the fixed return for the year ahead; the rate depends on the insurer's current investment portfolio. Fixed-rate annuities are generally very conservative investments; they typically buy government and corporate bonds as well as residential mortgages. Since you're locking in an interest rate, however, your fixed-rate annuity won't beat inflation.

Warning: Many fixed-rate annuities pay enticingly high rates in the first year of the contract as a lure. Afterward, your return falls considerably, often by three or more percentage points. One way to assess how an insurer treats its investors after the first year is to ask for the company's **interest rate floor**—the minimum interest rate you'll receive from the contract. With most fixed-rate contracts, the interest rate is guaranteed to be at least 5% a year. If you find one much lower, you can probably do better elsewhere.

The return on a **variable-rate annuity**, by contrast, fluctuates with the stock, bond, and money markets. Consequently, a variable-rate annuity offers the potential for much higher returns than a fixed-rate contract, but at greater risk. Variable-rate annuities are in essence mutual funds wrapped inside insurance contracts; again, the earnings are tax-deferred if you buy a deferred annuity. The insurance usually consists of a guarantee that your heirs will get back what you invested.

The insurer offers an assortment of stock, bond, and money-market funds, called **subaccounts** in annuity lingo, and gives you the responsibility of choosing among them. Established mutual fund companies such as Fidelity and Neuberger Berman run the subaccount portfolios. The typical annuity offers about seven subaccounts, with a variety of investment objectives. Some annuities, however, boast more than 30 investment options. Within the stock category, you may be offered a selection of aggressive growth, blue-chip, and international funds, among others. Within the bond funds, you might choose among corporate, government, and high-yield portfolios. You can allocate your money as you see fit and switch among subaccounts with no charge, usually by making a telephone call.

With most investments, you do the majority of your research when you put in your money. Annuity investors, however, may also have to plan carefully when they are ready to cash out. That might be sooner than you think: Once surrender charges have expired, you can take your money out of the company that built up your account without penalty and take it to a competing insurer offering better terms. Provided you keep your money in an annuity, you won't have to pay the 10% early-withdrawal tax penalty to the IRS. You will, however, have to fill out the IRS's 1035 exchange form, which your new insurance company will be only too pleased to give you.

Before considering any withdrawal or payout from your annuity, you need to understand **annuitizing**—turning over the accumulated value of your annuity to an insurer in return for fixed monthly income. Annuitizing has a distinct tax advantage: It lets you further postpone paying taxes on some of the earnings you have accrued. Each check you receive is considered only partly earnings; the rest is your original principal. You pay taxes only on the earnings and only as you receive them. If you want to annuitize for the certainty of getting a specific amount of income each year, you'll have to decide among three more choices:

- **Life annuity.** By choosing a standard life annuity, you guarantee yourself a lifetime income. Since the payments expire when you die, however, you're also betting on how long you will live. If you die before the insurer thinks you will, you won't get all the annuity income you were entitled to receive. This option may not be appropriate if, say, your spouse will be counting on receiving the annuity income after you die.
- **Joint-and-survivor annuity.** If you can afford to receive 5% or so less in your monthly checks, you can instruct the insurer to make sure your spouse or another dependent will keep getting paid after you die—for as long as your beneficiary is alive. If you outlive the other person named in the annuity, you'll keep getting checks until you die. A joint-and-survivor annuity is sensible for most couples.

- **Life-with-certain-period annuity.** This option assures you of a lifetime income while also guaranteeing payments for a set period of time, usually 10 years. If you die within that time, your beneficiary collects the remaining payments.

The other way to pull money out of your annuity is by setting up a **systematic withdrawal plan**. With this method, you tell the insurance company how much cash to send you from your account each month. Systematic withdrawal offers flexibility; at any time you can raise, lower, or stop the payments as well as annuitize. However, with this method your account could run out of money someday. What's more, cash paid out in a systematic plan is usually fully taxable until you have drained all your earnings from the annuity account.

You will probably fare better in the long run with a variable-rate annuity than a fixed-rate one, provided you select the right company and that you have at least 10 years to go before you'll need the money. That will give you enough time to ride out any short-term market dips as well as avoid any onerous surrender charges. To start your search for the best annuity for you, get the latest issue of a reliable annuity publication. For information on variable annuities, order Morningstar's *Variable Annuity/Life Performance Report* (800-735-0700; www.morningstar.com) or check out T. D. Waterhouse (800-622-3699; www.tdwaterhouse.com). For a list of fixed annuities, buy *Comparative Annuity Reports* (916-487-7863) or visit www.annuityscout.com. You may be able to find some or all of these publications in your public library or other sources online. When selecting an annuity, look for one with:

- **A solid insurer behind it.** Don't even consider an annuity unless it is offered by an insurer rated at least A+ for financial soundness by A. M. Best, AA− by Moody's Investors Service, or AA− by Standard & Poor's. Your annuity salesman can provide these ratings, or you can find them in large public libraries.
- **Proven performance.** To make your first cut in choosing a deferred annuity, compare the record of subaccounts in the contract with the average returns for their investment category over each of the past three years. You can generally find these figures in the *Variable Annuity/Life Performance Report.* If the subaccounts that interest you haven't been around for three years, pass. Similarly, cross off any annuity that doesn't break out its returns this way. Make sure to get performance figures after expenses have been deducted from the results. Any decent insurance agent or stockbroker selling annuities should be glad to help you compare the performance of variable annuity accounts.

- **Relatively low expenses.** In general, be wary of annuities with total expenses that exceed about 2% annually. That said, you needn't avoid an annuity with a strong investment performance simply because its fees are a bit above this benchmark. Your agent or annuity salesman can show you a breakdown of the contract's annual expenses.

  Consider buying an annuity directly from a **low-load insurer** who doesn't use a traditional sales force and thus doesn't have as many selling expenses to pass on to policyholders. A few discount brokerages and mutual fund operators, such as Fidelity, have teamed up with insurance companies in recent years to offer annuities with low or no sales and surrender charges.

- **A bailout provision.** Essential for fixed-rate annuity holders, this contract clause gives you one to three months to transfer your money to another annuity without penalty if your interest rate drops by a preset amount, usually one percentage point or more.

CHAPTER 17

How to Invest in Real Estate

There are at least five reasons why individual investors should consider sinking some cash into real estate once they've built a solid portfolio of stocks and bonds:

- **Real estate is an inflation hedge.** When overall consumer prices rise, the value of so-called **paper investments** such as bonds sometimes fails to keep pace. Historically, however, the value of **hard assets** like real estate has kept pace with or outrun inflation. That's because real estate, as a basic necessity, will always maintain its relative value against other assets as their prices rise.

- **Real estate historically lowers your overall investment risk and raises your returns.** Less risk, but bigger returns? Sounds like a mistake, right? It's not. Earl Osborn at the investment advisory firm Bingham Osborn & Scarborough in San Francisco has done numerous studies showing that real estate actually stabilizes an investment portfolio while increasing returns.

    For example, an investor who put 80% of his money into stocks and 20% into real estate from 1973 to 2000 would have earned more than 13.1% a year. Had he stuck solely with stocks, his annualized return would have averaged around 12.9%. What is more important, the portfolio with real estate in the mix actually experienced 7% less volatility. That's a fancy way of saying that his investments didn't bounce up and down as much as the stock-only portfolio. It's worth noting, however, that Osborn defines real estate as shares of real estate investment trusts, a type of stock, which is among the safest ways for individuals to play the real estate game, as you'll read later on in this chapter.

- **Real estate generates income.** Buildings and apartments can produce significant and reliable cash flows when they are rented out to other people who live or work in them. This is true whether you own the property yourself or invest passively through real estate trusts, mutual funds, or limited partnerships. And reliable income is extremely valuable for investors.

- **Real estate is stable.** Forget the temporary upheavals in home prices. Over the long run, real estate has proven to be quicker to rise in value than to fall. Barring war or natural disaster, real estate holds its value or rises steadily in price over time. You can't say that about all investment alternatives.

- **Real estate is a core asset.** Companies may rise and fall, but real estate endures. That's why land remains the practical and emotional foundation of most of the world's great fortunes. It's also why the U.S. government has encouraged home ownership through the deductibility of mortgage interest.

Despite these advantages, making a profit in real estate is no simple matter. A complicated array of national and local factors affects real estate values and investment returns. These include changes in tax laws, interest rate swings, regional and local economic trends, population shifts, building codes, and supply and demand within individual markets. Adding to the confusion are the numerous and varied ways you can choose to invest in real estate.

Ways to Invest in Real Estate

Today there are seven main ways to put real estate into your portfolio. Three of them—real estate mutual funds, real estate investment trusts (REITs), and real estate limited partnerships—don't involve owning a piece of land or building by yourself. Rather, investors own shares of one sort or another in legal entities that in turn own the properties. Four others—rental property, vacation homes, time-shares, and raw land—are "real" real estate, if you will—actual land or structures that you can walk through, on, or over and call your own. You can personally increase their value. All seven of these real estate investments are as different from each other as a skyscraper in Manhattan is from 40 acres of Kansas farmland. Here's how to sort them out, from the most conservative option to the riskiest:

Real Estate Mutual Funds

Given the complexities of investing in real estate, the best choice for most individuals is to buy shares in a mutual fund that specializes in it. Like stock mutual funds (described in Chapter 14), real estate funds pool individuals' money and invest it. Real estate mutual funds invest primarily in the shares of real estate investment trusts (REITs), which develop and manage a diversified portfolio of commercial office buildings, apartment complexes, shopping centers, and other projects. The mutual funds also buy shares of real estate–related companies such as home builders, hotels, and nursing homes. By joining forces with other investors, you enjoy distinct advantages over those lone wolves who venture into the real estate market themselves. Of course, real estate mutual funds, like other stock funds, offer no guaranteed returns. In fact, you could very well lose money in these funds over the course of a year. The average real estate mutual fund lost 15.8% on average in 1998 followed by a 3.6% loss in 1999. These funds, however, offer substantial returns over the long run. Several, for instance, earned more than 23% over a recent three-year period. Among the most important pluses of investing in real estate mutual funds are the following four:

1. **Professional management at an affordable price.** Ordinarily, you couldn't interest a money manager in minding your real estate portfolio unless you had at least a six-figure sum to invest. With real estate funds, though, you can ordinarily get in the door for as little as $100. Every fund comes with its own investment management team that can spend the time needed to understand the vagaries of individual real estate investment trusts and real estate–related stocks as well as the far-flung real estate markets that affect them. Some real estate fund managers invest all over the world, not just in the United States. Naturally, this kind of expert management comes at a price, but a reasonable one: The manager typically takes 0.5% to 1.5% of a fund's assets each year as an advisory fee. There may also be an initial up-front sales charge of roughly 7%.
2. **Liquidity.** You can get into and out of a real estate mutual fund easily, with a call to your stockbroker or the fund itself. You cannot, however, write checks on most real estate mutual funds. Other real estate investments, as you'll see, are not nearly as friendly to buyers or sellers as real estate funds.
3. **Diversification.** Real estate funds spread your money among a wide variety of regions, industries, and securities. Consequently, you're not at the mercy of one particular property doing well. Unlike real estate limited partnerships, however, these funds do not invest directly in land or buildings.

4. Income. Because they invest heavily in REITs that pay high dividends, most real estate funds offer investors high yields as well, generally ranging from 3% to 8%.

The process of choosing the right real estate mutual fund is far simpler than choosing a stock fund, since just a handful of funds specialize in real estate. Among them, two stand out as having solid track records: Cohen & Steers Realty Shares (800-437-9912; www.cohenandsteers.com) and Columbia Real Estate Equity Fund (800-547-1707; www.columbiafunds.com).

Real Estate Investment Trusts (REITs)

Real estate investment trusts (REITs) are publicly traded stocks that invest in office buildings, apartment complexes, industrial facilities, shopping centers, and other commercial spaces. REITs were created for small investors who don't have the money to spend on down payments and mortgages but nonetheless want to own real estate. Each REIT pools the money raised from investors and invests it in a diversified portfolio of real estate assets, similar to the way a stock mutual fund pools shareholders' money to invest in stocks. The trusts, in fact, are stocks, and most trade on the major stock exchanges or over-the-counter.

The REIT industry has a history of highs and lows, which doesn't negate the fact that over the long run REITs have proven to be a reliable and safe way for individuals to invest in real estate. That's because REITs offer:

- **Low-cost entry into an expensive business.** REITs let you become a part owner or financier of several pieces of commercial, residential, or industrial real estate. If you bought them directly, each might cost anywhere from $50,000 to several million dollars in down payments alone. You pay only the commissions that a stockbroker would charge if you bought shares in a company like IBM or General Motors. On the other hand, real estate limited partnerships, discussed later in the chapter, are burdened with front-end sales charges and management fees that take a nasty bite out of your long-term profits. REITs are also less picky about their investors, while many partnership deals come with minimum purchase requirements or financial suitability tests that lock out some investors.
- **Reliable income and capital appreciation over the long term.** By law, REITs must pass along to shareholders 90% of each year's operating profits in regular divi-

dend payments. As a result, REIT shares often yield more than most other types of stocks and provide a predictable income stream—as long as the REIT's underlying properties or mortgages are profitable. REITs also hold out the prospect of capital appreciation, just like any other stock, so you can score a profit when you sell the shares. The flip side of this, of course, is that when the stock market is taking a dive, REIT shares tend to fall, too. As a rule, REIT share prices usually rise and fall in value with the direction of the stock market, not the overall U.S. real estate market. So if you buy only one REIT, you're taking on more risk than if you buy a group of them or a real estate mutual fund.

- **Easy access to your money.** Another advantage of REITs is that they are easy to get into and out of. Owning real estate directly by being a landlord or investing in a limited partnership usually means tying up your money for many years. When you're ready to sell, you may have to wait a while to get an attractive price. When you want to get your money out of a REIT, you simply call your broker and sell your shares like any other stock.

You can get a list of all publicly traded REITs, as well as other information about the industry, from the National Association of Real Estate Investment Trusts (800-362-7348; www.nareit.org). The most important thing to know about the subject, however, is that there are three basic types of REITs, but only one—equity REITs—that you need to consider seriously. They are:

1. **Equity REITs.** These REITs, which typically yield between 4% and 8%, use their money primarily to buy income-producing property—in other words, property with rent-paying tenants. They are generally the best choice for investors who want long-term capital appreciation and current income. They're also the most appropriate form of real estate investing if you're looking to diversify your portfolio without spending much time. What's more, since real estate values rise over the long run, equity REITs offer a good inflation hedge.

   Some equity REITs focus on certain types of properties or invest only in specific regions of the country, while others spread their assets across geographic and industry borders. There are REITs that invest in deals put together by independent developers and REITs that buy, develop, and manage property themselves. Your best bet is to stick with REITs that focus on specific types of real estate or particular regions, as well as those that develop and manage their own properties.

   The first step in picking an equity REIT is to get a prospectus or annual report from your stockbroker or the REIT itself. Look at the section that describes what the trust owns and the location of its properties. Make sure you're comfortable owning the types of buildings in the REIT, whether they're shopping centers, nursing homes, apartment buildings, or something else. Make sure, too, that you're content owning them in San Antonio, Los Angeles, Washington, D.C., or wherever the REIT has its holdings. (If the REIT tends to buy real estate in your part of the country and you're optimistic about the economic growth prospects in your area, you may have a winner that you'll also feel comfortable owning.) Be sure that the prospectus says the REIT has been in the business for at least five years. For safety's sake, you don't want to take a chance on a new company or executives without expertise. What's more, if the REIT has been around for a while, you will be able to examine its performance records and its history of dividend increases. Restrict your equity REIT investing to ones whose dividends have been growing and are being paid out from the rental income of the properties in the portfolio. Avoid REITs that come up with the income for their dividends mostly by selling property or using the company's cash reserves.

2. **Mortgage REITs.** This breed of REIT lends money to developers and buyers and makes its profits from charging interest. More specifically, mortgage REITs originate or buy mortgages on commercial properties. Though they typically offer yields of 6% to 15%, mortgage REITs offer little capital appreciation potential because they don't own much property, if any. Moreover, if its borrowers hit trouble spots or even default, a mortgage REIT's share price can plummet. In other words, though the yields of mortgage REITs are generally higher than those of equity REITs, so are their risks. Also, mortgage REITs tend to behave more like bonds than real estate, so they offer little diversification if you're looking to broaden your portfolio from traditional stock and fixed-income investments.

3. **Hybrid REITs.** As the name suggests, these REITs are a little bit equity and a little bit mortgage; they own property and make loans. Here again, you are lessening your potential for capital appreciation while exposing yourself to potential mortgage defaults. You do, however, stand a stronger chance of raking in capital gains from hybrid REITs than you do from mortgage REITs.

Real Estate Limited Partnerships

Limited partnerships remain a fairly popular way to invest in real estate. The major reason, in all likelihood, is that stockbrokers and financial planners who push high-commission limited partnerships sometimes stress their profit potential and underplay their risks. Luckily that's been getting harder to do, since in recent years newspapers and magazines have been full of stories of pushy brokers and partnerships gone bust. Indeed, over the past few years hundreds of thousands of investors have filed dozens of lawsuits because they believe brokers duped them into investing billions of dollars in dud partnerships.

For as little as $1,000, limited partnerships offer individual investors the chance to invest in high-rise office buildings, apartment houses, medical centers, motels, or shopping malls. Unlike real estate mutual funds and REITs, limited partnerships come with steep commissions and can be extremely difficult to sell. So before you invest in a partnership, consider fully whether you can better meet your goals through mutual funds or REITs. For most investors, limited partnerships are an unnecessarily risky way to diversify into real estate or to generate steady income. Their chief advantage over mutual funds and REITs: tax breaks, though the breaks aren't nearly as great as they were in the early 1980s.

Briefly, a partnership is a business organization comprising a **general partner**, who runs the limited partnership's daily business, and **limited partners**, who put up most or all of the money. Limited partners receive income, capital gains, tax benefits, and losses generated by the partnership. You are called a limited partner because your liability in the partnership is limited to the amount of money that you invest. You are also protected from legal action against the partnership.

In a **specified partnership**, the general partner explains in advance how the organization will operate and what properties (or at least what types of properties) it will buy. A **blind pool partnership** does not set out its investment strategy. You must trust the general partner to spend your money wisely. As a rule, blind pools are inadvisable, unless the general partner is, say, your father or someone else you would trust with the keys to your house or combination to your safe.

Now about that advantage of limited partnership: taxes. Unlike many other investments, a limited partnership pays no taxes. Because all income, capital gains and losses, and tax breaks are passed through to the limited partners, you pay taxes only at your own individual rate. By contrast, if you own stock in a corporation that pays dividends, you are, in effect, taxed twice on the company's profits: first when the company is taxed as a corporation and then again when you pay taxes on your dividends.

This tax feature made real estate limited partnerships extremely popular in the early '80s, when they were viewed primarily as tax shelters. At that time individual tax rates were far higher than they are today, so upper-income people desperately sought ways to shield their income from the IRS. Because partnerships pass through all their tax benefits to the partners, investors plowed billions of dollars into limited partnerships to secure write-offs against their regular earned income. The juiciest tax benefits came from real estate depreciation—writing off part of the value of the property each year—and real estate tax credits, which can allow people to write off more than they invested in the programs. However, many of these deals were unprofitable, and when the Tax Reform Act of 1986 eliminated most of the tax shelters, many partnerships fell apart. Investors wound up holding limited partnership shares that were often barely worth the paper they were printed on, let alone their original price.

Today, two types of real estate limited partnerships can still offer some generous tax goodies. The first is a **low-income housing partnership**. This type of partnership invests in apartment complexes designed specifically for low- to moderate-income residents, as designated by the government. Provided that the partnership meets all the government standards, limited partners can be eligible for tax credits of as much as 9% of their investment for newly built housing projects and 4% for existing properties. A tax credit is much better than a deduction since it directly reduces your tax bill; a $2,000 credit will reduce your tax bill by $2,000. The low-income housing tax credits, however, are limited to investors with adjusted gross incomes of less than $250,000. In addition, if you've ever dealt with government rules and regulations, you know they can be maddening. So it's quite possible that a sponsor of a low-income housing partnership won't meet the government standards and its investors then won't get their anticipated tax benefits. While low-income properties do generate income, the amount of the rent is generally modest. Capital gains may occur once the partnership liquidates and sells its holdings, generally after 10 years.

The other type of real estate tax shelter is a **historic rehabilitation limited partnership**. Here, the partners put their money to work renovating buildings that the U.S. Department of the Interior has certified as historic. If the partnership's projects meet the government's strict architectural standards—not very easy to do—limited partners may be able to qualify for a 20% investment tax credit each year for 10 years. Again, these tax credits are far more valuable than tax deductions, since they reduce your taxes dollar for dollar. Something to keep in mind before scurrying for this shelter, though, is that these partnerships don't generate income; however, if the renovated property appreciates during the period the partnership owns it (generally a decade), the limited partners can realize capital gains after the sale of the building.

If you want to invest in a real estate partnership primarily for steady income and possible capital gains, rather than for tax breaks, you ought to invest in a conservative **equity real estate partnership**. This investment pools money from limited partners and buys existing, occupied buildings in the hopes of increasing rents as leases are renewed and then selling the properties for a profit in five to 10 years. For bigger potential capital gains but smaller income and greater risk, you could invest instead in a real estate partnership that will build properties, lease them out, and eventually sell them. Another type of real estate partnership, known as a **mortgage partnership**, loans money to property developers instead of owning buildings outright. The partnership secures a steady source of income for its partners in the form of mortgage payments— assuming that the developers don't default on their mortgages. Like mortgage REITs, these partnerships don't offer you much in the way of capital gains.

Real estate limited partnerships come in two basic forms: **public programs** or **private placement programs**. Public programs typically include thousands of individual investors who hand over as little as $1,000 or so. These public partnerships, which generally last from five to 12 years before they disband, are registered with the Securities and Exchange Commission and state regulatory authorities. They generally invest in numerous projects and are consequently highly diversified. Private placements, on the other hand, are not registered with the SEC, invest in just one or a few properties, and generally cannot be sold to more than a few dozen investors, all wealthy (you need to prove your financial suitability to a broker or planner in order to get into the private placement). These partnerships, which can last anywhere from three to 20 years, are generally riskier than public programs but offer the potential for greater profits.

One of the major drawbacks of investing in limited partnerships are the fees you will pay, both when you put in your money and throughout the life of the partnership. For starters, the brokerage firms who sell limited partnerships charge up-front commissions that generally range from 8% to 10% of your investment. In addition, most partnerships charge between 3% and 4% of assets each year for management fees. Many partners also levy an incentive fee, often as high as 15%, every time the partnership sells a piece of property. The theory is that the fee provides incentive for the general partner to get the highest sales price possible when selling off the partnership's assets.

Getting your money out of a limited partnership without taking a financial bath can be a struggle, too. First of all, your partnership shares aren't tracked in the paper, unlike the shares of a REIT or a real estate mutual fund, which can be sold immediately after you call to redeem them. From time to time the general partner will estimate the value of the shares and send you his opinion. You won't necessarily get paid this amount if you want to sell your shares before the partnership dissolves, however. Instead you'll receive whatever a buyer is willing to pay for them—assuming you can find a buyer. (There is an exception: **master limited partnerships**, which operate like traditional partnerships except that they trade on exchanges like any other stock.)

If you want to withdraw from a partnership early, you will most likely have to sell your stake in the secondary market. More than a dozen firms buy and sell units of existing partnerships there, often at a large discount to their original value.

Still interested? Consider these pointers before you invest:

- **Be prepared for the risks involved.** That means answering "Yes" to the following questions: Can you afford to potentially lose your entire investment? Can you afford to go without the money you're planning to invest for the entire estimated life of the partnership? Do you fit the investor suitability standards listed in the partnership's offering memorandum? If you answered "No" to any of these questions, you can't afford to invest.

- **Stick with existing partnerships.** Opt for one that is at least three years old and is on solid financial footing. That means, among other criteria, that the partnership's cash flows are covering its expenses with at least some money left over for income distributions. You either can search online or ask your broker. Be wary if he begins pushing his firm's house-brand partnerships; brokers often get bonuses to sell these products, and that's exactly how many of the recent partnership lawsuits got started.

- **Go with an experienced general partner.** Before investing in any partnership, get a prospectus laying out the deal. Scour this document closely for information about the general partner—to whom, after all, you will be entrusting your money. Specifically, you want a partner with similar projects already well along. A successful apartment complex developer, for instance, may not know a thing about building or buying shopping malls. By definition, a firm with an experienced general partner has probably been in business for at least five to 10 years—the longer the better.

- **Stay out of the blind pools.** Evaluating partnerships is tricky enough when you know what properties are owned or are being sought. When you don't know, it's like throwing money down a well and hoping it doesn't get wet.

- **Avoid highly leveraged partnerships.** Even after they've raised money from investors like you, many partnership sponsors borrow money to finance projects. The advantage in using someone else's money as leverage, like this, is that the potential return on your investment is higher. However, the disadvantage is that a larger cash flow from the properties will be required to make payments on the debt before the limited partners get any returns. These kinds of partnerships are for high-fliers only.

- **Steer clear of partnerships with high fees.** Above average fees and incentive fees are usually a clue that your general partner does not have your best interest at heart. Ask your broker or planner to show you how a partnership's fees compare with those of similar programs.

- **Ask an objective pro for advice.** Before investing in a partnership, go over the deal with your lawyer, financial planner, or accountant, or ask some other independent, trustworthy adviser to look over the terms and give you objective advice. Don't rely exclusively on the broker or investment adviser selling you the partnership shares, since she'll receive a hefty commission from the sale and won't be completely disinterested.

Rental Property

Now, you're about to enter the realm of dirt-under-the-fingernails real estate investing. With rental properties and the other alternatives that follow, you'll be doing most of the work yourself. You'll also have a chance personally to increase the value of your investment. Of all the hands-on real estate investments, residential rental property is the most attractive for individuals. Raw land doesn't generate rent or go up in value unless someone is willing to develop it. High-rise office buildings and shopping centers typically require more money and expertise than most amateur real estate investors possess. On the other hand, down payments on apartment houses are often within the reach of the average investor.

These days, residential rental real estate offers some of the best tax breaks around, plus the chance to earn 10% or more annually in income and capital gains. However, investing in a rental property is not the same as choosing a house for yourself. First, other people have to live there, so your taste doesn't matter a whit. The prospect for appreciation, which may not matter much to you when buying a home to live in, is an essential factor to consider when shopping for investment property. You must also calculate how much income you can reasonably expect the property to generate and whether that amount will cover your operating costs (mortgage payments, maintenance, and insurance, to name just three).

Investing in rental property is such a hands-on proposition that only people who have plenty of time and energy should consider it. Becoming a landlord means locating the right property, arranging financing, making repairs and improvements (or getting someone to do them), finding tenants, and collecting rent. Don't be discouraged, though. Anyone who takes the time to learn the rules of property investment can make it work and perhaps make a bundle. Here's a quick rundown of those rules:

1. **Get the best price you can.** Ideally you want to pay no more than 80% of the building's market value. To determine the value, work with an appraiser or a real estate agent who will check recent sales prices of comparable places. You might even consider joining a local real estate club to better familiarize yourself with the market. There are more than 100 of these kinds of groups around the country. (You can try searching for them online.)

2. **Buy property that will be easy to rent.** Choose a house or apartment in the best neighborhood within your price range, where the crime rate is low and the nearby properties are clean. Drive through a neighborhood during the day and at night to

get a feel for these factors. You should also check with the local police to assess the level of criminal activity in the area. You generally want to choose a property that has broad rental appeal; unusual, modern-looking structures may appeal to your artistic nature, but not to many others.

You're better off owning property close to home, for two reasons. First, even if you can afford to hire someone to manage your property, you will almost certainly want to visit the place regularly. That's a lot easier to do by car than by plane. Second, you will more likely understand the dynamics of the real estate market in your own back-yard than in another region of the country. So stick close to your home turf—say, no more than an hour's drive from your business or home.

3. **Buy property that is likely to appreciate.** Although real estate appreciation is influenced by such national factors as the level of mortgage rates and the overall economy, the market conditions you really need to understand are those where you want to buy. You can get information on regional and metropolitan prices from the National Association of Realtors (800-874-6500; www.nar.realtor.com). Ask local real estate brokers for more specific information on prices in a given area if you need it.

If your goal is to beat the average appreciation rate in your area, you may want to invest in a property that is a little run-down and fix it up on your own. Generally, for every dollar of repair you put into a dump, you can expect to gain $2 to $5 when you sell it as a palace. Make sure, however, that you don't get yourself in too deep. A house that requires a fresh coat of paint, new shutters, or light fixtures is fine, but you'll most likely want to avoid buildings in need of major repairs like a new foundation or a plumbing makeover. Chances are that you won't recoup enough on resale to justify the cost of such major face-lifts. It's worth spending the $250 to $2,000 that a building inspector will charge—depending on the size of the structure—to estimate how much work will be needed and how much it will cost. Your real estate broker can tell you if the increased value of the house after you repair it would make the investment worthwhile.

Your chances of selling property at a profit will be greatly improved if you buy it cheap. A smart way to do that is to keep an eye out for sellers in a hurry to unload their buildings. The real estate section of your local newspaper will invariably carry ads with phrases such as "Need to sell in a hurry." You can also ask friends and co-workers if they know of anyone moving to another city who is anxious to sell quickly and cheaply. Another strategy: Search through legal journals for notices of foreclosure sales. You can ask about these sales at your local bank, savings and loan, or credit union, too. Or you can call the Federal National Mortgage Association (800-732-6643; www.fanniemae.com) for a list of local foreclosed properties that it's selling. In any case, you'll want to be sure you know what a property is really worth. To find a qualified real estate appraiser, check your local Yellow Pages, contact the Appraisal Institute (312-335-4100; www.appraisalinstitute.com) and ask for its membership directory, or log onto www.appraiserlist.com.

In addition, ask local real estate agents for a list of the area's communities or neighborhoods that have the shortest resale time for residential properties. Such places are seller's markets that push property values higher. These days, single-family rental houses typically take about three months to sell.

Also, get the area's vacancy rate from a real estate agent or online. If it's around 5%, you can probably rent your property easily. If it's 7% to 10%, you may have trouble. Above 10%, forget it—unless you're getting a steal and think the neighborhood will turn around. Then buy and cross your fingers.

4. **Buy property that is profitable.** Your building should ideally produce a rental stream that will throw off income after it covers your mortgage installments, property taxes, maintenance, and insurance expenses. There's a simple formula for figuring this out. Divide the total selling price by the gross annual income and come up with the **rent multiplier**.

Rent Multiplier

$$\frac{\text{Selling price}}{\text{Gross annual rental}} = \text{Rent Multiplier}$$

For example, say a four-unit apartment is selling for $250,000 and generates $25,000 in annual rent. The formula would go like this:

$$\frac{\$250,000}{\$25,000} = 10$$

The rent multiplier would be 10.

In other words, the building is selling for 10 times the annual gross rental, or has a rent multiplier of 10. Generally, avoid property that is selling for more than seven or eight times gross annual rental. That's because it is more than likely to produce a negative cash flow; put another way, such a property will require you to spend more money than you take in. Worthwhile residential properties are those that generate enough rental income to pay your big operating expenses—mortgage, maintenance, and taxes—while you wait for your investment to appreciate. As a rule, you don't want to buy a building if the carrying costs are more than the income it produces, no matter how little you'll have to pay for it. The exception is if you can afford to pay the difference for as long as it takes the investment to rise in value and you're in a high enough tax bracket to make the wait worthwhile.

For a more detailed way to check out the rental numbers before you buy, after you find a property you like, fill out the worksheet on pages 390–391.

5. **Buy property with more than one tenant.** As with any investment, diversification is essential with rental property—even if you own only one building. You do not want to be beholden to the whims of one deadbeat hard-luck case. So buy buildings with as many rental units as you can afford. Your income will then be higher, your cost per apartment will be lower, and a vacancy won't wipe out your income. If a small, six-unit dwelling is too expensive, begin with a duplex or triplex, sometimes called a two-family or three-family house. These units generally cost more than single-family houses, but they also generate more income. For example, you might pay $200,000 for a duplex in the same neighborhood where single-family houses cost about $150,000. If you charge each tenant $900 a month per unit and take in $1,800, you'll fare a lot better than if you were getting even $1,200 for a single-family house. By investing 33% more, you have increased your rent by 50%, and if one of your tenants leaves, you would still collect $900 a month.

6. **Keep your ownership costs down.** Stipulate in the lease, for example, that a tenant pay for utilities or for minor repairs. The best way to hold down costs is to arrange for easy financing terms. You generally can get a better interest rate on your mortgage if you live in the property, providing your building has more than one unit and fewer than six. Bankers generally consider any apartment house with six units or more as investment property. This is an important distinction since bankers are likely to insist on tougher terms if you are borrowing for investment than if you are taking out a mortgage on a house you'll occupy. Lenders generally ask for a 10% to 20% larger down payment for investment properties with fewer than six units than they require of home buyers. For larger buildings, a 20% to 30% down payment is standard. It's also likely that if you don't live in the building you will be charged half a percentage point more in mortgage interest and an additional point in loan fees.

If you think you'll be able to raise rents substantially within two to three years of buying a building, you might keep your mortgage payments down initially by negotiating a fixed-rate, graduated-payment loan. Like an adjustable-rate mortgage, this loan will let you make lower monthly payments at the outset than with a standard

HOW TO CHECK THE RENTAL'S NUMBERS BEFORE YOU BUY

Pay close attention to two figures. On line 11 you'll find the annual return you can expect on the cash you invest, after the building is in rentable condition. You're looking for a figure that's at least double the one-year CD rate. On line 14 you'll get the overall projected return on your investment. If it's 10% or more, buy.

1. a) Annual rents $_____
   b) Allowance for $_____
       vacancies and
       uncollected rents
       (typically 5%)

2. Net rents (line 1a $_____
   minus line 1b)

3. Annual deductible $_____
   operating expenses
   excluding mortgage
   payments—such as
   your repairs and
   maintenance (typically
   10% of net rents),
   property taxes,
   insurance, management
   fees of 7% to 10%

4. Net operating income $_____
   before mortgage
   expense (line 2 minus
   line 3)

5. Annual mortgage $_____
   interest payment

6. Annual pretax cash $_____
   flow (line 4 minus
   line 5)

7. Annual property
   depreciation (cost of
   the building, but not
   the land, divided by
   27.5 years) $_____

8. Tax loss or gain (line
   6 minus line 7) $_____

9. Annual tax loss or tax
   due (line 8 multiplied
   by your combined
   federal, state, and city
   tax rates) $_____

10. After-tax cash flow
    (line 6 plus or minus
    line 9) $_____

11. Cash-on-cash return
    (line 10 divided by
    cash invested)   _____%

12. Projected one-year
    gain in price (purchase
    price multiplied by the
    estimated 12-month
    percentage increase in
    value) $_____

13. Projected total return
    for year (line 10 plus
    line 12) $_____

14. Return on investment
    (line 13 divided by
    cash invested)   _____%

Source: Michael P. Sampson, professor of taxation at American University and author of *Tax Guide for Residential Real Estate.*

fixed mortgage. Locking in the rate, however, guarantees that you won't run the risk that carrying costs will rocket skyward if interest rates shoot up in the future. Many real estate pros warn against taking out an adjustable mortgage since it makes it harder for you to project your future expenses. If it's the only mortgage you can qualify for, though, be sure the interest rate can't rise by more than six percentage points over the life of the loan.

You may also be eligible for low-interest or low–down payment loans offered through federal, state, and local governments. For example, you might qualify for a lower mortgage rate if you invest in a marginal neighborhood that is being rehabilitated. Or you might be able to negotiate a smaller down payment than you would get from a bank by purchasing property in a government foreclosure sale. You can find out about federal loan programs from the U.S. Department of Housing and Urban Development (202-708-1112; www.hud.gov). Your state housing authority will give you information about state and local loan programs.

7. **Manage your property yourself.** Once you've located the property with the best potential returns, arranged the financing, and closed the deal, you're still left with the chore of managing your investment. You can hire a professional property-management firm, but you'll sacrifice as much as 10% to 15% of your gross rental income for the privilege. Professional management may be worth the cost if your building generates income exceeding your expenses; otherwise, try to manage the property yourself. To find tenants, place an ad in your local newspaper or post a note on the bulletin board of grocery stores and colleges. Be certain to check any potential tenant's employment record and references from previous landlords. Even if you think you've fully vetted your prospects, you may wind up with some who don't pay their rent. Therefore it's smart to budget 2% to 10% of your rental income, depending on the turnover rate in the neighborhood, to cover the costs of deadbeat tenants. Such costs will include not only missing rent, but any potential enforcement or legal action you may choose to take. (Being a landlord can be an ugly business sometimes.) Set aside another 2% to 10% for repairs, and expect the occasional nighttime or weekend call from a frantic tenant, demanding that you fix whatever has just broken.

8. **Take advantage of tax breaks.** The hassles of owning rental property may not seem worth it until tax time. Then, wow! Becoming a real estate investor can really ax your taxes. Of the assorted tax breaks, depreciation is by far the most valuable. Typically, you could choose the straight-line depreciation method, in which you deduct the cost of the building over 27.5 years. Commercial real estate gets written off over 39 years. The IRS publishes standards for different items that make up a building, giving each a minimum number of years over which you could deduct the total

value. You can also deduct many of the expenses you incur, including the cost of mortgage interest, property taxes, insurance, maintenance, and transportation to your property. Check on www.irs.gov for details.

Middle-income taxpayers get a special break for investing in rental real estate. If your adjusted gross income is less than $100,000, you can write off against your earned income as much as $25,000 a year from your rental real estate losses as long as you actively manage your property (setting rents, choosing your tenants, that sort of thing). This tax break phases out until your adjusted gross income hits $150,000; at that point it vanishes.

Vacation Homes

One of the most enduring fantasies for many American homeowners is to own a vacation home—preferably up in the mountains or near a lake or the ocean. Not only do you have a restful retreat from the pressures of your daily life, but the house pays for itself because you rent it out when you're not using it, generating enough cash to cover your expenses and maybe throw off a little extra income on the side. After a few years the value of your piece of paradise ideally rises enough so that you realize a dandy profit when you decide to sell it.

That's the fantasy, anyway. The reality is often quite different. Many vacation homes never generate enough income to cover their costs, let alone produce profits for owners. What's more, for every vacation property that triples in value over time, there are two that rise no more than the average piece of real estate—and some even lose value.

This does not mean that vacation homes are a bad idea. Indeed, for people with realistic expectations, vacation homes can prove to be among the most enjoyable of investments. You just need to go into this world of real estate with both eyes wide open.

Before you buy a second home, it is crucial that you understand the tax consequences. Most of the tax benefits associated with owning your primary residence apply to a vacation home—providing you use it solely for your personal pleasure. You can deduct mortgage interest, property taxes, and, if you're unlucky enough to have them, casualty losses. These deductions, however, are limited to your first and second homes only.

Should you decide to rent out your vacation home for part of the year, the tax laws start getting complicated. Now the rules vary according to how long you rent out the property and how much you use it personally.

- **If you rent out your home for no more than 14 days a year, you'll owe no taxes on the rental income you get.** You can still deduct the mortgage interest and property taxes.

- **If you rent out the home for more than 14 days during the year, your rental income is taxed at your regular income tax rate.** You will, however, be able to write off expenses that you incurred as a landlord, such as depreciation and operating costs like advertising for tenants and the upkeep on the property.

- **If you rent out the home for more than 14 days but also use it yourself for more than 14 days or for more than 10% of the number of days you rent the home—whichever is greater (whew!)—you can still treat your vacation home as a second home since the IRS will consider it to be your personal residence.** That means mortgage interest and property taxes on the vacation home will be deductible to the extent that the house is for your use and not a rental. Likewise, you can deduct expenses related to the rental portion of the house only up to the amount of the rental income. For example, if you have $10,000 in rental expenses but only $5,000 in rental income, you can deduct only $5,000 in expenses. Fortunately you can carry over any excess write-offs to a future year when you have excess rental income.

- **If you limit your personal use of the home to 14 days or 10% of the number of days the home is rented, whichever is greater, then the home will be considered a rental property and not as a residence.** As a result, mortgage interest attributable to your personal use of the home is considered consumer interest and thus no longer deductible. However, you may be able to deduct rental expenses in excess of rental income. As noted previously, the IRS may let you deduct up to $25,000 of business losses from your adjusted gross income as long as you actively rent and maintain the property. You qualify for the full $25,000 write-off if your adjusted gross income is less than $100,000; the tax benefit is phased out for incomes of $100,000 to $150,000. If you earn more than $150,000, you can deduct rental business losses only against rental income, but not against regular income from your job or other types of investments. (There's an exception to this limitation for people in the real estate business; they can deduct rental business losses against income regardless of how much they earn.) Rental business losses, by the way, mean your expenses for maintaining the property—which include depreciation, painting, yard maintenance, repairs, and property taxes. You can also factor in the costs of any trips you take to inspect or repair the property. However, don't try to disguise personal use of your home as inspection trips. Reason: The IRS may not let you claim the house as a rental property if you take advantage of your visitation rights.

Once you understand the thorny tax issues concerning second homes, ask yourself the following questions before you take the plunge and buy a place:

1. **Can I afford it?** As a rule, your combined mortgage payments, homeowners insurance, and property taxes for your primary and vacation homes should not exceed 33% of your gross annual income. Otherwise you could find yourself underwater financially. Moreover, the total payments on all your mortgages and other long-term debts should not exceed 40% of your gross income.

   A lender will probably insist you make a down payment of 20% vs. as little as 10% for a primary residence. That's because financial institutions believe they're taking on bigger risks by lending money to people who won't be living in, and taking care of, their homes full-time. So they want more equity in the vacation homes from the start. You may even be told to put down 25% if you plan to rent out the property. Expect to pay one-quarter to one-half of a percentage point more for a mortgage on a second home than for the mortgage on a primary residence. Because your hideaway may be off the beaten track and frequently empty, your total homeowners insurance costs may run 50% higher than for a primary residence selling for a similar price. If you rent out the home, expect to pay roughly 20% extra to cover the potential damage while tenants are there.

2. **Do I want a house or would I prefer a condominium?** Condos are usually cheaper than a detached single-family house, but they are harder to sell. Their prices typically don't rise as much, either. Condos also are generally smaller than single-family houses. The bottom line: Condos are best suited for people who view their second homes primarily for personal use.

3. **Is the home in a desirable location?** There are several factors to consider when answering this question. Resist the temptation to look for a house in a resort area merely because you enjoyed your vacation there this past summer. Take a reality check. For instance, if the trip back and forth from your principal home would be unbearable on a regular basis and you're looking for a place you could escape to any weekend, you need to scout out a more accessible spot. The same reasoning applies even if you're planning to use the home mostly as a rental. Don't figure you can start a new vacation trend by buying in some out-of-the-way spot. You're best off purchasing a place where vacationers want to vacation and one with a proven rental record. Not only will you know that people have chosen to rent the place previously, you'll have a built-in list of potential future renters. You should also pay close attention to location because you'll want a place that repairmen, couriers, gardeners, and rental agents can get to easily. Generally, stick with homes that are within a half day's drive of a major population center.

Before buying a home, it's worth your while to talk with local government officials in an area you're considering. In winter resort areas, for example, a police officer can tell you how often your street or road gets plowed—secluded homes may be left adrift for many days. In a beachfront community, ask city officials about the shoreline's erosion pattern, since you'll want to avoid buying a home that might eventually require an expensive retaining wall.

4. **Do I have a reliable real estate and rental agent?** Local real estate agents can be helpful in a number of ways. For example, they can clue you in about area real estate trends, the best neighborhoods, and other important factors you may know little about. You'll need a top-notch rental agent if you want to limit your involvement in the day-to-day management of a vacation home. For example, a proficient agent can find renters for you, collect rent from them, clean up between tenants, and even make minor repairs. The agent's commission typically runs between 15% and 25% of the rent, so you'll have to decide how much all of these services are worth.

5. **Are the house and its contents in good shape?** The same rules that apply when you buy a primary residence hold when you're buying a vacation home—that means a solid foundation and roof, adequate plumbing, and good insulation. A home inspector can give you a complete description of the condition of the home. Remember to consider your potential renters when furnishing the place. Sturdy is important, since many strangers with no investment in the house will be plopping on your chairs, beds, and couches. Stylish counts, too, if you want return business. Just think what you would want on vacation, in terms of attractive furnishings, modern appliances, and air-conditioning. Then make sure your place has it.

6. **Am I paying the right price?** A knowledgeable real estate agent can help you here. Ask the agent for the average number of days houses are on the market—two to four months is typical—and how much the seller has dropped his asking price. Sellers in languishing markets will often accept low bids. Before you make one, though, ask yourself why the market is languishing. The local vacation home market may be whispering to you: "Don't buy here. The place is on the skids!"

Ask your agent about auctions. These sales are common among banks with foreclosed homes, developers with unsold properties, and even homeowners in a hurry to sell (though you ought to ask why they're going this route). Auctioned homes generally sell for 10% to 45% of their list prices. If you plan to buy at auction, bring a certified check, usually ranging from $2,500 to $10,000 (but be sure to check for details by calling the auction house). Within a week you'll need to come up with any remaining balance that equals 10% to 15% of the purchase price. You will have 45 to 60 days to find a mortgage.

Time-Shares

Buying a **time-share** generally means plunking down anywhere from $5,000 to $20,000 for a designated chunk of time—typically one week—at a specific place, generally a condo in a resort area. There are two types of time-shares. The most common is a **fee simple plan**, which gives you title to a portion of the property and ownership of your week there year after year. The other kind of time-share, a **right-to-use plan**, grants you the right to occupy your slot only for a specific number of years.

There's something innately alluring about time-shares: the ability to guarantee prepaid vacation accommodations for a week or more annually at a resort you'd enjoy repeatedly or, if you want, trade your week or location for another one. After all, when you have a time-share, you don't have the hassle of making reservations or the disappointment of having to stay at a so-so hotel because the one you wanted was booked. What's more, one day when you decide to sell the place, you can theoretically make a handsome profit. The cost? In addition to the purchase price, you'll owe an annual maintenance fee averaging $300 or so and subject to increase.

There are now more than 1,000 condominium and hotel time-share resorts in the United States and another thousand or so overseas. Millions of Americans have bought time-shares in the past two decades. For many, however, these investments have caused more heartache than happiness. That's because unprincipled fast-buck artists have plagued the time-share industry. Some are hustlers who disappear after being paid. Others are fast-talking marketers who exaggerate or even lie to close the deal. Still others are honest developers who lack the resources or experience to adequately manage time-shares.

Many owners have also learned that the solid initial attraction of time-shares can melt away. You may grow tired of visiting the same resort year after year. Or you may not always be able to schedule your vacation during that same week in August. You may also find that trading your time-share with someone else isn't so easy either. As real estate investments, time-shares often come up short. Though time-shares in some popular resorts have been resold for two or three times the original price, those are the exceptions, not the rule. Indeed, thousands of time-share owners have struggled to find buyers because the time-share salesmen in their resorts have steered potential buyers to new, unsold units. It's not unusual to swallow losses of 35% to 60% of your investment when you unload your time-share property. In short, time-shares provide an object lesson of why you should never mix business with pleasure.

If you're still interested in buying a time-share, pay close attention to the following rules:

- **Proceed with caution.** Don't surrender to a hard sell and buy on the spot. Instead, rent a few times in the development that appeals to you. Be sure to go during the week you think you'd want to own. These test visits will help you determine if you would really want to spend time there year after year after year.
- **Buy one- or two-bedroom units.** Smaller or larger ones will be harder to sell later.
- **Buy time during the peak season in a popular area.** This will enhance your chances of swapping your unit, renting it out, or selling it.
- **Buy in a place that's easy to reach.** If the location is remote, you may be discouraging potential swappers or buyers.
- **Don't overpay.** If you are buying a fee simple unit, don't pay more than 10 times the going rate for a comparable week in a local hotel or rental apartment. You can get those figures from newspaper ads or from a real estate agent. For a right-to-use time-share, divide the sales price by the number of years offered. If the amount is less than the cost of the equivalent rental, you're getting a good deal. Before buying from the developer, see whether a time-share resale agent is listing equivalent accommodations at the same project. If so, you may be able to swing a better deal on the price.
- **Buy from a proven developer.** Stick with experience and you'll be less likely to find your vacation spoiled by poor maintenance, bad management, or unforeseen lawsuits. Big developers—such as Marriott, Hilton, and Disney—are also more likely to run rental or resale offices to help you when you want to sell. Fully check out the time-share and the developer. Ask for customer references and then interview several of them. Check the firm's reputation further with the attorney general's office or any appropriate state agency that keeps an eye on time-sharing.
- **Investigate your ability to swap your time-share before you buy.** For information about time-share trades, call the two biggest exchange services: Resort Condominium International (800-338-7777; www.rci.com) and Interval International (305-666-1861; www.resortdeveloper.com).

Before signing any agreement, take home copies of the proposed contract, schedule of maintenance fees, and, if there is one, the developer's disclosure statement or offering memorandum. Scour the sales contract or other materials for a statement of your rights should the resort run into difficulty. If you're buying a fee simple time-share, you'll want to know when the title will become free of any claims by the property's lenders. In most cases there won't be clear title until you've paid in full and a certain percentage of weeks in your unit is sold. In a right-to-use contract, you will want a nondisturbance clause that ensures that the property's mortgage holder recognizes your occupancy rights in case of a foreclosure on the property. Make sure the same clause is in the time-share's mortgage or construction loan. If it isn't, the clause in your sales contract won't hold up.

Be sure that the developer is obligated to reserve a portion of your maintenance fee for major repairs and replacements, too. Otherwise you may face heavy special assessments in later years. The developer should be required to ante up for this fund an amount equal to the number of all unsold time-share weeks.

Have a real estate attorney familiar with the rules of time-sharing review any agreements before you sign. If you don't know of such a pro, ask your attorney to refer you to one. Most states that regulate time-shares—not all do—require the developer to give you at least three days to cancel your contract without penalty, but you'll want to have your lawyer write in such an escape clause if it's not already included.

Raw Land

Who hasn't watched the spread of cities and suburbs in this country and wished he'd had the foresight to buy a chunk of land 20 years ago and wait for developers to start a bidding war over the property? Success stories based on such prescience are common in the world of land speculation. Unfortunately, so are stories of unmitigated failure. Many speculators have bought land only to find that the interstate they were expecting wound up detouring 15 miles to the north. Others have learned that the cost of buying raw land—financing, property taxes, and insurance—was far greater than they had expected. And what about those unsuspecting souls who bought Florida swampland from fast-talking salesmen? So it should come as no surprise to you that raw land is the riskiest of all real estate investments.

Indeed, land speculation is suitable only if you have extra money you can afford to lose and you can wait years for appreciation—typically 10 years or more. Unlike other types of real estate, raw land won't pay you annual income; the payoff, if any, comes only when you sell. Still, if you can afford to tie up your money for years and you invest wisely, the profit potential in buying undeveloped land is huge. Some general rules for land grabbers:

• **Do the math.** Empty land that seems to be just sitting there is actually busy gobbling up money. When buying a parcel, you'll need to come up with a down payment and then mortgage payments, property taxes, and insurance premiums year after year. So you can't calculate the true profit potential of any land deal until you first determine the costs of owning the land. Start by totaling the preceding expenses and add any other charges you might have to pay, such as environmental studies or swamp drainage. As a rough rule, land values have to double every four or five years just to keep up with the ongoing costs of ownership. Therefore it's essential to work with a real estate agent to estimate the sort of price appreciation common in the area you're considering.

- **Know what the land is worth.** Land values vary dramatically from region to region and from year to year. For example, one lot that is suitable for residential development might run anywhere from $10,000 to $100,000. Farmland, on the other hand, is generally cheaper; it typically runs between $1,000 and $5,000 an acre. Whatever your pleasure, have any property appraised before you make a bid. (To find an appraiser, see page 388.) Ask the appraiser to tell you not only how much the property is worth today, but its expected future value, given local development and population patterns.

- **Have plenty of cash on hand.** Banks routinely make loans for purchases of raw land, but they require unusually high down payments to help lessen their risks. Expect to put down a minimum of 25% of the total cost and as much as 40%.

- **Be wary of out-of-the-way bargains.** There's usually an excellent reason why acres in the middle of nowhere are selling so cheaply: They're in the middle of nowhere. Forgive the cliché, but location is the most important factor to consider when buying undeveloped property. Check with local government authorities to see if the area's population is growing or if there is a shortage of land available for development. Ask these officials, as well as local builders and developers, how long it will take anticipated development to reach your particular plot of land.

- **Understand the local land-use trends.** It won't do you much good to own land suitable only for industrial use if local developers want property for building apartment houses. So make sure you understand the realistic potential of any parcel you're considering. Also, be certain that the local zoning board agrees with your estimation. If you think your land is perfect for a shopping mall, but the area is zoned for tract houses, you'll be out of luck. Sometimes zoning laws can be changed, however. So if you face a zoning problem, ask town officials whether you could get a rezoning. Remember to factor into your original cost analysis any expenses for lawyers and government fees.

   Find out, too, whether any nearby developments might affect your property. Generally, new schools and shopping malls are good neighbors; nuclear waste dumps and prisons are bad ones.

- **Seeing is believing.** Never buy land without visiting the property. Brochures, off-site sales presentations, or videotapes are not sufficient. They reveal only what the developer wants prospective buyers to see. You need to walk the property and check out things like the terrain, view, and path of the sun.

- **There's no place like home.** Playing the land speculation game is tough enough without losing the home-field advantage. So stick to properties in your own region. You'll have a much better shot at figuring out development and population growth trends than if you buy in a place you can barely pronounce.
- **Turn over rocks.** Not literally, of course. It's nearly as important to know, however, what's under your land as what you might put on it. Get a percolation test to determine how well your property drains. Test the land for environmental hazards such as toxic waste and to determine the property's ability to support buildings. Seemingly solid land can sometimes be little more than quicksand. Expect to pay several thousand dollars for all these tests; it's money well spent, though. When investing in raw land just as with any other type of real estate, early expense and effort can save you from later losses and lament.

SECTION FOUR

YOUR FAMILY FINANCES

CHAPTER 18

How to Get the Best Deals When You Spend Your Money

By now you've learned how to be a savvy saver, a diligent debtor, and an intelligent investor. Now for the fun part: smart spending. Don't worry. You're not about to read a lecture on how to be a tightwad or the importance of buying generic foods. Who wants to live like that? In fact, you'll find out when it makes sense to pay up to 30% more for an item. You will also learn how to negotiate like a pro, use the Internet to hunt down bargains, and get the best deals when you shell out big bucks. In addition, you'll see how to give away some of your money to charities without getting scammed in the process. With so many charity scandals in recent years, that kind of knowledge is essential.

How to Negotiate the Price of Just About Anything

For decades car shoppers have just said "No" to sticker prices. Their battle cry: "Let's make a deal." But lately, thanks largely to easily accessible information about pricing on the Internet, consumers are now savvier and negotiating has become more mainstream. So whether you're in the market for a car, a vacation, or a sofa, it pays to be an informed consumer. Instant recall of competitors' prices is the best ammunition for negotiators. These 10 other strategies can also help you wrangle great deals.

1. **Haggle late in the day.** That's when cranky store owners and hotel managers are eager to close a deal and make that one last sale.

2. **Buy in quantity if you can.** A customer who wants three dresses often has more leverage in getting better prices than the shopper buying just one.

3. **Pay cash.** The green stuff is like music to many merchants, who can lose 6% to 15% on purchases charged with credit cards. Pay the old-fashioned way and ask for a 10% cash rebate.

4. **Be polite.** Never call the merchandise "inferior." A breezy attitude will win you negotiating points faster than an obnoxious pitch.

5. **Be cool.** Don't be overly eager to snare a particular item. That's a sure way to quash a deal. If you're dreamy-eyed over that antique wall unit, a dealer may figure you'll eventually break down and pay full price.

6. **Offer to buy the floor model or a recently discontinued item.** Shoppers at electronic stores often use this technique. With new stereo, TV, and personal computer models rolling out every few months, it's smart to consider outmoded floor models. Many stores will sell floor models or recently discontinued items for 15% to 30% off the price of new items. Not a bad deal, considering that floor models are usually in perfectly good condition and typically come with full manufacturer warranties. Just be sure to carefully inspect the item for nicks and scratches and give it a test drive so you don't wind up being unpleasantly surprised when you bring it home.

7. **Barter with the big boys, too.** No haggling at department stores? These days, that's a myth. You'll have to get past the sales associate, however. The person with markdown authority is the department manager. Whenever you can summon one (to, say, point out a stain on a sweater), you may succeed in bringing down the price. At the biggies, your best bets for price breaks are on big-ticket items such as overstocked jewelry and furniture; clothes and furnishings that have lingered unsold for months; soiled items; and items with missing buttons or other imperfections.

8. **Know when and where to go to bid down big-ticket items.** Notice how the price of ski parkas melts when temperatures rise? Many store items have seasonal price fluctuations. You can wrestle down the prices even farther when the weather or retailing climate renders them duds. Some examples:
   - Look for end-of-season sales on clothing such as wool coats and cashmere sweaters, which can slice prices by more than 50%.
   - Get up to 30% off freezers and refrigerators in January or June.
   - Snap up a personal computer and related equipment in November and December, when manufacturers slash prices by 25% or more to unload inventory.

- Bargain hard for the fur coat of your dreams during March and August.
- Shop for discounted air conditioners in February and September.

9. **Negotiate for services, too.** Most negotiators vie for things. By ignoring costly services, however, hagglers win only half the battle. Ask for lower prices or special deals at your dry cleaner, tailor, or hairdresser.

10. **Use the Internet to amass key information about product prices and descriptions.** You'll be well equipped to haggle if you know not only what other traditional stores are charging on a product you want to buy, but also what kind of cyber deals there are. Don't forget, bricks-and-mortar shops are hotly competing with online stores, so you may be able to use a price you see online to talk down a shopkeeper or store manager. If you want to buy a patio table, for example, go to the Web sites run by bricks-and-mortar stores such as Crate & Barrel (www.crateandbarrel.com), as well as online stores such as Patio.com (www.patio.com). You can also get a broad range of prices at **shopping bots**, which are sites that search hundreds of other Web sites for the best prices. BotSpot (www.botspot.com) is a site dedicated to helping you find the right shopping bot, with links to nearly 50 of them.

Smart Shopping Tips for Car Buyers

For most people, few shopping experiences are as aggravating and intimidating as buying a car. (Some people get a kick out of trying to outsmart car dealers. Good for them.) Even before stepping into a showroom, a car buyer has to sort out a multitude of issues: Should I buy American? Japanese? European? How big an options package do I really need? Would I be better off leasing? What about buying a used car instead of a new one? How much will insurance set me back? What's the repair record for this model? Which of the nation's 22,000 dealers will give me the best price? Should I just go to a no-haggle dealer or perhaps hire a car-buying service to pay the least? What about automobile financing?

To make matters worse, not all customers are treated alike. It's no secret that dealers routinely offer male shoppers better prices than female buyers, and that whites have traditionally paid less than minorities. Such unlawful discrimination only underscores the value of being a knowledgeable car shopper. Follow these tips to help smooth the bumps on a car-buying journey that's riddled with potholes:

• **Set a budget.** A hot rod may look tempting. If your budget calls for a mere get-about, though, you won't regret sacrificing form for function. To figure a budget, decide first how much you can shell out for a down payment. As a rule, you should try to put down at least 20% and finance the rest over as short a term as possible (four years or less is best). Bear in mind that a car is not like a home, which almost always appreciates over time. Rather, it is a depreciating asset that's sure to lose value from the moment you drive it off the lot. In fact, the average new car maintains less than 60% of its value after five years; utility vehicles tend to keep their value best. So to avoid being stuck with a car worth less than the outstanding balance on your loan, you'll want to pay off your note as quickly as possible.

    There's another advantage to making a hefty down payment. Your 20% ante will help you win more favorable financing than a down payment of 10% or less—as much as a full percentage point lower at most banks and credit unions. On a four-year loan, that can save you several hundred dollars. You can easily find out how different interest rates would impact your monthly payment on a number of Web sites that are chockful of information for car shoppers. Carpoint (www.carpoint.com), a section of Microsoft's Web site MSN.com; Bankrate (www.bankrate.com), a consumer-finance site; and IntelliChoice (www.intellichoice.com), a California automotive research firm, each have calculators to compute monthly payments. You simply plug in variables such as the amount of your down payment, length of loan, and interest rate on the loan, and they compute how much you would have to shell out each month. The following table shows what your monthly payment would be on three- and four-year automobile loans of $15,000 to $25,000 at interest rates between 7.5% and 9%.

YOUR MONTHLY CAR PAYMENT

	Interest Rate			
	7.50%	8.00%	8.50%	9.00%
3 Years				
$15,000	$467	$470	$474	$477
$20,000	$622	$627	$631	$636
$25,000	$778	$784	$789	$795
4 Years				
$15,000	$363	$366	$370	$373
$20,000	$484	$488	$493	$498
$25,000	$605	$611	$617	$622

- **Get your financing first.** Don't let the tail wag the dog. Shopping for money before price gives you a reality check about how much car you can afford. By doing things in reverse, some drivers may be tempted to fall for a car that's bigger than their wallet, then wind up struggling to find ways to pay for it. When financing your wheels, you have four loan options: your bank, your credit union, the car dealership, or online lenders. Shop each for the best possible rates and terms. The best way to get going is to get a feel for the market by surfing the Web. Check average rates in the U.S. and in your region. You can find average daily rates on the Carpoint, Bankrate, and Intelli-Choice Web sites mentioned above, as well as on sites run by Consumer Reports (www.consumerreports.org), which has made its name giving unbiased reviews and reports on consumer products, and Edmunds (www.edmunds.com), which has published new and used vehicle information since 1966.

  Next, check with your local banks and credit unions, the dealership, and online lenders to find out what rate they'll give you. Lending Web sites, such as E-Loan (www.eloan.com) and the LendingTree (www.lendingtree.com), have worksheets that ask you to plug in information about your financing needs and some details about the car you're interested in. In return, it will list a number of loans you may qualify for, including interest rates, loan term, and other details.

  Before you settle on financing, though, look through listings of rebates and offers for cut-rate dealer financing, which may save you a bundle and minimize your financing needs. Carpoint's *Passenger Car Rebate Report* and IntelliChoice's *Rebates & Incentives*, both online, include free comprehensive listings.

- **Figure your car's target price and negotiate from there.** At dealers who negotiate, only suckers pay sticker price. Savvy shoppers aim to pay 3% to 4% over the dealer's cost for cars listing for less than $20,000 and 6% to 7% more than invoice for more expensive models. For example, the dealer's cost on a car with a $10,000 sticker price is probably around $9,000. So if you wanted to buy it, you'd set a target price of roughly $9,280. Generally, the pricier the car, the less you're likely to shave off. You can get the dealer's cost of most models from IntelliChoice's *The Complete Car Cost Guide*, a reference book available at most libraries. Or, you can visit the IntelliChoice Web site. Under its "New Cars" section, you can choose a car model and the site will list the dealer's cost, the sticker price, and a reasonable target price.

- **Consider no-haggle pricing.** Take-it-or-leave-it pricing is a tactic that General Motors introduced successfully with its Saturn line. The setup offers option-packed cars at one price, with no room for bargaining. Ostensibly, these vehicles go for 6% over the dealer's invoice, for a savings of half off traditional markups. While buying without negotiating won't necessarily yield the best price, you may want to give a little just to save on stress.

These days, you will find most no-haggle car dealers online, which makes the experience even more convenient. If this kind of shopping suits you, take a look at CarsDirect.com (www.carsdirect.com), Autoweb.com (www.autoweb.com), Auto-Nation.com (www.autonation.com), or Carpoint (www.carpoint.com).

- **Be compulsive about total cost, not monthly payments.** Too often, car shoppers try to determine "How much will I pay each month?" rather than "How much will this car cost me over time?" To drive away with the best deal, however, you'll want to estimate the car's total **five-year ownership cost.** This is how much you'll pay to own and operate the car. Get this: In just five years, the average car costs more to own and operate than its original price. A total ownership figure takes into account projected depreciation plus what you'll pay for financing, insurance, repairs, gas, and registration fees. Stack one similarly priced model against the next and you may well find that the total ownership cost swings greatly. For instance, the 2001 Acura Integra GS-R two-door coupe, with a sticker price of $22,300, had a total ownership cost of $37,065, according to IntelliChoice. The 2001 Subaru Legacy GT4 sedan was priced slightly higher at $22,895, but had a lower total ownership cost of $33,243.

  Car shoppers can get data about total ownership costs from many sources. Several publications, including MONEY and *Consumer Reports*, publish annual car rankings that feature this important benchmark. You can also find ownership costs listed for free on some Web sites, such as IntelliChoice and Carpoint.

- **Just say "No" to extended warranties.** Chances are your dealer will push an extended warranty. This contract can cost anywhere from $500 to $2,000 and is designed to cover any repairs you need after your limited factory warranty expires. Dealers love this little invention because it generates huge profits. For drivers, though, the deal isn't so sweet. Most carmakers these days offer excellent basic warranties covering your car repairs, most parts, and roadside assistance for three years or 36,000 miles, whichever comes first. Luxury cars usually cover you for four years and 50,000 miles. So why pay up front for something that won't gear up for three years down the road, if at all? A better idea: Fund your own warranty by keeping spare cash in the bank or a money-market fund.

- **Get the best price on your old mount.** Before you accept a dealer's offer for any trade-in cars, do your homework. The best no-cost route is to browse online. You can find trade-in prices at sites run by Kelley Blue Book (www.kbb.com), Edmunds, IntelliChoice, and Carpoint. For those who prefer print over free online services, pick up a copy of *New Cars & Trucks* or *Used Cars & Trucks* (published by Edmunds; $9.99) at your local bookstore. Then head to a few used-car lots for bids. If your dealer is offering significantly less than the used-car dealers, you might want to sell the car on your own. Sure, it's more work, but the do-it-yourself approach can often bring you 20% more than a trade-in.

• **Buy at the end of a model year.** Unless you're eyeing a car in heavy demand (in which case you may be forced to pay sticker), it generally pays to buy at the end of a model year. That's when most car dealers clear their lots to make room for newer models and are especially eager to bargain. This rule doesn't apply if you expect to trade in your car after a year. Since your car will quickly be "last year's model," you'll suffer a full year's depreciation in just a few short months. That will be bad news when you sell or trade in.

• **Use a buying or shopping service.** You're not up for a showdown in the showroom? There are still ways to get a cut-rate car. **Buying services**, the personal shoppers of the auto world, will hunt down the best price, then order and deliver your vehicle for a fee. More than 30 such services exist nationwide, and their $250 to $500 fees are still low enough to let you drive home a deal. Don't, however, confuse these types with car brokers. A broker's allegiance may be questionable, since he or she gets dealer commissions on top of fees paid by you. You can get more information about buying services by calling the National Association of Buyers' Agents (800-517-2277) or visiting its Web site (www.naba.com).

If you want someone simply to do some price legwork before closing the deal yourself, other services can help. The oldest is CarBargains (800-475-7283), which for $190 will pull in bids from five or more dealers in your area to get rock-bottom price quotes on one or two models.

How to Close a Great Lease Deal

It's easy to get rattled by the decision of whether to buy or lease a car. In the past, leasing almost always proved more costly than buying. These days, however, automakers and dealers are pushing leases like mad and luring many would-be buyers. In some cases their deals can be the cheaper way to go. Trouble is, if you don't know what you're doing, you can get taken for a ride. State attorneys general across the country have been flooded with complaints from customers who think they weren't told the whole truth about leasing from their dealers.

In a typical lease arrangement, you make preset monthly payments over a specific period of time, just as you would on a car loan. Because you're paying for a fraction of the car's value—its value over the time when you lease it—monthly payments are generally lower than comparable car loan payments. At the end of the lease term, you may buy the vehicle for a predetermined price.

Leasing, however, is a tricky proposition, unlike a straight car sale. Dealers often fail to provide shoppers with the underlying financial terms of a lease; instead, they're apt to focus on low monthly payments and little or no money down. Making things more complicated are terms the dealer may toss around, like capitalized cost and residual cost.

Before getting tangled up in the leasing process, consider whether leasing is really the best move for you. The answer is probably "Yes" if you are a certain type of driver. Strong lease candidates are people who like to trade models every few years, use their cars for business (lessees get deeper tax deductions than owners), drive infrequently (less than 12,000–15,000 miles per year), or lack the dough for a sizable cash down payment (at least 20% of the car's price). Drivers planning to keep the same set of wheels for five years or more, however, can almost always save by buying.

Once you decide to lease, cruise the Sunday paper for offers in your area. As you read, remember that the best leases combine several factors: low down payments, a fair selling price, and affordable monthly payments. To cut such a deal, though, you need to be armed with reliable information. You can get the monthly payment and the length of the lease from the ads. Figuring out the crucial money terms—the true interest rate and the car's capitalized cost—will take some dealer prodding and pencil pushing.

The key is to figure your **total lease cost**. Basically, the total cost is the difference between the car's value today (its selling price or **capitalized cost**) and its value at the end of the lease (its **residual value**), plus interest. You can't do much about the car's residual value, but you certainly can drive the selling cost south. Do your best to negotiate for a selling price or capitalized cost that's roughly 4% higher than the dealer's cost.

Another money-saving factor is the interest rate on your lease. Oddly, dealers may express your interest rate as some baffling decimal, like .00025. This is known as the **money factor**. Don't be put off by it. Simply multiply this number by 24 to arrive at the real-world annual interest rate (in this example, 6%).

There are five other key lease points to remember:

1. **Be sure you're comfortable with the term of your lease.** If you decide to back out of a lease early, you may (ouch!) be stuck with all remaining payments. In case you're in doubt about how long you'll be needing wheels, go for a shorter rather than longer lease term. Assuming you can afford it, you'll be wise to take a term that's as long as the manufacturer's "bumper-to-bumper warranty"—typically two or three years—in order to avoid paying any hefty repair bills yourself.

2. **Reduce pesky up-front costs.** Many leases require a truckload of cash up front. Top siphons: down payments, security deposits, and a check for the first month of

your contract. The last one is nonnegotiable. But the amount you're asked to pay for the other two is up for discussion. Just think: By getting your dealer to shave or eliminate the down payment, you can invest that money and make it work for you.

3. **Go for a factory-subsidized lease.** Cruise for a knock-out deal that's underwritten by the manufacturer. These are almost always superior arrangements, since carmakers can afford to set interest rates that are way below average. Some manufacturer-subsidized leases are attractive because the carmakers build in a high residual value. These types of leases, typically offered by Japanese carmakers, don't last long, however. Manufacturers usually tout subsidized leases for three to six months.

4. **Lease early in the model year.** Remember the advice for car buyers to shop late in the model year for the best price? With leases you turn that tip on its head. Lease early as opposed to late in the model year. Otherwise you're sure to hit mid-year price hikes, which in turn produce higher total costs and monthly payments. The best months to get a lease are October, November, and December, when you can snag next year's model.

5. **Drive a hard bargain and read the fine print.** Just as you'd haggle with a dealer over a car's sticker price in a purchase, do the same with your lease deal. Once you've chosen a specific model, call or visit at least five or six dealers to comparison shop. Even if you can't manage to get a lower monthly payment, you can always ask the dealer to knock a few hundred dollars off the purchase price, assuming you do intend to buy at lease end, or drop the down payment.

How to Get Great Deals When You Travel

Travelers today have the deck stacked in their favor. Here, too, the Internet has heated up the competition, driving hotels, airlines, and cruises to offer sweeter deals that will attract travelers bent on finding a bargain. Plus: A flurry of hotel building in the late '90s has widened travelers' choices without expanding their wallets. Add to that frequent flier programs and generous family package deals and the dream vacation suddenly looks like a reality.

The travel game has grown complicated, however. Airfares seem to change by the minute. Frequent flier deals come with more fine print than an insurance policy. Some airlines don't work with travel agents; others are making travel agents charge their customers for service. Some travel bargains demand that you make some compromises in your plans. And though travel Web sites are filled with deals and pricing information, wading through them can feel like a full-time job. You'll navigate your way to the best deals, however, by following these strategies:

- **Get smart about travel agents.** Whether you travel often or infrequently, a trusty travel agent can be a valuable asset. With the assistance of speedy computer reservations systems, an agent can coordinate your itinerary with speed and skill. What's more, your agent will know your frequent flier memberships, where you like to sit on a plane, whether you prefer no-smoking hotel rooms, if you normally order special airline meals, and what kind of rental car you prefer. In return, your agent typically receives commissions of 5% to 11% from the air carriers, hotels, and car rental companies he or she books.

   Though their services have traditionally been free, some agents now charge fees to issue inexpensive airline tickets or create complex trips. Loyal customers, however, may be exempt from these fees. So if you already have a reliable pro, stay put. When shopping around for a new agent (and you should try out several), ask him or her to spell out any service charges. Even if the agency charges its customers, you may be able to skirt the fees by presenting yourself as a potential long-term client who will bring in a lot of business. Also, if you are a customer who travels more than once a year and you get hit with a fee, ask the agent for a refund. You just might get it.

- **Wise up on travel Web sites.** You can find it all online—airfares, car rental deals, hotel rates, family packages, cruise itineraries, and more. So much, in fact, that surfing for travel deals can be a mind-numbing, hours-long experience. But if you know where to look, you can quickly get a good feel for market prices and avoid having to call each airline, hotel, and car rental service individually to check on rates. Among the most comprehensive, reliable travel sites that give you up-to-date information on travel deals, as well as online booking services, are Travelocity.com (www.travelocity.com), Orbitz.com (www.orbitz.com), and Expedia.com (www.expedia.com). Amid the thousands of other sites devoted to travel, there are a number that are useful when it comes to specific tasks, such as finding a last-minute fare or package deal. You will see some recommended as you read on.

- **Buy a package.** A package that bundles airfares, hotels, and ground transportation is usually the best way to save on a vacation. Available mainly through travel agents and directly through some airlines, these getaways can cost just half of what you'd pay for the pieces separately. Even so, it's smart to comparison shop. That's because agents typically buy packages from wholesalers or tour packagers, many of whom sell nearly identical trips. If you use a travel agent or surf the Web, be sure to get price quotes for the same vacation from several tour packagers. When shopping the airlines yourself by calling their 800 numbers or checking their Web sites, request a brochure on any specific area and compare your options. Then head to a travel agent to see if he or she can do better. If you don't mind waiting until the last minute, you can find the biggest discounts online at the travel Web sites Site59 (www.site59.com), LastMinuteTravel.com (www.lastminutetravel.com), and 11thHourVacations.com (www.11thhourvacations.com). These sites specialize in last-minute discounted package deals including hotel, airfare, car rental, and sometimes even dinner at a local restaurant.

- **Snag the lowest airfare.** Amazingly, the major airline carriers make more than 20,000 fare changes each day. So getting the cheapest fare available requires a careful strategy and a bit of luck. Your best bet for getting a quick snapshot of airfares is by checking out the Travelocity, Expedia, or Edmunds Web sites, which are great tools for finding the lowest published airfares. To increase the odds that you're landing the best possible rate, ask for price quotes from two or three travel agencies. Be sure to mention if you saw any lower rates advertised online so the agencies can try to match or beat them.

As a rule, reserving two weeks or even five days in advance will get you a better fare than flying last minute. Flexible travelers stand to save even more. The less picky you are about carriers, departure dates, and airports, for instance, the better your chance of flying in a cheap seat. An example: Traveling west to Los Angeles, fliers can save $50 to $150 by routing to nearby John Wayne Airport in Orange County.

Another way to fly on the cheap is to look for special last-minute airline-sponsored deals. You can find many by calling the airlines, but the quickest route is to go to deal-packed Web sites run by Bestfares.com (www.bestfares.com) and SmarterLiving (www.smarterliving.com). These list the times, dates, airlines, and rates of special offers, and update deals daily. What's more, they often list deals that are only advertised on the Internet. You can sometimes save as much as 50% or more off of regular fares on these Internet-only deals. But you have to be flexible about when you travel and which airports you will use.

Is Paris calling? Maybe Tokyo? Vacationers to foreign destinations shouldn't miss out on the deals from **consolidators**. These companies buy tickets from the airlines at wholesale and sell them to the public at substantial discounts. You can save up to 50% off competing fares by booking with a consolidator, or bucket shop, as they're also called. You'll spot their postage-stamp-size ads in the Sunday paper, or your travel agent can arrange for such a ticket. You can also check out online consolidators Cheap Tickets (www.cheaptickets.com) and Lowestfare.com (www.lowestfare.com). Once booked, however, these fares are usually nonrefundable, with no itinerary changes allowed.

When fare wars erupt, play your cards carefully. If a full-page ad trumpeting cheap fares inspires you to pack, don't book right away. Other carriers may soon match the price or undercut it by a notch or two. Wait a day or two after the brouhaha, then shop around.

- **Book discounted hotel rooms.** Seasoned travelers never pay a hotel's published or "rack" rate. No wonder. In large cities like New York and Los Angeles, standard hotel tariffs—including eye-popping taxes—can easily push a bill to $200 per night, before minibar. The good news for travelers is that hotels rarely are filled to capacity. On average, U.S. hotels fill only about 60% of their rooms on any given night. This leaves miles of room for negotiating unless you're traveling during peak season or run into a major convention.

  Start your hotel rate hunt with your travel agent. Large agencies, especially, often have relationships with specific hotels and can arrange discounts of 20% to 50%. Also check out the Travelocity and Expedia sites, to get an idea of going rates. Your next smartest move, assuming you've got a few hotels in mind, is to call each one directly and ask for the best deal in the house. Virtually anyone can qualify for the "corporate rate," which is about 10% less than rack rates. Don't stop at that, though. Deeper discounts for weekends or special promotions may be available for up to 50% off. By calling the hotel directly—as opposed to its centralized, toll-free corporate reservationist in some other city—you may happen upon a manager. If business is slow, he or she may cut you an impromptu deal. No matter what rate you get, though, request a better one when checking in.

  To get a decent hotel room at a rock-bottom price, check out a **hotel consolidator**. Like their airline counterparts, hotel wholesalers scoop up room blocks cheaply and pass on to guests the savings—routinely 25% to 65%. The choice of hotels in a given city may be limited, although you're almost always assured a first-class room. You won't find hotel consolidators widely advertised, however. Two of the oldest and largest hotel wholesalers in the United States: Hotel Reservations Network (800-964-6835; www.hoteldiscounts.com) and Express Hotel Reservations (800-356-1123; www.express-res.com).

- **Travel during the off-season to save 40% or more.** In travel, as in comedy, timing is everything. If at all possible, try to vacation when it isn't high season at your destination and rates are at their annual peak. Most areas in the United States, the Caribbean, and Europe have high and low seasons dictated by a number of factors, such as weather, holidays, and visitor traffic. The seasonal difference you'll pay can vary wildly. Consider: When traveling to a Caribbean island, you can save 40% or perhaps a bit more by visiting from March to September. For information on high and low seasons in a particular area, call its department of tourism or the local convention and visitors' bureau.

- **To set sail, book through a cruise-only agent.** Whether sailing to the Caribbean or Alaska, travelers who book the major cruise lines in advance (as far as a year ahead) can anchor discounts of up to 30%. You can get an even more generous offer by dealing with a cruise-only agent; cruise specialists help passengers get deals of 50% off. As a bonus, they can sometimes upgrade you to a better cabin class. Check for cruise-only agents in the Sunday travel sections of major newspapers.

- **Join a travel club.** After paying annual fees of $25 to $100, travel club members get access to some tremendous hotel, dining, car rental, cruise, and tour discounts—often up to 50%. There's no fancy footwork or third-party booking involved. Instead, you're likely to get some combination of membership cards, directories, and fat coupon books; it's up to you to provide club credentials when making reservations. Two of the largest travel clubs are Entertainment Publications (800-285-5525; www.entertainment.com; for hotels, restaurants, rental cars, and attractions nationwide) and Premier Dining (800-346-3241; dining only).

- **Haggle for a car rental deal.** Yes, it is often difficult to drive a great bargain off the rental lot. Even when you think you're getting a decent rate—whoops, the fine print proves you wrong. For instance, most car rental companies offer discounted weekend rates, but if you wind up keeping the car into the week, you may jeopardize the deal. Your best strategy, if you have the stomach and patience for it, is to visit the desks of several rental agencies upon landing at an airport even if you've booked ahead. Ask for a lower price and you just might get one, especially if you've lucked into a slow business day. Be sure to mention any discounts you're entitled to receive, such as a corporate rate, a special price for being an AAA member, or a discount for being a senior citizen.

How to Be a Smart Medical Consumer

With corporate employers cutting back on health benefits while the cost of medical care spirals, you need to be an aggressive health consumer these days. Earlier chapters offered advice about choosing among managed-care providers, shopping for health insurance, and using your employer's flexible spending account. These tips will take you the next step:

- **Check your hospital bills.** Here's a shocker: As many as nine in 10 hospital bills are inaccurate, with consumers and insurers usually left holding the bag. The errors aren't tiny, either. Overcharges typically run 5% to 7% of most bills, which works out to $500 to $700 on the average $10,000 hospital bill. To avoid a rip-off at the hospital, either you, a friend, or a relative should keep a diary of your daily expenses in the medical center. Begin your tally on the day you check in, noting every charge from each aspirin prescribed to every test you take. Upon checking out, compare your notes with your itemized bill, looking for any suspicious or suspiciously high entries. Among the most frequent errors to watch for: inaccurate charges, such as typos (turning a $5 pill into a $50 one); duplicate charges, where you're charged more than once for the same service or item; and phantom charges for things you simply never received. Hospitals are busy places, and honest billing mistakes happen a lot. If you find any discrepancies, ask your hospital's billing department for an explanation.
- **Try ambulatory or urgent-care centers.** Too often, Americans use the local emergency room for basic health needs. To avoid getting stuck with a bill your insurer won't pay, treat broken bones and flu symptoms at one of more than 4,000 ambulatory care centers nationwide. These privately run clinics can help you save about 20% on noncritical illnesses and injuries. You can locate a center near you by visiting the North American Association for Ambulatory Urgent Care Web site (www.nafac.com).
- **Question the need for diagnostic tests.** Usually, your doctor knows best. But since many physicians have a financial stake in diagnostic laboratories, they may have a vested interest in a few extra X-rays, too. Of course, no patient should pass up a potentially lifesaving test. Still, it is important to ask your doctor to carefully explain the purpose of any costly tests such as MRIs.
- **Explore nontraditional therapies.** More and more employee health plans are covering alternative healing methods such as chiropractic adjustments, acupuncture, and vitamin therapy. Clearly, the demand exists for these treatments; roughly one in three Americans has sought such care. Even if therapies such as hypnosis or homeopathy aren't covered by your plan, you may want to check them out—they're relative bargains. Nontraditional healing methods cost an average of about $30 per session versus $75 for the typical M.D.'s bill.
- **Don't expect to pay less for drugs on the Internet.** There are a number of online drugstores these days that let you order your prescriptions with the click of a mouse. Among the most popular are the online-only store Drugstore.com (www.drugstore.com) and the traditional CVS stores' Web site (www.cvs.com). While these sites are extremely convenient, don't expect to save. According to a recent University of Pennsylvania study, Viagra and Propecia were being sold for an average 10%

more online than at five traditional Philadelphia pharmacies. As with any online shopping venture, be wary when buying prescription drugs. Bypass sites that don't let you pose questions to a pharmacist by e-mail or telephone, or don't list a U.S. mailing address and phone number. And never have a prescription written by a doctor on the Web who never has examined you and doesn't have full access to your health records.

• **An ounce of prevention . . .** Yes, it does beat a pound of cure. To avoid the need for costly health care, be sure to get regular physical exams and checkups. For women, these include annual Pap smears and, if you're over 40, mammograms. Men should get screened for signs of prostate cancer every year starting at age 50.

Using the Internet to Shop for Deals

It used to be that consumers visited a couple of stores or scanned a few newspaper ads to compare prices on an item before buying. Now, thanks to the Internet, it's not uncommon for people to compare prices at half a dozen stores or more. As a result, consumers are better educated than they ever have been, and are much more likely to find a good deal, whether online or offline.

Unfortunately, though, there's no rule of thumb for where you will find the best deals. Prices are all over the map, and changing constantly. One day you may find the lowest price on a book at an online-only store like Amazon.com (www.amazon.com) and the next day it might be at your local bookshop.

So the best advice is to comparison shop on the Web, and also visit your neighborhood bricks-and-mortar stores. To save you time online, give some of the online shopping bots a try, such as MySimon (www.mysimon.com) or Yahoo! Shopping (shopping. yahoo.com). They search thousands of online retailers and deliver you the most competitive prices.

If you're willing to spend a little more time at the computer, roll up your sleeves and check out the world of **online auctions**. EBay (www.ebay.com) is the biggest and most popular auction site, though you can try out an auction bot such as BidXS (www.bidxs.com) to search some 300 auction sites for products. Online auctions are quite safe. The main drawbacks are that they take time, and the items being sold are generally used and you don't really know what shape a product is in until you get your hands on it.

Finding Furniture Bargains

How would you like to save 30% to 80% off manufacturers' suggested list prices for furniture? It's easier than you think. The secret is shopping the showrooms and stores in central North Carolina towns such as High Point and Hickory. That's where nearly two-thirds of America's furniture is made. It's best to do your North Carolina furniture shopping in person. After all, that's the only way you can see and test out the furniture. Try not to go in mid-April or mid-October, though. During those periods, the industry holds its biannual home furnishings show in the area and the place is a zoo. Visit in March and September and you'll be able to get some terrific discounts by purchasing last season's items. Bring your checkbook, too. High Point stores typically insist on deposits of 25% to 50% by check or money order. To fly to the High Point area, you'll want to book a flight into Greensboro's Piedmont Triad International Airport or Charlotte International Airport.

You don't have to travel for the bargains, though. Quite a few of the furniture discounters take phone or online orders. For a directory of the stores, get a copy of *The Fine Furniture and Furnishings Discount Shopping Guide* ($15.95; P.O. Box 973, Bloomfield Hills, MI. 48303; or order online at www.amazon.com or Barnes & Noble's site, www.bn.com).

When It Pays to Pay More

So far, you've read quite a bit about saving money when you shop. Sometimes, however, it makes sense to pay full retail price—as long as the value is there. For instance, you should be glad to pay top dollar for an item or service you expect will perform for quite a while. A perfect example: mattresses. Scrimp a little now and you could be suffering from back pain for years.

It's also worth paying full freight when the product is far superior to the competition or one of a kind. Case in point: top-of-the-line sports equipment. Custom-made clothing, fine jewelry, and art will set you back a bit, but the quality usually more than compensates for the cost. In fact, the jewelry and art may even appreciate over time.

Finally, safety is almost always worth the price. Sure you'll pay a little more for organic food or lawn care. However, you may sleep better knowing that your family will cut its contact with chemicals or pesticides. The same holds for a worthwhile home alarm system.

Checking Out Charities

Perhaps you've dialed in during a charity telethon, sponsored a colleague at work for a walkathon, or simply been torn about dropping a quarter in a homeless person's cup. Americans are fairly generous, in fact, contributing roughly $900 per household annually to good works. Yet with so many seemingly worthy recipients of your dollars, the choices may become blurred. Indeed, some 320,000 new "charities" spring up each year. Just how wisely would each use your donation?

Given the growth of charity scams and frauds in recent years, you'll want to investigate any charitable group thoroughly. During national crises, such as the attacks on the World Trade Center and the Pentagon in 2001, phony charities sprang up virtually overnight, purporting to send money, food, and gifts to victims and their families.

These general guidelines can help ensure that your dollars end up in deserving hands:

- **Gather information.** Never agree to make a charitable donation over the phone to a group you don't know. Instead, ask the caller to send you materials about the charity. If the group is legit, you'll receive the mailing. If it isn't, you'll get a song-and-dance over the phone about how the cost of such mailings is prohibitive and why you should make a donation now. Such callers often want little more than to get your credit-card number.

  Before giving any of your hard-earned money to a charity, no matter how worthy it appears, read its brochures, annual reports, or other printed information about the group. They should clearly explain the charity's mission and give you some background on its officers. Before contributing, you'll probably want to make sure you're in tune with a charity's philosophy, political bent, and methods for achieving its goals. The material also should plainly state the group's tax status. This matters, since you can take a charitable write-off for donations only to groups defined as 501c(3)s under the federal tax code—as well as to churches and synagogues. The term "nonprofit" is irrelevant here. Lobbying groups are nonprofits, but unless they also qualify as charitable institutions, any money you give to them is not deductible.

- **Find out how the group spends its money.** A key barometer of the worthiness of a charity is the percentage of its income spent on actual good works. As a giver, you'll want to be sure that at least 70% of a group's total budget goes to the programs it claims to support. With truly well-managed groups, such as the American Red Cross and the Boy Scouts of America, this figure stays fairly consistent from year to year. A smaller charity should be willing to send you data showing exactly how much money it took in during the previous year and how much it spent on programs.

- **Give appropriately.** If you're inspired to make a gift after checking out a charity, your next task is to do it properly. Avoid scam artists and ensure proper documentation for your tax write-off by writing a check for your donations. (By law, in order to deduct a contribution of more than $250, you must get written documentation from the charity.) Never agree to write your check to an individual, however. Use only the formal name of the group or its fund-raising arm.

- **Make sure the group can address all of your concerns.** Evasive answers to your questions may signal that something's amiss. Any bona fide charity will cheerfully answer your questions about its programs, donations, fund-raisers, and leadership. If you still have questions or concerns about a charitable group, you may want to contact the watchdog groups that police the charity front. Each keeps tabs on dozens of charities and rates them based on their program spending and administration. One is the BBB Wise Giving Alliance, which is affiliated with the Better Business Bureau (4200 Wilson Blvd., Arlington, VA 22203; www.give.org). You can order a complimentary copy of the group's publication, *The Better Business Bureau Wise Giving Guide*, online. Another helpful organization is the American Institute of Philanthropy (4905 Del Ray Ave., Bethesda, MD 20814; www.charitywatch.org). You can order a copy of the AIP *Rating Guide and Watchdog Report* for $3 online or through the mail. To investigate local groups, call the Better Business Bureau in your city. This agency can tell you whether consumers have recently filed any complaints about a charity that solicits donations in your area.

Avoiding Other Consumer Scams

Chances are you've recently opened your mailbox or your e-mail account and found a suspicious-looking note exclaiming:

"CONGRATULATIONS! YOU HAVE BEEN SELECTED FOR A CARIBBEAN CRUISE! TO CLAIM YOUR PRIZE, CALL . . . "

If this sounds familiar to you, count yourself among the millions of Americans who are targeted annually for consumer scams.

Each year, con artists siphon about $100 billion from trusting victims' pockets. Reaching out by mail, phone, and computer online services, rip-off artists creatively spin new ploys daily. Typically, they prey on vulnerable types such as the elderly or people with poor credit. Their games are often more than annoying, they're illegal. Any con artist using the mail system is committing a felony that's punishable with jail time.

Using common sense can help you ferret out the legitimate offers from the scams. For starters, one old saw is still valid: If it sounds too good to be true, it probably is. Never give your credit-card number over the phone to unsolicited callers. Don't dial in on a 900-number ploy, either, no matter what the offer. These lines charge several dollars per minute and often exist to line the pockets of crooks. Never buy anything from a Web site unless you know the business is legitimate. If you're cautious but get conned anyway, contact the National Fraud Information Center by telephone or through its Web site (800-876-7060; www.fraud.org) to find out more about your rights and any recourse you may have.

Among the top consumer scams to avoid:

- **"Guaranteed" prize offers.** Don't fall for any postcard or phone call alerting you to a "guaranteed" prize. Typically, this is an invitation to pay for some inferior product or vacation. Any notice requiring you to put up money or dial a 900 number is only a guarantee that you'll be ripped off.
- **Credit-card heists.** Fraudulent credit-card purchases cost consumers and issuers $3 billion each year. Many credit cards are simply stolen, but a crook doesn't even need to lift your card to wreak havoc. A credit-card receipt bears your name and account number—often that's all the information a thief needs to make purchases in your name. The best defense is to keep an eye on all your cards and credit-card transaction receipts. Request your carbons from salespeople, then tear them up. Destroy all old cards, too. If your monthly credit-card statement fails to arrive on time, don't chalk it up to a postal error. It could have been stolen, so call the card company right away to check.
- **Phony job opportunities.** Beware anyone touting rich job offers if you merely provide your résumé and a few hundred dollars. Most legitimate employment agencies do not charge a fee, and none should charge a fee for supposed "job listings."
- **Home repair scams.** Here's a prime example of how con artists prey on the weak. In these scams, the targets often are recent victims of disasters such as earthquakes, fires, or floods. The MO can take various forms. Some "contractors" are phonies who show up, demand a fee, then disappear. Others may be qualified and do actual work—but the work they do winds up being costly and unnecessary.

The best way to check out a contractor is to first make sure that he or she is properly licensed. You can find this out from your state's licensing board. Also, ring up the local Better Business Bureau to check for its record of customer complaints. Next, call several former clients and ask them about the quality of work performed, if the job was completed on time, and if it came in on budget. To make sure a contractor's references are legit, ask if you can drop by to inspect the work yourself. Before proceeding with the job, get at least three different estimates, with the terms of the contract hammered out in writing. In addition to clarifying costs, completion dates, and payment schedules, the contract should be specific about the quality of materials to be used.

- **Investment muggings.** In the world of investing, there is no such thing as a sure thing. Remember this advice the next time you're solicited for some "investment opportunity of the century" hyping sky-high returns and little or no risk. Think you're too smart for that? Maybe. Even sophisticated investors get duped by phony financial offers, though. Indeed, financial fraud costs Americans more than $10 billion each year. Ploys can range from fake high-yielding bonds to worthless stocks, stamps, and real estate deals. Lately, investment scammers have been poaching on the online services, trapping unsuspecting users.

  Bear in mind, these schemes are often elaborate and can seem quite convincing. Crafty con artists may even send phony performance records for the "investment" you've made. To avoid getting fleeced, take your time making all investment decisions. If the company is unknown to you, gather written information on the opportunity and ask for an annual report or prospectus. You might also ask your banker, broker, and local Better Business Bureau if they know anything about the investment in question. Have doubts about a so-called broker's pitch? Find out if he is licensed or has a complaint record by calling the National Association of Securities Dealers (800-289-9999) or contact NASD Dispute Resolution, Inc., at www.nasdadr.com.

- **Loan scams.** Consumers with bad credit may get hit with dubious opportunities for loans or credit cards. Your tip-off: The application is not like most others. For instance, most credit-card companies don't charge an application fee. The exceptions are some secured credit cards, which demand collateral. Application fees on loans are fairly common, but watch out for any that sound exorbitant. Also, beware lenders who tout a "guaranteed" acceptance once you've forked over some dough. Another loan ploy involves 900 numbers. If you're asked to dial one for a loan application form, don't. That's just a shady way of charging you for information that may prove useless.

- **Trips to nowhere.** You probably wouldn't fall for a trip to, say, the Fountain of Youth. Yet there are plenty of bum travel "deals," so you need to be on guard. One common scam beckons newspaper readers to take a cruise or Caribbean vacation. Would-be travelers are asked to fork over a "deposit" by credit card over the phone, then are told to book their trip later. Sometimes callers are promised open-ended tickets. Of course, the trips never materialize. To avoid such trickery, deal only with established agents you know.

- **Online ploys to get you to buy just about anything.** It's easy to imagine: You come across a snazzy-looking Web site that advertises a rock-bottom price on a set of golf clubs you've been thinking about buying. You plug in your credit-card number, and two months later you're still waiting for the UPS truck to show up. Well, wise up. Be suspicious if you see no contact information for a company running the site, or if you're asked for any personal information other than a password, shipping information, and a credit-card number. Only order on a secure site—look for an unbroken key or padlock icon, which indicate that the information you send will be encrypted. If you're unsure of a site's legitimacy, your best move is to avoid it.

What You Can Get for Free and How to Find It

If you relish a mere deal, you'd probably swoon over a freebie. As it happens, these days companies are bending over backward to win customer loyalty, and that means there's a surprising variety of loot for the taking. You just need to know where and how to look. Want advice on the house from a top-notch financial planner? No problem. Free samples of new cosmetics? They're yours. Companies shell out roughly $7 billion a year on freebies. To get your share of free stuff and more, you can:

- **Be a guinea pig.** Companies and even local stores can be obsessive about testing new products and services. After all, they can't afford flops. To avoid marketing fiascoes, most firms do extensive product research. That's where you come in. For instance, long-distance telephone carriers have been known to offer cold cash—as much as $100—for trying their services. Hotels and restaurants sometimes pay the tab for ordinary folks to anonymously sample their food and lodging.

   Primed to help out with such important work? Then crack open the Yellow Pages for clues. Look under "Market Research," and call the listed firms to ask when they will next need volunteers for surveys, polls, or focus groups. If you're selected, you'll likely receive some good stuff, including cash, free items, and coupons.
- **Flaunt your good taste.** Quick, name a product you've recently tried and simply adored. Did you (a) keep your opinion to yourself, (b) recommend it to others, or (c) drop a line to the company brass, letting them in on your new allegiance? If you answered "c," you're catching on. If you responded to both "b" and "c" and mentioned "b" in your letter, give yourself a hand. Companies love good word of mouth. Share your feelings about a product or service and you may be richly rewarded.

   Hotels, food companies, airlines, and restaurants are particularly flattered to receive fan mail. They sometimes lavish loyal, vocal customers with coupons for free or discounted meals, stays, and flights. So speak up. If the target of your praise is a small store or local hotel, put your compliments in writing to the manager. For the products and services of larger stores and chains, write directly to corporate headquarters, addressing the note to the CEO or to customer service.

- **Seek out free information.** Believe it or not, you can get an impressive education on somebody else's nickel. Here are just a few examples. Recreational Equipment, Inc. (REI), the outdoorsmen's store and catalog, routinely holds free seminars on rock climbing, camping, and kayaking. Over at Home Depot, the ultimate retailer for house tinkerers, you can learn to build just about anything at the free clinics offered at the firm's 280 stores nationwide. Even at your local library, there's probably a shelf devoted to videos you can borrow for free. These are typically videos focused on public service, ranging from safety for kids to health and family issues.

  You can also get loads of free information online that you would otherwise have to pay for. Some newspapers, such as the *New York Times*, give you free access to their daily news online. And if you want information from a site that requires you to sub-scribe, take advantage of any free trials before you shell out any dough. If they don't advertise a trial, call the business to ask for one. (If its contact information isn't listed on the site, avoid the site altogether. One sign of an illegitimate Web site is an absence of contact information.)

  Professionals like lawyers, financial advisers, and accountants often dispense advice without charge, too. Most, for instance, offer free initial consultations. Others, as a community service, hold free or low-cost seminars at local colleges or libraries.

- **Celebrate on somebody else.** Got a birthday soon? An anniversary or graduation coming up? Ripe opportunities await those not shy about sharing the news. This doesn't just apply at McDonald's, where anyone presenting proof of his or her birthday can have a free meal on Ronald. (You can find the toll-free numbers of most large companies by dialing 1-800-555-1212.) New moms can rack up valuable coupons for diapers, formula, and bottles by dialing up baby-minded companies to share the news—especially about multiple births. Traveling honeymooners can often get bumped to an airplane's first-class section by informing the gate agent about their recent nuptials. If you loved the place where you stayed as honeymooners, give them a ring. Many hotels will offer you a free night's stay on your anniversary to repeat the experience.

- **Browse the Web for giveaways.** Before you buy software or sign up for fee-based online services, find out if you can get what you want for free. For example, sites such as Dealnews (www.dealnews.com) and Where-to-Save (www.where-to-save.com) will keep you up-to-date on offers for free software, among other products. Absolute-lyFreebies.com (www.absolutelyfreebies.com) and Value Freebies (www.valuefreebies.

com) link you to sites with giveaways on cyber products and cyber services such as electronic greeting cards, virtual flowers, and college scholarship searches.

- **Score points for your loyalty.** Be sure to join any frequent buyer programs that reward your patronage with freebies. The best examples are airline frequent flier programs. Hotels, long-distance carriers, and credit-card companies also offer similar programs. In fact, the list of businesses offering rebates to loyal customers is growing by the day.

CHAPTER 19

How to Handle Money as a Couple

Love is sticky stuff. It links people; it's the symbol of connection. Money is the opposite. The symbol of separation, money buys us freedom from the control of another person. Yet dealing with money issues during courtship is one of the best ways to cement your relationship, even if the issue is as simple as deciding who pays for pizza. Openness about financial matters early on helps ensure that the two of you won't come to an unhappy parting later, quarreling over assets.

Like it or not, when you join together as a couple—married or living together—you're also forming a financial partnership. As with any new enterprise, the partners must discuss goals, establish some sort of spending plan, and sort out personal differences. Truth is, embarking on a marital partnership is infinitely more complicated than opening up a restaurant with your mate. Marriage, after all, involves children, parents, and issues of personal intimacy as well as daily issues of getting and spending. In addition, talking about the family's money can bring out tangled feelings about how well or badly you've been treated in the past by those you love.

Even the coolest of couples are likely to encounter some hot money buttons early on. Almost every couple starting out together discovers a wide variance in their beliefs about what they need today and what they ought to put aside for tomorrow.

Differences of opinion, and the compromises you each make to bridge them, become the basis for setting up your financial life. Don't look to financial experts for ironclad rules about whether you should have joint or separate checking accounts, savings that are merged or kept resolutely apart. There are absolutely no absolutes here except one: Do what you and your partner are comfortable doing. In the meantime, while you're working to discover what financial choices please you both, follow two fundamental guidelines to construct the necessary delicate balance:

1. **Give each other some financial space.**
2. **Play fair.** While you must play fair, you and your spouse must both be actively involved in your financial affairs—even if one spouse prefers not getting involved in the family's financial affairs.

Some aspects of money handling will change as you move into different periods of your life together. While you will be spending, earning, borrowing, saving, and investing continually, the importance of each will shift at different life stages:

- **Newlyweds.** Getting married usually represents a major change in your financial lifestyle. If you follow the statistical norm and wed in your mid-twenties, your earnings will probably be at their lowest in your adult life—at least until after you retire. From the start, you and your new spouse need to have frank discussions about money. Put all your assets on the table, then portion out joint and separate responsibilities—who will pay the bills, balance the bank statements, and handle the mechanics of saving and investing. Both of you should share in the work. Take into account, however, who has more time, talent, and interest in the tasks.

   Choose whether you prefer separate or joint bank accounts, and reserve the right to change your mind later on. Young couples with no assets and little income often live from paycheck to paycheck, pooling nearly all their resources just to make ends meet. When earnings and assets rise, more affluent marrieds may establish both joint and separate savings and investment accounts, perhaps reflecting different risk tolerances, a family inheritance, or simply personal preference. Discuss what works best for both of you.

   Establish the habit of setting aside an hour or so every week or two for a regular "business meeting" in which you thrash out ongoing financial issues and new ones that may have arisen.

   This is the time that you and your partner are probably beginning to set long-term goals, like coming up with the down payment for a house. So saving money takes on new importance. Try to sock away 10% of your combined pretax incomes, if you can. Impossible? Then try a strategy of saving 4% to 8% of your gross in your twenties and doubling that percentage when you reach your thirties and forties. Once you have a reasonable emergency fund—say, three to six months' worth of living expenses—start a systematic investment program and be sure to make the most of any tax-advantaged retirement savings plans that your employer(s) may offer.

- **When baby makes three—or four—and expenses soar.** Family responsibilities bring new needs for financial protection. Update your will (if you haven't made one, get to it pronto). Check that you have adequate life insurance on the family bread-winner(s). You don't need to buy a life insurance policy for your newborn, despite what some pushy life insurance agents insist. The purpose of life insurance is to replace lost income after the policyholder dies.

   During this period of your life, your earnings are rising but your expenses are probably mounting even faster. You'll want to start the newborn's college fund, but first you have to pay those rising medical bills and hack away at your credit-card balances. The biggest danger at this point in your life is that you will overuse credit and under-plan for future needs. If you're feeling swamped, sit down with your partner and establish some realistic family financial goals—small upcoming ones, if that's all you can manage. Put them down on paper; it makes the commitment stick. Divide difficult, long-term objectives into a series of reachable, short-term targets. For example, instead of saying "We need to save $100,000 for Max's college tuition in 15 years," say "We need to start investing $250 a month in a mutual fund for Max's future college tuition bills." If you can't afford your heart's desire now, don't cross that goal off your wish list forever. Just downsize a bit or schedule it for a more distant date. Maybe you'll buy that first house in two years, rather than in two months. The important thing is to set your goals and work on meeting them. You can even get the kids involved once they reach age seven or so (see Chapter 20).

- **Beyond the college crunch.** Hang tough. When the tuition bills stop, your borrowing, scrimping, and financial pressure will slacken. At that time (if not earlier), saving and investing become the main financial event. Review your investment plans periodically with your partner and see if you're on track toward a comfortable retirement. A software program could come in handy.

   Another possible concern: your aging parents and their financial needs. You can prevent trouble later on by exploring their financial and other concerns now. As you'll see in Chapter 21, it's a smart idea to have an honest discussion with your parents about their current finances and their financial prospects for the rest of their lives. You'll also want to find out from them where they keep their savings and investments, which credit cards and loans they have, and whom they use as financial advisers, in case of an emergency. This way you can help ensure that if their health or mind deteriorates, their debts will be paid and they'll get all their investment, pension, and Social Security checks. Naturally, you and your partner should share with each other the same kind of information about your separate and combined finances.

- **Pre-retirement.** This is the time to consolidate your financial assets and nail down your future security. With luck, you're earning more money than you even thought possible 30 years ago. You're considering tax-reduction ideas, new investment opportunities, perhaps even a vacation home that will become a retirement haven. You may be thinking about volunteer work to continue when you retire or contemplating a move to an area with a lower cost of living and warmer climate. The major mistake you can make now is not saving enough to supplement your future pension and Social Security income. A second consideration: Readjust your life insurance. You may need less coverage or even none at all after the kids are on their own.

- **Preserving assets.** Making your money last is critical at this stage. Once upon a time, your kids' needs may have dominated your living and spending patterns. Now it's more likely that the health and welfare of you and your partner are pressing considerations in determining your spending, borrowing, investing, and lifestyle. Discuss with your children your wishes for your future living arrangements if you one day can no longer take care of yourself. Would you want to be moved to a nursing home? If so, which one? Would you prefer in-home health care? Would you want to move in with your adult child? Finally, you and your spouse must together face difficult questions of how you will manage—financially and otherwise—after one of you dies. Will your children need to supplement your income? What living arrangements will each of you make? If you have followed the guidelines in this book over the decades, however, and had a modicum of luck to complement your efforts, your reward should be a comfortable self-sufficiency in your final years.

Resolving Money Arguments

The first step toward resolving chronic financial quarrels is identifying patterns that need changing. Washington, D.C., psychotherapist Olivia Mellan teaches contentious couples the process of depolarization—that is, how to bridge their opposing tendencies. The most productive approach, she finds, is to talk about feelings and dynamics first and hard facts afterward. Here are some tips to follow:

- **Pick a nonstressful time to talk, like an afternoon at the beach.** Then, share your early experiences with money. Recall the ways your parents spent, saved, talked, or screamed about money. Confide the financial worries that grip you and discuss what money represents to you: Security? Power? Independence? Dishonesty?

Learning to translate the different messages that money sends to each of you can reduce friction.

- **Describe the financial behaviors you admire in your partner.** Yes, you can share judgments and criticisms of each other, but get past them quickly. Move on to the positive aspects of your mate's behavior and spell them out in detail.

- **Establish goals—separately.** Better still, each of you should independently set three types of goals. Write up a list of short-, medium-, and long-term goals for yourself and your partner. Then put it aside for at least a week before reviewing it. When each of you has a list, rank the goals in three groups: (1) the ones that are most important; (2) the goals you could live without if necessary; and (3) the items you could relinquish more easily. Set a tentative date for accomplishing each goal. At the same time, put a price tag on each one and figure out how the two of you will earn, save, or otherwise come up with the money necessary to accomplish your goals.

- **Finally, share your goal lists with your spouse.** If there are major divergences, try to work them out so that both of you can get most of what you want. Ultimately you'll want to meld both wish lists into a set of joint goals. Work out a timetable, put down some preliminary numbers, and start turning those dreams into reality. If a few goals seem unattainable, try slicing them into a series of smaller steps and work on those.

WHERE TO GO FOR HELP

Three places to look for advice on money issues in your marriage:

Prevention and Relationship Enhancement Program (PREP)
Contact: 800-366-0166 to sign up for a seminar in Colorado or for a referral.

American Association for Marriage and Family Therapy
Contact: 202-452-0109 or www.aamft.org for a referral.

Association for Financial Counseling and Planning Education
Contact: 614-485-9650 or www.afcpe.org for a referral.

Special Concerns for Unwed Couples

The phrase "unmarried domestic partners" may conjure up memories of hippies in the '60s, but today's reality is quite different: Some 5.5 million households are headed by couples who are not married to each other. In 2000, 47% of men and 42% of women over the age of 35 were unmarried partners.

More than most people, young unwed partners are often slow to plan. But this reluctance can boomerang badly, causing serious damage to one or both of the people involved. When things go wrong—illness strikes, you decide to break up, your partner dies—you might find yourself having to deal with financial issues for the first time in relatively uncharted legal territory, with few of the protections or financial privileges accorded to married couples.

Certain financial precautions are in order from the start of your live-in relationship. In the early stages, when one or both of you may not be fully committed to couplehood, it's best to own little or nothing jointly and to keep most of your cash in separate accounts, to minimize future disputes over joint property. Both of you can contribute equally to a shared checking account for common expenses like the rent or mortgage, food, and utilities. If there's a major income disparity—you make $35,000 a year but your lover brings in $75,000—then chip in proportional amounts.

As the relationship ripens, you and your partner may want to draw up a **living-together agreement** to avert painful surprises in the future. In this document, address such issues as how you'll own property, if you'll hold income in joint or individual accounts, and what will happen if you separate. If your financial lives are comparatively uncomplicated, this could be a homemade document drawn to clarify your arrangements. Once you start building up assets and income, however, you might want to hire a matrimonial or family lawyer. This attorney can draw up a contract stating that all property acquired while you live together, other than that which either of you receives as a gift or inheritance, is to be owned jointly. Any income derived from such property would also be owned jointly. In addition, the agreement could stipulate that should you break up, voluntarily or involuntarily, the property will be sold and the proceeds divided, unless you both agree otherwise at that time.

The apartment you rent or the home you share can be a particular locus of contention if you come to a parting of the ways. The key point to remember is that the property belongs only to the person whose name is on the lease or the deed, regardless of who makes rent or mortgage payments. If the named person leaves, dies, or ends the romance, the partner has no legal right to remain in the home. For mutual protection, both names can go on the lease or deed. Remember, though, that each person will then become legally liable for the entire amount owed if the partner doesn't pay up.

Buying a home can be a disconcerting experience, especially if you are gay. Although it is against the law for a seller to reject an offer or a lender to deny a mortgage because a couple is unmarried or gay, you could face tacit discrimination. Once you find a house, condo, or co-op to buy, you will have to choose between two legal arrangements if you plan to buy the place jointly. Joint ownership with right of survivorship means that you and your lover own the property and one of you will inherit it immediately if the other dies. Ownership as tenants in common means that each person owns a half share of the home. If you die, half the property will go to your next of kin unless a will specifies otherwise. Be sure to talk through this issue together to avoid painful future surprises.

In the event that you and your lover split after decades of devotion, the biggest financial pitfall is likely to be the equitable division of retirement assets. This can be a disaster if you've been paying most of the household bills while your companion has been plumping up his or her retirement account. A carefully drawn living-together contract can go a long way toward protecting both of you, particularly the financially vulnerable partner.

You may also want to grant your partner a **durable power of attorney**, allowing him or her to make financial decisions for you if you become incompetent. Similarly, you probably will want to get a **health care proxy**, a document that permits a non-relative to make medical decisions for an incapacitated patient. This will also give your lover the right to visit should you end up in a hospital intensive care unit—an entitlement normally limited to close family members. In addition, draw up a will to provide for your companion, since he or she will have no automatic rights of inheritance. If you need a kick to get you to the attorney's office, imagine this scene or a close variation: You own a house that you share with a lover whom your family has never accepted; you die without a will and those relatives automatically inherit the love nest. Not a pretty picture for your beloved.

Wills, trusts, and other estate-planning tools are all steps toward getting you the legal protections that a married couple would receive automatically. Because the law doesn't step in to resolve conflicting demands or ensure equitable distribution among unmarried couples after separation or death, it is critical that the two of you work together on your financial affairs, perhaps with a lawyer and CPA or financial adviser. The more you settle now, the less chance for confusion later—which is a fine state of affairs for any twosome.

TO MARRY OR NOT TO MARRY

Living together is no longer a precursor of wedding bells; it's now a lifelong alternative to marriage. Over the past decade the number of unmarried couples living together grew 72% to 5.5 million couples, according to the U.S. Census Bureau. Here are the financial pluses and minuses of both arrangements:

If you get married, you . . .

+ Are eligible for spousal employee benefits—including health insurance.
+ May qualify for lower car insurance rates.
+ Can file negligence or malpractice suits if your spouse is hurt or disabled.
+ Will not have to pay estate taxes on inheritance from your spouse.
+ Will probably qualify for your deceased spouse's pension or Social Security benefits.
− Must pay the marriage income tax penalty (to be phased out by 2009).
− May have to pay the high costs of divorce if you break up.
− Will receive a lower Social Security benefit (in a dual-income marriage).
− May not be eligible to continue receiving pension or Social Security benefits of your deceased previous spouse.

If you live together, you . . .

+ Will not have to pay marriage income tax penalty.
+ Can skirt the legal entanglements of divorce.
+ Will continue receiving pension and Social Security benefits of deceased previous spouse.
− May not be eligible for spousal employee benefits.
− Will not be automatically named guardian of your partner's child, if your partner should die.
− Do not have automatic visitation rights to see your partner in intensive or critical care units of hospitals.
− Will have to pay estate taxes if the estate you inherit from your deceased partner is worth more than $1 million (in 2002).

Planning a Divorce

If you and your soon-to-be ex become enmeshed in unrelenting quarrels, you might want to seek a professional divorce mediator to smooth your parting. Marriage or family therapists, financial planners, even attorneys, may be trained to serve as divorce mediators. Lawyers usually charge their standard hourly fee. Therapists, psychologists, social workers, and ministers generally have lower fees; some even offer sliding scales based on your ability to pay. A simple divorce mediation, limited to financial affairs rather than custody issues, might involve two to eight one-hour sessions at $100 to $350 an hour, depending on where you live. The mediator will work with the two of you to carve out a compromise but will not take sides. The result probably will be faster, cheaper, and less rancorous than a solution carved out by warring lawyers. After mediation, use a lawyer to review the agreement you reached and to file the necessary legal papers.

In uncomplicated cases, if you and your ex-partner are equally committed to going through the process with minimum damage, you might consider handling your own divorce. Suitable candidates: couples in their twenties or thirties who have little or no property and either have no children or have agreed on who'll get custody. In some states, such as Arizona, California, and Texas, independent paralegals run thriving businesses handling divorce paperwork for their customers for fees of a few hundred dollars. To find such a service, check the classifieds in your telephone book or local newspaper under the headings "Divorce Assistance" or "Lawyer Alternatives."

Even if you can handle your own divorce, however, it may be wiser not to do so. It's best to seek legal help—either for a limited consultation or for ongoing representation—if you are confused about your legal rights or overwhelmed by the financial complexities. Certainly consult a lawyer if your spouse files legal papers that seem to contradict the facts or spirit of your prior agreements and discussions. If your divorce is complicated because you have hard-to-value assets, are engaged in bankruptcy proceedings, or are disputing ownership of valuable property, don't hesitate to get the specialized help you need from an attorney, accountant, real estate agent, or financial planner.

The traditional "big three" considerations of divorce are alimony, child support, and property settlements. Here are the basics about all of them:

- **Alimony.** This is the amount of money one ex-spouse is legally bound to give the other under a decree of divorce, separate maintenance, or written separation agreement. In general, alimony is treated as taxable income for the person who gets it, while the one writing the alimony checks can usually deduct the periodic payments. Unrestricted alimony is rarely awarded these days. More likely, a spouse who hasn't worked outside the home (or hasn't done so recently) will get some degree of support for a limited time. The amount and duration of alimony increasingly are determined by each party's earning ability, the length of the marriage, and the recipient's nonmonetary contribution to the union. Some counties have adopted financial schedules to help judges determine equitable support levels. But you and your ex-spouse can make your own arrangements outside of court that differ from the guidelines.

- **Child support.** If you have a child and are divorcing, even though you and your ex cease being husband and wife, your roles as parents continue. Each state sets its own guidelines for determining child support. Two factors are usually paramount: the child's needs and the parent's ability to pay. In order to prevent kids from suffering financially, child support payments must continue until the youngest child is 18 or 21, depending on state law. Child support payments are neither taxable to the recipient nor deductible by the payer.

  To compute the amount you or your spouse might be required to pay, get a copy of your state's support formula from a court clerk or attorney. Then calculate the income of both parents and the needs of your children that your state factors into its support formula. Your award may differ from the norm if the noncustodial parent has a notably high or low income or if either parent has remarried or has a live-in mate.

  When estimating their kids' future expenses, wise parents consider costs that go beyond the scope of the typical formula. By including a cost-of-living adjustment clause in the settlement agreement, for example, parents can ensure that inflation won't erode the buying power of future child support. It may also prevent a return to court to seek an upward adjustment of the amount a few years down the line, with the attendant expense and aggravation. In addition, make sure you and your soon-to-be ex decide who will pay for the following: your children's health insurance; future higher-education costs (if you're aiming to send your children to Ivy League schools, be sure your ex-spouse understands the level of contribution he or she will be expected to contribute); medical expenses and deductibles not covered by the support formula; and special school expenses such as class trips, activities fees, sports uniforms, and equipment.

  Determine, too, how your children's expenses will be met if you or your ex-husband or -wife dies or becomes disabled. You may require that one or both parents maintain life insurance and disability coverage at least until the children turn 21 or complete their education.

- **Property settlements.** These are one-time transfers of cash or other assets upon divorce. You can undoubtedly quickly identify some of your shared property—the house, the car, the checking and savings accounts. To get your fair share of the joint pie, however, consider the less obvious assets: the value of a professional license, the cash value of life insurance, your spouse's businesses or hobbies, the gold coins or savings bonds in the safe-deposit box, even such things as stock options, frequent flier miles, season tickets, and club memberships.

When it comes to dividing the assets, state laws consider the nature and duration of the partnership. Rulings vary widely depending on the judge and your state. In the community property states (Arizona, California, Idaho, Louisiana, Nevada, New Mexico, Texas, and Washington, with similar legislation in Wisconsin), each spouse is co-owner of any property acquired by either spouse during the marriage if a joint effort was made in acquiring the property. Any gifts or inheritances that one person received during the marriage are usually excluded, but growth in those assets may be considered joint property if the spouse contributed significantly to the increase. (Community property laws differ among the states, however, so if you are a resident of one, be sure to learn about the specific regulations that apply.)

Remember that you may well have rights to your partner's pension assets as part of the divorce settlement. In community property states, only the portion of the retirement plans earned during the marriage is subject to division. In most other states, a court would consider all retirement benefits in arriving at an equitable distribution of the marital assets.

If both of you have pension plans and Individual Retirement Accounts, the simplest solution is for each of you to keep the accounts that are in your own name. Should the amounts be vastly unequal, you can make up the difference in the way you divvy up other assets. Another option is for each of you to keep a specific portion of the plan (or plans). This choice is a bit more complex, since a lawyer must then draw up something called a **Qualified Domestic Relations Order** (or **QDRO**, pronounced "quadro") for a judge to approve. This is an order from the court to the retirement plan administrator, explaining how the pension plan's benefits are to be assigned to each party in a divorce. The options include an immediate distribution to an IRA owned by the alternate payee; monthly payments at retirement age; or an immediate full payout, in which case the alternate payee will owe income taxes on the money. You probably don't need a QDRO to make an immediate transfer from your spouse's IRA to your own, however, or for a payment directly to you. But if you get an IRA distribution and do not roll it over within 60 days, you will owe income tax on the amount you receive plus a 10% premature distribution penalty if you are under age 59½.

As for Social Security, if you were married for 10 years or longer, you will be eligible to collect benefits based on your ex-spouse's earnings record when you reach age 62, assuming you have been divorced for at least two years and have not remarried. Those benefits are equal to half the amount your former spouse is eligible to collect, including the period after your marriage was dissolved. If you have worked for a number of years, your Social Security benefits based on your own earnings record may be greater than the derivative benefit based on your former spouse's earnings. In that case you'll want to collect benefits based on your own record, since you can't get both.

When the divorce agreement has been signed and sealed, you may be ready to take a deep breath—and perhaps a celebratory glass of bubbly. Don't lighten up quite yet, however. While you have scaled the major hurdles, there may still be a few stumbling blocks to navigate. For instance, you may have to:

- **Examine your insurance policies.** If your ex-spouse is named beneficiary of your life insurance, change the designation to your children or other heirs. Reconsider the amounts of your life and disability coverage, too. You may need more coverage if you are about to become the sole financial support for your children, or less if the principal aim of the insurance was to provide for your spouse. If you have a car, make sure you have auto insurance in your own name. You may need new homeowners or renters insurance as well.
- **Update your will.** You'll probably want to exclude your ex-mate and choose new heirs. At the same time, destroy any powers of attorney or health care proxies you may have given your ex-spouse and decide if you want someone else to have them instead.
- **Unbundle your joint accounts.** Take your spouse's name off savings, brokerage, and other accounts, according to your property settlement agreement. Similarly, cancel joint credit cards, phone cards, and the like. Otherwise your ex-spouse can continue to use them and you will be financially responsible for the bills.
- **Spread the news.** Friends and relatives probably know already, but you might also want to inform your children's teachers, the pediatrician, your landlord, and perhaps even potential matchmakers.

Reducing Financial Risk in Remarriage

Love may be lovelier the second time around, but it's also more complex. Most of the 1.7 million Americans a year who remarry will bring to the altar their own children and assets, commitments, and obligations—in short, the emotional and financial baggage of adult life. The first marriage is nearly always still exacting some kind of payment from at least one spouse, not to mention the lingering wounds and emotional scars. For all these reasons, don't rush to merge your financial lives as you pass from courtship to cohabiting and remarriage. Take time to build up trust and deal with problems as they arise.

An honest airing of priorities combined with careful planning, however, can help smooth the choppy passages. Before you exchange new rings, tell each other what you own and what you owe. Discuss your long- and short-term goals and objectives. Before your families blend, lay out each spouse's financial responsibilities. Then, create a plan to accommodate them. If each parent pays only for his or her progeny, for example, you will need to keep separate budgets for everything, plus another set of numbers if you have children with your new mate.

The toughest question is likely to be whether to merge your assets and liabilities completely, partially, or not at all. If you keep financial assets separate, you may need legal advice to ward against the automatic commingling of property under some state laws. The best way to do this is by executing a so-called **property status agreement**— either as part of a premarital agreement or after you're married—noting who owns what and forfeiting any spousal claims to specified assets.

Many financial advisers and attorneys favor **prenuptial contracts** for their clients who are about to start second marriages. These documents often make sense intellectually, though drafting them may have a chilling effect emotionally. While prenups primarily discuss property arrangements, you can include more mundane topics as well, right down to how you share the housework or who will get custody of Fido if the marriage goes to the dogs. Later, if unforeseen events trigger the need, you and your spouse may decide to draw up a postmarital agreement, dealing with the same sorts of issues.

Whether you and your partner decide on a written agreement before or after the nuptial day, certain rules apply. First, consult an attorney to make sure the document conforms to your state's laws. Second, remember that both parties must enter freely into the agreement—well in advance of the wedding date if it's a prenup, lest it smack of coercion. Finally, full disclosure of the assets, liabilities, and obligations of your financial life is imperative. If the court believes one of you is trying to sell the other a false bill of goods, the judge may well strike down the agreement in the event of divorce.

Estate planning poses particularly delicate problems for blended families, since parents may want to protect their biological offspring without neglecting or offending their new spouse and stepchildren. Even if your new partner has promised to provide for your kids as if they were his or her own, you may still feel queasy. After all, mythmakers from the Brothers Grimm to Walt Disney have helped create a pretty bad rap for stepparents.

One way to keep your legacy intact is to direct your lawyer to draft a **trust** naming your children as beneficiaries. (For more on trusts, see Chapter 12.) Upon your death, the assets you've designated will fund the trust, which will be managed by a trustee of your choice. The money can then be parceled out in lump sums when the kids reach the ages you specify. If you want your new spouse to enjoy the benefits of the wealth while he or she is still living, draft a so-called **bypass trust**. After your death, your spouse can get any income thrown off by your legacy and, with the trustee's approval, withdraw part of the principal if he or she needs it to pay for important expenses such as medical bills. When your spouse dies, the assets will then flow directly to your children.

At the same time you're redoing wills, review your life insurance to protect your extended family. Consider changing beneficiary designations on existing policies and retirement plans, just as you did after your divorce. Eyeball other forms of insurance, too, for duplications and omissions in coverage. If your new mate comes equipped with a teenage road devil, for instance, make sure your auto policy reflects the fact.

Keeping your new house in order may involve some unexpected strains. Blended families, bulging with kids from two marriages or more, frequently find themselves squeezed to cover the steep child care costs and other living expenses that accompany large households. Moreover, the two-tiered nature of many blended families—older children from first unions, toddlers from the new marriage—means that parents may face child-rearing expenses over many more years than other households do. In particular, the kids' college costs may well soak up all or most of the money that the parents might have used for their retirement.

If that unhappy choice sounds familiar to you, try cutting your spending by at least 5%. Small economies can make a bigger difference than you think. Even so, many parents will still have to make tough choices between fully funding their own retirement years or bankrolling their kids' education. Only you and your mate can make this decision, of course. From a financial perspective, however, it's much wiser to provide for your retirement. There are plenty of educational compromises you and your teenager can consider, including community colleges, state schools, and loan and grant programs. What's more, the kids will eventually make it on their own if they have the ambition. Your retirement, on the other hand, is ultimately your own responsibility.

CHAPTER 20

Kids and Money

Contemporary kids appear to have a startling financial sophistication: They know that money doesn't grow on trees—it comes from automated teller machines. When parents say they can't afford a toy, credit-wise moppets urge Mom and Dad to charge it.

But for all that, most kids' actual understanding of personal money management runs not much deeper than that of Bart Simpson in the cartoon *The Simpsons*. Parents complain that children spend all their money on junk, don't know the value of a dollar, and cannot save a dime. If you have any doubt that some instruction is in order, consider this:

A 2000 survey by the Jump$tart Coalition for Personal Financial Literacy, measuring 12th graders' knowledge of personal finance basics, found on average that only 51.9 % of the questions were answered correctly, a failing grade based upon the typical grade scale used by schools. A 1999 study by the National Council on Economic Education, the nation's leading provider of economic education materials and resources for teachers, found that only 38% of high school students understood the purpose of the stock markets is to bring together the buyers and sellers of securities.

Yet the Y generation needs to learn financial know-how more than any in recent memory. For one thing, they encounter—or at least covet—serious money sooner than their predecessors did. In the '60s, youngsters may have wheeled around on no-gear Schwinn bikes costing $50, but their 2000 counterparts often hunger for mountain bikes retailing for $300 or more. By the dawn of the twenty-first century, teenagers were shelling out a total of more than $155 billion a year. Most of it goes for food, clothes, and entertainment, says Teenage Research Unlimited, a market research firm in North-brook, Ill. Though most teens say they want to salt away funds for college, more than half save nothing at all, except for more expensive purchases.

So what does it take to teach your kids the skills and discipline they need to make the American dream come true for them? The most successful financial training devices are the same four simple strategies that have been deployed by parents since the Ozzie and Harriet era:

1. Give youngsters an allowance, to prove to them that there are limits to spending power.
2. Pay them for out-of-the-ordinary chores, to show that effort produces rewards.
3. Encourage them to save, so they become accustomed to delaying gratification.
4. Teach them the basics of investing, so they have the opportunity to make their savings grow faster.

But far and away the most powerful teaching tool is parental example. If you give money to your kid grudgingly, that conveys something to your offspring. So, too, if you're in a constant frazzle over your maxed-out credit cards. Whether you donate to charity, return the difference when a cashier hands you too much change, or brag at the dinner table about cleverly cheating on your taxes—these daily choices ram home important messages to your kids on a regular basis. Your offspring will pay far more attention to what you practice than to what you preach, so your first task is to set the pattern you want them to follow.

Your second obligation is to draw an honest picture of the family's finances, so your kids understand that the green stuff doesn't grow behind the slots in bank machines. No, you don't have to reveal your precise income or net worth for Junior to trumpet around the schoolyard. But you should discuss some of the financial choices the family is facing. Example: "We're not getting a new car for a while because we're building a college fund for your sister." Over time, the young ones will develop a sense that there are limits to what they—and the family—can spend.

Early on—through your example—teach them the difference between things the family wants and things the family needs. Older kids—age nine and up—should be invited to express opinions on family financial options presented to them.

The following guidelines will help you enrich your kids' financial education at every age and stage. Be warned, though: The suggestions below require time and attention to implement.

Starting Out: Toddlers to Preteens

At this age, your child can start learning basic home economics, money trade-offs, and key financial concepts such as saving money and spending limits. The specifics on what you can do to help:

- **Teach the basics early.** By trusting your own imagination, you can devise simple situations to teach rudimentary money skills to your preschooler. At the supermarket, for instance, he can count apples as he puts them in the plastic bag. Give him the necessary dollars to pay for the apples, get a receipt—then let him keep a few coins in change for himself. Rugrats love to push buttons: Let yours punch in the numbers at the ATM while you explain where the dollars come from. Real-world experience, not merely explanation, increases a child's understanding.

  By age five, a child can usually recognize pennies and perhaps nickels, dimes, and other coins. Don't be dismayed if your preschooler thinks a nickel is worth more than a dime, however. A young child almost always thinks that larger coins are worth more than smaller ones. A seven-year-old won't choose the nickel over the dime, can generally name all the coins, and will know how many pennies are in each.

  Older children begin getting more interested in money, perhaps even saving for a future purchase. Take advantage of this curiosity by involving your child in simple projects. She can help you clip grocery coupons and then track down the items at the store. Give her the cents you save and encourage her to put them in her piggy bank or savings account. If your child asks why you are buying the jar with the red label and not the blue one, explain that yours is cheaper, tastier, thicker, or vitamin enriched. Make use of everyday opportunities—a visit to the mall, a stop at the bank—to give your children a sense of where money comes from, where it goes, and why. Even when you leave for the office in the morning, you can help your preschooler understand that you must work to earn the money needed to help pay for the house, the food—and, yes, her toys.

- **Give your child a regular allowance.** By the time children can count—about age five or six—they are ready for that all-American financial institution, the weekly allowance. Surveys suggest that only a minority of kids get a regular stipend, though child-development experts strongly favor the practice. No-allowance youngsters mainly nag for cash as needed or get haphazard handouts. Parents may be surprised to learn that youngsters much prefer a regular income and that they are less likely to run out of cash and more likely to save when they have a regular income. They also feel more independent.

Settling on the appropriate sum for the first allowance is the parents' next decision—not an easy one, either. You'll want to consider your child's age, your household income, and the affluence of the community where you live. The average allowance for six- to eight-year-olds is $2 or so a week. The amount should be enough for the child to purchase a candy bar or other small treat for himself (under your supervision), with some change left for the piggy bank. To make amounts grow faster, you might offer to match any coins saved and put your money plus his into an interest-bearing savings account.

An easy rule of thumb is to give a dollar a week for each grade a child is in. (Another one is a dollar for every year of their age.) However, this may not be enough for older children.) Be open and clear about what the money is to cover. Decide if the young recipient can spend the whole amount for fun or if she must save part of the money to cover contributions to the church or synagogue or future purchases.

By third grade a child can generally comprehend the difference between fixed and discretionary expenses. Expand the allowance to cover one or two essentials such as school lunch and bus fare but still allow some recreational spending. Then if he blows his lunch money on baseball cards, stifle your pity (or annoyance) and show him how to make a peanut-butter sandwich to brown-bag from home. As he gets older, increase the allowance annually—perhaps on a birthday or when the child is promoted to a higher grade. When students reach age 10, parents can start doling out a dollar or two for each year of a youngster's age, depending on what he will be expected to pay for. These more princely sums may be expected to cover a wider range of both fun stuff and necessities.

As much as possible, let your children disburse their money as they wish. Setting narrow limits for how they can spend defeats the purpose of the allowance. You, of course, retain veto power over any purchase that's unsafe, unhealthy, or in violation of your family's principles. Apart from that, don't fret if they go a little wild at first. They'll simmer down once they realize that no more money is forthcoming to bail them out. Let them live with their mistakes, rather than shield them from the disagreeable consequences. Loans should be rare and are best given only to kids who are age nine or older. If you decide to permit advances (all of us come up short occasionally), charge some token interest—a dime on each dollar, say—so your child learns early that credit carries a price. Alternatively, you could have the child pay you back within a specified time period and owe you a "free" laundry folding or lawn mowing as "interest."

While you should let a child live with his own spending mistakes, take a tougher line when your offspring are careless with expensive stuff that you have provided. If, for example, your daughter forgets to lock her bike and it's stolen, don't replace it immediately. Let her feel the loss for a while—and perhaps buy a cheaper bike next time or let her chip in with part of her allowance. If your son owes $12 for a lost library book, let him pay out of his savings. No savings? Then let him take on extra jobs around the house to earn the $12.

Child psychologists and financial experts generally discourage tying the basic allowance to the performance of routine household chores. Your son or daughter should carry out those tasks as part of ordinary family duty. While experts discourage linking the regular allowance to simple tasks, they almost uniformly applaud paying a child for taking on special projects around the house.

Your intuition is probably the best guide as to which tasks are part of being a family member, and therefore done free, and which ones are beyond the call of duty. Some parents pay youngsters for cleaning the bathrooms but not for table setting or walking the dog. Baby-sitting might be done free in the late afternoon, performed for a "family discount" on weeknights, but command full market rate on Saturday nights.

One caveat: Don't be super-nitpicky about the way household jobs are performed. You want the work, paid or unpaid, to be a positive experience that your child will be eager to repeat. Also, there is no need to lavish cold cash on your children to reward high marks at school or exemplary behavior. Some things should be done for their own sake; otherwise you're encouraging a young blackmailer-in-training to expect a payoff for every positive action. If your child has made some monumental effort sitting still during the four-hour car trip to your cousin's house, honor the accomplishment by baking his favorite cake or going to a ball game together.

Don't cut off your child's allowance "earnings" as punishment—that merely encourages the notion that bad behavior is a negotiable item and not simply unacceptable. When your child misbehaves, one appropriate recourse is to banish access to the TV or take away other privileges, rather than cutting the weekly handout.

- **Encourage saving.** By age six or so, your child is ready (with your help and your signature) to open a savings account. Before marching your youngster downtown, however, check with a bank officer first. Sadly, many commercial institutions no longer accept small deposits even from kids, or they charge punitive fees. If you decide to proceed, ask a bank representative what identification is required, since the policy varies among institutions. Typically, you will have to provide identification for yourself (a driver's license will do) and a Social Security number for your child. The most relaxed regulations are typically found at credit unions, and many of them welcome small accounts.

If you're willing for your youthful saver to bank by mail, the Young Americans Bank in

Denver (311 Steele St., Denver, CO 80206; 303-321-2265; www.theyoungamericans. org) is a child-friendly institution that offers services for anyone up to age 22. (It is part of the Young Americans Education Foundation.) Kids can open accounts in person or by mail with a minimum deposit of $10. The Young Americans Bank has everything an adult bank has including savings and checking accounts, loans, ATMs, and credit cards.

If you have a pint-size plutocrat with serious money on hand—say, more than $1,000—you might help her invest in U.S. savings bonds, a certificate of deposit, or a no-load money-market fund to attain a higher return than standard passbook savings accounts provide.

In addition to establishing formal savings accounts for their offspring, many parents attach strings to the weekly allowance to encourage (or enforce) regular thrift. One popular device is the so-called three-jar system, which takes myriad variations among different families. Typically, a chunk of the weekly income is allocated to one container for spending, a second is for charitable donations, and a third (and possibly a fourth) is for savings (which may be divided into short-term and long-term).

To soften the sting and make saving more palatable, help establish a savings goal— something the child longs to do or own. It could be a puppy, a leather jacket, or just a small toy that his heart is set on. Once the price (or the child's share of the price) is established, you two can discuss how much might be saved from the allowance each week and how much might be earned from extra chores or outside jobs.

On the sticky question of savings withdrawals, you will have to be the referee. A reasonable compromise is to make a clear distinction at the start between short-term and long-term savings goals—putting some funds aside for a new CD player, say, and reserving other dollars for college expenses.

Freer Rein: The Teen Years

This is the time to start edging your youngsters toward financial independence. It's when you should initiate discussions about paying for college education or technical training, allow him or her to take on a part-time job and open a checking account, and get a credit card in her name on your account. Perhaps most important, it's your last chance to keep your kid from developing bad money habits he might later regret. Here's how to set your teen straight about money:

- **Share your spending decisions.** Let adolescents participate in the family's more complex buying decisions. If you decide to get a new car, for example, read consumer magazines with your kids and discuss what models and options offer true value for money. Talk with them about how you plan to pay for the purchase. If you're getting a car loan, let them see that you're shopping around to compare interest rates and other terms. Similarly, if you are buying a house, keep them abreast of the bidding and counterbidding that go on, even if you shield them from the actual amounts involved. Money is a marker of family values, and teens should learn that the expenditure of big money warrants a big investment of time and thought.

- **Discuss the cost of future education.** Sometime in junior high, your child should begin learning about how you plan to pay for his future education—especially if you'll require his help. If you can afford to pay only for the local technical school or community college, say so. That gives teenagers time to earn money if they want to go somewhere else or to boost their grades to qualify for scholarship money. Plus, when children understand the limits of the family's resources, they are likely to take their studies and their grades more seriously.

  Review savings plans that you have in place for your child's education. If there are substantial sums in a savings account that might earn more in a CD or other conservative investment, make the switch. The earlier you and your teen start planning for his future education or training for the real-world job market, the better the chances that your joint efforts will turn dreams into reality.

- **Expand the allowance.** You're virtually certain to pony up more pocket money as your child grows more independent.

  A 2000 Rand youth poll found that 13- to 15-year-old boys had an average weekly allowance of $33.80 (girls averaged $39.65 a week); 16- to 19-year-old boys got $48.74 (girls: $52.15). Most of the money slips away fast—on food and snacks, clothing, movies, and entertainment. Around 70% say they save a portion of their personal income; however, 71% of that saving is on a short-term basis (two to three months) for something like a bike, stereo, or computer. Only 22% say they are saving for a long-term goal such as college, a car, or a vacation.

  To prevent squandermania at your house, impose some structure on your adolescent's spending. The early teens are a good time to switch from a weekly stipend to a monthly one, so your potentially prodigal son will learn to budget money over longer periods of time. The allowance should be large enough for him to manage most spending for clothes, gifts, fast-food meals, entertainment, and related pleasures. Once a spending plan is established, though, make your teen stick to it. If she blows her budget on designer jeans and can't afford a jacket, let her chill out. She won't make the same mistake twice.

As your teen matures, continue to extend the time between pay periods and further increase the scope of what the allowance covers. For instance, you might exclude clothing from the monthly stipend and instead provide a clothing allowance twice a year, before school starts in the fall and again in the spring. By the mid- to late teens, your child should be managing most of the spending events of his life—just as he signs up for SATs on his own and arranges his social agenda. Managing his money is, after all, essentially a microcosm for managing his life.

To prepare for budgeting during the post–high school years, let your teenager spend a summer or a semester monitoring expenses, either by recording money spent in a small notebook or by using a computer-based personal finance program such as Quicken or Managing Your Money. Then, with your teen, draw up a list of all the income he has (from allowances, jobs, and gifts) and all the expenses he should shoulder. To bridge the gap between income and outgo, decide together where expenses can be cut and how much income should be raised to bridge the gap. The goal is to have your teen stay on a budget for at least six months without having to ask a parent for financial help before he flies the family nest for college or a job.

• **Limit your teen's work hours.** According to a 2001 UPROMISE study, *Learning and Earning: Working in College*, 57% of college students age 16 to 24 work full- or part-time. On average, working college students put in 25 hours a week at the job and earn $7.50 an hour.

But that juicy income can carry hidden costs in terms of academic performance and attention to school activities. The UPROMISE survey reports that college students who worked part-time, around 10 hours a week, generally eliminate only non-productive activities such as watching television because of their work. In addition, students who work part-time have a slightly higher GPA than similar students. On the other hand, full-time employment (35 hours or more per week) has a negative effect on students' studies. Of students who work full-time, 36% report work reduces class choices, 40% say it limits their class schedule, 30% say work limits the number of classes they take, and 26% report it limits access to the library.

You also shouldn't let your high-school-age children sacrifice their current education (and possibly their chances of getting into a good college) just to support a flashy car, a clotheshorse habit—or worse. Be vigilant about hours. High school sophomores can probably handle a 10-hour workweek; juniors and seniors can usually manage 15 hours. Remind the new worker, however, that school is his primary responsibility. If grades slip, give him one report card period to bring them back up—or require him to resign from the workplace.

If your teen is dead set on earning money, and many high schoolers are, let him start with a summer job to harvest both money and career-related experience. Or have him start his own summer business like tutoring, baby-sitting, baking, or car or lawn care. Such work might also give him a really clear idea of what he doesn't want to do for a living. Many students have come off summers toiling in food service or retail sales, making little more than the minimum wage, with a strong determination to prepare for something better than another junk job.

If your son or daughter starts making money, offer some guidance on how to handle this newfound affluence. Before the first paycheck arrives, set up an income-allocation plan with your teen. This will force him to manage his salary more seriously. The 2001 *Parents, Youth & Money Survey*, conducted by the American Savings Education Council, reported that 38% of parents say that their 15- to 17-year-olds are saving for college tuition. Don't hesitate to ask your future scholar to contribute—he'll take college and his grades more seriously. One caveat, though: Don't eliminate your child's allowance when he takes an outside job. Doing so will only send the message that he was better off accepting your handout without exerting himself.

Taking increased responsibility is the name of the game as the child is finishing high school. When kids hit their late teens, many parents expect them to pay their own way for much of the fun stuff that allowances covered in the earlier years. According to the 2001 *Parents, Youth & Money Survey,* 58% of parents say they require their child to save some of the money he or she receives from allowance, paid employment, or other sources.

- **Encourage volunteering as an alternative to work.** Don't overlook the value in nonpaid extracurricular activities. In particular, don't let your teens waste a summer vacation sitting around the house. By planning ahead, parents and kids can make sure the child does something enriching every summer, something that broadens his or her horizons beyond the local mall. Remember, colleges look favorably at students who volunteer their time to help others. For leads, your child can try the school placement office, churches, service organizations such as the Lions or Kiwanis, and local government officials who administer job training programs. If one of these avenues pays off, you might agree to increase the child's allowance or compensate for the forgone earnings in some other fashion.

- **Introduce checking accounts and credit cards.** Before your child packs off to college, give him practice in handling those two essential tools of adult life: a checking account and a credit card. Let him reconcile the monthly bank statements himself. Keep resources finite, however: Don't agree to cover bounced checks or overdraft charges.

Opinions vary on whether a teen needs a credit card, but many parents like the security that plastic provides their child in emergencies. One way to get teens started—under your supervision—is with a secured credit card, where you or your child pays a deposit of $500 or so and then the cardholder can charge only up to that amount. You can also have a card issued in your child's name on the account in which you are the primary cardholder. (His or her expenses will show up on your bill, so it's easy to monitor spending.)

Debit, cash, or stored-value cards for teens are available. With most of these cards, parents transfer money into an online account, which kids 13 and older tap with a credit-card lookalike. Any store or Web site that accepts Visa or MasterCard will take the secured versions of these cards. Since the money is already in the account, there are no interest or finance charges, but there may be an annual fee.

If you opt to give your child a stored-value card or a traditional credit card, review the monthly bill with him. Make sure he purchased everything that is charged on the card, then discuss whether to make a full or partial payment. If you opt for a credit card, insist that the balance be paid in full each month. On rare and special occasions—the skis that he's been dreaming of have finally gone on sale—the limit might be stretched to three months, but let him swallow the finance charges. Well before your teen leaves the nest for college, make sure he understands the meaning of credit-card finance charges, grace periods, minimum payments, and late fees.

- **Teach basic investing concepts.** Some children take to the financial markets at an early age; others don't. But many parents find youngsters get more curious about investing when they reach their teens. If you really want to engage your offspring in the stock market, you're best off using real money, either yours or theirs, once you're assured of their genuine interest. It's hard for anyone to stay interested in a hypothetical portfolio for long.

Smart investors of any age look at things they know, so you can tap into your teen's enthusiasm for fast food, sporting goods, or computers. Let him make his own investment decisions—using, say, 10% to 20% of his savings. You will have to do the actual buying and selling, though. Under state laws, a minor isn't legally permitted to trade securities, so you'll have to purchase the shares and hold them in your name as the child's custodian. The securities then legally belong to the youngster, but you are nominally in charge until he reaches the legal age specified under state law (usually 18 or 21).

A few brokers will execute a child's buy and sell orders directly, particularly if they are acquainted with the parents and if the young customer knows what he or she is doing. Some brokers say that kids often are more rational and less emotional about investing decisions than adults are. In particular, they're more willing to cut their losses and admit when they've made a mistake.

Mutual funds might, in truth, make more sense for the fledgling investor, since they offer diversity and professional management. But funds are a tougher concept for teens to get a handle on, since they, as shareholders, don't directly own a piece of an individual company. One mutual fund that works specifically to teach children is SteinRoe Young Investor (800-403-KIDS; www.steinroe.com for a prospectus). The fund seeks long-term capital appreciation by investing 65% of its portfolio in companies that affect kids' lives. The rest of its holdings consist of companies that make products kids enjoy, such as toys or computer software. There is no sales commission, and investors receive an owner's manual full of investing information, a coloring book for younger kids, teaching materials for parents, and a certificate with the child's name on it. The minimum investment is $500, if you agree to have a fixed amount of at least $50 deposited automatically into the fund from a checking account each month.

A tax reminder: Until your son or daughter turns 14, the first $750 of his or her investment income is tax-free (in 2002) and the next $750 is taxed at the child's rate, usually 10%. But the rest of the money is taxed at your top rate. After the child turns 14 the "kiddie tax" no longer applies, and he or she starts paying federal tax on all income and capital gains at his or her own rate rather than yours.

Cutting Purse Strings: The College Years

Once your child reaches college age, you need to make abundantly clear in advance which expenses you will cover and which are your child's responsibility. And if your son or daughter doesn't know much about credit cards by now, this is the time to explain the rules and the risks of plastic. How to do it right:

• **Negotiate a realistic spending plan.** The summer before your child heads off to college, begin discussing a budget so your freshman-to-be knows exactly how much is available to spend. Don't just set an overall limit; draw up a list of the types of expenses you will and won't be willing to cover and set spending limits for each category. You might want to segregate certain critical necessities—textbooks, for example—and agree to pay for them separately. That way your young scholar won't be tempted to skimp on buying basic texts because he overspent on pizza. If you can afford it, you may want to foot most or all of the bills yourself and reserve your child's nest egg for graduate school, buying a house, or some other significant milestone. The important point is that you make clear up front how you expect to divide the financial responsibilities.

For convenience, have your child open a checking account at a bank where you have an account. You can then easily disburse funds either by telephone or by depositing money into her account in your branch. Whatever amount you agree to contribute, parcel out the funds periodically rather than writing a lump-sum check for the year. Fiscal discipline is tough if a student spender has to manage a single payout over many months. You'll be the best judge when your young adult is ready to manage larger amounts paid over a longer duration.

Initially, have your new collegian keep detailed records of where all the money is going. By Christmas break (or earlier, if problems arise), you can check the records to see where the budget needs to be revised—or if Junior's spending habits need reining in. Once the basic budgeting plan is established, it should set the pattern, with only minor modifications, until graduation.

- **Uses and abuses of credit.** Once kids hit the campus, they're fair game for credit-card issuers. In recent years, Citibank, American Express, Discover, and others have been flooding them with applications for pre-approved plastic, some of which carry interest rates of 15% or more. College kids age 18 or older need little more than a student ID to get a card with a credit line ranging from a few hundred dollars to several thousand. Nearly all the credit-issuing standards that apply to adults are waived for collegians—sometimes with dubious results. A 2000 Student Monitor survey reported that two-thirds of college students have a credit card in their own name. Nearly 83% of those students paid their own bills and 58% said they paid their monthly bill in full. The average amount of the 42% who carried a balance was $577. And 16% reported a balance of $1,000 or more.

Used judiciously, however, credit cards can help college students build a sound credit history, which will make it easier for them to get a job, rent an apartment, and obtain other kinds of credit after they graduate. In addition, they are convenient, safer than cash, and accepted more readily than checks, particularly if you are away from home. Without one, it's nearly impossible to rent a car or buy an airline ticket.

Consequently, despite the risk of getting carried away with newfound financial freedom, it makes sense for your collegian to have a card of his own and start building his own credit history. But as insurance for yourself, don't co-sign your child's accounts. If you do, his late payments could damage your credit report. (If he is carrying a card on an account where you are the primary cardholder, the bill will be sent to you, which is useful for monitoring his expenses. But you'll have to write the check and then dun him for payment.)

To limit the risk of debt piling up, restrict your child to one card in his own name—two max. Emphasize that credit cards are for limited use—textbooks and airline tickets, for example—or for emergencies. If your kid's in doubt about what qualifies as an emergency, tell him this: nothing that you can eat, drink, listen to, or wear on your back.

Warn your inexperienced cardholder that the terms of credit-card contracts are growing ever more complex. Many issuers, for example, have introduced so-called tiered rates, in which they commonly charge a lower interest rate for new purchases and a higher one for cash advances. Three other doubtful deals that card issuers have been pushing:

1. **Phony no-fee cards.** These spare you an annual fee, then sock it to you with other charges such as cash advances at interest rates above 20%.
2. **Cards that offer cut rates to big spenders.** This is not the lesson you want your freshman to be learning. Besides, when you read the fine print, it often turns out that moderate spenders are paying rates that are no deal at all.
3. **Teaser-rate cards.** These advertise rock-bottom interest rates that last only a few months before they're abruptly boosted by 10 percentage points or more.

Your son or daughter also needs to be aware of the harm that a bad credit rating can do. Explain that credit bureaus begin keeping tabs on the balance and payments as soon as a card is issued. Many creditors assess late fees if payment is not received by a certain date each month. This date (which varies among creditors) typically ranges from zero to 14 days beyond the payment due date. And be sure to mention that records of late-payment fees can remain part of your credit history for as long as seven years, hurting your chances of getting an apartment, a mortgage, car or education loans, and sometimes even utilities.

CHAPTER 21

Your Parents and Money

If you grew up in a financially secure home, you're probably more accustomed to accepting help from your parents than wondering what kind of help they might need from you. No matter how you were brought up, however, the issue of your aging parents' finances is an important one. Even if your mother and father are well off now—and especially if they're not—your parents may need your economic support or advice someday. Figuring out in advance whether your parents are likely to be financially independent for the rest of their lives will not only ease their later years, it will let you anticipate how their needs may affect your own financial future.

Whether or not your parents have plenty of money, you may need to offer other kinds of assistance—with housing, money management, and medical care—as their physical or mental powers wane. Contemplating these needs, too, can save both you and your parents from making the wrong decisions in an emergency.

Helping your parents can be a ticklish task. People who grew up during the Great Depression, as perhaps your parents did, came of age before the word "entitlements" entered our vocabulary and long before family secrets were routinely bared on *Oprah*. As a result, your parents may feel that their financial situation is their problem—and their business. They might also fear that your gentle questioning of their finances is little more than a covert attempt to extract money from them either before they die or after. Your parents could also be reluctant to divulge any information about their financial status, even though you would need details about their income and expenses in order to assess their solvency. In short, helping your parents with their money is as much a psychological exercise for you and them as a financial one.

If possible, try to discuss your parents' finances with your folks while they are feeling fairly flush and healthy. That's probably when they're in their early sixties. The longer you wait, the more serious the financial problems could become and the harder it may be for you to do much. For instance, if you don't have a talk with your father about money and he develops Alzheimer's, his memory may be too fuzzy to give you the guidance you need to get his finances in order.

How to Know Whether They Need Your Help

Unless your parents ask for your succor or you spot signals that they need it, you'll have to use your own instincts to decide whether to offer a hand. There are some clues that suggest it's time to step in, one way or another. If your normally fastidious parents start leaving their home a mess or you notice deteriorating personal hygiene, your mother and father are quietly saying: "I can't or won't take care of myself now." Also, the next time you visit your parents, take a look at their mail stack on the q.t. If you see unopened letters postmarked months ago or second or third billing notices from creditors, that's another strong hint that your services could be needed. One thing you could do to help: Get their mutual fund and dividend checks, Social Security payments, and any pension checks direct deposited into the bank. Pay close attention to any slippage in your parents' health. If you notice that your mother's vision is going, for instance, you may want to hire someone to help her with the chores. You might even offer to help write out checks for her bills—with her checks. Be certain, too, that your parents are getting any medication they need and not going without just to save money. If you're fairly certain that your offer to help will be taken kindly, by all means speak up. Otherwise it's probably better to keep mum until you feel your parents' health or welfare is at stake. Authority and dignity are especially crucial to older people, who often worry about losing both in their later years.

Talking Things Over

There's no best way to broach the subject of your parents' finances. One hint offered by psychologists: Draw up your own living will (see Chapter 12) and discuss it with your parents. This may ease the off-putting implication that they're the only ones who need to think about incapacitation. After they've helped you formalize your intentions, it may be easier to ask if they, too, might want to contemplate the future.

Otherwise, getting the ball rolling depends largely on the relationship between you and your parents. You might be able simply to plunge in, acknowledging your awkwardness but explaining the reasons for your questions. Alternatively, you may be more comfortable hiring a third party, such as a financial planner, to conduct a family financial discussion lasting two hours or longer. Try to find one who has experience conducting intergenerational planning sessions. So if you already work with a financial planner and admire his competence and style, you can ask him to be the discussion leader. If not, locate a planner who specializes in retirement issues; for advice on finding a reputable planner, see Chapter 3.

It's best to include all immediate family members in your financial talk with your parents. This way you'll head off possible misunderstandings about the point or nature of the conversation or any resentments about your taking the lead.

To keep this delicate talk on track, draw up a list of the questions you need answered. Start with the least sensitive ones and work up to the toughest ones, as shown below.

Questions to Ask Your Parents

- **Who are your advisers?** Be sure to get a list of the names and addresses or phone numbers of all the advisers they have, including their lawyer, broker, accountant, primary-care physician, and insurance agents. If they lack financial advisers but could use some, offer to introduce them to yours. Or tell them to read Chapter 3 of this book. You'll want to develop a close relationship with your parents' advisers since you may need to work with them at some point. In addition, you will find out if any of the advisers is in any way hurting your parents financially.
- **Where are your personal records kept?** You're looking here for the location of your parents' safe-deposit box; insurance policies; wills and any trusts; brokerage, bank, and mutual fund statements; and copies of their tax returns. Tell your parents that

you're asking not because you want to see these documents right now, but because you may need to review them at some time in the future. Do not ask for details about the contents of the will; if your parents want you to know how much you'll get after they die, they'll tell you. Learning about your parents' records will also suggest to you whether your mother and father own unnecessary insurance policies such as duplicate health insurance coverage or a life insurance policy that they can cancel.

- **What are your monthly expenses?** Tell your folks that you don't need the figures down to the nearest decimal point. You just want to know their rough outlays each month to be sure they have enough income to pay their bills, cover their essential expenses, and have something left over.
- **What is your income, and what are its sources?** This question could touch a nerve. So make it clear that you aren't looking for their exact gross income, just a rough idea so that you know how they're faring financially. It will help if your parents tell you which stocks, bonds, mutual funds, and real estate investments they own, the rough value of them, and why they are holding on to them. You also should find out whose name the investments are in, since there may be some estate-planning implications. If your parents seem to be open about discussing their investments, ask them for the numbers of their brokerage accounts and mutual funds, too; you may need these vital figures someday. If not, ask them to keep a written record of this information with their will.
- **Have you done any estate planning?** Would you like to do some? Here, you're just trying to find out whether your parents want to get their estate in order.
- **Where would you like to live if you couldn't keep living in your present home?** A section later in this chapter discusses housing alternatives for the elderly and offers some suggestions.
- **What life-prolonging measures, if any, would you want taken if you became terminally ill or hopelessly incapacitated?** This topic is critically important. By discussing it, you'll be certain that you'll know your parents' wishes should the occasion arise. (A fuller description of this topic follows.)
- **What funeral arrangements, if any, have you made?** Grim? Yes. Essential? Absolutely.

Don't criticize any answers you get from your parents. If you see areas that could use improvement or that your mother and father simply haven't thought about, note that the matter may warrant further consideration in the future.

Take notes during the discussion or, if no one objects, tape-record it. That way, if any confusion arises, you or any of the other participants can double-check what was said.

Documents That Could Help (also see Chapter 12)

If you and your parents foresee a time when you may have to start paying their bills, handling their investments, or possibly even sell their home for them, consider enlisting the help of a lawyer to draw up a document known as a **durable power of attorney** (also called a **health care power of attorney**). While many parents simply add an adult child's name to their bank accounts or other assets to facilitate access, doing so is not a great idea. If you're sued or get a divorce, some of your parents' assets ultimately could wind up in the hands of a creditor or your ex-spouse. What's more, if you apply for financial assistance (including college aid), your parents' assets may disqualify you. A durable power of attorney, by contrast, will give you the right to manage your parents' financial affairs while keeping all their assets in their names.

Don't wait to create a durable power of attorney until your parents start failing, though. In order to sign this document, your parents must be of sound mind. If they're reluctant to give you discretion over their affairs while they're still capable, have the lawyer add a "springing" clause, which gives you authority only if a judge in domestic relations court deems them incompetent. Such a clause, however, can create delays and complications, which is exactly what you're trying to avoid.

Virtually any lawyer can draw up a durable power of attorney for you. If you have many questions or special circumstances, however, you may prefer an expert in a specialty called **elder law**. For the name of an elder law practitioner, call your state bar association, or the National Academy of Elder Law Attorneys (520-881-4005; www.naela.org), or the Eldercare Locator (800-677-1116; www.aoa.gov/elderpage/locator.html).

In an era when modern medicine can extend the lives of hopelessly ill patients seemingly indefinitely, many older people reject the financial and emotional costs of an artificially prolonged existence. Others, however, covet the full arsenal of care. Whichever camp your parents are in, help ensure that their wishes are followed at the end of life by having them sign so-called **advance directives** such as **living wills** and **health care proxies**. The process is easy, quick, and doesn't require a lawyer.

The main difference between the two documents is whom they empower to act for them. A living will, which is for terminally ill patients, gives authority to doctors. A health care proxy, which also covers nonterminal situations such as comas, gives authority to anyone your parents have designated in writing. Both documents are recognized in most states. Alabama and Alaska acknowledge only living wills, while Massachusetts, Michigan, and New York recognize just health care proxies. For details on individual state laws plus free forms that fit each state's legal requirements, get in touch with Partnership for Caring, a national nonprofit group that works to improve the quality of care at the end of life (800-989-9455; www.partnershipforcaring.org).

Once the advance directives are signed, don't let your parents stow away their only copy in a safe-deposit box or some other place that's hard to reach in an emergency. Have them give copies to their doctor and to you, and suggest they keep a copy handy in their home.

Finances and Money Management

Assuming your parents are strong and healthy, chances are the only help they'll need, if any, is managing their money. If, like many older people, your parents generally stick to what's safe and familiar in their financial lives, you may find that they haven't created a retirement budget or an investment strategy. Instead they're just doing what they've always done and crossing their fingers. As a result, they may be too liberal in their spending and too conservative in their investing. By reviewing their budget with them, you may discover that your parents are paying for things that may no longer justify their expense, such as a large life insurance policy, a second car, or a pricey country club membership. Naturally they'll have to make all final decisions. Your parents may find, however, that scrutinizing their budget together will produce found money.

Similarly, if you find that your parents are keeping virtually all their cash in safety-first investments such as Treasury bills, bank certificates of deposit, and U.S. savings bonds, there's a lot you can do to help them boost their returns. Taking a few smart investment steps can easily up your parents' income by 10% or more. As a result, they'll be able to worry less about whether their money will last.

Explain to your parents that professional money managers recommend that retirees keep a significant portion of their portfolio in stocks to counteract the asset-diminishing effects of inflation. If they seem unmoved, try this: If inflation grows by 5% a year, their cash will lose half its value in 18 years. Stocks, of course, historically outpace inflation. How much of your parents' money should be in stocks? That depends on how much they have, how much extra income they need, and their risk tolerance. As a rule of thumb, however, the percentage of their portfolio in stocks should be the number you get when you subtract your younger parent's age from 100. For example, for a 70-year-old, the amount would be 30%.

It's wise to steer your parents toward mutual funds for their equity investments, rather than individual stocks that they—or you—will have to actively manage. Ask to borrow the prospectuses of any mutual funds your parents are considering. That way both you and your parents will understand what they're buying. If your parents don't know how to select a mutual fund and don't want to start learning, find out from them what kinds of risks they're willing to take and start hunting for a fund yourself. The mutual fund performance rankings in publications like MONEY, *Business Week, Barron's*, and the *Wall Street Journal* will help you find funds with strong long-term performance records.

Be sure to consider your parents' tax bracket when you or they choose investments. If they are in a high tax bracket and require extra income, tax-exempt municipal bonds and bond funds may well offer better returns than taxable bonds and CDs. To see whether taxables or tax-frees are better, do this calculation with your parents: 1 minus their tax bracket (0.30 for the 30% bracket, for example) multiplied by the taxable yield they could get today. The result is the percentage yield they'd have to earn tax-free to beat what they could get from a taxable investment. If municipals are yielding more than that, they ought to be in munis.

One major source of extra cash for many retirees is the equity in their homes. According to U.S. Census data, people age 65 to 74 have an average of $48,000 in home equity. If your parents are willing to consider moving, they may be able to generate a considerable cash infusion by selling their home and moving to a smaller house or an apartment. Up to $250,000 in capital gains per person (or $500,000 per couple) will be tax-free.

Even if they're not interested in moving, your mother and father may be able to tap their equity with a so-called **reverse mortgage**. Offered by banks in a handful of states, as well as by some local community agencies, reverse mortgages let your parents keep living in their home while collecting monthly payments generated by a loan secured by up to 100% of their equity. Reverse mortgages can be for a fixed term, say, five or 10 years, or for your parents' lifetime. After the period is up, the loan must be repaid, generally by selling the home. The size of the payments to the homeowner depends on the length of time chosen, the value of the home, closing costs, expected appreciation, and the mortgage interest rate. For instance, at a 10% interest rate, $100,000 in home equity might generate $800 a month for five years, $500 a month for 10 years, and about $350 a month for the rest of the life of a 75-year-old owner. For more information about reverse mortgages, contact AARP at 800-209-8085; www.aarp.org/revmort.

Another way your parents can tap their equity without moving: You buy their home and then rent it back to them. Be careful, though. Purchasing the home presents complicated tax ramifications for you. In general, this arrangement—called a **sale-leaseback**—makes sense for you only if your parents' proceeds on the sale can produce more income than you need to charge for rent to cover your expenses. The reason: If you charge too little rent, you may run afoul of IRS regulations requiring investors to charge fair market value for property rentals to qualify for tax deductions. Without write-offs, the transaction probably won't pay for you. Have an accountant figure out the actual cost and benefits of such a deal before you proceed.

Your parents may also be able to get some assistance from federal or state programs for the elderly, depending on their income. For instance, they might qualify for Supplemental Security Income, available to people over 65 with low incomes and few assets— assets can't exceed $2,000 for singles and $3,000 for couples, though Social Security excludes homes, personal belongings, and some other holdings. They could also qualify for free Medicaid coverage for medical expenses, prescription drug subsidies, lower utility rates, or home meal delivery. To find out what programs might benefit your parents, call your state department on aging, usually a division of the human services agency. The office is usually listed under "State Government" in your telephone book.

Your Parents and Your Taxes

You can also help your parents extract more income from their assets by sharing the cost of investments with them. With a so-called **split-interest purchase**, you and your parents buy an income-producing investment, such as a bond. They receive all the income while they're alive; after their death you receive any capital gains. The IRS has strict rules governing such transactions, so it's best to check with a tax pro—preferably a tax attorney—before entering into such an agreement with your parents.

If your parents' income is quite low, you may be able to get some sizable tax benefits in exchange for giving them direct financial support. For example, if your father has taxable income of less than roughly $2,500, and you provide more than 50% of his support, you can legally deduct him as a dependent on your own tax return and claim a dependency exemption. What's more, if your dad qualifies as your dependent, you can add any of his medical expenses to yours when determining if you can write off such costs. Normally it's extremely difficult to claim medical deductions since the expenses must exceed 7.5% of your adjusted gross income before you can deduct any of them. If you and your siblings jointly support your parents, and each of you contributes at least 10% but no more than 50% to their well-being, you can rotate the annual personal and medical deductions among yourselves; only one person can claim your parents in any year, however. Remember, too, that if your employer offers a dependent-care flexible spending account, you can use the FSA to help support your parents if they meet the dependency qualifications. Check with your company benefits office.

For short-term emergencies, you may want to make a gift or a loan to your parents. A gift is simpler, if you can afford to part with the money. You can give each of your parents up to $11,000 a year without triggering federal gift taxes. It's best to spell out the terms of the gift in writing.

Should you and your parents prefer that you lend them money to be repaid in the future, however, things get a little trickier. If you'll be lending less than $10,000, you can charge as much or as little interest as you choose—even no interest. The written agreement must say when the money will be repaid, though. For larger loans, the IRS demands that you charge at least what's known as the **applicable federal rate**. The government changes the interest rate periodically; you can find the current federal rate in the *Wall Street Journal* around the 20th of the month. Generally, the rate is lowest on loans shorter than three years, a bit higher on loans of three to nine years, and the highest for longer loans. You will also have to pay taxes on the interest you get. To make an interest-free loan of more than $10,000 but less than $100,000, you'll usually have to report as taxable income to the IRS the forgone interest or an amount equal to your parents' investment income, whichever is less.

When you draw up a loan agreement, specify all the terms, including the amount and length of the loan, any collateral, and, if you're charging interest, the interest rate. The advantage of such a formal agreement is that in case your parents become unable to repay the loan, you may be able to deduct up to $3,000 a year of the lost cash as a bad debt on your tax return. If you feel that your parents would be offended by a request to sign this kind of document, however, or that repayment is unlikely, stick with a gift.

Helping with Medical Insurance

Even if your parents don't need money, they may welcome your help finding and managing their medical insurance. They might want to take advantage of a relatively new service: firms that process the filing of health insurance claims for you. Keeping track of all the forms from doctors, insurers, pharmacies, and hospitals can be dizzying. Typically, claims-filing services charge a flat fee of about $200 a year or a percentage of what they collect. You or your parents could check with local senior agencies and groups or the nearest chapter of the AARP. Make sure your parents don't sign over the right to have checks issued directly to a claims service. One reputable firm in this business is Medical

Insurance Claims (800-355-2662; www.miconline.com), which charges 15% to collect claims totaling $500 or less and 10% for claims over $500.

In general, the medical insurance issues your parents face will depend primarily on their age.

- **If they're under 65:** Unless your parents have medical coverage from a former employer, the availability and perhaps the cost of health insurance are likely to be a major problem for them. Although a few states have tried to make it easier for older consumers to buy insurance—by requiring, for instance, that insurers offer coverage to anyone who asks—the fact is that people over 50 pay health insurance premiums costing two to four times the cost for people under 30. That can easily come to $5,000 a year or more for a couple. Unfortunately, there's not much your parents can do about cost except to shop carefully for the best deal. One way that they might do this is by paying Quotesmith, a policy shopping service, to search for the best, least expensive coverage (800-556-9393; www.quotesmith.com). (For more on insurance, check out the insurance section in Chapter 2.)

  If your parents haven't looked into managed-care plans such as health maintenance organizations (HMOs), encourage them to do so. While premiums may be a bit higher than for traditional plans, the out-of-pocket costs are far lower for those who use a lot of medical services, as older people often do. Unfortunately, only about a third of HMOs accept individual members. In addition, some areas of the country, particularly the central plains, have few HMOs. So if your parents live in one, their choice of plans may be limited. Chapter 2 describes in detail the best ways to check out an HMO generally.

- **If they're 65 or older:** Most Americans age 65 or older have federal health coverage through Medicare. As of this writing (in 2002), the annual premium for Part A Medicare can go as high as $300, but you will not be required to pay if you or your spouse have had 40 or more quarters of Medicare-covered employment. It pays 100% of hospital bills after a deductible (currently $792). Medicare Part B pays up to 80% of doctor bills for a monthly premium of $54 (in 2002). Medicare also offers some coverage for many other medical needs such as lab tests, home health care, convalescent nursing home care, and personal medical equipment. Unfortunately, payment limits are often low. In fact, since its establishment 30 years ago, Medicare's value has eroded. Today the program pays only about a third of beneficiaries' average expenses. If your parents—or you—are having trouble understanding their Medicare coverage or running into problems getting reimbursed, ask the Medicare Rights Center (800-333-4114; www.medicarerights.org) for free help. This nonprofit group publishes informational pamphlets, answers questions, and even goes to bat for Medicare recipients.

Your parents could get supplemental coverage by joining a **Medicare-qualified HMO**. Unlike most Medigap policies, many Medicare HMOs provide some coverage for things Medicare won't cover, such as prescription drugs and eyeglasses. They also avoid paperwork and often offer low copayments and no deductibles. However, despite the term "Medicare-qualified," an HMO open to people over 65 is likely to be no better or worse than another HMO. Here again, it's best to do some investigating before signing up. Medicare beneficiaries should go one step farther, however, and seek out HMO members on Medicare to find out if the intensive medical needs of seniors are well met in the plan.

In some states, Medicare recipients can purchase **Medicare Select** coverage, which gives them lower premiums or greater benefits if they agree to patronize doctors and other medical providers in a specified managed-care network. Savings differ among states, which run their own networks, but range from 10% to 30% over standard Medicare coverage with its unrestricted choice of providers.

Another way your parents can beef up their Medicare coverage is by purchasing a supplemental health insurance policy known as a **Medigap policy**, which can cost between $900 and $3,000 a year per person.

To help your parents decide among various Medigap alternatives, make sure they or you get a detailed list of benefits included under each offer. Then go over each policy to see which benefits are most desirable to them and their cost. For example, only three of the 10 standard Medigap policies offer coverage for prescription drugs. For a $49 survey of the benefits and premiums of all the Medigap policies sold in your parents' age range, contact Weiss Ratings (800-289-9222; www.weissratings.com).

A key tip: If your parents have significant medical problems and plan to buy a Medigap policy, make sure they sign up for one within six months of turning 65. During this brief window, according to federal law, no one can be turned down for a Medigap policy or be charged more than anyone else the same age.

SIX WAYS YOUR PARENTS CAN REDUCE THEIR MEDICAL COSTS

Health care costs can be a huge expense for your parents. However, they may be able to slice their medical bills by taking some of the following advice:

1. **Patronize doctors who agree to accept the amount stipulated by Medicare as their full fee.** Even doctors who don't accept Medicare's stipulated fee, however, can charge no more than 15% above it.
2. **Seek out free or low-cost medical screenings.** Hospitals, state health departments, and other community groups typically offer these services.
3. **For savings of 5% to 40% on prescription drugs, look into mail-order purchasing services.** The AARP Pharmacy Service (800-456-2226; www.aarppharmacy. com) and 1-800-Pharmacy (800-374-2762; www.1800pharmacy.net) are two of the large mail-order pharmacies.
4. **Ask your doctor or pharmacist whether there are generic versions of your prescriptions.** Generics can save as much as 70% of the price of brand-name prescription drugs.
5. **Comparison shop at local pharmacies.** Typically, drugstore chains don't charge as much as independent pharmacies.
6. **Use a modest income and the absence of Medigap insurance as bargaining tools to negotiate low rates from hospitals, doctors, and labs.** There's no guarantee that you'll be able to bring down the charges, but it doesn't hurt to ask.

A Guide for Long-Term Care

Neither Medicare nor Medigap covers the cost of nonmedical care in a nursing home or at home. Yearly costs for such services can easily top $55,000, and can be much more, depending on where you live, potentially impoverishing a spouse or wiping out an inheritance. Medicaid, the government health insurance program for the indigent, pays for long-term care only for individuals whose income and assets put them at poverty levels. As a result, many older people wonder whether they should try to head off this catastrophic expense in one of two ways: either stashing their wealth in so-called **Medicaid trusts** to impoverish themselves, at least on paper, or buying insurance against the cost of long-term care.

For most people, the answer to both questions is probably no. Let's start with the Medicaid trusts. In the past few years Congress has stringently tightened the rules under which people who transfer their assets to others can receive Medicaid. Currently, such transfers must take place at least 36 months before Medicaid qualification begins, and the money in a trust must be so out of reach that its sponsor is literally, not just legally, impoverished. Under the extreme conditions, few parents are likely to be interested.

Long-term-care (LTC) insurance is a bit more complicated. The cost of premiums for these policies depends on how old you are when you buy the coverage. At age 50, a standard long-term-care policy paying $80 per day in a nursing home and $40 for care at home might run between $500 and $1,000 a year, depending on other features. If you wait until you're 65 to buy that same policy, however, the cost jumps to between $1,000 and $2,200 a year. By age 79, when the possibility of entering a nursing home for a prolonged period starts to increase dramatically, premiums run $4,000 to $7,200 a year. Don't forget, that's per person; if both of your parents are living, those figures would double. While sellers of LTC policies argue that starting early is the key to affordability, they ignore the fact that a younger policyholder also pays premiums much longer—for an expense he may never incur.

A more reasonable way to look at the issue is to examine how much money is at stake and what it would cost to protect it. (Keep in mind that as long as one spouse is living in the family home, the other can receive Medicaid without selling the home, provided the Medicaid recipient meets other asset and income qualifications.) For a couple with assets under $100,000, aside from their home, paying hefty premiums indefinitely makes little sense. With assets above $500,000 or so, an elderly person can probably pay his or her long-term-care costs without exhausting the family legacy.

If your parents' assets are somewhere in between $100,000 and $500,000, the issue of buying a long-term-care policy comes down to cash flow. If the yearly cost of one LTC insurance premium or two (one per spouse) would put such a large crimp in your parents' budget that their standard of living would plummet, tell them to forget the inheritance and enjoy themselves. Alternatively, you and your siblings might consider chipping in to pay for the insurance yourselves. By the way, the insurer won't care how old you are if you're buying the policy for your parents. The premium is based on the beneficiary's age.

Should you decide to start shopping for a long-term-care policy for your parents, consider their particular circumstances carefully. For example, most elderly people prefer to remain at home as long as possible, making policies with home care benefits very desirable. If your parent lives in an area without any agencies providing home care or lives alone, however, home care probably will not be much of an option. In that case, paying for a home care benefit is a waste. Similarly, policies with inflation protection that increase benefits periodically are usually a fine idea for buyers under age 75, although they're at least 50% more expensive than policies with flat benefits. After age 75, however, the average lifespan is short enough that inflation becomes a minor threat. Then the extra coverage is not worth the substantial extra cost.

Increasingly, your parents can also buy long-term-care coverage as a benefit offered by a life insurance policy or an annuity. The advantage of this kind of arrangement is that even if they never need long-term care, their premium will provide other benefits, such as a savings fund or a death stipend. These policies also often offer complete discretion on how long-term-care benefits are spent. They merely provide a specified maximum amount per day or month that can be used for nursing home care, home care, retrofitting a private home, or even paying a relative to provide needed services. The drawbacks, however, are that your parents will pay premiums for life insurance they may not want or need, and they'll incur steep withdrawal penalties if they cancel the coverage after only a few years.

Finding Your Parents Housing

Even the most independent seniors may eventually lose the ability or desire to live on their own. As your parents' physical or mental agility flags or they simply begin to feel lonely, they may need to rethink their living arrangements. Depending on their situation, the best choice might be a retirement enclave for active seniors, an elder care community for people needing personal assistance, help in their home or yours, or, in more extreme situations, a nursing home. The best facilities often have waiting lists of three months to two years. So the sooner you and your parents start investigating them, the better. Below, a rundown of the options:

- **For active seniors.** If your parents need little more than companionship, recreation, and a low-maintenance household, they may be drawn to an **active-adult retirement community** such as Sun City in Arizona or any of the hundreds of similar developments around the country. Bear in mind, however, that these projects offer little for residents needing a lot of personal care or medical attention. Should your parents move into one of these developments and require serious medical attention down the road, they may have to move again. These kinds of facilities may be perfect interim arrangements, though, if you and your siblings plan eventually to move your parents in with one of you. The cost of these types of communities can vary tremendously. Some have no entry fees and charge between $1,000 and $4,000 a month. Others require an entry fee of $17,000 to nearly $300,000 and charge $500 to $1,000 a month. Part-time living assistance or nursing care may be available, for something like $75 to $150 a day. Otherwise it's best to look farther down the road toward a time when your parents may be less independent than they are now.

A **continuing care (or life-care) retirement community** (**CCRC**) is one type of development especially appropriate for active seniors who might like help with daily functions in the future. CCRCs offer a range of services, including independent apartments, personal assistance and medical care, and even nursing home care. A continuing care community is like an insurance policy, since it accepts only seniors who are currently able to live independently but who want to be assured of receiving services if they become dependent later in life. The cost: an admission fee of $75,000 to $250,000, plus a monthly fee that starts at an average of $1,346 for a one-bedroom apartment and rises to an average of $4,040 for full-time nursing care.

There are two reasons for the huge range between the least and most expensive continuing care facilities. Some of the communities are far more luxurious than others, offering golf courses, pools, and sometimes even on-site brokerages and banks. Also, some CCRCs include part or all of the projected costs of future services in their fees, while others charge for them only as you use them. Although there are several hundred CCRCs across the country, not all provide value or high-quality services. Many of the best are accredited by the American Association of Homes and Services for the Aging. For a list of accredited communities, plus information on how to evaluate a CCRC, contact the association (202-783-2242; www.aahsa.com).

Don't let your parents sign up for a continuing care community until their lawyer or financial adviser first reviews its financial statements and admittance contract. It's essential to know how much money would be refunded if your parents moved. You'll also want to know what would happen if, sadly, your parents could no longer afford to live there.

- **For seniors needing help with daily activities.** If your parents are not in robust health but don't need the extensive personal and medical services provided in a nursing home, **assisted-living facilities** may be the answer. Residents live either in apartments or private rooms and receive meals, housekeeping services, laundry service, and professional supervised medical care. As with CCRCs, costs depend on accommodations and the services provided. Assisted-living facilities don't always require entrance fees, which could be as much as $5,000. Monthly rent is usually $2,500 or so. For more information, contact the Assisted Living Federation of America (703-691-8100; www.alfa.org).

  Residential care communities are a close cousin to assisted-living facilities. Sometimes known as personal-care homes or homes for the aged, they can be quite small—the tiniest hold two to 10 people. Residents live in private rooms and pay $350 to $4,000 a month.

  Adult foster care sounds like a friendly alternative. Your parents, assuming they're healthy, get taken into someone else's home and pay $500 to $3,000 a month. Trouble is, the adult foster care business is largely unregulated. Be careful here.

- **For seniors needing continuing medical care.** If your parents are infirm but don't want to move into a nursing home, they may be happiest with **home care**. That home could be theirs or yours. Constructing a downstairs bedroom and bath in their home and bringing in the daily services of a housekeeper and home health care attendant may be just enough to allow your parents to remain in their own home. While such help can easily run to $100 a day or more, it may be cheaper and less upsetting than a move to another location.

Bringing a parent in to live with you can yield the same advantages, though it can also create major emotional problems for both of you. It's probably best to agree to such an arrangement on a temporary basis rather than risk making your parent feel let down if it doesn't work out.

One way to ease tensions in a multigeneration household is with **adult day care**. Senior centers or for-profit businesses in many areas run programs in which elders get recreation, companionship, meals, and sometimes minor medical attention in a safe setting for eight hours or so a day. Encouraging your parent to have interests and relationships outside your family can enhance everyone's ability to live together. The typical daily cost of adult day care varies depending on where you live.

There's no way to make choosing a **nursing home** easy for either you or a parent who needs too much care to remain in his home or yours. You can probably avoid what both of you fear most—poor quality care—by choosing a facility carefully. Time is your best ally. Though most nursing home admissions occur after a medical emergency such as a fall or a stroke, you can foresee many others. If your parent is becoming increasingly frail or is in the throes of worsening Alzheimer's disease, begin your search by asking for recommendations from health care professionals who work with the elderly. Try to restrict your selection of nursing homes to ones near the home of either a relative or a friend who could drop in from time to time. If a nursing home operator knows that someone might be visiting your mother at any time, you'll raise the chances that your parent will get the attention she so much deserves.

Tour the facilities mentioned. The nursing home should, of course, be clean and the staff cheerful and compassionate. Look for more subtle indicators, though. For instance, most nursing homes will have bedridden and mentally disturbed patients, so if you don't see any, it means they're hidden away. That's a bad sign. Scan menus and activities to make sure they reflect adult tastes and interests—scallopini and chamber music, not spaghetti and construction paper art. Similarly, you will want to see some flexibility in timetables, rather than rigid scheduling.

Though most nursing homes do not openly discriminate against the indigent, it will be easier to get your parent into a quality home if he is paying the bills directly. However, make sure the home accepts Medicaid in case your parent's resources eventually disappear. Nursing homes have no entry fees, and their rates range: The national average is $45,000 to $55,000 a year. (For more info, see the Web site sponsored by the American Health Care Association at www.ahca.org.)

WHERE TO GO FOR HELP

The following four resources can help you choose an appropriate home for your parents:

- **A state unit on aging can provide free information on services for the elderly in the state.** For the location of the unit closest to your parents, call the National Association of State Units on Aging (202-898-2578).
- **The Eldercare Locator** (800-677-1116; www.aoa.gov/elderpage/locator.html), sponsored by the U.S. Administration on Aging, will direct you to community programs in your parents' area.
- **The Consumers' Directory of Continuing Care Retirement Communities,** published by the American Association of Homes and Services for the Aging, has profiles of more than 550 nonprofit CCRCs throughout the United States as well as worksheets and checklists to help prospective residents compare costs and features among facilities (800-508-9442; www.aahsa.org).
- **AARP (formerly known as the American Association of Retired Persons)** has free materials on dozens of subjects, including retrofitting a home for an elderly person, evaluating continuing care communities, and buying long-term-care insurance. (For a catalog of publications, write AARP Fulfillment Services, 601 E St. N.W., Washington, DC 20049 or go to the Web site at www.aarp.org.)

Helping Out When You're Far Away

More than three-quarters of the elderly with adult children live within 50 miles of at least one offspring. If your parents are in the other 25%, however, or in the 5% who are 1,000 miles or more from their nearest child, offering support from a distance can be anything from a strain to a nightmare. Faraway parents can be a source of constant worry and periodic crises. For many families the best solution is having the parents move closer. This can often be accomplished painlessly at the time your parents decide to sell their home for something smaller. By bringing them for a visit and a tour of nearby retirement facilities, you may be able to lure them to your area.

Otherwise you'll have to find someone to look out for your parents on your behalf. If neither you nor they have much spare money, try to enlist either a kindly neighbor or a government or volunteer assistance program to look after them for free or for a small fee. Your best solution is probably a combination of the two. First, call local government agencies serving the aging to see if they can refer you to home care services supported by government or charitable funds. Then, if there's a neighbor your parents like and trust, consider asking that person to be your eyes and ears to make sure your parents are getting all they need.

If you can afford it, hire a **professional care manager** or a **geriatric care manager** to make sure someone is looking after your parents at all times. You can often find these specialists, generally social workers with training in gerontology, through local agencies that serve the aging. A care manager will secure and supervise all the care your parents need. If necessary, she (most are women) will find a driver or housekeeper for your parents—even someone who will be sure that your parents' bills are paid on time. Professional care managers charge an hourly fee of $60 to $150; the initial, overall long-term-care plan might run $500 or more. Naturally, you need to make sure that the care manager herself is competent and honest. Credentials count, so look for individuals licensed in social work or psychology who have studied gerontology in a recognized academic program and who have experience and references. For the names of professionals in your parents' area who have met these criteria, contact:

- **The National Association of Professional Geriatric Care Managers** (520-881-8008; www.caremanager.org) or **Aging Network Services** (301-657-4329; www.agingnets.com).

Other organizations that keep updated on laws that protect the elderly and regulate facilities for assisted living:

- **The National Center for Assisted Living** (www.ncal.org). You can download a summary of your state's laws for assisted-living facilities, as well as information on contacting regulators.
- **HC Pro** (www.hcpro.com). This site posts state-by-state summaries of pending legislation, lawsuits, staffing concerns, and other issues that affect assisted-living and CCRC residents.
- **American Seniors Housing Association** (202-237-2900). Its $50 guide, *Seniors Housing State Regulatory Handbook 2001*, provides the most current breakdown of assisted-living and CCRC state regulations and contacts.

Once you know that your parents are all right, you can then get back to making sure your finances are on track, as well.

INDEX

TALKING MONEY

Everything You Need to Know about Your Finances and Your Future
by Jean Chatzky

Today everyone is talking about money: how to spend it, how to save it, and how to invest it. But how much of this wall-to-wall money talk really makes sense? And how does all of it affect you? Now *Today* show financial expert and MONEY magazine columnist Jean Chatzky brings her down-to-earth style to a book for real people with real issues about money. In this amazingly concise and easy-to-understand guide, she tells you what you need to know about all money matters. So grab a cup of coffee, pull up a chair, and start . . . *Talking Money*.

"When it comes to your personal finances, Jean Chatzky tells you exactly what you need to know—in language you can understand!"

—KATIE COURIC, coanchor of NBC News *Today*

CAR SHOPPING MADE EASY

Buying or Leasing, New or Used: How to Get the Car You Want
at the Price You Want to Pay
by Jerry Edgerton

MONEY magazine knows that buying a car isn't what it used to be: It's more expensive, more complicated, more daunting—and requires more extensive research than ever before. Now MONEY brings together in one book all the facts that every car buyer needs to know. Completely updated and revised, this classic guide shows you how you can easily use online resources to find the right car and the right deal for you. Learn how to get the inside track to buying or leasing a great new or used car and save lots of money—by using the Internet!

"Authoritative . . . easy to use."

—*Newsday*

more . . .

401(k): TAKE CHARGE OF YOUR FUTURE
by Eric Schurenberg

Everyone knows the benefits of a 401(k) plan, but not everyone knows how to invest in it, manage it, change it, and keep it on track for maximum results. Written by a national expert on retirement planning, this book will answer all your questions as it shows you how to establish goals and avoid common mistakes. Fully illustrated with graphs and charts and written in easy-to-understand language, this guide will set you on the right course to financial security.